I AM THAT

I AM THAT

Talks with
SRI NISARGADATTA MAHARAJ

Translated
from the Marathi taperecordings by
MAURICE FRYDMAN

Revised and edited by
SUDHAKAR S. DIKSHIT

THE ACORN PRESS
Durham, North Carolina

Originally published by Chetana Pvt. Ltd., Bombay, in 1973. Published by arrangement with Chetana, in the USA and Canada, by The Acorn Press, Box 3279, Durham, NC 27715-3279.

First American hard cover edition 1982;
reprinted 1984, 1985, 1986.
First published in paperback 1988;
reprinted 1990, 1992, 1994, 1996, 1997,
1999, 2002, 2004, 2005, 2006, 2008.

ISBN 0-89386-022-0
Library of Congress Catalog Card No. 81-66800

Photographs by Jitendra Arya.

Printed in the United States of America.

*That in whom reside all beings and who
resides in all beings, who is the giver of
grace to all, the Supreme Soul of the
universe, the limitless being — I am that .*
                                    Amritbindu Upanishad

*That which permeates all, which
nothing transcends and which, like the
universal space around us, fills
everything completely from within and
without, that Supreme non-dual Brahman
— that thou art.*

                              Sankaracharya

(For books of related interest, see the list following p. 550)

O

Foreword

That there should be yet another edition of I AM THAT is not surprising, for the sublimity of the words spoken by Sri Nisargadatta Maharaj, their directness and the lucidity with which they refer to the Highest have already made this book a literature of paramount importance. In fact, many regard it as the only book of spiritual teaching really worth studying.

There are various religions and systems of philosophy which claim to endow human life with meaning. But they suffer from certain inherent limitations. They couch into fine-sounding words their traditional beliefs and ideologies, theological or philosophical. Believers, however, discover the limited range of meaning and applicability of these words, sooner or later. They get disillusioned and tend to abandon the systems, in the same way as scientific theories are abandoned, when they are called in question by too much contradictory empirical data.

When a system of spiritual interpretation turns out to be unconvincing and not capable of being rationally justified, many people allow themselves to be converted to some other system. After a while, however, they find limitations and contradictions in the other system also. In this unrewarding pursuit of acceptance and rejection what remains for them is only scepticism and agnosticism, leading to a fatuous way of living, engrossed in mere gross utilities of life, just consuming material goods. Sometimes, however, though rarely, scepticism gives rise to an intuition of a basic reality, more fundamental than that of words, religions or philosophic systems. Strangely, it is a positive aspect of scepticism. It was in such a state of scepticism, but also having an intuition of the basic reality, that I happened to read Sri Nisargadatta Maharaj's I AM THAT. I was at once struck by the finality and unassailable certitude of his words. Limited by their very nature though words are, I found the utterances of Maharaj transparent, polished windows, as it were.

No book of spiritual teachings, however, can replace the presence of the teacher himself. Only the words spoken directly to you by the Guru shed their opacity completely. In the Guru's presence the last boundaries drawn by the mind vanish. Sri Nisargadatta Maharaj is indeed such a Guru. He is not a preacher, but he provides precisely those indications which the seeker needs. The reality which emanates from him is inalienable and Absolute. It is authentic. Having experienced the verity of his words in the pages of I AM THAT, and being inspired by it, many from the West have found their way to Maharaj, to seek enlightenment.

Maharaj's interpretation of truth is not different from that of Jnana Yoga/Advaita Vedanta. But, he has a way of his own. The multifarious forms around us, says he, are constituted of the five elements. They are transient, and in a state of perpetual flux. Also they are governed by the law of causation. All this applies to the body and the mind also, both of which are transient and subject to birth and death. We know that only by means of the bodily senses and the mind can the world be known. As in the Kantian view, it is a correlate of the human knowing subject, and, therefore, has the fundamental structure of our way of knowing. This means that time, space and causality are not 'objective', or extraneous entities, but mental categories in which everything is moulded. The existence and form of all things depend upon the mind. Cognition is a mental product. And the world as seen from the mind is a subjective and private world, which changes continuously in accordance with the restlessness of the mind itself.

In opposition to the restless mind, with its limited categories — intentionality, subjectivity, duality etc. — stands supreme the limitless sense of 'I am'. The only thing I can be sure about is,that 'I am'; not as a thinking 'I am' in the Cartesian sense, but without any predicates. Again and again Maharaj draws our attention to this basic fact in order to make us realize our 'I am-ness' and thus get rid of all self-made prisons. He says: The only true statement is 'I am'. All else is mere inference. By no effort can you change the 'I am' into 'I am-not'.

Behold, the real experiencer is not the mind, but myself, the light in which everything appears.Self is the common factor at the root of all experience, the awareness in which everything happens. The entire field of consciousness is only as a film, or a speck, in 'I am'. This 'I am-ness' is, being conscious of consciousness, being aware of itself. And it is indescribable, because it has no attributes. It is only being my self, and being my self is all that there is. Everything that exists, exists as my self. There is nothing which is different from me. There is no duality and, therefore, no pain. There are no problems. It is the sphere of love, in which everything is perfect. What happens, happens spontaneously, without intentions—like digestion, or the growth of the hair. Realize this, and be free from the limitations of the mind.

Behold, the deep sleep in which there is no notion of being this or that. Yet 'I am' remains. And behold the eternal *now*. Memory seems to bring things to the present out of the past, but all that happens does happen in the present only. It is only in the timeless *now* that phenomena manifest themselves. Thus, time and causation do not apply in reality. *I am* prior to the world, body and mind. *I am* the sphere in which they appear and disappear. *I am* the source of them all, the universal power by which the world with its bewildering diversity becomes manifest.

In spite of its primevality, however, the sense of 'I am' is not the Highest. It is not the Absolute. The sense, or taste of 'I am-ness' is not absolutely beyond time. Being the essence of the five elements, it, in a way, depends upon the world. It arises from the body, which, in its turn, is built by food, consisting of the elements. It disappears when the body dies, like the spark extinguishes when the incense stick burns out. When pure awareness is attained, no need exists any more, not even for 'I am', which is but a useful pointer, a direction-indicator towards the Absolute. The awareness 'I am' then easily ceases. What prevails is that which cannot be described, that which is beyond words. It is this 'state' which is most real, a state of pure potentiality, which is prior to everything. The 'I am' and the universe are mere reflections of it. It is this reality which a *jnani* has realized.

The best that you can do is to listen attentively to the *jnani* — of whom Sri Nisargadatta is a living example — and to trust and believe him. By such listening you will realize that his reality is your reality. He helps you in seeing the nature of the world and of the 'I am'. He urges you to study the workings of the body and the mind with solemn and intense concentration, to recognize that you are neither of them and to cast them off. He suggests that you return again and again to 'I am' until it is your only abode, outside of which nothing exists; until the ego as a limitation of 'I am', has disappeared. It is then that the highest realization will just happen effortlessly.

Mark the words of the *jnani,* which cut across all concepts and dogmas. Maharaj says: "Until one becomes self-realized, attains to knowledge of the self, transcends the self, until then, all these cock-and-bull stories are provided, all these concepts."* Yes, they are concepts, even 'I am' is, but surely there are no concepts more precious. It is for the seeker to regard them with the utmost seriousness, because they indicate the Highest Reality. No better concepts are available to shed all concepts.

I am thankful to Sudhakar S.Dikshit, the editor, for inviting me to write the Foreword to this new edition of I AM THAT and thus giving me an opportunity to pay my homage to Sri Nisargadatta Maharaj, who has expounded highest knowledge in the simplest, clearest and the most convincing words.

Philosophical Faculty   Douwe Tiemersma
Erasmus Universiteit
Rotterdam, Holland

June, 1981

* Evening Talk. October 2. 1979. recorded by Josef Nauwelaerts of Antverp. Belgium.

Who is Nisargadatta Maharaj?

When asked about the date of his birth the Master replied blandly that he was never born!

Writing a biographical note on Sri Nisargadatta Maharaj is a frustrating and unrewarding task. For, not only the exact date of his birth is unknown, but no verified facts concerning the early years of his life are available. However, some of his elderly relatives and friends say that he was born in the month of March 1897 on a full moon day, which coincided with the festival of Hanuman Jayanti, when Hindus pay their homage to Hanuman, also named Maruti, the monkey-god of Ramayana fame. And to associate his birth with this auspicious day his parents named him Maruti.

Available information about his boyhood and early youth is patchy and disconnected. We learn that his father, Shivrampant, was a poor man, who worked for some time as a domestic servant in Bombay and, later, eked out his livelihood as a petty farmer at Kandalgaon, a small village in the back woods of Ratnagiri district of Maharashtra. Maruti grew up almost without education. As a boy he assisted his father in such labours as lay within his power — tended cattle, drove oxen, worked in the fields and ran errands. His pleasures were simple, as his labours, but he was gifted with an inquisitive mind, bubbling over with questions of all sorts.

His father had a Brahmin friend named Vishnu Haribhau Gore, who was a pious man and learned too from rural standards. Gore often talked about religious topics and the boy Maruti listened attentively and dwelt on these topics far more than anyone would suppose. Gore was for him the ideal man — earnest, kind and wise.

When Maruti attained the age of eighteen his father died, leaving behind his widow, four sons and two daughters. The meagre income from the small farm dwindled further after the old man's death and was not sufficient to feed so many mouths. Maruti's elder brother left the village for Bombay in search of work and he followed shortly after. It is said that in Bombay he worked for a few months as a low-paid junior clerk in an office, but resigned the job in disgust. He then took to petty trading as a haberdasher and started a shop for selling children's clothes, tobacco and hand-made country cigarettes. This business is said to have flourished in course of time, giving him some sort of financial security. During this period he got married and had a son and three daughters.

Childhood, youth, marriage, progeny — Maruti lived the usual humdrum and eventless life of a common man till his middle age, with no inkling at all of the sainthood that was to follow. Among his friends during this period was one Yashwantrao Baagkar, who was a devotee of Sri Siddharameshwar Maharaj, a spiritual teacher of the *Navnath Sampradaya, a sect of Hinduism. One evening Baagkar took Maruti to his Guru and that evening proved to be the turning point in his life. The Guru gave him a *mantra* and instructions in meditation. Early in his practice he started having visions and occasionally even fell into trances. Something exploded within him, as it were, giving birth to a cosmic consciousness, a sense of eternal life. The identity of Maruti, the petty shopkeeper, dissolved and the illuminating personality Sri Nisargadatta emerged.

Most people live in the world of self-consciousness and do not have the desire or power to leave it. They exist only for themselves; all their effort is directed towards achievement of self-satisfaction and self-glorification. There are, however, seers, teachers and revealers who, while apparently living in the same world, live simultaneously in another world also — the world of cosmic consciousness, effulgent with infinite knowledge. After his illuminating experience Sri Nisargadatta Maharaj started living such a dual life. He conducted his shop, but ceased to be a profit-minded merchant. Later, abandoning his family and business he became a mendicant, a pilgrim over the vastness and variety of the Indian religious scene. He walked barefooted on his way to the Himalayas where he planned to pass the rest of his years in quest of an eternal life. But he soon retraced his steps and came back home comprehending the futility of such a quest. Eternal life, he perceived, was not to be sought for; he already had it. Having gone beyond the I-am-the-body idea, he had acquired a mental state so joyful, peaceful and glorious that everything appeared to be worthless compared to it. He had attained self-realization.

Uneducated though the Master is, his conversation is enlightened to an extraordinary degree. Though born and brought up in poverty, he is the richest of the rich, for he has the limitless wealth of perennial knowledge, compared to which the most fabulous treasures are mere tinsel. He is warm-hearted and tender, shrewdly humorous, absolutely fearless and absolutely true — inspiring, guiding and supporting all who come to him.

Any attempt to write a biographical note on such a man is frivolous and futile. For he is not a man with a past or future; he is the living present — eternal and immutable. He is the self that has become all things.

o o o

Translator's Note

I met Sri Nisargadatta Maharaj some years back and was impressed with the spontaneous simplicity of his appearance and behaviour and his deep and genuine earnestness in expounding his experience.

However humble and difficult to discover his little tenement in the backlanes of Bombay, many have found their way there. Most of them are Indians, conversing freely in their native language, but there were also many foreigners who needed a translator. Whenever I was present the task would fall to me. Many of the questions put and answers given were so interesting and significant that a tape-recorder was brought in. While most of the tapes were of the regular Marathi-English variety, some were polyglot scrambles of several Indian and European languages. Later, each tape was deciphered and translated into English.

It was not easy to translate verbatim and at the same time avoid tedious repetitions and reiterations. It is hoped that the present translation of the tape-recordings will not reduce the impact of this clear-minded, generous and in many ways an unusual human being.

A Marathi version of these talks, verified by Sri Nisargadatta Maharaj himself, has been separately published.

Bombay,   Maurice Frydman
October 16, 1973   Translator

Editor's Note

The present edition of I AM THAT is a revised and re-edited version of the 101 talks that appeared in two volumes in earlier editions. Not only the matter has now been re-set in a more readable typeface and with chapter headings, but new pictures of Sri Nisargadatta Maharaj have been included and the appendices contain some hitherto unpublished valuable material.

I draw special attention of the reader to the contribution entitled 'Nisarga Yoga' (Appendix I), in which my esteemed friend, the late Maurice Frydman, has succinctly presented the teaching of Maharaj. Simplicity and humility are the keynotes of his teachings, as Maurice observes. The Master does not propound any intellectual concept or doctrine. He does not put forward any pre-conditions before the seekers and is happy with them as they are. In fact Sri Nisargadatta Maharaj is peculiarly free from all disparagement and condemnation; the sinner and the saint are merely exchanging notes; the saint has sinned, the sinner can be sanctified. It is time that divides them; it is time that will bring them together. The teacher does not evaluate; his sole concern is with 'suffering and the ending of suffering'. He knows from his personal and abiding experience that the roots of sorrow are in the mind and it is the mind that must be freed from its distorting and destructive habits. Of these the identification of the self with its projections is most fatal. By precept and example Sri Nisargadatta Maharaj shows a short-cut, a-logical but empirically sound. It operates, when understood.

Revising and editing of I AM THAT has been for me a pilgrimage to my inner self—at once ennobling and enlightening. I have done my work in a spirit of dedication, with great earnestness. I have treated the questions of every questioner as mine own questions and have imbibed the answers of the Master with a mind emptied of all it knew. However, in this process of what may be called a two-voiced meditation, it is possible that at places I may have failed in the cold-blodded punctiliousness about the syntax and punctuation, expected of an editor. For such lapses, if any, I seek forgiveness of the reader.

Before closing, I wish to express my heart-felt thanks to Professor Douwe Tiemersma of the Philosophical Faculty Erasmus. Universiteit, Rotterdam, Holland for contributing a new Foreword to this edition. That he acceeded to my request promptly makes me feel all the more grateful.

Bombay,   Sudhakar S. Dikshit
July 1981   Editor

Contents

xix

The seeker is he who is in search of himself.

Give up all questions except one: 'Who am I?' After all, the only fact you are sure of is that you are. The 'I am' is certain. The 'I am this' is not. Struggle to find out what you are in reality.

To know what you are, you must first investigate and know what you are not.

Discover all that you are not — body, feelings, thoughts, time, space, this or that — nothing, concrete or abstract, which you perceive can be you. The very act of perceiving shows that you are not what you perceive.

The clearer you understand that on the level of mind you can be described in negative terms only, the quicker will you come to the end of your search and realize that you are the limitless being.

Sri Nisargadatta Maharaj

The Sense of 'I am'

Questioner: It is a matter of daily experience that on waking up the world suddenly appears. Where does it come from?

Maharaj: Before anything can come into being there must be somebody to whom it comes. All appearance and disappearance presupposes a change against some changeless background.

Q: Before waking up I was unconscious.

M: In what sense? Having forgotten, or not having experienced? Don't you experience even when unconscious? Can you exist without knowing? A lapse in memory: is it a proof of non-existence? And can you validly talk about your own non-existence as an actual experience? You cannot even say that your mind did not exist. Did you not wake up on being called? And on waking up, was it not the sense 'I am' that came first? Some seed consciousness must be existing even during sleep, or swoon. On waking up the experience runs: 'I am — the body — in the world.' It may appear to arise in succession but in fact it is all simultaneous, a single idea of having a body in a world. Can there be the sense of 'I am' without being somebody or other?

Q: I am always somebody with its memories and habits. I know no other 'I am'.

M: Maybe something prevents you from knowing? When you do not know something which others know, what do you do?

Q: I seek the source of their knowledge under their instruction.

M: Is it not important to you to know whether you are a mere body, or something else? Or, maybe nothing at all? Don't you see that all your problems are your body's problems — food, clothing, shelter, family, friends, name, fame, security, survival — all these lose their meaning the moment you realize that you may not be a mere body.

Q: What benefit there is in knowing that I am not the body?

M: Even to say that you are not the body is not quite true. In a way you are all the bodies, hearts and minds and much more. Go deep into the sense of 'I am' and you will find. How do you find a thing you have mislaid or forgotten? You keep it in your mind until you recall it. The sense of being, of 'I am' is the first to emerge. Ask yourself whence it comes, or just watch it quietly. When the mind stays in the 'I am', without moving, you enter a state which cannot be verbalized but can be experienced. All you need to do is to try and try again. After all the sense 'I am' is always with you, only you have attached all kinds of things to it — body, feelings, thoughts, ideas, possessions etc. All these self-identifications are misleading. Because of them you take yourself to be what you are not.

Q: Then what am I?

M: It is enough to know what you are not. You need not know what you are. For, as long as knowledge means description in terms of what is already known, perceptual, or conceptual, there can be no such thing as self-knowledge, for what you are cannot be described, except as total negation. All you can say is: 'I am not this, I am not that'. You cannot meaningfully say 'this is what I am'. It just makes no sense. What you can point out as 'this' or 'that' cannot be yourself. Surely, you can not be 'something' else. You are nothing perceivable, or imaginable. Yet, without you there can be neither perception nor imagination. You observe the heart feeling, the mind thinking, the body acting; the very act of perceiving shows that you are not what you perceive. Can there be perception, experience, without you? An experience must 'belong'. Somebody must come and declare it as his own. Without an experiencer the experience is not real. It is the experiencer that imparts reality to experience. An experience which you cannot have, of what value is it to you?

Q: The sense of being an experiencer, the sense of 'I am', is it not also an experience?

M: Obviously, every thing experienced is an experience. And in every experience there arises the experiencer of it. Memory creates the illusion of continuity. In reality each experience has its own experiencer and the sense of identity is due to the common factor at the root of all experiencer-experience relations. Identity and continuity are not the same. Just as each flower has its own colour, but all colours are caused by the same light, so do many experiencers appear in the undivided and indivisible awareness, each separate in memory, identical in essence. This essence is the root, the foundation, the timeless and spaceless possibility' of all experience.

Q: How do I get at it?

M: You need not get at it, for you *are* it. It will get at you, if you give it a chance. Let go your attachment to the unreal and the real will swiftly and smoothly step into its own. Stop imagining yourself being or doing this or that and the realization that you are the source and heart of all will dawn upon you. With this will come great love which is not choice or predilection, nor attachment, but a power which makes all things love-worthy and lovable.   •••

2

Obsession with the Body

Questioner: Maharaj, you are sitting in front of me and I am here at your feet. What is the basic difference between us?

Maharaj: There is no basic difference.

Q: Still there must be some real difference, I come to you, you do not come to me.

M: Because you imagine differences, you go here and there in search of 'superior' people.

Q: You too are a superior person. You claim to know the real, while I do not.

M: Did I ever tell you that you do not know and, therefore, you are inferior? Let those who invented such distinctions prove them. I do not claim to know what you do not. In fact, I know much less than you do.

Q: Your words are wise, your behaviour noble, your grace all-powerful.

M: I know nothing about it all and see no difference between you and me. My life is a succession of events, just like yours. Only I am detached and see the passing show as a passing show, while you stick to things and move along with them.

Q: What made you so dispassionate?

M: Nothing in particular. It so happened that I trusted my Guru. He told me I am nothing but my self and I believed him. Trusting him, I behaved accordingly and ceased caring for what was not me, nor mine.

Q: Why were you lucky to trust your teacher fully, while our trust is nominal and verbal?

M: Who can say? It happened so. Things happen without cause and reason and, after all, what does it matter, who is who? Your high opinion of me is your opinion only. Any moment you may change it. Why attach importance to opinions, even your own?

Q: Still, you are different. Your mind seems to be always quiet and happy. And miracles happen round you.

M: I know nothing about miracles, and I wonder whether nature admits exceptions to her laws, unless we agree that everything is a miracle. As to my mind, there is no such thing. There is consciousness in which everything happens. It is quite obvious and within the experience of everybody. You just do not look carefully enough. Look well, and see what I see.

Q: What do you see?

M: I see what you too could see, here and now, but for the wrong focus of your attention. You give no attention to your self. Your mind is all with things, people and ideas, never with your self. Bring your self into focus, become aware of your own existence. See how you function, watch the motives and the results of your actions. Study the prison you have built around yourself, by inadvertence. By knowing what you are not, you come to know your self. The way back to your self is through refusal and rejection. One thing is certain: the real is not imaginary, it is not a product of the mind. Even the sense 'I am' is not continuous, though it is a useful pointer; it shows where to seek, but not what to seek. Just have a good look at it. Once you are convinced that you cannot say truthfully about your self anything except 'I am', and that nothing that can be pointed at, can be your self, the need for the 'I am' is over — you are no longer intent on verbalizing what you are. All you need is to get rid of the tendency to define your self. All definitions apply to your body only and to its expressions. Once this obsession with the body goes, you will revert to your natural state, spontaneously and effortlessly. The only difference between us is that I am aware of my natural state, while you are bemused. Just like gold made into ornaments has no advantage over gold dust, except when the mind makes it so, so are we one in being — we differ only in appearance. We discover it by being earnest, by searching, enquiring, questioning daily and hourly, by giving one's life to this discovery. ●●●

The Living Present

Questioner: As I can see, there is nothing wrong with my body nor with my real being. Both are not of my making and need not be improved upon. What has gone wrong is the 'inner body', call it mind, consciousness, *antahkarana*, whatever the name.

Maharaj: What do you consider to be wrong with your mind?

Q: It is restless, greedy of the pleasant and afraid of the unpleasant.

M: What is wrong with its seeking the pleasant and shirking the unpleasant? Between the banks of pain and pleasure the river of life flows. It is only when the mind refuses to flow with life, and gets stuck at the banks, that it becomes a problem. By flowing with life I mean acceptance — letting come what comes and go what goes. Desire not, fear not, observe the actual, as and when it happens, for you are not what happens, you are to whom it happens. Ultimately even the observer you are not. You are the ultimate potentiality of which the all-embracing consciousness is the manifestation and expression.

Q: Yet, between the body and the self there lies a cloud of thoughts and feelings, which neither serve the body nor the self. These thoughts and feelings are flimsy, transient and meaningless, mere mental dust that blinds and chokes, yet they are there, obscuring and destroying.

M: Surely, the memory of an event cannot pass for the event itself. Nor can the anticipation. There is something exceptional, unique, about the present event, which the previous, or the coming do not have. There is a livingness about it, an actuality; it stands out as if illumined. There is the 'stamp of reality' on the actual, which the past and future do not have.

Q: What gives the present that 'stamp of reality'?

M: There is nothing peculiar in the present event to make it different from the past and future. For a moment the past was actual and the future will become so. What makes the present so different? Obviously, my presence. I am real for I am always *now,* in the present, and what is with me now shares in my reality. The past is in memory, the future — in imagination. There is nothing in the present event itself that makes it stand out as real. It may be some simple, periodical occurrence, like the striking of the clock. In spite of our knowing that the successive strokes are identical, the present stroke is quite different from the previous one and the next — as remembered, or expected. A thing focussed in the now is with me, for I am ever present; it is my own reality that I impart to the present event.

Q: But we deal with things remembered as if they were real.

M: We consider memories, only when they come into the present. The forgotten is not counted until one is reminded — which implies bringing into the *now.*

Q: Yes, I can see there is in the now some unknown factor that gives momentary reality to the transient actuality.

M: You need not say it is unknown, for you see it in constant operation. Since you were born, has it ever changed? Things and thoughts have been changing all the time. But the feeling that what is now is real has never changed, even in dream.

Q: In deep sleep there is no experience of the present reality.

M: The blankness of deep sleep is due entirely to the lack of specific memories. But a general memory of well-being is there. There is a difference in feeling when we say 'I was deeply asleep' from 'I was absent'.

Q: We shall repeat the question we began with: between life's source and life's expression (which is the body), there is the mind and its ever-changeful states. The stream of mental states is endless, meaningless and painful. Pain is the constant factor. What we call pleasure is but a gap, an interval between two painful states. Desire and fear are the weft and warp of living, and both are made of pain. Our question is: can there be a happy mind?

M: Desire is the memory of pleasure and fear is the memory of pain. Both make the mind restless. Moments of pleasure are merely gaps in the stream of pain. How can the mind be happy?

Q: That is true when we desire pleasure or expect pain. But there are moments of unexpected, unanticipated joy. Pure joy, uncontaminated by desire — unsought, undeserved, God-given.

M: Still, joy is joy only against a background of pain.

Q: Is pain a cosmic fact, or purely mental?

M: The universe is complete and where there is completeness, where nothing lacks, what can give pain?

Q: The universe may be complete as a whole, but incomplete in details.

M: A part of the whole seen in relation to the whole is also complete. Only when seen in isolation it becomes deficient and thus a seat of pain. What makes for isolation?

Q: Limitations of the mind, of course. The mind cannot see the whole for the part.

M: Good enough. The mind, by its very nature, divides and opposes. Can there be some other mind, which unites and harmonizes, which sees the whole in the part and the part as totally related to the whole?

Q: The other mind — where to look for it?

M: In the going beyond the limiting, dividing and opposing mind. In ending the mental process as we know it. When this comes to an end, that mind is born.

Q: In that mind, the problem of joy and sorrow exist no longer?

M: Not as we know them, as desirable or repugnant. It becomes rather a question of love seeking expression and meeting with obstacles. The inclusive mind is love in action, battling against circumstances, initially frustrated, ultimately victorious.

Q: Between the spirit and the body, is it love that provides the bridge?

M: What else? Mind creates the abyss, the heart crosses it. ●●●

Real World is Beyond the Mind

Questioner: On several occasions the question was raised as to whether the universe is subject to the law of causation, or does it exist and function outside the law. You seem to hold the view that it is uncaused, that everything, however small, is uncaused, arising and disappearing for no known reason whatsoever.

Maharaj: Causation means succession in time of events in space, the space being physical or mental. Time, space, causation are mental categories, arising and subsiding with the mind.

Q: As long as the mind operates, causation is a valid law.

M: Like everything mental, the so-called law of causation contradicts itself. No thing in existence has a particular cause; the entire universe contributes to the existence of even the smallest thing; nothing could be as it is without the universe being what it is. When the source and ground of everything is the only cause of everything, to speak of causality as a universal law is wrong. The universe is not bound by its content, because its potentialities are infinite; besides it is a manifestation, or expression of a principle fundamentally and totally free.

Q: Yes, one can see that ultimately to speak of one thing being the only cause of another thing is altogether wrong. Yet, in actual life we invariably initiate action with a view to a result.

M: Yes, there is a lot of such activity going on, because of ignorance. Would people know that nothing can happen unless the entire universe makes it happen, they would achieve much more with less expenditure of energy.

Q: If everything is an expression of the totality of causes, how can we talk of a purposeful action towards an achievement?

M: The very urge to achieve is also an expression of the total universe. It merely shows that the energy potential has risen at a particular point. It is the illusion of time that makes you talk of causality. When the past and the future are seen in the timeless *now*, as parts of a common pattern, the idea of cause-effect loses its validity and creative freedom takes its place.

Q: Yet, I cannot see how can anything come to be without a cause.

M: When I say a thing is without a cause, I mean it can be without a particular cause. Your own mother was not needed to give you birth; you could have been born from some other woman. But you could not have been born without the sun and the earth. Even these could not have caused your birth without the most important factor: your own desire to be born. It is desire that gives birth, that gives name and form. The desirable is imagined and wanted and manifests itself as something tangible or conceivable. Thus is created the world in which we live, our personal world. The real world is beyond the mind's ken; we see it through the net of our desires, divided into pleasure and pain, right and wrong, inner and outer. To see the universe as it is, you must step beyond the net. It is not hard to do so, for the net is full of holes.

Q: What do you mean by holes? And how to find them?

M: Look at the net and its many contradictions. You do and undo at every step. You want peace, love, happiness and work hard to create pain, hatred and war. You want longevity and overeat, you want friendship and exploit. See your net as made of such contradictions and remove them — your very seeing them will make them go.

Q: Since my seeing the contradiction makes it go, is there no causal link between my seeing and its going?

M: Causality, even as a concept, does not apply to chaos.

Q: To what extent is desire a causal factor?

M: One of the many. For everything there are innumerable causal factors. But the source of all that is, is the Infinite Possibility, the Supreme Reality, which is in you and which throws its power and light and love on every experience. But, this source is not a cause and no cause is a source. Because of that, I say everything is uncaused. You may try to trace how a thing happens, but you cannot find out why a thing *is* as it is. A thing is as it is, because the universe is as it is.   ●●●

5

What is Born must Die

Questioner: Is the witness-consciousness permanent or not?

Maharaj: It is not permanent. The knower rises and sets with the known. That in which both the knower and the known arise and set, is beyond time. The words permanent or eternal do not apply.

Q: In sleep there is neither the known, nor the knower. What keeps the body sensitive and receptive?

M: Surely you cannot say the knower was absent. The experience of things and thoughts was not there, that is all. But the absence of experience too is experience. It is like entering a dark room and saying: 'I see nothing'. A man blind from birth knows not what darkness means. Similarly, only the knower knows that he does not know. Sleep is merely a lapse in memory. Life goes on.

Q: And what is death?

M: It is the change in the living process of a particular body. Integration ends and disintegration sets in.

Q: But what about the knower. With the disappearance of the body, does the knower disappear?

M: Just as the knower of the body appears at birth, so he disappears at death.

Q: And nothing remains?

M: Life remains. Consciousness needs a vehicle and an instrument for its manifestation. When life produces another body, another knower comes into being.

Q: Is there a causal link between the successive body-knowers, or body-minds?

M: Yes, there is something that may be called the memory body, or causal body, a record of all that was thought, wanted and done. It is like a cloud of images held together.

Q: What is this sense of a separate existence?

M: It is a reflection in a separate body of the one reality. In this reflection the unlimited and the limited are confused and taken to be the same. To undo this confusion is the purpose of Yoga.

Q: Does not death undo this confusion?

M: In death only the body dies. Life does not, consciousness does not, reality does not. And the life is never so alive as after death.

Q: But does one get reborn?

M: What was born must die. Only the unborn is deathless. Find what is it that never sleeps and never wakes, and whose pale reflection is our sense of 'I'.

Q: How am I to go about this finding out?

M: How do you go about finding anything? By keeping your mind and heart on it. Interest there must be and steady remembrance. To remember what needs to be remembered is the secret of success. You come to it through earnestness.

Q: Do you mean to say that mere wanting to find out is enough? Surely, both qualifications and opportunities are needed.

M: These will come with earnestness. What is supremely important is to be free from contradictions: the goal and the way must not be on different levels; life and light must not quarrel; be-

haviour must not betray belief. Call it honesty, integrity, whole-
ness; you must not go back, undo, uproot, abandon the conquered ground. Tenacity of purpose and honesty in pursuit will
bring you to your goal.

Q: Tenacity and honesty are endowments, surely! Not a trace
of them I have.

M: All will come as you go on. Take the first step first. All blessings come from within. Turn within. 'I am' you know. Be with it
all the time you can spare, until you revert to it spontaneously.
There is no simpler and easier way.   •••

6

Meditation

Questioner: All teachers advise to meditate. What is the purpose of meditation?

Maharaj: We know the outer world of sensations and actions,
but of our inner world of thoughts and feelings we know very little. The primary purpose of meditation is to become conscious
of, and familiar with, our inner life. The ultimate purpose is to
reach the source of life and consciousness.

Incidentally, practice of meditation affects deeply our character. We are slaves to what we do not know; of what we know we
are masters. Whatever vice or weakness in ourselves we discover and understand its causes and its workings, we overcome it by the very knowing; the unconscious dissolves when
brought into the conscious. The dissolution of the unconscious

releases energy; the mind feels adequate and become quiet.

Q: What is the use of a quiet mind?

M: When the mind is quiet, we come to know ourselves as the pure witness. We withdraw from the experience and its experiencer and stand apart in pure awareness, which is between and beyond the two. The personality, based on self-identification, on imagining oneself to be something: 'I am this, I am that', continues, but only as a part of the objective world. Its identification with the witness snaps.

Q: As I can make out, I live on many levels and life on each level requires energy. The Self by its very nature delights in everything and its energies flow outwards. Is not the purpose of meditation to dam up the energies on the higher levels, or to push them back and up, so as to enable the higher levels to prosper also?

M: It is not so much the matter of levels as of *gunas* (qualities). Meditation is a *sattvic* activity and aims at complete elimination of *tamas* (inertia) and *rajas* (motivity). Pure *sattva* (harmony) is perfect freedom from sloth and restlessness.

Q: How to strengthen and purify the *sattva*?

M: The *sattva* is pure and strong always. It is like the sun. It may seem obseured by clouds and dust, but only from the point of view of the perceiver. Deal with the causes of obscuration, not with the sun.

Q: What is the use of *sattva*?

M: What is the use of truth, goodness, harmony, beauty? They are their own goal. They manifest spontaneously and effortlessly, when things are left to themselves, are not interfered with, not shunned, or wanted, or conceptualized, but just experienced in full awareness. Such awareness itself is *sattva*. It does not make use of things and people — it fulfils them.

Q: Since I cannot improve *sattva*, am I to deal with *tamas* and *rajas* only? How do I deal with them?

M: By watching their influence in you and on you. Be aware of them in operation, watch their expressions in your thoughts, words and deeds, and gradually their grip on you will lessen and the clear light of *sattva* will emerge. It is neither a difficult, nor a protracted process; earnestness is the only condition of success.   ●●●

7

The Mind

Questioner: There are very interesting books written by apparently very competent people, in which the illusoriness of the world is denied (though not its transitoriness). According to them, there exists a hierarchy of beings, from the lowest to the highest; on each level the complexity of the organism enables and reflects the depth, breadth and intensity of consciousness, without any visible or knowable culmination. One law supreme rules throughout: evolution of forms for the growth and enrichment of consciousness and manifestation of its infinite potentialities.

Maharaj: This may or may not be so. Even if it is, it is only so from the mind's point of view, but in fact the entire universe *(mahadakash)* exists only in consciousness *(chidakash)*, while I have my stand in the Absolute *(paramakash)*. In pure being consciousness arises; in consciousness the world appears and disappears. All there *is* is me, all there *is* is mine. Before all beginnings, after all endings — I am. All has its being in me, in the 'I am', that shines in every living being. Even not-being is unthinkable without me. Whatever happens, I must be there to witness it.

Q: Why do you deny being to the world?

M: I do not negate the world. I see it as appearing in consciousness, which is the totality of the known in the immensity of the unknown.

What begins and ends is mere appearance. The world can be said to appear, but not to *be*. The appearance may last very long on some scale of time, and be very short on another, but ultimately it comes to the same. Whatever is time bound is momentary and has no reality.

Q: Surely, you see the actual world as it surrounds you. You seem to behave quite normally!

M: That is how it appears to you. What in your case occupies the entire field of consciousness, is a mere speck in mine. The world lasts, but for a moment. It is your memory that makes you think that the world continues. Myself, I don't live by memory. I see the world as it is, a momentary appearance in consciousness.

Q: In *your* consciousness?

M: All idea of 'me' and 'mine', even of 'I am' is in consciousness.

Q: Is then your 'absolute being' *(paramakash)* un-consciousness?

M: The idea of un-consciousness exists in consciousness only.

Q: Then, how do you know you are in the supreme state?

M: Because I am in it. It is the only natural state.

Q: Can you describe it?

M: Only by negation, as uncaused, independent, unrelated, undivided, uncomposed, unshakable, unquestionable, unreachable by effort. Every positive definition is from memory and, therefore, inapplicable. And yet my state is supremely actual and, therefore, possible, realizable, attainable.

Q: Are you not immersed timelessly in an abstraction?

M: Abstraction is mental and verbal and disappears in sleep, or swoon; it reappears in time; I am in my own state *(swarupa)* timelessly in the *now*. Past and future are in the mind only — I am *now*.

Q: The world too is *now*.

M: Which world?

Q: The world around us.

M: It is your world you have in mind, not mine. What do you know of me, when even my talk with you is in your world only? You have no reason to believe that my world is identical with yours. My world is real, true, as it is perceived, while yours appears and disappears, according to the state of your mind. Your world is something alien, and you are afraid of it. My world is myself. I am at home.

Q: If you are the world, how can you be conscious of it? Is not the subject of consciousness different from its object?

M: Consciousness and the world appear and disappear together, hence they are two aspects of the same state.

Q: In sleep I am not, and the world continues.

M: How do you know?

Q: On waking up I come to know. My memory tells me.

M: Memory is in the mind. The mind continues in sleep.

Q: It is partly in abeyance.·

M: But its world picture is not affected. As long as the mind is there, your body and your world are there. Your world is mind-made, subjective, enclosed within the mind, fragmentary, temporary, personal, hanging on the thread of memory.

Q: So is yours?

M: Oh, no. I live in a world of realities, while yours is of imaginings. Your world is personal, private, unshareable, intimately your own. Nobody can enter it, see as you see, hear as you hear, feel your emotions and think your thoughts. In your world you are truly alone, enclosed in your ever-changing dream, which you take for life. My world is an open world, common to all, accessible to all. In my world there is community, insight, love, real quality; the individual is the total, the totality — in the individual. All are one and the One is all.

Q: Is your world full of things and people as is mine?

M: No, it is full of myself.

Q: But do you see and hear as we do?

M: Yes, I appear to hear and see and talk and act, but to me it just happens, as to you digestion or perspiration happens. The body-mind machine looks after it, but leaves me out of it. Just as you do not need to worry about growing hair, so I need not worry about words and actions. They just happen and leave me unconcerned, for in my world nothing ever goes wrong.   ●●●

8
The Self Stands Beyond Mind

Questioner: As a child fairly often I experienced states of complete happiness, verging on ecstasy: Later, they ceased, But since I came to India they reappeared, particularly after I met you. Yet these states, however wonderful, are not lasting. They come and go and there is no knowing when they will come back.

Maharaj: How can anything be steady in a mind which itself is not steady?

Q: How can I make my mind steady?

M: How can an unsteady mind make itself steady? Of course it cannot. It is the nature of the mind to roam about. All you can do is to shift the focus of consciousness beyond the mind.

Q: How is it done?

M: Refuse all thoughts except one: the thought 'I am'. The mind will rebel in the beginning, but with patience and perseverance it will yield and keep quiet. Once you are quiet, things will begin to happen spontaneously and quite naturally, without any interference on your part.

Q: Can I avoid this protracted battle with my mind?

M: Yes, you can. Just live your life as it comes, but alertly, watchfully, allowing everything to happen as it happens, doing the natural things the natural way, suffering, rejoicing — as life brings. This also is a way.

Q: Well, then I can as well marry, have children, run a business. . . . be happy.

M: Sure. You may or may not be happy, take it in your stride.

Q: Yet I want happiness.

M: True happiness cannot be found in things that change and pass away. Pleasure and pain alternate inexorably. Happiness comes from the self and can be found in the self only. Find your real self (swarupa) and all else will come with it.

Q: If my real self is peace and love, why is it so restless?

M: It is not your real being that is restless, but its reflection in the mind appears restless because the mind is restless. It is just like the reflection of the moon in the water stirred by the wind. The wind of desire stirs the mind and the 'me', which is but a reflection of the Self in the mind, appears changeful. But these ideas of movement, of restlessness, of pleasure and pain are all in the mind. The Self stands beyond the mind, aware, but unconcerned.

Q: How to reach it?

M: You are the Self, here and now Leave the mind alone, stand aware and unconcerned and you will realize that to stand alert but detached, watching events come and go, is an aspect of your real nature.

Q: What are the other aspects?

M: The aspects are infinite in number. Realize one, and you will realize all.

Q: Tell me some thing that would help me.

M: You know best what you need!

Q: I am restless. How can I gain peace?

M: For what do you need peace?

Q: To be happy.

M: Are you not happy now?

Q: No, I am not.

M: What makes you unhappy?

Q: I have what I don't want, and I want what I don't have.

M: Why don't you invert it: want what you have and care not for what you don't have?

Q: I want what is pleasant and don't want what is painful.

M: How do you know what is pleasant and what is not?

Q: From past experience, of course.

M: Guided by memory you have been pursuing the pleasant and shunning the unpleasant. Have you succeeded?

Q: No, I have not. The pleasant does not last. Pain sets in again.

M: Which pain?

Q: The desire for pleasure, the fear of pain, both are states of distress. Is there a state of unalloyed pleasure?

M: Every pleasure, physical or mental, needs an instrument. Both the physical and mental instruments are material, they get tired and worn out. The pleasure they yield is necessarily limited in intensity and duration. Pain is the background of all your pleasures. You want them because you suffer. On the other hand, the very search for pleasure is the cause of pain. It is a vicious circle.

Q: I can see the mechanism of my confusion, but I do not see my way out of it.

M: The very examination of the mechanism shows the way. After all, your confusion is only in your mind, which never rebelled so far against confusion and never got to grips with it. It rebelled only against pain.

Q: So, all I can do is to stay confused?

M: Be alert. Question, observe, investigate, learn all you can about confusion, how it operates, what it does to you and others. By being clear about confusion you become clear of confusion.

Q: When I look into myself, I find my strongest desire is to create a monument, to build something which will outlast me. Even when I think of a home, wife and child, it is because it is a lasting, solid, testimony to myself.

M: Right, build yourself a monument. How do you propose to do it?

Q: It matters little what I build, as long as it is permanent.

M: Surely, you can see for yourself that nothing is permanent. All wears out, breaks down, dissolves. The very ground on which you build gives way. What can you build that will outlast all?

Q: Intellectually, verbally, I am aware that all is transient. Yet, somehow my heart wants permanency. I want to create something that lasts.

M: Then you must build it of something lasting. What have you that is lasting? Neither your body nor mind will last. You must look elsewhere.

Q: I long for permanency, but I find it nowhere.

M: Are you, yourself, not permanent?

Q: I was born, I shall die.

M: Can you truly say you were not before you were born and can you possibly say when dead: 'Now I am no more'? You cannot say from your own experience that you are not. You can only say 'I am'. Others too cannot tell you 'you are not'.

Q: There is no 'I am' in sleep.

M: Before you make such sweeping statements, examine carefully your waking state. You will soon discover that it is full of gaps, when the mind blanks out. Notice how little you remember even when fully awake. You cannot say that you were not conscious during sleep. You just don't remember. A gap in memory is not necessarily a gap in consciousness.

Q: Can I make myself remember my state of deep sleep?

M: Of course! By eliminating the intervals of inadvertence during your waking hours you will gradually eliminate the long interval of absent-mindedness, which you call sleep. You will be aware that you are asleep.

Q: Yet, the problem of permanency, of continuity of being, is not solved.

M: Permanency is a mere idea, born of the action of time. Time again depends on memory. By permanency you mean unfailing memory through endless time. You want to eternalize the mind, which is not possible.

Q: Then what is eternal?

M: That which does not change with time. You cannot eternalize a transient thing — only the changeless is eternal.

Q: I am familiar with the general sense of what you say. I do not crave for more knowledge. All I want is peace.

M: You can have for the asking all the peace you want.

Q: I am asking.

M: You must ask with an undivided heart and live an integrated life.

Q: How?

M: Detach yourself from all that makes your mind restless. Renounce all that disturbs its peace. If you want peace, deserve it.

Q: Surely everybody deserves peace.

M: Those only deserve it, who don't disturb it.

Q: In what way do I disturb peace?

M: By being a slave to your desires and fears.

Q: Even when they are justified?

M: Emotional reactions, born of ignorance or inadvertence, are never justified. Seek a clear mind and a clean heart. All you need is to keep quietly alert, enquiring into the real nature of yourself. This is the only way to peace. ●●●

Responses of Memory

Questioner: Some say the universe was created. Others say that it always existed and is for ever undergoing transformations. Some say it is subject to eternal laws. Others deny even causality. Some say the world is real. Others — that it has no being whatsoever.

Maharaj: Which world are you enquiring about?

Q: The world of my perceptions, of course.

M: The world you can perceive is a very small world indeed. And it is entirely private. Take it to be a dream and be done with it.

Q: How can I take it to be a dream? A dream does not last.

M: How long will your own little world last?

Q: After all, my little world is but a part of the total.

M: Is not the idea of a total world a part of your personal world? The universe does not come to tell you that you are a part of it. It is you who have invented a totality to contain you as a part. In fact all you know is your own private world, however well you have furnished it with your imaginations and expectations.

Q: Surely, perception is not imagination!

M: What else? Perception is recognition, is it not? Something entirely unfamiliar can be sensed, but cannot be perceived. Perception involves memory.

Q: Granted, but memory does not make it illusion.

M: Perception, imagination, expectation, anticipation, illusion — all are based on memory. There are hardly any border lines between them. They just merge into each other. All are responses of memory.

Q: Still, memory is there to prove the reality of my world.

M: How much do you remember? Try to write down from memory what you were thinking, saying and doing on the 30th of the last month.

Q: Yes, there is a blank.

M: It is not so bad. You do remember a lot — unconscious memory makes the world in which you live so familiar.

Q: Admitted that the world in which I live is subjective and partial. What about you? In what kind of world do *you* live?

M: My world is just like yours. I see, I hear, I feel, I think, I speak and act in a world I perceive, just like you. But with you it is all, with me it is almost nothing. Knowing the world to be a part of myself, I pay it no more attention than you pay to the food you have eaten. While being prepared and eaten, the food is separate from you and your mind is on it; once swallowed, you become totally unconscious of it. I have eaten up the world and I need not think of it any more.

Q: Don't you become completely irresponsible?

M: How could I? How can I hurt something which is one with me. On the contrary, without thinking of the world, whatever I do will be of benefit to it. Just as the body sets itself right unconsciously, so am I ceaselessly active in setting the world right.

Q: Nevertheless, you are aware of the immense suffering of the world?

M: Of course I am, much more than you are.

Q: Then what do you do?

M: I look at it through the eyes of God and find that all is well.

Q: How can you say that all is well? Look at the wars, the exploitation, the cruel strife between the citizen and the state.

M: All these sufferings are man-made and it is within man's power to put an end to them. God helps by facing man with the results of his actions and demanding that the balance should be restored. *Karma* is the law that works for righteousness; it is the healing hand of God.   •••

10

Witnessing

Questioner: I am full of desires and want them fulfilled. How am I to get what I want?

Maharaj: Do you deserve what you desire? In some way or other you have to work for the fulfilment of your desires. Put in energy and wait for the results.

Q: Where am I to get the energy?

M: The desire itself is energy.

Q: Then why does not every desire get fulfilled?

M: Maybe it was not strong enough and lasting.

Q: Yes, that is my problem. I want things, but I am lazy when it comes to action.

M: When your desire is not clear nor strong, it cannot take shape. Besides, if your desires are personal, for your own enjoyment, the energy you give them is necessarily limited; it cannot be more than what you have.

Q: Yet, often ordinary persons do attain what they desire.

M: After desiring it very much and for a long time. Even then, their achievements are limited.

Q: And what about unselfish desires?

M: When you desire the common good, the whole world desires with you. Make humanity's desire your own and work for it. There you cannot fail.

Q: Humanity is God's work, not mine. I am concerned with myself. Have I not the right to see my legitimate desires fulfilled? They will hurt no one. My desires are legitimate. They are right desires, why don't they come true?

M: Desires are right or wrong according to circumstances· it depends on how you look at them. It is only for the individual that a distinction between right and wrong is valid.

Q: What are the guide-lines for such distinction? How am I to know which of my desires are right and which are wrong?

M: In your case desires that lead to sorrow are wrong and those which lead to happiness are right. But you must not forget others. Their sorrow and happiness also count.

Q: Results are in the future. How can I know what they will be?

M: Use your mind. Remember. Observe. You are not different from others. Most of their experiences are valid for you too. Think clearly and deeply, go into the entire structure of your desires and their ramifications. They are a most important part of your mental and emotional make-up and powerfully affect your actions. Remember, you cannot abandon what you do not know. To go beyond yourself, you must know yourself.

Q: What does it mean to know myself? By knowing myself what exactly do I come to know?

M: All that you are not.

Q: And not what I am?

M: What you are, you already are. By knowing what you are not, you are free of it and remain in your own natural state. It all happens quite spontaneously and effortlessly.

Q: And what do I discover?

M: You discover that there is nothing to discover. You are what you are and that is all.

Q: But ultimately what am I?

M: The ultimate denial of all you are not.

Q: I do not understand!

M: It is your fixed idea that you must be something or other, that blinds you.

Q: How can I get rid of this idea?

M: If you trust me, believe when I tell you that you are the pure awareness that illumines consciousness and its infinite content. Realize this and live accordingly. If you do not believe me, then go within, enquiring 'What am I'? or, focus your mind on 'I am', which is pure and simple being.

Q: On what my faith in you depends?

M: On your insight into other people's hearts. If you cannot look into my heart, look into your own.

Q: I can do neither.

M: Purify yourself by a well-ordered and useful life. Watch over your thoughts, feelings, words and actions. This will clear your vision.

Q: Must I not renounce every thing first, and live a homeless life?

M: You cannot renounce. You may leave your home and give trouble to your family, but attachments are in the mind and will not leave you until you know your mind in and out. First thing first — know yourself, all else will come with it.

Q: But you already told me that I am the Supreme Reality. Is it not self-knowledge?

M: Of course you are the Supreme Reality! But what of it? Every grain of sand is God; to know it is important, but that is only the beginning.

Q: Well, you told me that I am the Supreme Reality. I believe you. What next is there for me to do?

M: I told you already. Discover all you are not. Body, feelings, thoughts, ideas, time, space, being and not-being, this or that — nothing concrete or abstract you can point out to is you. A mere verbal statement will not do — you may repeat a formula endlessly without any result whatsoever. You must watch yourself continuously — particularly your mind — moment by moment, missing nothing. This witnessing is essential for the separation of the self from the not-self.

Q: The witnessing — is it not my real nature?

M: For witnessing, there must be something else to witness. We are still in duality!

Q: What about witnessing the witness? Awareness of awareness?

M: Putting words together will not take you far. Go within and discover what you are not. Nothing else matters.   ●●●

11

Awareness and Consciousness

Questioner: What do you do when asleep?
Maharaj: I am aware of being asleep.

Q: Is not sleep a state of unconsciousness?
M: Yes, I am aware of being unconscious.

Q: And when awake, or dreaming?
M: I am aware of being awake, or dreaming.

Q: I do not catch you. What exactly do you mean? Let me make my terms clear: by being asleep I mean unconscious, by being awake I mean conscious, by dreaming I mean conscious of one's mind, but not of the surroundings.
M: Well, it is about the same with me. Yet, there seems to be a difference. In each state you forget the other two, while to me there is but one state of being, including and transcending the three mental states of waking, dreaming and sleeping.

Q: Do you see in the world a direction and a purpose?
M: The world is but a reflection of my imagination. Whatever I want to see, I can see. But why should I invent patterns of creation, evolution and destruction? I do not need them. The world is in me, the world is myself. I am not afraid of it and have no desire to lock it up in a mental picture.

Q: Coming back to sleep. Do you dream?
M: Of course.

Q: What are your dreams?
M: Echoes of the waking state.

Q: And your deep sleep?

M: The brain consciousness is suspended.

Q: Are you then unconscious?

M: Unconscious of my surroundings — yes.

Q: Not quite unconscious?

M: I remain aware that I am unconscious.

Q: You use the words 'aware' and 'conscious'. Are they not the same?

M: Awareness is primordial; it is the original state, beginning-less, endless, uncaused, unsupported, without parts, without change. Consciousness is on contact, a reflection against a surface, a state of duality. There can be no consciousness without awareness, but there can be awareness without consciousness, as in deep sleep. Awareness is absolute, consciousness is relative to its content; consciousness is always of something. Consciousness is partial and changeful, awareness is total, change-less, calm and silent. And it is the common matrix of every experience.

Q: How does one go beyond consciousness into awareness?

M: Since it is awareness that makes consciousness possible, there is awareness in every state of consciousness. Therefore, the very consciousness of being conscious is already a movement in awareness. Interest in your stream of consciousness takes you to awareness. It is not a new state. It is at once recognized as the original, basic existence, which is life itself, and also love and joy.

Q: Since reality is all the time with us, what does self-realization consist of?

M: Realization is but the opposite of ignorance. To take the world as real and one's self as unreal is ignorance, the cause of sorrow. To know the self as the only reality and all else as temporal and transient is freedom, peace and joy. It is all very simple. Instead of seeing things as imagined, learn to see them as they are. When you can see everything as it is, you will also see yourself as you are. It is like cleansing a mirror. The same mirror that shows you the world as it is, will also show you your own face. The thought 'I am' is the polishing cloth. Use it.   ●●●

12

The Person is not Reality

Questioner: Kindly tell us how you realized.
Maharaj: I met my Guru when I was 34 and realized by 37.

Q: What happened? What was the change?
M: Pleasure and pain lost their sway over me. I was free from desire and fear. I found myself full, needing nothing. I saw that in the ocean of pure awareness, on the surface of the universal consciousness, the numberless waves of the phenomenal worlds arise and subside beginninglessly and endlessly. As consciousness, they are all me. As events they are all mine. There is a mysterious power that looks after them. That power is awareness, Self, Life, God, whatever name you give it. It is the foundation, the ultimate support of all that is, just like gold is the basis for all gold jewellery. And it is so intimately ours! Abstract the name and shape from the jewellery and the gold becomes obvious. Be free of name and form and of the desires and fears they create, then what remains?

Q: Nothingness.
M: Yes, the void remains. But the void is full to the brim. It is the eternal potential as consciousness is the eternal actual.

Q: By potential you mean the future?
M: Past, present and future — they are all there. And infinitely more.

Q: But since the void is void, it is of little use to us.
M: How can you say so? Without breach in continuity how can there be rebirth? Can there be renewal without death? Even the darkness of sleep is refreshing and rejuvenating. Without death we would have been bogged up for ever in eternal senility.

Q: Is there no such thing as immortality?

M: When life and death are seen as essential to each other, as two aspects of one being, that is immortality. To see the end in the beginning and beginning in the end is the intimation of eternity. Definitely, immortality is not continuity. Only the process of change continues. Nothing lasts.

Q: Awareness lasts?

M: Awareness is not of time. Time exists in consciousness only. Beyond consciousness where are time and space?

Q: Within the field of your consciousness there is your body also.

M: Of course. But the idea 'my body', as different from other bodies, is not there. To me it is 'a body', not 'my body', 'a mind', not 'my mind'. The mind looks after the body all right, I need not interfere. What needs be done is being done, in the normal and natural way.

You may not be quite conscious of your physiological functions, but when it comes to thoughts and feelings, desires and fears, you become acutely self-conscious. To me these too are largely unconscious. I find myself talking to people, or doing things quite correctly and appropriately, without being very much conscious of them. It looks as if I live my physical, waking life automatically, reacting spontaneously and accurately.

Q: Does this spontaneous response come as a result of realization, or by training?

M: Both. Devotion to your goal makes you live a clean and orderly life, given to search for truth and to helping people, and realization makes noble virtue easy and spontaneous, by removing for good the obstacles in the shape of desires and fears and wrong ideas.

Q: Don't you have desires and fears any more?

M: My destiny was to be born a simple man, a commoner, a humble tradesman, with little of formal education. My life was of the common kind, with common desires and fears. When, through my faith in my teacher and obedience to his words, I realized my true being, I left behind my human nature to look after itself, until its destiny is exhausted. Occasionally an old reaction, emotional or mental, happens in the mind, but it is at once noticed and discarded. After all, as long as one is burdened with a person, one is exposed to its idiosyncrasies and habits.

Q: Are you not afraid of death?

M: I am dead already.

Q: In what sense?

M: I am double dead. Not only am I dead to my body, but to my mind too.

Q: Well, you do not look dead at all!

M: That's what you say! You seem to know my state better than I do!

Q: Sorry. But I just do not understand. You say you are bodyless and mindless, while I see you very much alive and articulate.

M: A tremendously complex work is going on all the time in your brain and body, are you conscious of it? Not at all. Yet for an outsider all seems to be going on intelligently and purposefully. Why not admit that one's entire personal life may sink largely below the threshold of consciousness and yet proceed sanely and smoothly?

Q: Is it normal?

M: What is normal? Is your life — obsessed by desires and fears, full of strife and struggle, meaningless and joyless — normal? To be acutely conscious of your body is it normal? To be torn by feelings, tortured by thoughts: is it normal? A healthy body, a healthy mind live largely unperceived by their owner; only occasionally, through pain or suffering they call for attention and insight. Why not extend the same to the entire personal life? One can function rightly, responding well and fully to whatever happens, without having to bring it into the focus of awareness. When self-control becomes second nature, awareness shifts its focus to deeper levels of existence and action.

Q: Don't you become a robot?

M: What harm is there in making automatic, what is habitual and repetitive? It is automatic anyhow. But when it is also chaotic, it causes pain and suffering and calls for attention. The entire purpose of a clean and well-ordered life is to liberate man from the thraldom of chaos and the burden of sorrow.

Q: You seem to be in favour of a computerized life.

M: What is wrong with a life which is free from problems? Personality is merely a reflection of the real. Why should not the reflection be true to the original as a matter of course, automatically? Need the person have any designs of its own? The life of which it is an expression will guide it. Once you realize that the person is merely a shadow of the reality, but not reality itself, you cease to fret and worry. You agree to be guided from within and life becomes a journey into the unknown.   •••

where are you focused?

13

The Supreme, the Mind and the Body

Questioner: From what you told us it appears that you are not quite conscious of your surroundings. To us you seem extremely alert and active. We cannot possibly believe that you are in a kind of hypnotic state, which leaves no memory behind. On the contrary, your memory seems excellent. How are we to understand your statement that the world and all it includes does not exist, as far as you are concerned.

Maharaj: It is all a matter of focus. Your mind is focussed in the world; mine is focussed in reality. It is like the moon in daylight

— when the sun shines, the moon is hardly visible. Or, watch how you take your food. As long as it is in your mouth, you are conscious of it; once swallowed, it does not concern you any longer. It would be.troublesome to have it constantly in mind until it is eliminated. The mind should be normally in abeyance — incessant activity is a morbid state. The universe works by it-self — that I know. What else do I need to know?

Q: So a *gnani* knows what he is doing only when he turns his mind to it; otherwise he just acts, without being concerned.

M: The average man is not conscious of his body as such. He is conscious of his sensations, feelings and thoughts. Even these, once detachment sets in, move away from the centre of con-sciousness and happen spontaneously and effortlessly.

Q: What then is in the centre of consciousness?

M: That which cannot be given name and form, for it is without quality and beyond consciousness. You may say it is a point in consciousness, which is beyond consciousness. Like a hole in the paper is both in the paper and yet not of paper, so is the supreme state in the very centre of consciousness, and yet beyond consciousness. It is as if an opening in the mind through which the mind is flooded with light. The opening is not even the light. It is just an opening.

Q: An opening is just void, absence.

M: Quite so. From the mind's point of view, it is but an opening for the light of awareness to enter the mental space. By itself the light can only be compared to a solid, dense, rocklike, homogeneous and changeless mass of pure awareness, free from the mental patterns of name and shape.

Q: Is there any connection between the mental space and the supreme abode?

M: The supreme gives existence to the mind. The mind gives existence to the body.

Q: And what lies beyond?

M: Take an example. A venerable Yogi, a master in the art of longevity, himself over 1000 years old, comes to teach me his art. I fully respect and sincerely admire his achievements, yet all I can tell him is: of what use is longevity to me? I am beyond time. However long a life may be, it is but a moment and a dream. In the same way I am beyond all attributes. They appear and disappear in my light, but cannot describe me. The universe is all names and forms, based on qualities and their differences, while I am beyond. The world is there because I am, but I am not the world.

Q: But you are living in the world!

M: That's what you say! I know there is a world, which includes this body and this mind, but I do not consider them to be more "mine" than other minds and bodies. They are there, in time and space, but I am timeless and spaceless.

Q: But since all exists by your light, are you not the creator of the world?

M: I am neither the potentiality nor the actualization, nor the actuality of things. In my light they come and go as the specks of dust dancing in the sunbeam. The light illumines the specks, but does not depend on them. Nor can it be said to create them. It cannot be even said to know them.

Q: I am asking you a question and you are answering. Are you conscious of the question and the answer?

M: In reality I am neither hearing nor answering. In the world of events the question happens and the answer happens. Nothing happens to me. Everything just happens.

Q: And you are the witness?

M: What does witness mean? Mere knowledge. It rained and now the rain is over. I did not get wet. I know it rained, but I am not affected. I just witnessed the rain.

Q: The fully realized man, spontaneously abiding in the supreme state, appears to eat, drink and so on. Is he aware of it, or not?

M: That in which consciousness happens, the universal consciousness or mind, we call the ether of consciousness. All the objects of consciousness form the universe. What is beyond both, supporting both, is the supreme state, a state of utter stillness and silence. Whoever goes there, disappears. It is unreachable by words, or mind. You may call it God, or *Parabrahman,* or Supreme Reality, but these are names given by the mind. It is the nameless, contentless, effortless and spontaneous state, beyond being and not being.

Q: But does one remain conscious?

M: As the universe is the body of the mind, so is consciousness the body of the supreme. It is not conscious, but it gives rise to consciousness.

Q: In my daily actions much goes by habit, automatically. I am aware of the general purpose, but not of each movement in detail. As my consciousness broadens and deepens, details tend to recede, leaving me free for the general trends. Does not the same happens to a *gnani,* but more so?

M: On the level of consciousness — yes. In the supreme state, no. This state is entirely one and indivisible, a single solid block of reality. The only way of knowing it is to *be* it. The mind cannot reach it. To perceive it does not need the senses; to know it, does not need the mind.

Q: That is how God runs the world.

M: God is not running the world.

Q: Then who is doing it.?

M: Nobody. All happens by itself. You are asking the question and you are supplying the answer. And you know the answer when you ask the question. All is a play in consciousness. All divisions are illusory. You can know the false only. The true you must yourself *be.*

Q: There is the witnessed consciousness and there is the witnessing consciousness. Is the second the supreme?

M: There are the two — the person and the witness, the observer. When you see them as one, and go beyond, you are in the supreme state. It is not perceivable, because it is what makes perception possible. It is beyond being and not being. It is neither the mirror nor the image in the mirror. It is what *is* — the timeless reality, unbelievably hard and solid.

Q: The *gnani* — is he the witness or the Supreme?

M: He is the Supreme, of course, but he can also be viewed as the universal witness.

Q: But he remains a person?

M: When you believe yourself to be a person, you see persons everywhere. In reality there are no persons, only threads of memories and habits. At the moment of realization the person ceases. Identity remains, but identity is not a person, it is inherent in the reality itself. The person has no being in itself; it is a reflection in the mind of the witness, the 'I am', which again is a mode of being.

Q: Is the Supreme conscious?

M: Neither conscious nor unconscious, I am telling you from experience.

Q: *Pragnanam Brahma.* What is this *Pragna?*

M: It is the un-selfconscious knowledge of life itself.

Q: Is it vitality, the energy of life, livingness?

M: Energy comes first. For everything is a form of energy. Consciousness is most differentiated in the waking state. Less so in dream. Still less in sleep. Homogeneous — in the fourth state. Beyond is the inexpressible monolithic reality, the abode of the *gnani*.

Q: I have cut my hand. It healed. By what power did it heal?

M: By the power of life.

Q: What is that power?

M: It is consciousness. All is conscious.

Q: What is the source of consciousness?

M: Consciousness itself is the source of everything.

Q: Can there be life without consciousness?

M: No, nor consciousness without life. They are both one. But in reality only the Ultimate *is*. The rest is a matter of name and form. And as long as you cling to the idea that only what has name and shape exists, the Supreme will appear to you non-existing. When you understand that names and shapes are hollow shells without any content whatsoever, and what is real is nameless and formless, pure energy of life and light of consciousness, you will be at peace — immersed in the deep silence of reality.

Q: If time and space are mere illusions and you are beyond,

please tell me what is the weather in New York. Is it hot or raining there?

M: How can I tell you? Such things need special training. Or,
just travelling to New York. I may be quite certain that I am
beyond time and space, and yet unable to locate myself at will
at some point of time and space. I am not interested enough; I
see no purpose in undergoing a special Yogic training. I have
just heard of New York. To me it is a word. Why should I know
more than the word conveys? Every atom may be a universe, as
complex as ours. Must I know them all? I can — if I train.

Q: In putting the question about the weather in New York,
where did I make the mistake?

M: The world and the mind are states of being. The supreme is
not a state. It pervades all states, but it is not a state of something else. It is entirely uncaused, independent, complete in itself, beyond time and space, mind and matter.

Q: By what sign do you recognize it?

M: That's the point that it leaves no traces. There is nothing to
recognize it by. It must be seen directly, by giving up all search
for signs and approaches. When all names and forms have
been given up, the real is with you. You need not seek it. Plura-
lity and diversity are the play of the mind only. Reality is one.

Q: If reality leaves no evidence, there is no speaking about it.

M: It *is*. It cannot be denied. It is deep and dark, mystery
beyond mystery. But it *is,* while all else merely happens.

Q: Is it the Unknown?

M: It is beyond both, the known and the unknown. But I would
rather call it the known, than the unknown. For whenever something is known, it is the real that is known.

Q: Is silence an attribute of the real?

M: This too is of the mind. All states and conditions are of the
mind.

Q: What is the place of *samadhi*?

M: Not making use of one's consciousness is *samadhi*. You just
leave your mind alone. You want nothing, neither from your
body nor from your mind.   ●●●

14

Appearances and the Reality

Questioner: Repeatedly you have been saying that events are causeless, a thing just happens and no cause can be assigned to it. Surely everything has a cause, or several causes. How am I to understand the causelessness of things?

Maharaj: From the highest point of view the world has no cause.

Q: But what is your own experience?

M: Everything is uncaused. The world has no cause.

Q: I am not enquiring about the causes that led to the creation of the world. Who has seen the creation of the world? It may even be without a beginning, always existing. But I am not talking of the world. I take the world to exist — somehow. It contains so many things. Surely, each must have a cause, or several causes.

M: Once you create for yourself a world in time and space, governed by causality, you are bound to search for and find causes for everything. You put the question and impose an answer.

Q: My question is very simple: I see all kinds of things and I understand that each must have a cause, or a number of causes. You say they are uncaused — from your point of view. But, to you nothing has being and, therefore, the question of causation does not arise. Yet you seem to admit the existence of things, but deny them causation. This is what I cannot grasp. Once you accept the existence of things, why reject their causes?

M: I see only consciousness, and know everything to be but consciousness, as you know the picture on the cinema screen to be but light.

Q: Still, the movements of light have a cause.

M: The light does not move at all. You know very well that the movement is illusory, a sequence of interceptions and colourings in the film. What moves is the film — which is the mind.

Q: This does not make the picture causeless. The film is there, and the actors with the technicians, the director, the producer, the various manufacturers. The world is governed by causality. Everything is inter-linked.

M: Of course, everything is inter-linked. And therefore everything has numberless causes. The entire universe contributes to the least thing. A thing is as it is, because the world is as it is. You see, you deal in gold ornaments and I — in gold. Between the different ornaments there is no causal relation. When you re-melt an ornament to make another, there is no causal relation between the two. The common factor is the gold. But you cannot say gold is the cause. It cannot be called a cause, for it causes nothing by itself. It is reflected in the mind as 'I am', as the ornament's particular name and shape. Yet all is only gold. In the same way reality makes everything possible and yet nothing that makes a thing what it is, its name and form, comes from reality.

But why worry so much about causation? What do causes matter, when things themselves are transient? Let come what comes and let go what goes — why catch hold of things and enquire about their causes?

Q: From the relative point of view, everything must have a cause.

M: Of what use is the relative view to you? You are able to look from the absolute point of view — why go back to the relative? Are you afraid of the absolute?

Q: I am afraid. I am afraid of falling asleep over my so-called absolute certainties. For living a life decently absolutes don't help. When you need a shirt, you buy cloth, call a tailor and so on.

M: All this talk shows ignorance.

Q: And what is the knower's view?

M: There is only light and the light is all. Everything else is but a picture made of light. The picture is in the light and the light is in the picture. Life and death, self and not-self — abandon all these ideas. They are of no use to you.

Q: From what point of view you deny causation? From the relative — the universe is the cause of everything. From the absolute — there is no thing at all.

M: From which state are you asking?

Q: From the daily waking state, in which alone all these discussions take place.

M: In the waking state all these problems arise, for such is its nature. But, you are not always in that state. What good can you do in a state into which you fall and from which you emerge, helplessly. In what way does it help you to know that things are causally related — as they may appear to be in your waking state?

Q: The world and the waking state emerge and subside together.

M: When the mind is still, absolutely silent, the waking state is no more.

Q: Words like God, universe, the total, absolute, supreme are just noises in the air, because no action can be taken on them.

M: You are bringing up questions which you alone can answer.

Q: Don't brush me off like this! You are so quick to speak for the totality, the universe and such imaginary things! They cannot come and forbid you to talk on their behalf. I hate those irresponsible generalizations! And you are so prone to personalize them. Without causality there will be no order; nor purposeful action will be possible.

M: Do you want to know all the causes of each event? Is it possible?

Q: I know it is not possible! All I want to know is if there are causes for everything and the causes can be influenced, thereby affecting the events?

M: To influence events, you need not know the causes. What a roundabout way of doing things! Are you not the source and the end of every event? Control it at the source itself.

Q: Every morning I pick up the newspaper and read with dismay that the world's sorrows — poverty, hatred and wars — continue unabated. My questions are concerning the fact of sorrow, the cause, the remedy. Don't brush me off saying that it is Buddhism! Don't label me. Your insistence on causelessness removes all hope of the world ever changing.

M: You are confused, because you believe that you are in the world, not tne world in you. Who came first — you or your parents? You imagine that you were born at a certain time and place, that you have a father and a mother, a body and a name. This is your sin and your calamity! Surely you can change your world if you work at it. By all means, work. Who stops you? I have never discouraged you. Causes or no causes, you have made this world and you can change it.

Q: A causeless world is entirely beyond my control.

M: On the contrary, a world of which you are the only source and ground is fully within your power to change. What is created can be always dissolved and re-created. All will happen as you want it, provided you really want it.

Q: All I want to know is how to deal with the world's sorrows.

M: You have created them out of your own desires' and fears, you deal with them. All is due to your having forgotten your own being. Having given reality to the picture on the screen, you love its people and suffer for them and seek to save them. It is just not so. You must begin with yourself. There is no other way. Work, of course. There is no harm in working.

Q: Your universe seems to contain every possible experience. The individual traces a line through it and experiences pleasant and unpleasant states. This gives rise to questioning and seeking, which broaden the outlook and enable the individual to go beyond his narrow and self-created world, limited and self-centered. This personal world can be changed — in time. The universe is timeless and perfect.

M: To take appearance for reality is a grievous sin and the cause of all calamities. You are the all-pervading, eternal and infinitely creative awareness — consciousness. All else is local and temporary. Don't forget what you are. In the meantime work to your heart's content. Work and knowledge should go hand in hand.

Q: My own feeling is that my spiritual development is not in my hands. Making one's own plans and carrying them out leads nowhere. I just run in circles round myself. When God considers the fruit to be ripe, He will pluck it and eat it. Whichever fruit seems green to Him will remain on the world's tree for another day.

M: You think God knows you? Even the world He does not know.

Q: Yours is a different God. Mine is different. Mine is merciful. He suffers along with us.

M: You pray to save one, while thousands die. And if all stop dying, there will be no space on earth

Q: I am not afraid of death. My concern is with sorrow and suffering. My God is a simple God and rather helpless. He has no power to compel us to be wise. He can only stand and wait.

M: If you and your God are both helpless, does it not imply that the world is accidental? And if it is, the only thing you can do is to go beyond it. ●●●

15

The *Gnani*

Questioner: Without God's power nothing can be done. Even you would not be sitting here and talking to us without Him.

Maharaj: All is His doing, no doubt. What is it to me, since I want nothing? What can God give me, or take away from me? What is mine is mine and was mine even when God was not. Of course, it is a very tiny little thing, a speck — the sense 'I am', the fact of being. This is my own place, nobody gave it to me. The earth is mine; what grows on it is God's.

Q: Did God take the earth on rent from you?

M: God is my devotee and did all this for me.

Q: Is there no God apart from you?

M: How can there be? 'I am' is the root, God is the tree. Whom am I to worship, and what for?

Q: Are you the devotee or the object of devotion?

M: Am neither, I am devotion itself.

Q: There is not enough devotion in the world.

M: You are always after the improvement of the world. Do you really believe that the world is waiting for you to be saved?

Q: I just do not know how much I can do for the world. All I can do, is to try. Is there anything else you would like me to do?

M: Without you is there a world? You know all about the world, but about yourself you know nothing. You yourself are the tools of your work, you have no other tools. Why don't you take care of the tools before you think of the work?

Q: I can wait, while the world cannot.

M: By not enquiring you keep the world waiting.

Q: Waiting for what?

M: For somebody who can save it.

Q: God runs the world, God will save it.

M: That's what you say! Did God come and tell you that the world is His creation and concern and not yours?

Q: Why should it be my sole concern?

M: Consider. The world in which you live, who else knows about it?

Q: You know. Everybody knows.

M: Did anybody come from outside of your world to tell you? Myself and everybody else appear and disappear in your world. We are all at your mercy.

Q: It cannot be so bad! I exist in your world as you exist in mine.

M: You have no evidence of my world. You are completely wrapped up in the world of your own making.

Q: I see. Completely, but — hopelessly?

M: Within the prison of your world appears a man who tells you that the world of painful contradictions, which you have created, is neither continuous nor permanent and is based on a misapprehension. He pleads with you to get out of it, by the same way by which you got into it. You got into it by forgetting what you are and you will get out of it by knowing yourself as you are.

Q: In what way does it affect the world?

M: When you are free of the world, you can do something about it. As long as you are a prisoner of it, you are helpless to change it. On the contrary, whatever you do will aggravate the situation.

Q: Righteousness will set me free.

M: Righteousness will undoubtedly make you and your world a comfortable, even happy place. But what is the use? There is no reality in it. It cannot last.

Q: God will help.

M: To help you God must know your existence. But you and your world are dream states. In dream you may suffer agonies. None knows them, and none can help you.

Q: So all my questions, my search and study are of no use?

M: These are but the stirrings of a man who is tired of sleeping. They are not the causes of awakening, but its early signs. But, you must not ask idle questions, to which you already know the answers.

Q: How am I to get a true answer?

M: By asking a true question — non-verbally, but by daring to live according to your lights. A man willing to die for truth will get it.

Q: Another question. There is the person. There is the knower of the person. There is the witness. Are the knower and the witness the same, or are they separate states?

M: The knower and the witness are two or one? When the knower is seen as separate from the known, the witness stands alone. When the known and the knower are seen as one, the witness becomes one with them.

Q: Who is the *gnani*? The witness or the supreme?

M: The *gnani* is the supreme and also the witness. He is both being and awareness. In relation to consciousness he is awareness. In relation to the universe he is pure being.

Q: And what about the person? What comes first, the person or the knower.

M: The person is a very small thing. Actually it is a composite, it cannot be said to exist by itself. Unperceived, it is just not there. It is but the shadow of the mind, the sum total of memories. Pure being is reflected in the mirror of the mind, as knowing. What is known takes the shape of a person, based on memory and habit. It is but a shadow, or a projection of the knower onto the screen of the mind.

Q: The mirror is there, the reflection is there. But where is the sun?

M: The supreme is the sun.

Q: It must be conscious.

M: It is neither conscious nor unconscious. Don't think of it in terms of consciousness or unconsciousness. It is the life, which contains both and is beyond both.

Q: Life is so intelligent. How can it be unconscious?

M: You talk of the unconscious when there is a lapse in memory. In reality there is only consciousness. All life is conscious, all consciousness — alive.

Q: Even stones?

M: Even stones are conscious and alive.

Q: The worry with me is that I am prone to denying existence to what I cannot imagine.

M: You would be wiser to deny the existence of what you imagine. It is the imagined that is unreal.

Q: Is all imaginable unreal?

M: Imagination based on memories is unreal. The future is not entirely unreal.

Q: Which part of the future is real and which is not?

M: The unexpected and unpredictable is real.   •••

16

Desirelessness, the Highest Bliss

Questioner: I have met many realized people, but never a liberated man. Have you come across a liberated man, or does liberation mean, among other things, also abandoning the body?

Maharaj: What do you mean by realization and liberation?

Q: By realization I mean a wonderful experience of peace,

goodness and beauty, when the world makes sense and there is an all-pervading unity of both substance and essence. While such experience does not last, it cannot be forgotten. It shines in the mind, both as memory and longing. I know what I am talking about, for I have had such experiences.

By liberation I mean to be permanently in that wonderful state. What I am asking is whether liberation is compatible with the survival of the body.

M: What is wrong with the body?

Q: The body is so weak and shortlived. It creates needs and cravings. It limits one grievously.

M: So what? Let the physical expressions be limited. But liberation is of the self from its false and self-imposed ideas; it is not contained in some particular experience, however glorious.

Q: Does it last for ever?

M: All experience is time bound. Whatever has a beginning must have an end.

Q: So liberation, in my sense of the word, does not exist?

M: On the contrary, one is always free. You are, both conscious and free to be conscious. Nobody can take this away from you. Do you ever know yourself non-existing, or unconscious?

Q: I may not remember, but that does not disprove my being occasionally unconscious.

M: Why not turn away from the experience to the experiencer and realize the full import of the only true statement you can make: 'I am'?

Q: How is it done?

M: There is no 'how' here. Just keep in mind the feeling 'I am', merge in it, till your mind and feeling become one. By repeated attempts you will stumble on the right balance of attention and affection and your mind will be firmly established in the thought-feeling 'I am'. Whatever you think, say, or do, this sense of immutable and affectionate being remains as the ever-present background of the mind.

Q: And you call it liberation?

M: I call it normal. What is wrong with being, knowing and acting effortlessly and happily? Why consider it so unusual as to expect the immediate destruction of the body? What is wrong with the body that it should die? Correct your attitude to your body and leave it alone. Don't pamper, don't torture. Just keep it going, most of the time below the threshold of conscious attention.

Q: The memory of my wonderful experiences haunts me. I want them back.

M: Because you want them back, you cannot have them. The state of craving for anything blocks all deeper experience. Nothing of value can happen to a mind which knows exactly what it wants. For nothing the mind can visualize and want is of much value.

Q: Then what is worth wanting?

M: Want the best. The highest happiness, the greatest freedom. Desirelessness is the highest bliss.

Q: Freedom from desire is not the freedom I want. I want the freedom to fulfil my longings.

M: You are free to fulfil your longings. As a matter of fact, you are doing nothing else.

Q: I try, but there are obstacles which leave me frustrated.

M: Overcome them.

Q: I cannot, I am too weak.

M: What makes you weak? What is weakness? Others fulfil their desires, why don't you?

Q: I must be lacking energy.

M: What happened to your energy? Where did it go? Did you not scatter it over so many contradictory desires and pursuits? You don't have an infinite supply of energy.

Q: Why not?

M: Your aims are small and low. They do not call for more. Only God's energy is infinite — because He wants nothing for Himself. Be like Him and all your desires will be fulfilled. The higher your aims and vaster your desires, the more energy you will have for their fulfilment. Desire the good of all and the universe will work with you. But if you want your own pleasure, you must earn it the hard way. Before desiring, deserve.

Q: I am engaged in the study of philosophy, sociology and education. I think more mental development is needed before I can dream of self-realization. Am I on the right track?

M: To earn a livelihood some specialized knowledge is needed. General knowledge develops the mind, no doubt. But if you are going to spend your life in amassing knowledge, you build a wall round yourself. To go beyond the mind, a well-furnished mind is not needed.

Q: Then what is needed?

M: Distrust your mind, and go beyond.

Q: What shall I find beyond the mind?

M: The direct experience of being, knowing and loving.

Q: How does one go beyond the mind?

M: There are many starting points — they all lead to the same goal. You may begin with selfless work, abandoning the fruits of action; you may then give up thinking and end in giving up all desires. Here, giving up *(tyaga)* is the operational factor. Or, you may not bother about any thing you want, or think, or do and just stay put in the thought and feeling 'I am', focussing 'I am' firmly in your mind. All kinds of experience may come to you — remain unmoved in the knowledge that all perceivable is transient, and only the 'I am' endures.

Q: I cannot give all my life to such practices. I have my duties to attend to.

M: By all means attend to your duties. Action, in which you are not emotionally involved and which is beneficial and does not cause suffering will not bind you. You may be engaged in several directions and work with enormous zest, yet remain inwardly free and quiet, with a mirror-like mind, which reflects all, without being affected.

Q: Is such a state realizable?

M: I would not talk about it, if it were not. Why should I engage in fancies?

Q: Everybody quotes scriptures.

M: Those who know only scriptures know nothing. To know is to *be*. I know what I am talking about; it is not from reading, or hearsay.

Q: I am studying Sanskrit under a professor, but really I am only reading scriptures. I am in search of self-realization and I came to get the needed guidance. Kindly tell me what am I to do?

M: Since you have read the scriptures, why do you ask me?

Q: The scriptures show the general directions but the individual needs personal instructions.

M: Your own self is your ultimate teacher *(sadguru)*. The outer teacher (Guru) is merely a milestone. It is only your inner teacher, that will walk with you to the goal, for he is the goal.

Q: The inner teacher is not easily reached.

M: Since he is in you and with you, the difficulty cannot be serious. Look within, and you will find him.

Q: When I look within, I find sensations and perceptions, thoughts and feelings, desires and fears, memories and expectations. I am immersed in this cloud and see nothing else.

M: That which sees all this, and the nothing too, is the inner teacher. He alone *is,* all else only appears to be. He is your own self *(swarupa),* your hope and assurance of freedom; find him and cling to him and you will be saved and safe.

Q: I do believe you, but when it comes to the actual finding of this inner self, I find it escapes me.

M: The idea 'it escapes me', where does it arise?

Q: In the mind.

M: And who knows the mind.

Q: The witness of the mind knows the mind.

M: Did anybody come to you and say: 'I am the witness of your mind'?

Q: Of course not. He would have been just another idea in the mind.

M: Then who is the witness?

Q: I am.

M: So, you know the witness because you are the witness. You need not see the witness in front of you. Here again, to *be* is to know.

Q: Yes, I see that I am the witness, the awareness itself. But in which way does it profit me?

M: What a question! What kind of profit do you expect? To know what you are, is it not good enough?

Q: What are the uses of self-knowledge?

M: It helps you to understand what you are not and keeps you free from false ideas, desires and actions.

Q: If I am the witness only, what do right and wrong matter?

M: What helps you to know yourself is right. What prevents, is wrong. To know one's real self is bliss, to forget — is sorrow.

Q: Is the witness-consciousness the real Self?

M: It is the reflection of the real in the mind *(buddhi)*. The real is beyond. The witness is the door through which you pass beyond.

Q: What is the purpose of meditation?

M: Seeing the false as the false, is meditation. This must go on all the time.

Q: We are told to meditate regularly.

M: Deliberate daily exercise in discrimination between the true and the false and renunciation of the false is meditation. There are many kinds of meditation to begin with, but they all merge finally into one.

Q: Please tell me which road to self-realization is the shortest.

M: No way is short or long, but some people are more in earnest and some are less. I can tell you about myself. I was a simple man, but I trusted my Guru. What he told me to do, I did. He told me to concentrate on 'I am' — I did. He told me that I am beyond all perceivables and conceivables — I believed. I gave him my heart and soul, my entire attention and the whole of my spare time (I had to work to keep my family alive). As a result of faith and earnest application, I realized my self *(swarupa)* within three years.

You may choose any way that suits you; your earnestness will determine the rate of progress.

Q: No hint for me?

M: Establish yourself firmly in the awareness of 'I am'. This is the beginning and also the end of all endeavour.   •••

17

The Ever-present

Questioner: The highest powers of the mind are understanding, intelligence and insight. Man has three bodies — the physical, the mental and the causal *(prana, mana, karana)*. The physical reflects his being; the mental — his knowing and the causal — his joyous creativity. Of course, these are all forms in consciousness. But they appear to be separate, with qualities of their own. Intelligence *(buddhi)* is the reflection in the mind of the power to know *(chit)*. It is what makes the mind knowledgeable. The brighter the intelligence, the wider, deeper and truer the knowledge. To know things, to know people and to know oneself are all functions of intelligence: the last is the most important and contains the former two. Misunderstanding oneself and the world leads to false ideas and desires, which again lead to bondage. Right understanding of oneself is necessary for freedom from the bondage of illusion. I understand all this in theory, but when it comes to practice, I find that I fail hopelessly in my responses to situations and people and by my inappropriate reactions I merely add to my bondage. Life is too quick for my dull and slow mind. I do understand but too late, when the old mistakes have been already repeated.

Maharaj: What then is your problem?

Q: I need a response to life, not only intelligent, but also very quick. It cannot be quick unless it is perfectly spontaneous. How can I achieve such spontaneity?

M: The mirror can do nothing to attract the sun. It can only keep bright. As soon as the mind is ready, the sun shines in it.

Q: The light is of the Self, or of the mind?

M: Both. It is uncaused and unvarying by itself and coloured by the mind, as it moves and changes. It is very much like a cinema. The light is not in the film, but the film colours the light and makes it appear to move by intercepting it.

Q: Are you now in the perrect state?

M: Perfection is a state of the mind, when it is pure. I am beyond the mind, whatever its state, pure or impure. Awareness is my nature; ultimately I am beyond being and non-being.

Q: Will meditation help me to reach your state?

M: Meditation will help you to find your bonds, loosen them, untie them and cast your moorings. When you are no longer attached to anything, you have done your share. The rest will be done for you.

Q: By whom?

M: By the same power that brought you so far, that prompted your heart to desire truth and your mind to seek it. It is the same power that keeps you alive. You may call it Life or the Supreme.

Q: The same power kills me in due course.

M: Were you not present at your birth? Will you not be present at your death? Find him who is always present and your problem of spontaneous and perfect response will be solved.

Q: Realization of the eternal and an effortless and adequate response to the ever-changing temporary event are two different and separate questions. You seem to roll them into one. What makes you do so?

M: To realize the Eternal is to become the Eternal, the whole, the universe, with all it contains. Every event is the effect and the expression of the whole and is in fundamental harmony with the whole. All response from the whole must be right, effortless and instantaneous.

It cannot be otherwise, if it is right. Delayed response is wrong response. Thought, feeling and action must be one and simultaneous with the situation that calls for them.

Q: How does it come?

M: I told you already. Find him who was present at your birth and will witness your death.

Q: My father and mother?

M: Yes, your father-mother, the source from which you came. To solve a problem you must trace it to its source. Only in the dissolution of the problem in the universal solvents of enquiry and dispassion, can its right solution be found.　　●●●

18
To Know What you Are, Find What you Are Not

Questioner: Your way of describing the universe as consisting of matter, mind and spirit is one of the many. There are other patterns to which the universe is expected to conform, and one is at a loss to know which pattern is true and which is not. One ends in suspecting that all patterns are only verbal and that no pattern can contain reality. According to you, reality consists of three expanses: The expanse of matter-energy (mahadakash), the expanse of consciousness (chidakash) and of pure spirit (paramakash). The first is something that has both movement and inertia. That we perceive. We also know that we perceive —

we are conscious and also aware of being conscious. Thus, we have two: matter-energy and consciousness. Matter seems to be in space while energy is always in time, being connected with change and measured by the rate of change. Consciousness seems to be somehow here and now, in a single point of time and space. But you seem to suggest that consciousness too is universal — which makes it timeless, spaceless and impersonal. I can somehow understand that there is no contradiction between the timeless and spaceless and the here and now, but impersonal consciousness I cannot fathom. To me consciousness is always focalized, centered, individualized, a person. You seem to say that there can be perceiving without a perceiver, knowing without a knower, loving without a lover, acting without an actor. I feel that the trinity of knowing, knower and known can be seen in every movement of life. Consciousness implies a conscious being, an object of consciousness and the fact of being conscious. That which is conscious I call a person. A person lives in the world, is a part of it, affects it and is affected by it.

M: Why don't you enquire how real are the world and the person?

Q: Oh, no! I need not enquire. Enough if the person is not less real than the world in which the person exists.

M: Then what is the question?

Q: Are persons real, and universals conceptual, or are universals real and persons imaginary?

M: Neither are real.

Q: Surely, I am real enough to merit your reply and I am a person.

M: Not when asleep.

Q: Submergence is not absence. Even though asleep, I am.

M: To be a person you must be self-conscious. Are you so always?

Q: Not when I sleep, of course, nor when I am in a swoon, or drugged.

M: During your waking hours are you continually self-conscious?

Q: No, Sometimes I am absent-minded, or just absorbed.

M: Are you a person during the gaps in self-consciousness?

Q: Of course I am the same person throughout. I remember myself as I was yesterday and yester year — definitely, I am the same person.

M: So, to be a person, you need memory?

Q: Of course.

M: And without memory, what are you?

Q: Incomplete memory entails incomplete personality. Without memory I cannot exist as a person.

M: Surely you can exist without memory. You do so — in sleep.

Q: Only in the sense of remaining alive. Not as a person.

M: Since you admit that as a person you have only intermittent existence, can you tell me what are you in the intervals in between experiencing yourself as a person?

Q: I am, but not as a person. Since I am not conscious of myself in the intervals, I can only say that I exist, but not as a person.

M: Shall we call it impersonal existence?

Q: I would call it rather unconscious existence; I am, but I do not know that I am.

M: You have said just now: 'I am, but I do not know that I am'. Could you possibly say it about your being in an unconscious state?

Q: No, I could not.

M: You can only describe it in the past tense: 'I did not know. I was unconscious', in the sense of not remembering.

Q: Having been unconscious, how could I remember and what?

M: Were you really unconscious, or you just do not remember?

Q: How am I to make out?

M: Consider. Do you remember every second of yesterday?

Q: Of course, not.

M: Were you then unconscious?

Q: Of course, not.

M: So, you are conscious and yet you do not remember?

Q: Yes.

M: Maybe you were conscious in sleep and just do not remember.

Q: No, I was not conscious. I was asleep. I did not behave like a conscious person.

M: Again, how do you know?

Q: I was told so by those who saw me asleep.

M: All they can testify to is that they saw you lying quietly with closed eyes and breathing regularly. They could not make out whether you were conscious or not. Your only proof is your own memory. A very uncertain proof it is!

Q: Yes, I admit that on my own terms I am a person only during my waking hours. What I am in between, I do not know.

M: At least you know that you do not know! Since you pretend not to be conscious in the intervals between the waking hours, leave the intervals alone. Let us consider the waking hours only.

Q: I am the same person in my dreams.

M: Agreed. Let us consider them together — waking and dreaming. The difference is merely in continuity. Were your dreams consistently continuous, bringing back night after night the same surroundings and the same people, you would be at a loss to know which is the waking and which is the dream. Henceforward, when we talk of the waking state, we shall include the dream state too.

Q: Agreed. I am a person in a conscious relation with a world.

M: Are the world and the conscious relation with it essential to your being a person?

Q: Even immured in a cave, I remain a person.

M: It implies a body and a cave. And a world in which they can exist.

Q: Yes, I can see. The world and the consciousness of the world are essential to my existence as a person.

M: This makes the person a part and parcel of the world, or vice versa. The two are one.

Q: Consciousness stands alone. The person and the world appear in consciousness.

M: You said: appear. Could you add: disappear?

Q: No, I cannot. I can only be aware of my and my world's appearance. As a person, I cannot say: 'the world is not'. Without a world I would not be there to say it. Because there is a world, I am there to say: 'there is a world'.

M: May be it is the other way round. Because of you, there is a world.

Q: To me such statement appears meaningless.

M: Its meaninglessness may disappear on investigation.

Q: Where do we begin?

M: All I know is that whatever depends, is not real. The real is truly independent. Since the existence of the person depends on the existence of the world and it is circumscribed and defined by the world, it cannot be real.

Q: It cannot be a dream, surely.

M: Even a dream has existence, when it is cognized and enjoyed, or endured. Whatever you think and feel has being. But it may not be what you take it to be. What you think to be a person may be something quite different.

Q: I am what I know myself to be.

M: You cannot possibly say that you are what you think yourself to be! Your ideas about yourself change from day to day and from moment to moment. Your self-image is the most changeful thing you have. It is utterly vulnerable, at the mercy of a passer by. A bereavement, the loss of a job, an insult, and your image of yourself, which you call your person, changes deeply. To know what you are you must first investigate and know what you are not. And to know what you are not you must watch yourself carefully, rejecting all that does not necessarily go with the basic fact: 'I am'. The ideas: I am born at a given place, at a given time, from my parents and now I am so-and-so, living at, married to, father of, employed by, and so on, are not inherent in the sense 'I am'. Our usual attitude is of 'I am this'. Separate consistently and perseveringly the 'I am' from 'this' or 'that', and try to feel what it means to *be,* just to *be,* without being 'this' or 'that'. All our habits go against it and the task of fighting them is long and hard sometimes, but clear understanding helps a lot. The clearer you understand that on the level of the mind you can be described in negative terms only, the quicker you will come to the end of your search and realize your limitless being.   •••

19
Reality lies in Objectivity

Questioner: I am a painter and I earn by painting pictures. Has it any value from the spiritual point of view?
Maharaj: When you paint, what do you think about?

Q: When I paint, there is only the painting and myself.
M: What are you doing there?

Q: I paint.
M: No, you don't. You see the painting going on. You are watching only, all else happens.

Q: The picture is painting itself? Or, is there some deeper 'me', or some god who is painting?
M: Consciousness itself is the greatest painter. The entire world is a picture.

Q: Who painted the picture of the world?
M: The painter is in the picture.

Q: The picture is in the mind of the painter and the painter is in the picture, which is in the mind of the painter who is in the picture! Is not this infinity of states and dimensions absurd? The moment we talk of picture in the mind, which itself is in the picture, we come to an endless succession of witnesses, the higher witness witnessing the lower. It is like standing between two mirrors and wondering at the crowd!

M: Quite right, you alone and the double mirror are there. Between the two, your forms and names are numberless.

Q: How do you look at the world?

M: I see a painter painting a picture. The picture I call the world, the painter I call God. I am neither. I do not create, nor am I created. I contain all, nothing contains me.

Q: When I see a tree, a face, a sunset, the picture is perfect. When I close my eyes, the image in my mind is faint and hazy. If it is my mind that projects the picture, why need I open my eyes to see a lovely flower and with eyes closed I see it vaguely?

M: It is because your outer eyes are better than your inner eyes. Your mind is all turned outward. As you learn to watch your mental world, you will find it even more colourful and perfect than what the body can provide. Of course, you will need some training. But why argue? You imagine that the picture must come from the painter who actually painted it. All the time you look for origins and causes. Causality is in the mind only; memory gives the illusion of continuity and repetitiveness creates the idea of causality. When things repeatedly happen together, we tend to see a causal link between them. It creates a mental habit, but a habit is not a necessity.

Q: You have just said that the world is made by God.

M: Remember that language is an instrument of the mind; it is made by the mind, for the mind. Once you admit a cause, then God is the ultimate cause and the world the effect. They are different, but not separate.

Q: People talk of seeing God.

M: When you see the world you see God. There is no seeing God, apart from the world. Beyond the world to see God is to be God. The light by which you see the world, which is God, is the tiny little spark: 'I am', apparently so small, yet the first and the last in every act of knowing and loving.

Q: Must I see the world to see God?

M: How else? No world, no God.

Q: What remains?

M: You remain as pure being.

Q: And what becomes of the world and of God?

M: Pure being *(avyakta).*

Q: Is it the same as the Great Expanse *(paramakash)?*

M: You may call it so. Words do not matter, for they do not reach it. They turn back in utter negation.

Q: How can I see the world as God? What does it mean to see the world as God?

M: It is like entering a dark room. You see nothing — you may touch, but you do not see — no colours, no outlines. The window opens and the room is flooded with light. Colours and shapes come into being. The window is the giver of light, but not the source of it. The sun is the source. Similarly, matter is like the dark room; consciousness — the window — flooding matter with sensations and perceptions, and the supreme is the sun, the source both of matter and of light. The window may be closed, or open, the sun shines all the time. It makes all the difference to the room, but none to the sun. Yet all this is secondary to the tiny little thing which is the 'I am'. Without the 'I am' there is nothing. All knowledge is about the 'I am'. False ideas about this 'I am' lead to bondage, right knowledge leads to freedom and happiness.

Q: Is 'I am' and 'there is' the same?

M: 'I am' denotes the inner, 'there is' — the outer. Both are based on the sense of being.

Q: Is it the same as the experience of existence?

M: To exist means to be something, a thing, a feeling, a thought, an idea. All existence is particular. Only being is universal, in the sense that every being is compatible with every other being. Existences clash, being — never. Existence means becoming, change, birth and death and birth again, while in being there is silent peace.

Q: If I create the world, why have I made it bad?

M: Everyone lives in his own world. Not all the worlds are equally good or bad.

Q: What determines the difference?

M: The mind that projects the world, colours it its own way. When you meet a man, he is a stranger. When you marry him, he becomes your own self. When you quarrel, he becomes your enemy. It is your mind's attitude that determines what he is to you.

Q: I can see that my world is subjective. Does it make it also illusory?

M: It is illusory as long as it is subjective and to that extent only. Reality lies in objectivity.

Q: What does objectivity mean? You said the world is subjective and now you talk of objectivity. Is not everything subjective?

M: Everything is subjective, but the real is objective.

Q: In what sense?

M: It does not depend on memories and expectations, desires and fears, likes and dislikes. All is seen as it is.

Q: Is it what you call the fourth state *(turiya)*?

M: Call it as you like. It is solid, steady, changeless, beginningless and endless, ever new, ever fresh.

Q: How is it reached?

M: Desirelessness and fearlessness will take you there.　●●●

20

The Supreme is Beyond All

Questioner: You say, reality is one. Oneness, unity, is the attribute of the person. Is then reality a person, with the universe as its body?

Maharaj: Whatever you may say will be both true and false. Words do not reach beyond the mind.

Q: I am just trying to understand. You are telling us of the Person, the Self and the Supreme. *(vyakti, vyakta, avyakta).* The light of Pure Awareness *(pragna)*, focussed as 'I am' in the Self *(jivatma),* as consciousness *(chetana)* illumines the mind *(antahkarana)* and as life *(prana)* vitalizes the body *(deha).* All this is fine as far as the words go. But when it comes to distinguishing in myself the person from the Self and the Self from the Supreme, I get mixed up.

M: The person is never the subject. You can see a person, but you are not the person. You are always the Supreme which appears at a given point of time and space as the witness, a bridge between the pure awareness of the Supreme and the manifold consciousness of the person.

Q: When I look at myself, I find I am several persons fighting among themselves for the use of the body.

M: They correspond to the various tendencies *(samskara)* of the mind.

Q: Can I make peace between them?

M: How can you? They are so contradictory! See them as they are — mere habits of thoughts and feelings, bundles of memories and urges.

Q: Yet they all say 'I am'.

M: It is only because you identify yourself with them. Once you realize that whatever appears before you cannot be yourself, and cannot say 'I am', you are free of all your 'persons' and their demands. The sense 'I am' is your own. You cannot part with it, but you can impart it to anything, as in saying: I am young. I am rich etc. But such self-identifications are patently false and the cause of bondage.

Q: I can now understand that I am not the person, but that which, when reflected in the person, gives it a sense of being. Now, about the Supreme? In what way do I know myself as the Supreme?

M: The source of consciousness cannot be an object in consciousness. To know the source is to *be* the source. When you realize that you are not the person, but the pure and calm witness, and that fearless awareness is your very being, you *are* the being. It is the source, the Inexhaustible Possibility.

Q: Are there many sources or one for all?

M: It depends how you look at it, from which end. The objects in the world are many, but the eye that sees them is one. The higher always appears as one to the lower and the lower as many to the higher.

Q: Shapes and names are all of one and the same God?

M: Again, it all depends on how you look at it. On the verbal level everything is relative. Absolutes should be experienced, not discussed.

Q: How is the Absolute experienced?

M: It is not an object to be recognized and stored up in memory. It is in the present and in feeling rather. It has more to do with the 'how' than with the 'what'. It is in the quality, in the value; being the source of everything, it is in everything.

Q: If it is the source, why and how does it manifest itself?

M: It gives birth to consciousness. All else is in consciousness.

Q: Why are there so many centres of consciousness?

M: The objective universe *(mahadakash)* is in constant movement, projecting and dissolving innumerable forms. Whenever a form is infused with life *(prana)*, consciousness *(chetana)* appears by reflection of awareness in matter.

Q: How is the Supreme affected?

M: What can affect it and how? The source is not affected by the vagaries of the river nor is the metal — by the shape of the jewellery. Is the light affected by the picture on the screen? The Supreme makes everything possible, that is all.

Q: How is it that some things do happen and some don't?

M: Seeking out causes is a pastime of the mind. There is no duality of cause and effect. Everything is its own cause.

Q: No purposeful action is then possible?

M: All I say is that consciousness contains all. In consciousness all is possible. You can have causes if you want them, in *your* world. Another may be content with a single cause — God's will. The root cause is one: the sense 'I am'.

Q: What is the link between the Self *(Vyakta)* and the Supreme *(Avyakta)?*

M: From the self's point of view the world is the known, the Supreme — the Unknown. The Unknown gives birth to the known, yet remains Unknown. The known is infinite, but the Unknown is an infinitude of infinities. Just like a ray of light is never seen unless intercepted by the specs of dust, so does the Supreme make everything known, itself remaining unknown.

Q: Does it mean that the Unknown is inaccessible?

M: Oh, no. The Supreme is the easiest to reach for it is your very being. It is enough to stop thinking and desiring anything, but the Supreme.

Q: And if I desire nothing, not even the Supreme?

M: Then you are as good as dead, or you are the Supreme.

Q: The world is full of desires. Everybody wants something or other. Who is the desirer? The person or the self?

M: The self. All desires, holy and unholy, come from the self; they all hang on the sense 'I am'.

Q: I can understand holy desires *(satyakama)* emanating from the self. It may be the expression of the bliss aspect of the *Sadchitananda* (Beingness — Awareness — Happiness) of the Self. But why unholy desires?

M: All desires aim at happiness. Their shape and quality depend on the psyche *(antahkarana)*. Where inertia *(tamas)* predominates, we find perversions. With energy *(rajas)*, passions arise. With lucidity *(sattva)* the motive behind the desire is goodwill, compassion, the urge to make happy rather than be happy. But the Supreme is beyond all, yet because of its infinite permeability all cogent desires can be fulfilled.

Q: Which desires are cogent?

M: Desires that destroy their subjects, or objects, or do not subside on satisfaction are self-contradictory and cannot be fulfilled. Only desires motivated by love, goodwill and compassion are beneficial to both the subject and object and can be fully satisfied.

Q: All desires are painful, the holy as well as the unholy.

M: They are not the same and pain is not the same. Passion is painful, compassion — never. The entire universe strives to fulfil a desire born of compassion.

Q: Does the Supreme know itself? Is the Impersonal conscious?

M: The source of all has all. Whatever flows from it must be there already in seed form. And as a seed is the last of innumerable seeds, and contains the experience and the promise of numberless forests, so does the Unknown contain all that was, or could have been and all that shall or would be. The entire field of becoming is open and accessible; past and future co-exist in the eternal *now*.

Q: Are you living in the Supreme Unknown?

M: Where else?

Q: What makes you say so?

M: No desire ever arises in my mind.

Q: Are you then unconscious?

M: Of course not! I am fully conscious, but since no desire cr fear enters my mind, there is perfect silence.

Q: Who knows the silence?

M: Silence knows itself. It is the silence of the silent mind, when passions and desires are silenced.

Q: Do you experience desires occasionally?

M: Desires are just waves in the mind. You know a wave when you see one. A desire is just a thing among many. I feel no urge to satisfy it, no action needs be taken on it. Freedom from desire means this: the compulsion to satisfy is absent.

Q: Why do desires arise at all?

M: Because you imagine that you were born, and that you will die if you do not take care of your body. Desire for embodied existence is the root-cause of trouble.

Q: Yet, so many *jivas* get into bodies. Surely it cannot be some error of judgement. There must be a purpose. What could it be?

M: To know itself the self must be faced with its opposite — the not-self. Desire leads to experience. Experience leads to discrimination, detachment, self-knowledge — liberation. And what is liberation after àll? To know that you are beyond birth and death. By forgetting who you are and imagining yourself a mortal creature, you created so much trouble for yourself that you have to wake up, like from a bad dream.

Enquiry also wakes you up. You need not wait for suffering; enquiry into happiness is better, for the mind is in harmony and peace.

Q: Who exactly is the ultimate experiencer — the Self or the Unknown?

M: The Self, of course.

Q: Then why introduce the notion of the Supreme Unknown?

M: To explain the Self.

Q: But is there anything beyond the Self?

M: Outside the Self there is nothing. All is one and all is contained in 'I am'. In the waking and dream states it is the person. In deep sleep and *turiya* it is the Self. Beyond the alert intentness of *turiya* lies the great, silent peace of the Supreme. But in fact all is one in essence and related in appearance. In ignorance the seer becomes the seen and in wisdom he is the seeing.

But why be concerned with the Supreme? Know the knowers and all will be known. ●●●

21

Who am I?

Questioner: We are advised to worship reality personified as God, or as the Perfect Man. We are told not to attempt the worship of the Absolute, as it is much too difficult for a brain-centered consciousness.

Maharaj: Truth is simple and open to all. Why do you complicate? Truth is loving and lovable. It includes all, accepts all, purifies all. It is untruth that is difficult and a source of trouble. It always wants, expects, demands. Being false, it is empty, always in search of confirmation and reassurance. It is afraid of and avoids enquiry. It identifies itself with any support, however weak and momentary. Whatever it gets, it loses and asks for more. Therefore put no faith in the conscious. Nothing you can see, feel, or think is so. Even sin and virtue, merit and demerit are not what they appear. Usually the bad and the good are matter of convention and custom and are shunned or welcomed, according to how the words are used.

Q: Are there not good desires and bad, high desires and low?

M: All desires are bad, but some are worse than others. Pursue any desire, it will always give you trouble.

Q: Even the desire to be free of desire?

M: Why desire at all? Desiring a state of freedom from desire will not set you free. Nothing can set you free, because you *are* free. See yourself with desireless clarity, that is all.

Q: It takes time to know oneself.

M: How can time help you? Time is a succession of moments; each moment appears out of nothing and disappears into nothing, never to reappear. How can you build on something so fleeting?

Q: What is permanent?

M: Look to yourself for the permanent. Dive deep within and find what is real in you.

Q: How to look for myself?

M: Whatever happens, it happens to you. What you do, the doer is in you. Find the subject of all that you are as a person.

Q: What else can I be?

M: Find out. Even if I tell you that you are the witness, the silent watcher, it will mean nothing to you, unless you find the way to your own being.

Q: My question is: How to find the way to one's own being?

M: Give up all questions except one: 'Who am I'? After all, the only fact you are sure of is that you *are*. The 'I am' is certain. The 'I am this' is not. Struggle to find out what you are in reality.

Q: I am doing nothing else for the last 60 years.

M: What is wrong with striving? Why look for results? Striving itself is your real nature.

Q: Striving is painful.

M: You make it so by seeking results. Strive without seeking, struggle without greed.

Q: Why has God made me as I am?

M: Which God are you talking about? What is God? Is he not the very light by which you ask the question? 'I am' itself is God. The seeking itself is God. In seeking you discover that you are neither the body nor mind, and the love of the self in you is for the self in all. The two are one. The consciousness in you and the consciousness in me, apparently two, really one, seek unity and that is love.

Q: How am I to find that love?

M: What do you love now? The 'I am'. Give your heart and mind to it, think of nothing else. This, when effortless and natural, is the highest state. In it love itself is the lover and the beloved.

Q: Everybody wants to live, to exist. Is it not self-love?

M: All desire has its source in the self. It is all a matter of choosing the right desire.

Q: What is right and what is wrong varies with habit and custom. Standards vary with societies.

M: Discard all traditional standards. Leave them to the hypocrites. Only what liberates you from desire and fear and wrong ideas is good. As long as you worry about sin and virtue you will have no peace.

Q: I grant that sin and virtue are social norms. But there may be also spiritual sins and virtues. I mean by spiritual the absolute. Is there such a thing as absolute sin or absolute virtue?

M: Sin and virtue refer to a person only. Without a sinful or virtuous person what is sin or virtue? At the level of the absolute there are no persons; the ocean of pure awareness is neither virtuous nor sinful. Sin and virtue are invariably relative.

Q: Can I do away with such unnecessary notions?

M: Not as long as you think yourself to be a person.

Q: By what sign shall I know that I am beyond sin and virtue?

M: By being free from all desire and fear, from the very idea of being a person. To nourish the ideas: 'I am a sinner'. 'I am not a sinner', is sin. To identify oneself with the particular is all the sin there is. The impersonal is real, the personal appears and disappears. 'I am' is the impersonal Being. I am this is the person. The person is relative and the pure Being — fundamental.

Q: Surely pure Being is not unconscious, nor is it devoid of discrimination. How can it be beyond sin and virtue? Just tell us, please, has it intelligence or not?

M: All these questions arise from your believing yourself to be a person. Go beyond the personal and see.

Q: What exactly do you mean when you ask me to stop being a person?

M: I do not ask you to stop being — that you cannot. I ask you only to stop imagining that you were born, have parents, are a body, will die and so on. Just try, make a beginning — it is not as hard as you think.

Q: To think oneself as the personal is the sin of the impersonal.

M: Again the personal point of view! Why do you insist on polluting the impersonal with your ideas of sin and virtue? It just does not apply. The impersonal cannot be described in terms of good and bad. It is Being — Wisdom — Love — all absolute. Where is the scope for sin there? And virtue is only the opposite of sin.

Q: We talk of divine virtue.

M: True virtue is divine nature *(swarupa)*. What you are really is your virtue. But the opposite of sin which you call virtue is only obedience born out of fear.

Q: Then why all effort at being good?

M: It keeps you on the move. You go on and on till you find God. Then God takes you into Himself — and makes you as He is.

Q: The same action is considered natural at one point and a sin at another. What makes it sinful?

M: Whatever you do against your better knowledge is sin.

Q: Knowledge depends on memory.

M: Remembering your self is virtue, forgetting your self is sin. It all boils down to the mental or psychological link between the spirit and matter. We may call the link psyche *(antahkarana)*. When the psyche is raw, undeveloped, quite primitive, it is subject to gross illusions. As it grows in breadth and sensitivity, it becomes a perfect link between pure matter and pure spirit and gives meaning to matter and expression to spirit.

There is the material world *(mahadakash)* and the spiritual *(paramakash)*. Between lies the universal mind *(chidakash)*, which is also the universal heart *(premakash)*. It is wise love that makes the two one.

Q: Some people are stupid, some are intelligent. The difference is in their psyche. The ripe ones had more experience behind them. Just like a child grows by eating and drinking, sleeping and playing, so is man's psyche shaped by all he thinks and feels and does, until it is perfect enough to serve as a bridge between the spirit and the body. As a bridge permits the traffic between the banks, so does the psyche bring together the source and its expression.

M: Call it love. The bridge is love.

Q: Ultimately all is experience. Whatever we think, feel, do, is experience. Behind it is the experiencer. So all we know consists of these two, the experiencer and the experience. But the two are really one — the experiencer alone is the experience. Still, the experiencer takes the experience to be outside. In the same way the spirit and the body are one; they only appear as two.

M: To the Spirit there is no second.

Q: To whom then does the second appear? It seems to me that duality is an illusion induced by the imperfection of the psyche. When the psyche is perfect, duality is no longer seen.

M: You have said it.

Q: Still I have to repeat my very simple question: who makes the distinction between sin and virtue?

M: He who has a body, sins with the body, he who has a mind, sins with the mind.

Q: Surely, the mere possession of mind and body does not compel to sin. There must be a third factor at the root of it. I come back again and again to this question of sin and virtue, because now-a-days young people keep on saying that there is no such thing as sin, that one need not be squeamish and should follow the moment's desire readily. They will accept neither tradition nor authority and can be influenced only by solid and honest thought.

If they refrain from certain actions, it is through fear of police rather than by conviction. Undoubtedly there is something in what they say, for we can see how our values change from place to place and time to time. For instance — killing in war is great virtue today and may be considered a horrible crime next century.

M: A man who moves with the earth will necessarily experience days and nights. He who stays with the sun will know no darkness. My world is not yours. As I see it, you all are on a stage performing. There is no reality about your comings and goings. And your problems are so unreal!

Q: We may be sleep-walkers, or subject to nightmares. Is there nothing you can do?

M: I am doing: I did enter your dreamlike state to tell you —

"Stop hurting yourself and others, stop suffering, wake up".

Q: Why then don't we wake up?

M: You will. I shall not be thwarted. It may take some time. When you shall begin to question your dream, awakening will be . not far away.   ●●●

22
Life is Love and Love is Life

Questioner: Is the practice of Yoga always conscious? Or, can it be quite unconscious, below the threshold of awareness?

Maharaj: In the case of a beginner the practice of Yoga is often deliberate and requires great determination. But those who are practising sincerely for many years, are intent on self-realization all the time, whether conscious of it or not. Unconscious *sadhana* is most effective, because it is spontaneous and steady.

Q: What is the position of the man who was a sincere student of Yoga for some time and then got discouraged and abandoned all efforts?

M: What a man appears to do, or not to do, is often deceptive. His apparent lethargy may be just a gathering of strength. The causes of our behaviour are very subtle. One must not be quick to condemn, not even to praise. Remember that Yoga is the work of the inner self *(vyakta)* on the outer self *(vyakti)*. All that the outer does is merely in response to the inner.

Q: Still the outer helps.

M: How much can it help and in what way? It has some control over the body and can improve its posture and breathing. Over the mind's thoughts and feelings it has little mastery, for it is itself the mind. It is the inner that can control the outer. The outer will be wise to obey.

Q: If it is the inner that is ultimately responsible for man's spiritual development, why is the outer so much exhorted and encouraged?

M: The outer can help by keeping quiet and free from desire and fear. You would have noticed that all advice to the outer is in the form of negations: don't, stop, refrain, forego, give up, sacrifice, surrender, see the false as false. Even the little description of reality that is given is through denials — 'not this, not this', *(neti, neti)*. All positives belong to the inner self, as all absolutes — to Reality.

Q: How are we to distinguish the inner from the outer in actual experience?

M: The inner is the source of inspiration, the outer is moved by memory. The source is untraceable, while all memory begins somewhere. Thus the outer is always determined, while the inner cannot be held in words. The mistake of students consists in their imagining the inner to be something to get hold of, and forgetting that all perceivables are transient and, therefore, unreal. Only that which makes perception possible, call it Life or *Brahman,* or what you like, is real.

Q: Must Life have a body for its self-expression?

M: The body seeks to live. It is not life that needs the body; it is the body that needs life.

Q: Does life do it deliberately?

M: Does love act deliberately? Yes and no. Life is love and love is life. What keeps the body together but love? What is desire, but love of the self? What is fear but the urge to protect? And what is knowledge but the love of truth? The means and forms may be wrong, but the motive behind is always love — love of the me and the mine. The me and the mine may be small, or may explode and embrace the universe, but love remains.

Q: The repetition of the name of God is very common in India. Is there any virtue in it?

M: When you know the name of a thing, or a person, you can find it easily. By calling God by His name you make Him come to you.

Q: In what shape does He come?

M: According to your expectations. If you happen to be unlucky and some saintly soul gives you a *mantra* for good luck and you repeat it with faith and devotion, your bad luck is bound to turn. Steady faith is stronger than destiny. Destiny is the result of causes, mostly accidental, and is therefore loosely woven. Confidence and good hope will overcome it easily.

Q: When a *mantra* is chanted, what exactly happens?

M: The sound of *mantra* creates the shape which will embody the Self. The Self can embody any shape — and operate through it. After all, the Self is expressing itself in action — and a *mantra* is primarily energy in action. It acts on you, it acts on your surroundings.

Q: The *mantra* is traditional. Must it be so?

M: Since times immemorial a link was created between certain words and corresponding energies and reinforced by numberless repetitions. It is just like a road to walk on. It is an easy way — only faith is needed. You trust the road to take you to your destination.

Q: In Europe there is no tradition of a *mantra,* except in some contemplative orders. Of what use is it to a modern young Westerner?

M:ʹNone, unless he is very much attracted. For him the right procedure is to adhere to the thought that he is the ground of all knowledge, the immutable and perennial awareness of all that happens to the senses and the mind. If he keeps it in mind all the time, aware and alert, he is bound to break the bounds of non-awareness and emerge into pure life, light and love. The idea — 'I am the witness only' will purify the body and the mind and open the eye of wisdom. Then man goes beyond illusion and his heart is free of all desires. Just like ice turns to water, and water to vapour, and vapour dissolves in air and disappears in space, so does the body dissolve into pure awareness *(chidakash)*, then into pure being *(paramakash)*, which is beyond all existence and non-existence.

Q: The realized man eats, drinks and sleeps. What makes him do so?

M: The same power that moves the universe, moves him too.

Q: All are moved by the same power: what is the difference?

M: This only: The realized man knows what others merely hear, but don't experience. Intellectually they may seem convinced, but in action they betray their bondage, while the realized man is always right.

Q: Everybody says 'I am'. The realized man too says 'I am'. Where is the difference?

M: The difference is in the meaning attached to the words 'I am'. With the realized man the experience: 'I am the world, the world is mine' is supremely valid — he thinks, feels and acts integrally and in unity with all that lives. He may not even know the theory and practice of self-realization, and be born and bred free of religious and metaphysical notions. But there will not be the least flaw in his understanding and compassion.

Q: I may come across a beggar, naked and hungry and ask him: 'Who are you?' He may answer: 'I am the Supreme Self'. 'Well', I say, 'since you are the Supreme, change your present state'. What will he do?

M: He will ask you: 'Which state? What is there that needs changing? What is wrong with me?

Q: Why should he answer so?

M: Because he is no longer bound by appearances, he does not identify himself with the name and shape. He uses memory, but memory cannot use him.

Q: Is not all knowledge based on memory?

M: Lower knowledge — yes. Higher knowledge, knowledge of Reality, is inherent in man's true nature.

Q: Can I say that I am not what I am conscious of, nor am I consciousness itself?

M: As long as you are a seeker, better cling to the idea that you are pure consciousness, free from all content. To go beyond consciousness is the supreme state.

Q: The desire for realization, does it originate in consciousness, or beyond?

M: In consciousness, of course. All desire is born from memory and is within the realm of consciousness. What is beyond is clear of all striving. The very desire to go beyond consciousness is still in consciousness.

Q: Is there any trace, or imprint, of the beyond on consciousness?

M: No, there cannot be.

Q: Then, what is the link between the two? How can a passage be found between two states which have nothing in common? Is not pure awareness the link between the two?

M: Even pure awareness is a form of consciousness.

Q: Then what is beyond? Emptiness?

M: Emptiness again refers only to consciousness. Fullness and emptiness are relative terms. The Real is really beyond — beyond not in relation to consciousness, but beyond all relations of whatever kind. The difficulty comes with the word 'state'. The Real is not a state of something else — it is not a state of mind or consciousness or psyche — nor is it something that has a beginning and an end, being and not being. All opposites are contained in it — but it is not in the play of opposites. You must not take it to be the end of a transition. It is itself, after the consciousness as such is no more. Then words 'I am man', or 'I am God' have no meaning. Only in silence and in darkness can it be heard and seen. ●●●

23

Discrimination leads to Detachment

Maharaj: You are all drenched for it is raining hard. In my world it is always fine weather. There is no night or day, no heat or cold. No worries beset me there, nor regrets. My mind is free of thoughts, for there are no desires to slave for.

Questioner: Are there two worlds?

M: Your world is transient, changeful. My world is perfect, changeless. You can tell me what you like about your world — I shall listen carefully, even with interest, yet not for a moment shall I forget that your world is not, that you are dreaming.

Q: What distinguishes your world from mine?

M: My world has no characteristics by which it can be identified. You can say nothing about it. I am my world. My world is myself. It is complete and perfect. Every impression is erased, every experience — rejected. I need nothing, not even myself, for myself I cannot lose.

Q: Not even God?

M: All these ideas and distinctions exist in your world; in mine there is nothing of the kind. My world is single and very simple.

Q: Nothing happens there?

M: Whatever happens in your world, only there it has validity and evokes response. In my world nothing happens.

Q: The very fact of your experiencing your own world implies duality inherent in all experience.

M: Verbally — yes. But your words do not reach me. Mine is a non-verbal world. In your world the unspoken has no existence.

In mine — the words and their contents have no being. In your world nothing stays, in mine — nothing changes. My world is real, while yours is made of dreams.

Q: Yet we are talking.

M: The talk is in your world. In mine — there is eternal silence. My silence sings, my emptiness is full, I lack nothing. You cannot know my world until you are there.

Q: It seems as if you alone are in your world.

M: How can you say alone or not alone, when words do not apply? Of course, I am alone for I am all.

Q: Are you ever coming into our world?

M: What is coming and going to me? These again are words. *am.* Whence am I to come from and where to go?

Q: Of what use is your world to me?

M: You should consider more closely your own world, examine it critically and, suddenly, one day you will find yourself in mine.

Q: What do we gain by it?

M: You gain nothing. You leave behind what is not your own and find what you have never lost — your own being.

Q: Who is the ruler of your world?

M: There are no ruler and ruled here. There is no duality whatsoever. You are merely projecting your own ideas. Your scriptures and your gods have no meaning here.

Q: Still you have a name and shape, display consciousness and activity.

M: In your world I appear so. In mine I have being only. Nothing else. You people are rich with your ideas of possession, of quantity and quality. I am completely without ideas.

Q: In my world there is disturbance, distress and despair. You seem to be living on some hidden income, while I must slave for a living.

M: Do as you please. You are free to leave your world for mine.

Q: How is the crossing done?

M: See your world as it is, not as you imagine it to be. Discrimination will lead to detachment; detachment will ensure right action; right action will build the inner bridge to your real being. Action is a proof of earnestness. Do what you are told diligently and faithfully and all obstacles will dissolve.

Q: Are you happy?

M: In your world I would be most miserable. To wake up, to eat, to talk, to sleep again — what a bother!

Q: So you do not want to live even?

M: To live, to die — what meaningless words are these! When you see me alive, I am dead. When you think me dead, I am alive. How muddled up you are!

Q: How indifferent you are? All the sorrows of our world are as nothing to you.

M: I am quite conscious of your troubles.

Q: Then what are you doing about them?

M: There is nothing I need doing. They come and go.

Q: Do they go by the very act of your giving them attention?

M: Yes. The difficulty may be physical, emotional or mental; but it is always individual. Large scale calamities are the sum of numberless individual destinies and take time to settle. But death is never a calamity?

Q: Even when a man is killed?

M: The calamity is of the killer.

Q: Still, it seems there are two worlds, mine and yours.

M: Mine is real, yours is of the mind.

Q: Imagine a rock and a hole in the rock and a frog in the hole. The frog may spend its life in perfect bliss, undistracted, undisturbed. Outside the rock the world goes on. If the frog in the hole were told about the outside world, he would say: 'There is no such thing. My world is of peace and bliss. Your world is a word structure only, it has no existence'. It is the same with you. When you tell us that our world simply does not exist, there is no common ground for discussion. Or, take another example. I go to a doctor and complain of stomach ache. He examines me and says: 'You are all right'. 'But it pains' I say. 'Your pain is mental' he asserts. I say 'It does not help me to know that my pain is mental. You are a doctor, cure me of my pain. If you cannot cure me, you are not my doctor.'

M: Quite right.

Q: You have built the railroad, but for lack of a bridge no train can pass. Build the bridge.

M: There is no need of a bridge.

Q: There must be some link between your world and mine.

M: There is no need of a link between a real world and an imaginary world, for there cannot be any.

Q: So what are we to do?

M: Investigate your world, apply your mind to it, examine it critically, scrutinize every idea about it; that will do.

Q: The world is too big for investigation. All I know is that I am, the world is, the world troubles me and I trouble the world.

M: My experience is that everything is bliss. But the desire for bliss creates pain. Thus bliss becomes the seed of pain. The entire universe of pain is born of desire. Give up the desire for pleasure and you will not even know what is pain.

Q: Why should pleasure be the seed of pain?

M: Because for the sake of pleasure you are committing many sins. And the fruits of sin are suffering and death.

Q: You say the world is of no use to us — only a tribulation. I feel it cannot be so. God is not such a fool. The world seems to me a big enterprise for bringing the potential into actual, matter into life, the unconscious into full awareness. To realize the supreme we need the experience of the opposites. Just as for building a temple we need stone and mortar, wood and iron, glass and tiles, so for making a man into a divine sage, a master of life and death, one needs the material of every experience. As a woman goes to the market, buys provisions of every sort, comes home, cooks, bakes and feeds her lord, so we bake ourselves nicely in the fire of life and feed our God.

M: Well, if you think so, act on it. Feed your God, by all means.

Q: A child goes to school and learns many things, which will be of no use to it later. But in the course of learning it grows. So do we pass through experiences without number and forget them all, but in the meantime we grow all the time. And what is a *gnani* but a man with a genius for reality! This world of mine cannot be an accident. It makes sense, there must be a plan behind it. My God has a plan.

M: If the world is false, then the plan and its creator are also false.

Q: Again, you deny the world. There is no bridge between us.

M: There is no need of a bridge. Your mistake lies in your belief that you are born. You were never born nor will you ever die, but you believe that you were born at a certain date and place and that a particular body is your own.

Q: The world is, I am. These are facts.

M: Why do you worry about the world before taking care of yourself? You want to save the world, don't you? Can you save the world before saving yourself? And what means being saved? Saved from what? From illusion. Salvation is to see things as they are. I really do not see myself related to anybody and anything. Not even to a self, whatever that self may be. I remain forever — undefined. I am within and beyond — intimate and unapproachable.

Q: How did you come to it?

M: By my trust in my Guru. He told me: 'You alone are' and I did not doubt him. I was merely puzzling over it, until I realized that it is absolutely true.

Q: Conviction by repetition?

M: By self-realization. I found that I am conscious and happy absolutely and only by mistake I thought I owed being-consciousness-bliss to the body and the world of bodies.

Q: You are not a learned man. You have not read much and what you read, or heard did perhaps not contradict itself. I am fairly well educated and have read a lot and I found that books and teachers contradict each other hopelessly. Hence whatever I read or hear, I take it in a state of doubt. 'It may be so, it may not be so' is my first reaction. And as my mind is unable to decide what is true and what is not, I am left high and dry with my doubts. In Yoga a doubting mind is at a tremendous disadvantage.

M: I am glad to hear it; but my Guru too taught me to doubt — everything and absolutely. He said: 'deny existence to everything except your self.' Through desire you have created the world with its pains and pleasures.

Q: Must it be also painful?

M: What else? By its very nature pleasure is limited and transitory. Out of pain desire is born, in pain it seeks fulfilment, and it ends in the pain of frustration and despair. Pain is the background of pleasure, all seeking of pleasure is born in pain and ends in pain.

Q: All you say is clear to me. But when some physical or mental trouble comes, my mind goes dull and grey, or seeks frantically for relief.

M: What does it matter? It is the mind that is dull or restless, not you. Look, all kinds of things happen in this room. Do I cause them to happen? They just happen. So it is with you — the roll of destiny unfolds itself and actualizes the inevitable. You cannot change the course of events, but you can change your attitude and what really matters is the attitude and not the bare event. The world is the abode of desires and fears. You cannot find peace in it. For peace you must go beyond the world. The root-cause of the world is self-love. Because of it we seek pleasure and avoid pain. Replace self-love by love of the Self and the picture changes. *Brahma* the Creator is the sum total of all desires. The world is the instrument for their fulfilment. Souls take whatever pleasure they desire and pay for them in tears. Time squares all accounts. The law of balance reigns supreme.

Q: To be a superman one must be a man first. Manhood is the fruit of innumerable experiences. Desire drives to experience. Hence at its own time and level desire is right.

M: All this is true in a way. But a day comes when you have amassed enough and must begin to build. Then sorting out and discarding *(viveka-vairagya)* are absolutely necessary. Everything must be scrutinized and the unnecessary ruthlessly destroyed. Believe me, there cannot be too much destruction. For in reality nothing is of value. Be passionately dispassionate — that is all.   ●●●

24

God is the All-doer, the *Gnani* a Non-doer

Questioner: Some Mahatmas (enlightened beings) maintain that the world is neither an accident nor a play of God, but the result and expression of a mighty plan of work aiming at awakening and developing consciousness throughout the universe. From lifelessness to life, from unconsciousness to consciousness, from dullness to bright intelligence, from misapprehension to clarity — that is the direction in which the world moves ceaselessly and relentlessly. Of course, there are moments of rest and apparent darkness, when the universe seems to be dormant, but the rest comes to an end and the work on consciousness is resumed. From our point of view the world is a dale of tears, a place to escape from, as soon as possible and by every possible means. To enlightened beings the world is good and it serves a good purpose. They do not deny that the world is a mental structure and that ultimately all is one, but they see and say that the structure has meaning and serves a supremely desirable purpose. What we call the will of God is not a capricious whim of a playful deity, but the expression of an absolute necessity to grow in love and wisdom and power, to actualize the infinite potentials of life and consciousness.

Just as a gardener grows flowers from a tiny seed to glorious perfection, so does God in His own garden grow, among other beings, men to supermen, who know and love and work along with Him.

When God takes rest *(pralaya),* those whose growth was not completed, become unconscious for a time, while the perfect ones, who have gone beyond all forms and contents of consciousness, remain aware of the universal silence. When the time comes for the emergence of a new universe, the sleepers wake up and their work starts. The more advanced wake up first and prepare the ground for the less advanced — who thus find forms and patterns of behaviour suitable for their further growth.

Thus runs the story. The difference with your teaching is this: you insist that the world is no good and should be shunned. They say that distaste for the world is a passing stage, necessary, yet temporary, and is soon replaced by an all-pervading love, and a steady will to work with God.

Maharaj: All you say is right for the outgoing *(pravritti)* path. For the path of return *(nivritti)* naughting oneself is necessary. My stand I take where nothing *(paramakash)* is; words do not reach there, nor thoughts. To the mind it is all darkness and silence. Then consciousness begins to stir and wakes up the mind *(chidakash)*, which projects the world *(mahadakash)*, built of memory and imagination. Once the world comes into being, all you say may be so. It is in the nature of the mind to imagine goals, to strive towards them, to seek out means and ways, to display vision, energy and courage. These are divine attributes and I do not deny them. But I take my stand where no difference exists, where things are not, nor the minds that create them. There I am at home. Whatever happens, does not affect me — things act on things, that is all. Free from memory and expectation, I am fresh, innocent and wholehearted. Mind is the great worker *(mahakarta)* and it needs rest. Needing nothing, I am unafraid. Whom to be afraid of? There is no separation, we are not separate selves. There is only one Self, the Supreme Reality, in which the personal and the impersonal are one.

Q: All I want is to be able to help the world.

M: Who says you cannot help? You made up your mind about what help means and needs and got your self into a conflict between what you should and what you can, between necessity and ability.

Q: But why do we do so?

M: Your mind projects a structure and you identify yourself with it. It is in the nature of desire to prompt the mind to create a world for its fulfilment. Even a small desire can start a long line of action; what about a strong desire? Desire can produce a universe; its powers are miraculous. Just as a small matchstick can set a huge forest on fire, so does a desire light the fires of manifestation. The very purpose of creation is the fulfilment of desire. The desire may be noble, or ignoble, space *(akash)* is neutral — one can fill it with what one likes: You must be very careful as to what you desire. And as to the people you want to help, they are in their respective worlds for the sake of their desires; there is no way of helping them except through their desires. You can only teach them to have right desires so that they may rise above them and be free from the urge to create and re-create worlds of desires, abodes of pain and pleasure.

Q: A day must come when the show is wound up; a man must die, a universe come to an end.

M: Just as a sleeping man forgets all and wakes up for another day, or he dies and emerges into another life, so do the worlds of desire and fear dissolve and disappear. But the universal witness, the Supreme Self never sleeps and never dies. Eternally the Great Heart beats and at each beat a new universe comes into being.

Q: Is he conscious?

M: He is beyond all that the mind conceives. He is beyond being and not being. He is the Yes and No to everything, beyond and within, creating and destroying, unimaginably real.

Q: God and the Mahatma are they one or two?

M: They are one.

Q: There must be some difference.

M: God is the All-Doer, the *gnani* is a non-doer. God himself does not say: 'I am doing all.' To Him things happen by their own nature. To the *gnani* all is done by God. He sees no difference between God and nature. Both God and the *gnani* know themselves to be the immovable centre of the movable, the eternal witness of the transient. The centre is a point of void and the witness a point of pure awareness; they know themselves to be as nothing, therefore nothing can resist them.

Q: How does this look and feel in your personal experience?

M: Being nothing, I am all. Everything is me, everything is mine. Just as my body moves by my mere thinking of the movement, so do things happen as I think of them. Mind you, I do nothing. I just see them happen.

Q: Do things happen as you want them to happen, or do you want them to happen as they happen?

M: Both. I accept and am accepted. I am all and all is me. Being the world I am not afraid of the world. Being all, what am I to be afraid of? Water is not afraid of water, nor fire of fire. Also I am not afraid because I am nothing that can experience fear, or can be in danger. I have no shape, nor name. It is attachment to a name and shape that breeds fear. I am not attached. I am nothing, and nothing is afraid of no thing. On the contrary, everything is afraid of the Nothing, for when a thing touches Nothing, it becomes nothing. It is like a bottomless well, whatever falls into it, disappears.

Q: Isn't God a person?

M: As long as you think yourself to be a person, He too is a person. When you are all, you see Him as all.

Q: Can I change facts by changing attitude?

M: The attitude is the fact. Take anger. I may be furious, pacing the room up and down; at the same time I know what I am, a centre of wisdom and love, an atom of pure existence. All subsides and the mind merges into silence.

Q: Still, you are angry sometimes.

M: With whom am I to be angry and for what? Anger came and dissolved on my remembering myself. It is all a play of *gunas* (qualities of cosmic matter). When I identify myself with them, I am their slave. When I stand apart, I am their master.

Q: Can you influence the world by your attitude? By separating yourself from the world you lose all hope of helping it.

M: How can it be? All is myself — can't I help myself? I do not identify myself with anybody in particular, for I am all — both the particular and the universal.

Q: Can you then help me, the particular person?

M: But I do help you always — from within. My self and your self are one. I know it, but you don't. That is all the difference — and it cannot last.

Q: And how do you help the entire world?

M: Gandhi is dead, yet his mind pervades the earth. The thought of a *gnani* pervades humanity and works ceaselessly for good. Being anonymous, coming from within, it is the more powerful and compelling. That is how the world improves — the inner aiding and blessing the outer. When a *gnani* dies, he is no more, in the same sense in which a river is no more when it merges in the sea; the name, the shape, are no more, but the water remains and becomes one with the ocean. When a *gnani* joins the universal mind, all his goodness and wisdom become the heritage of humanity and uplift every human being.

Q: We are attached to our personality. Our individuality, our being unlike others, we value very much. You seem to denounce both as useless. Your unmanifested, of what use is it to us?

M: Unmanifested, manifested, individuality, personality *(nirguna, saguna, vyakta, vyakti);* all these are mere words, points of view, mental attitudes. There is no reality in them. The real is experienced in silence. You cling to personality — but you are conscious of being a person only when you are in trouble — when you are not in trouble you do not think of yourself.

Q: You did not tell me the uses of the Unmanifested.

M: Surely, you must sleep in order to wake up. You must die in order to live, you must melt down to shape anew. You must destroy to build, annihilate before creation. The Supreme is the universal solvent, it corrodes every container, it burns through every obstacle. Without the absolute denial of everything the tyranny of things would be absolute. The Supreme is the great harmonizer, the guarantee of the ultimate and perfect balance — of life in freedom. It dissolves you and thus re-asserts your true being.

Q: It is all well on its own level. But how does it work in daily life?

M: The daily life is a life of action. Whether you like it or not, you must function. Whatever you do for your own sake accumulates and becomes explosive; one day it goes off and plays havoc with you and your world. When you deceive yourself that you work for the good of all, it makes matters worse, for you should not be guided by your own ideas of what is good for others. A man who claims to know what is good for others, is dangerous.

Q: How is one to work then?

M: Neither for yourself nor for others, but for the work's own sake. A thing worth doing is its own purpose and meaning. Make nothing a means to something else. Bind not. God does not create one thing to serve another. Each is made for its own sake. Because it is made for itself, it does not interfere. You are using things and people for purposes alien to them and you play havoc with the world and yourself.

Q: Our real being is all the time with us, you say. How is it that we do not notice it?

M: Yes, you are always the Supreme. But your attention is fixed on things, physical or mental. When your attention is off a thing and not yet fixed on another, in the interval you are pure being. When through the practice of discrimination and detachment *(viveka-vairagya),* you lose sight of sensory and mental states, pure being emerges as the natural state.

Q: How does one bring to an end this sense of separateness?

M: By focussing the mind on 'I am', on the sense of being, 'I am so-and-so' dissolves; '. am a witness only' remains and that too submerges in 'I am all'. Then the all becomes the One and the One — yourself, not to be separate from me. Abandon the idea of a separate 'I' and the question of 'whose experience?' will not arise.

Q: You speak from your own experience. How can I make it mine?

M: You speak of my experience as different from your experience, because you believe we are separate. But we are not. On a deeper level my experience is your experience. Dive deep within yourself and you will find it easily and simply. Go in the direction of 'I am'.   ●●●

25

Hold on to 'I am'

Questioner: Are you ever glad or sad? Do you know joy and sorrow?

Maharaj: Call them as you please. To me they are states of mind only, and I am not the mind.

Q: Is love a state of mind?

M: Again, it depends what you mean by love. Desire is, of course, a state of mind. But the realization of unity is beyond mind. To me, nothing exists by itself. All is the Self, all is myself. To see myself in everybody and everybody in myself most certainly is love.

Q: When I see something pleasant, I want it. Who exactly wants it? The self or the mind?

M: The question is wrongly put. There is no 'who'. There is desire, fear, anger, and the mind says — this is me, this is mine. There is no thing which could be called 'me' or 'mine'. Desire is a state of the mind, perceived and named by the mind. Without the mind perceiving and naming, where is desire?

Q: But is there such a thing as perceiving without naming?

M: Of course. Naming cannot go beyond the mind, while perceiving is consciousness itself.

Q: When somebody dies what exactly happens?

M: Nothing happens. Something becomes nothing. Nothing was, nothing remains.

Q: Surely there is a difference between the living and the dead. You speak of the living as dead and of the dead as living.

M: Why do you fret at one man dying and care little for the millions dying every day? Entire universes are imploding and ex-

ploding every moment — am I to cry over them? One thing is
quite clear to me: all that is, lives and moves and has its being in
consciousness and I am in and beyond that consciousness. I
am in it as the witness. I am beyond it as Being.

Q: Surely, you care when your child is ill, don't you?

M: I don't get flustered. I just do the needful. I do not worry
about the future. A right response to every situation is in my nature. I do not stop to think what to do. I act and move on. Results
do not affect me. I do not even care, whether they are good or
bad. Whatever they are, they are — if they come back to me, I
deal with them afresh. Or, rather, I happen to deal with them afresh. There is no sense of purpose in my doing anything. Things
happens as they happen — not because I make them happen,
but it is because I *am* that they happen. In reality nothing ever
happens. When the mind is restless, it makes *Shiva* dance, like
the restless waters of the lake make the moon dance. It is all
appearance, due to wrong ideas.

Q: Surely, you are aware of many things and behave according
to their nature. You treat a child as a child and an adult as an
adult.

M: Just as the taste of salt pervades the great ocean and every
single drop of sea-water carries the same flavour, so every experience gives me the touch of reality, the ever fresh realization
of my own being.

Q: Do I exist in your world, as you exist in mine?

M: Of course, you are and I am. But only as points in consciousness; we are nothing apart from consciousness. This
must be well grasped: the world hangs on the thread of
consciousness; no consciousness, no world.

Q: There are many points in consciousness; are there as many
worlds?

M: Take dream for an example. In a hospital there may be
many patients, all sleeping, all dreaming, each dreaming his
own private, personal dream, unrelated, unaffected, having one
single factor in common — illness. Similarly, we have divorced
ourselves in our imagination from the real world of common experience and enclosed ourselves is a cloud of personal desires

and fears, images and thoughts, ideas and concepts.

Q: This I can understand. But what could be the cause of the tremendous variety of the personal worlds?

M: The variety is not so great. All the dreams are superimposed over a common world. To some extent they shape and influence each other. The basic unity operates in spite of all. At the root of it all lies self-forgetfulness; not knowing who I am.

Q: To forget, one must know. Did I know who I am, before I forgot it?

M: Of course. Self-forgetting is inherent in self-knowing. Consciousness and unconsciousness are two aspects of one life. They co-exist. To know the world you forget the self — to know the self you forget the world. What is world after all? A collection of memories. Cling to one thing, that matters, hold on to 'I am' and let go all else. This is *sadhana*. In realization there is nothing to hold on to and nothing to forget. Everything is known, nothing is remembered.

Q: What is the cause of self-forgetting?

M: There is no cause, because there is no forgetting. Mental states succeed one another, and each obliterates the previous one. Self-remembering is a mental state and self-forgetting is another. They alternate like day and night. Reality is beyond both.

Q: Surely there must be a difference between forgetting and not knowing. Not knowing needs no cause. Forgetting presupposes previous knowledge and also the tendency or ability to forget. I admit I cannot enquire into the reason for not-knowing, but forgetting must have some ground.

M: There is no such thing as not-knowing. There is only forgetting. What is wrong with forgetting? It is as simple to forget as to remember.

Q: Is it not a calamity to forget oneself?

M: As bad as to remember oneself continuously. There is a state beyond forgetting and not-forgetting — the natural state. To remember, to forget — these are all states of mind, thought-bound, word-bound. Take for example, the idea of being born. I am told I was born. I do not remember. I am told I shall die. I do not expect it. You tell me I have forgotten, or I lack imagination. But I just cannot remember what never happened, nor expect the patently impossible. Bodies are born and bodies die, but what is it to me? Bodies come and go in consciousness and consciousness itself has its roots in me. I am life and mine are mind and body.

Q: You say at the root of the world is self-forgetfulness. To forget I must remember: What did I forget to remember? I have not forgotten that I am.

M: This 'I am' too may be a part of the illusion.

Q: How can it be? You cannot prove to me that I am not. Even when convinced that I am not — I am.

M: Reality can neither be proved nor disproved. Within the mind you cannot, beyond the mind you need not. In the real, the question 'what is real?' does not arise. The manifested *(saguna)* and unmanifested *(nirguna)* are not different.

Q: In that case all is real.

M: I am all. As myself all is real. Apart from me, nothing is real.

Q: I do not feel that the world is the result of a mistake.

M: You may say so only after a full investigation, not before. Of course, when you discern and let go all that is unreal, what remains is real.

Q: Does anything remain?

M: The real remains. But don't be mislead by words!

Q: Since immemorial time, during innumerable births, I build and improve and beautify my world. It is neither perfect, nor unreal. It is a process.

M: You are mistaken. The world has no existence apart from you. At every moment it is but a reflection of yourself. You create it, you destroy it.

Q: And build it again, improved.

M: To improve it, you must disprove it. One must die to live. There is no rebirth, except through death.

Q: Your universe may be perfect. My personal universe is improving.

M: Your personal universe does not exist by itself. It is merely a limited and distorted view of the real. It is not the universe that needs improving, but your way of looking.

Q: How do you view it?

M: It is a stage on which a world drama is being played. The quality of the performance is all that matters; not what the actors say and do, but how they say and do it.

Q: I do not like this *lila* (play) idea. I would rather compare the world to a work-yard in which we are the builders.

M: You take it too seriously. What is wrong with play? You have a purpose only as long as you are not complete *(purna);* till then completeness, perfection, is the purpose. But when you are complete in yourself, fully integrated within and without, then you enjoy the universe; you do not labour at it. To the disinte- grated you may seem working hard, but that is their illusion. Sportsmen seem to make tremendous efforts: yet their sole mo- tive is to play and display.

Q: Do you mean to say that God is just having fun, that he is engaged in purposeless action?

M: God is not only true and good, he is also beautiful *(satyam-shivam-sundaram).* He creates beauty — for the joy of it.

Q: Well, then beauty is his purpose!

M: Why do you introduce purpose? Purpose implies move- ment, change, a sense of imperfection. God does not aim at beauty — whatever he does is beautiful. Would you say that a flower is trying to be beautiful? It is beautiful by its very nature. Similarly God is perfection itself, not an effort at perfection.

Q: The purpose fulfils itself in beauty.

M: What is beautiful? Whatever is perceived blissfully is beauti- ful. Bliss is the essence of beauty.

Q: You speak of *Sat-Chit-Ananda.* That I am is obvious. That I know is obvious. That I am happy is not at all obvious. Where has my happiness gone?

M: Be fully aware of your own being and you will be in bliss consciously. Because you take your mind off yourself and make it dwell on what you are not, you lose your sense of well-being, of being well.

Q: There are two paths before us — the path of effort *(yoga marga)*, and the path of ease *(bhoga marga)*. Both lead to the same goal — liberation.

M: Why do you call *bhoga* a path? How can ease bring you perfection?

Q: The perfect renouncer *(yogi)* will find reality. The perfect enjoyer *(bhogi)* also will come to it.

M: How can it be? Aren't they contradictory?

Q: The extremes meet. To be a perfect Bhogi is more difficult than to be a perfect Yogi.

I am a humble man and cannot venture judgements of value. Both the Yogi and the Bhogi, after all, are concerned with the search for happiness. The Yogi wants it permanent, the Bhogi is satisfied with the intermittent. Often the Bhogi strives harder than the Yogi.

M: What is your happiness worth when you have to strive and labour for it? True happiness is spontaneous and effortless.

Q: All beings seek happiness. The means only differ. Some seek it within and are therefore called Yogis; some seek it without and are condemned as Bhogis. Yet they need each other.

M: Pleasure and pain alternate. Happiness is unshakable. What you can seek and find is not the real thing. Find what you have never lost, find the inalienable.   ●●●

26

Personality, an Obstacle

Questioner: As I can see, the world is a school of Yoga and life itself is Yoga practice. Everybody strives for perfection and what is Yoga but striving. There is nothing contemptible about the so-called 'common' people and their 'common' lives. They strive as hard and suffer as much as the Yogi, only they are not conscious of their true purpose.

Maharaj: In what way are your common people — Yogis?

Q: Their ultimate goal is the same. What the Yogi secures by renunciation *(tyaga)* the common man realizes through experience *(bhoga)*. The way of Bhoga is unconscious and, therefore, repetitive and protracted, while the way of Yoga is deliberate and intense and, therefore, can be more rapid.

M: Maybe the periods of Yoga and Bhoga alternate. First Bhogi, then Yogi, then again Bhogi, then again Yogi.

Q: What may be the purpose?

M: Weak desires can be removed by introspection and meditation, but strong, deep-rooted ones must be fulfilled and their fruits, sweet or bitter, tasted.

Q: Why then should we pay tribute to Yogis and speak slightingly of Bhogis? All are Yogis, in a way.

M: On the human scale of values deliberate effort is considered praiseworthy. In reality both the Yogi and Bhogi follow their own nature, according to circumstances and opportunities. The Yogi's life is governed by a single desire — to find the Truth; the Bhogi serves many masters. But the Bhogi becomes a Yogi and the Yogi may get a rounding up in a bout of Bhoga. The final result is the same.

Q: Buddha is reported to have said that it is tremendously important to have heard that there is enlightenment, a complete reversal and transformation in consciousness. The good news is compared to a spark in a shipload of cotton; slowly but relentlessly the whole of it will turn to ashes. Similarly the good news of enlightenment will, sooner or later, bring about a transformation.

M: Yes, first hearing *(shravana)*, then remembering *(smarana)*, pondering *(manana)* and so on. We are on familiar ground. The man who heard the news becomes a Yogi; while the rest continue in their Bhoga.

Q: But you agree that living a life — just living the humdrum life of the world, being born to die and dying to be born — advances man by its sheer volume, just like the river finds its way to the sea by the sheer mass of the water it gathers.

M: Before the world was, consciousness was. In consciousness it comes into being, in consciousness it lasts and into pure consciousness it dissolves. At the root of everything, is the feeling 'I am'. The state of mind: 'there is a world' is secondary, for to *be*, I do not need the world, the world needs me.

Q: The desire to live is a tremendous thing.

M: Still greater is the freedom from the urge to live.

Q: The freedom of the stone?

M: Yes, the freedom of the stone, and much more besides. Freedom unlimited and conscious.

Q: Is not personality required for gathering experience?

M: As you are now, the personality is only an obstacle. Self-identification with the body may be good for an infant, but true growing up depends on getting the body out of the way. Normally, one should outgrow body-based desires early in life. Even the Bhogi, who does not refuse enjoyments, need not hanker after the ones he has tasted. Habit, desire for repetition, frustrates both the Yogi and the Bhogi.

Q: Why do you keep on dismissing the person *(vyakti)* as of no importance? Personality is the primary fact of our existence. It occupies the entire stage.

M: As long as you do not see that it is mere habit, built on memory, prompted by desire, you will think yourself to be a person

— living, feeling, thinking, active, passive, pleased or pained. Question yourself, ask yourself. 'Is it so?' 'Who am I'? 'What is behind and beyond all this?' And soon you will see your mistake. And it is in the very nature of a mistake to cease to be, when seen.

Q: The Yoga of living, of life itself, we may call the Natural Yoga *(nisarga yoga)*. It reminds me of the Primal Yoga *(adhi yoga)*, mentioned in the Rig-Veda which was described as the marrying of life with mind.

M: A life lived thoughtfully, in full awareness, is by itself Nisarga Yoga.

Q: What does the marriage of life and mind mean?

M: Living in spontaneous awareness, consciousness of effortless living, being fully interested in one's life — all this is implied.

Q: Sharada Devi, wife of Sri Ramakrishna Paramahamsa, used to scold his disciples for too much effort. She compared them to mangoes on the tree which are being plucked before they are ripe. 'Why hurry?' she used to say. 'Wait till you are fully ripe, mellow and sweet.'

M: How right she was! There are so many who take the dawn for the noon, a momentary experience for full realization and destroy even the little they gain by excess of pride. Humility and silence are essential for a *sadhaka,* however advanced. Only a fully ripened *gnani* can allow himself complete spontaneity.

Q: It seems there are schools of Yoga where the student, after illumination, is obliged to keep silent for 7 or 12 or 15 or even 25 years. Even Bhagavan Sri Ramana Maharshi imposed on himself 20 years of silence before he began to teach.

M: Yes, the inner fruit must ripen. Until then the discipline, the living in awareness, must go on. Gradually the practice becomes more and more subtle, until it becomes altogether formless.

Q: Krishnamurti too speaks of living in awareness.

M: He always aims directly at the 'ultimate'. Yes, ultimately all Yogas end in your *adhi yoga*, the marriage of consciousness (the bride) to life (the bridegroom). Consciousness and being *(sad-chit)* meet in bliss *(ananda)*. For bliss to arise there must be meeting, contact, the assertion of unity in duality.

Q: Buddha too has said that for the attainment of *nirvana* one must go to living beings. Consciousness needs life to grow.

M: The world itself is contact — the totality of all contacts actualized in consciousness. The spirit touches matter and consciousness results. Such consciousness, when tainted with memory and expectation, becomes bondage. Pure experience does not bind; experience caught between desire and fear is impure and creates *karma*.

Q: Can there be happiness in unity? Does not all happiness imply necessarily contact, hence duality?

M: There is nothing wrong with duality as long as it does not create conflict. Multiplicity and variety without strife is joy. In pure consciousness there is light. For warmth, contact is needed. Above the unity of being is the union of love. Love is the meaning and purpose of duality.

Q: I am an adopted child. My own father I do not know. My mother died when I was born. My foster father, to please my foster mother, who was childless, adopted me — almost by accident. He is a simple man — a truck owner and driver. My mother keeps the house. I am 24 years now. For the last two and a half years I am travelling, restless, seeking. I want to live a good life, a holy life. What am I to do?

M: Go home, take charge of your father's business, look after your parents in their old age. Marry the girl who is waiting for you, be loyal, be simple, be humble. Hide your virtue, live silently. The five senses and the three qualities *(gunas)* are your eight steps in Yoga. And 'I am' is the Great Reminder *(mahamantra)*. You can learn from them all you need to know. Be attentive, enquire ceaselessly. That is all.

Q: If just living one's life liberates, why are not all liberated?

M: All are being liberated. It is not what you live, but how you live that matters. The idea of enlightenment is of utmost importance. Just to know that there is such possibility, changes one's entire outlook. It acts like a burning match in a heap of saw dust. All the great teachers did nothing else. A spark of truth can burn up a mountain of lies. The opposite is also true. The sun of truth remains hidden behind the cloud of self-identification with the body.

Q: This spreading the good news of enlightenment seems very important.

M: The very hearing of it, is a promise of enlightenment. The very meeting a Guru is the assurance of liberation. Perfection is life-giving and creative.

Q: Does a realized man ever think: 'I am realized?' Is he not astonished when people make much of him? Does he not take himself to be an ordinary human being?

M: Neither ordinary, nor extra-ordinary. Just being aware and affectionate — intensely. He looks at himself without indulging in self-definitions and self-identifications. He does not know himself as anything apart from the world. He is the world. He is completely rid of himself, like a man who is very rich, but continually gives away his riches. He is not rich, for he has nothing; he is not poor, for he gives abundantly. He is just property-less. Similarly, the realized man is egoless; he has lost the capacity of identifying himself with anything. He is without location, placeless, beyond space and time, beyond the world. Beyond words and thoughts is he.

Q: Well, it is deep mystery to me. I am a simple man.

M: It is you who are deep, complex, mysterious, hard to understand. I am simplicity itself, compared to you. I am what is — without any distinction whatsoever into inner and outer, mine and yours, good and bad. What the world is, I am; what I am the world is.

Q: How does it happen that each man creates his own world?

M: When a number of people are asleep, each dreams his own dream. Only on awakening the question of many different dreams arises and dissolves when they are all seen as dreams, as something imagined.

Q: Even dreams have a foundation.

M: In memory. Even then, what is remembered, is but another dream. The memory of the false cannot but give rise to the false. There is nothing wrong with memory as such. What is false is its content. Remember facts, forget opinions.

Q: What is a fact?

M: What is perceived in pure awareness, unaffected by desire and fear is fact.   ●●●

27

The Beginningless Begins Forever

Questioner: The other day I was asking you about the two ways of growth — renunciation and enjoyment *(yoga* and *bhoga)*. The difference is not so great as it looks — the Yogi renounces to enjoy; the Bhogi enjoys to renounce. The Yogi renounces first, the Bhogi enjoys first.

Maharaj: So what? Leave the Yogi to his Yoga and the Bhogi to his Bhoga.

Q: The way of Bhoga seems to me the better one. The Yogi is like a green mango, separated from the tree prematurely and kept to ripen in a basket of straw. Airless and overheated, it does get ripe, but the true flavour and fragrance are lost. The mango left on the tree grows to full size, colour and sweetness, a joy in every way. Yet somehow Yoga gets all the praises, and Bhoga — all the curses. As I see it, Bhoga is the better of the two.

M: What makes you say so?

Q: I watched the Yogis and their enormous efforts. Even when they realize, there is something bitter or astringent about it. They seem to spend much of their time in trances and when they speak, they merely voice their scriptures. At their best such *gnanis* are like flowers — perfect, but just little flowers, shedding their fragrance within a short radius. There are some others, who are like forests — rich, varied, immense, full of surprises, a world in themselves. There must be a reason for this difference.

M: Well, you said it. According to you one got stunted in his Yoga, while the other flourished in Bhoga.

Q: Is it not sc? The Yogi is afraid of life and seeks peace, while the Bhogi is adventurous, full of spirits, forward going. The Yogi is bound by an ideal, while the Bhogi is ever ready to explore.

M: It is a matter of wanting much or being satisfied with little. The Yogi is ambitious while the Bhogi is merely adventurous. Your Bhogi seems to be richer and more interesting, but it is not so in reality. The Yogi is narrow as the sharp edge of the knife. He has to be — to cut deep and smoothly, to penetrate unerringly the many layers of the false. The Bhogi worships at many altars; the Yogi serves none but his own true Self.

There is no purpose in opposing the Yogi to the Bhogi. The way of outgoing *(pravritti)* necessarily precedes the way of returning *(nivritti)*. To sit in judgement and allot marks is ridiculous. Everything contributes to the ultimate perfection. Some say there are three aspects of reality — Truth-Wisdom-Bliss. He who seeks Truth becomes a Yogi, he who seeks wisdom becomes a *gnani;* he who seeks happiness becomes the man of action.

Q: We are told of the bliss of non-duality.

M: Such bliss is more of the nature of a great peace. Pleasure and pain are the fruits of actions — righteous and unrighteous.

Q: What makes the difference?

M: The difference is between giving and grasping. Whatever the way of approach, in the end all becomes one.

Q: If there be no difference in the goal, why discriminate between various approaches?

M: Let each act according to his nature. The ultimate purpose will be served in any case. All your discriminations and classifications are quite all right, but they do not exist in my case. As the description of a dream may be detailed and accurate, though without having any foundation, so does your pattern fit nothing but your own assumptions. You begin with an idea and you end with the same idea under a different garb.

Q: How do you see things?

M: One and all are the same to me. The same consciousness *(chit)* appears as being *(sat)* and as bliss *(ananda):* Chit in movement is Ananda; Chit motionless is being.

Q: Still you are making a distinction between motion and motionlessness.

M: Non-distinction speaks in silence. Words carry distinctions. The unmanifested *(nirguna)* has no name, all names refer to the manifested *(saguna).* It is useless to struggle with words to express what is beyond words. Consciousness *(chidananda)* is spirit *(purusha),* consciousness is matter *(prakriti).* Imperfect spirit is matter, perfect matter is spirit. In the beginning as in the end, all is one.

All division is in the mind *(chitta);* there is none in reality *(chit).* Movement and rest are states of mind and cannot be without their opposites. By itself nothing moves, nothing rests. It is a grievous mistake to attribute to mental constructs absolute existence. Nothing exists by itself.

Q: You seem to identify rest with the Supreme State?

M: There is rest as a state of mind *(chidaram)* and there is rest as a state of being *(atmaram).* The former comes and goes, while the true rest is the very heart of action. Unfortunately, language is a mental tool and works only in opposites.

Q: As a witness, you are working or at rest?

M: Witnessing is an experience and rest is freedom from experience.

Q: Can't they co-exist, as the tumult of the waves and the quiet of the deep co-exist in the ocean.

M: Beyond the mind there is no such thing as experience. Experience is a dual state. You cannot talk of reality as an experience. Once this is understood, you will no longer look for being and becoming as separate and opposite. In reality they are one and inseparable, like roots and branches of the same tree. Both can exist only in the light of consciousness, which again, arises in the wake of the sense 'I am'. This is the primary fact. If you miss it, you miss all.

Q: Is the sense of being a product of experience only? The great saying (Mahavakya) *tat-sat* is it a mere mode of mentation?

M: Whatever is spoken is speech only. Whatever is thought is thought only. The real meaning is unexplainable, though experienceable. The Mahavakya is true, but your ideas are false, for all ideas *(kalpana)* are false.

Q: Is the conviction: 'I am That' false?

M: Of course. Conviction is a mental state. In 'That' there is no 'I am'. With the sense 'I am' emerging, 'That' is obscured, as with the sun rising the stars are wiped out. But as with the sun comes light, so with the sense of self comes bliss *(chidananda)*. The cause of bliss is sought in the 'not — I' and thus the bondage begins.

Q: In your daily life are you always conscious of your real state?

M: Neither conscious, nor unconscious. I do not need convictions. I live on courage. Courage is my essence, which is love of life. I am free of memories and anticipations, unconcerned with what I am and what I am not. I am not addicted to self-descriptions, *soham* and *brahmasmi* ('I am He', 'I am the Supreme') are of no use to me, I have the courage to be as nothing and to see the world as it is: nothing. It sounds simple, just try it!

Q: But what gives you courage?

M: How perverted are your views! Need courage be given? Your question implies that anxiety is the normal state and courage is abnormal. It is the other way round. Anxiety and hope are born of imagination — I am free of both. I am simple *being* and I need nothing to rest on.

Q: Unless you know yourself, of what use is your *being* to you? To be happy with what you are, you must know what you are.

M: Being shines as knowing, knowing is warm in love. It is all one. You imagine separations and trouble yourself with questions. Don't concern yourself overmuch with formulations. Pure being cannot be described.

Q: Unless a thing is knowable and enjoyable, it is of no use to me. It must become a part of my experience, first of all.

M: You are dragging down reality to the level of experience. How can reality depend on experience, when it is the very ground *(adhar)* of experience. Reality is in the very fact of experience, not in its nature. Experience is, after all, a state of mind, while being is definitely not a state of mind.

Q: Again I am confused! Is being separate from knowing?

M: The separation is an appearance. Just as the dream is not apart from the dreamer, so is knowing not apart from being. The dream is the dreamer, the knowledge is the knower, the distinction is merely verbal.

Q: I can see now that *sat* and *chit* are one. But what about bliss *(ananda)?* Being and consciousness are always present together, but bliss flashes only occasionally.

M: The undisturbed state of being is bliss; the disturbed state is what appears as the world. In non-duality there is bliss; in duality — experience. What comes and goes is experience with its duality of pain and pleasure. Bliss is not to be known. One is always bliss, but never blissful. Bliss is not an attribute.

Q: I have another question to ask: Some Yogis attain their goal, but it is of no use to others. They do not know, or are not able to share. Those who can share out what they have, initiate others. Where lies the difference?

M: There is no difference. Your approach is wrong. There are no others to help. A rich man, when he hands over his entire fortune to his family, has not a coin left to give a beggar. So is the wise man *(gnani)* stripped of all his powers and possessions. Nothing, literally nothing, can be said about him. He cannot help anybody, for he is everybody. He is the poor and also his poverty, the thief and also his thievery. How can he be said to help, when he is not apart? Who thinks of himself as separate from the world, let him help the world.

Q: Still, there is duality, there is sorrow, there is need of help. By denouncing it as mere dream nothing is achieved.

M: The only thing that can help is to wake up from the dream.

Q: An awakener is needed.

M: Who again is in the dream. The awakener signifies the beginning of the end. There are no eternal dreams.

Q: Even when it is beginningless?

M: Everything begins with you. What else is beginningless?

Q: I began at birth.

M: That is what you are told. Is it so? Did you see yourself beginning?

Q: I began just now. All else is memory.

M: Quite right. The beginningless begins forever. In the same way, I give eternally, because I have nothing. To be nothing, to have nothing, to keep nothing for oneself is the greatest gift, the highest generosity.

Q: Is there no self-concern left?

M: Of course I am self-concerned, but the self is all. In practice it takes the shape of goodwill, unfailing and universal. You may call it love, all-pervading, all-redeeming. Such love is supremely active — without the sense of doing. ●●●

28

All Suffering is Born of Desire

Questioner: I come from a far off country. I had some inner experiences on my own and I would like to compare notes.

Maharaj: By all means. Do you know yourself?

Q: I know that I am not the body. Nor am I the mind.

M: What makes you say so?

Q: I do not feel I am in the body. I seem to be all over the place, everywhere. As to the mind, I can switch it on and off, so to say. This makes me feel I am not the mind.

M: When you feel yourself everywhere in the world, do you remain separate from the world? Or, are you the world?

Q: Both. Sometimes I feel myself to be neither mind nor body, but one single all-seeing eye. When I go deeper into it, I find myself to be all I see and the world and myself become one.

M: Very well. What about desires? Do you have any?

Q: Yes, they come, short and superficial.

M: And what do you do about them?

Q: What can I do? They come, they go. I look at them. Sometimes I see my body and my mind engaged in fulfilling them.

M: Whose desires are being fulfilled?

Q: They are a part of the world in which I live. They are just as trees and clouds are there.

M: Are they not a sign of some imperfection?

Q: Why should they be? They are as they are, and I am as I am. How can the appearance and disappearance of desires affect me? Of course, they affect the shape and content of the mind.

M: Very well. What is your work?

Q: I am a probation officer.

M: What does it mean?

Q: Juvenile offenders are let off on probation and there are special officers to watch their behaviour and to help them get training and find work.

M: Must you work?

Q: Who works? Work happens to take place.

M: Do you need to work?

Q: I need it for the sake of money. I like it, because it puts me in touch with living beings.

M: What do you need them for?

Q: They may need me and it is their destinies that made me take up this work. It is one life, after all.

M: How did you come to your present state?

Q: Sri Ramana Maharshi's teachings have put me on my way. Then I met one Douglas Harding who helped me by showing me how to work on the 'Who am I?'

M: Was it sudden or gradual?

Q: It was quite sudden. Like something quite forgotten, coming back into one's mind. Or, like a sudden flash of understanding. 'How simple', I said, 'How simple; I'm not what I thought I am! I'm neither the perceived nor the perceiver; I'm the perceiving only'.

M: Not even the perceiving, but that which makes all this possible.

Q: What is love?

M: When the sense of distinction and separation is absent, you may call it love.

Q: Why so much stress on love between man and woman?

M: Because the element of happiness in it is so prominent.

Q: Is it not so in all love?

M: Not necessarily. Love may cause pain. You call it then compassion.

Q: What is happiness?

M: Harmony between the inner and the outer is happiness. On the other hand, self-identification with the outer causes is suffering.

Q: How does self-identification happen?

M: The self by its nature knows itself only. For lack of experience whatever it perceives it takes to be itself. Battered, it learns to look out *(viveka)* and to live alone *(vairagya)*. When right behaviour *(uparati)*, becomes normal, a powerful inner urge *(mukmukshutva)* makes it seek its source. The candle of the body is lighted and all becomes clear and bright *(atmaprakash)*.

Q: What is the real cause of suffering?

M: Self-identification with the limited *(vyaktitva)*. Sensations as such, however strong, do not cause suffering. It is the mind, bewildered by wrong ideas, addicted to thinking: 'I am this'. 'I am that', that fears loss and craves gain and suffers when frustrated.

Q: A friend of mine used to have horrible dreams night after night. Going to sleep would terrorise him. Nothing could help him.

M: Company of the truly good *(satsang)* would help him.

Q: Life itself is a nightmare.

M: Noble friendship *(satsang)* is the supreme remedy for all ills, physical and mental.

Q: Generally one cannot find such friendship.

M: Seek within. Your own self is your best friend.

Q: Why is life so full of contradictions?

M: It serves to break down mental pride. We must realize how poor and powerless we are. As long as we delude ourselves by what we imagine ourselves to be, to know, to have, to do, we are in a sad plight indeed. Only in complete self-negation there is a chance to discover our real being.

Q: Why so much stress on self-negation?

M: As much as on self-realization. The false self must be abandoned before the real self can be found.

Q: The self you choose to call false is to me most distressingly real. It is the only self I know. What you call the real self is a mere concept, a way of speaking, a creature of the mind, an attractive ghost. My daily self is not a beauty, I admit, but it is my own and only self. You say I am, or have, another self. Do you see it — is it a reality to you, or do you want me to believe what you yourself don't see?

M: Don't jump to conclusions rashly. The concrete need not be the real, the conceived need not be false. Perceptions based on sensations and shaped by memory imply a perceiver, whose nature you never cared to examine. Give it your full attention, examine it with loving care and you will discover heights and depths of being which you did not dream of, engrossed as you are in your puny image of yourself.

Q: I must be in the right mood to examine myself fruitfully.

M: You must be serious, intent, truly interested. You must be full of goodwill for yourself.

Q: I am selfish all right.

M: You are not. You are all the time destroying yourself, and your own, by serving strange gods, inimical and false. By all means be selfish — the right way. Wish yourself well, labour at what is good for you. Destroy all that stands between you and happiness. Be all — love all — be happy — make happy. No happiness is greater.

Q: Why is there so much suffering in love?

M: All suffering is born of desire. True love is never frustrated. How can the sense of unity be frustrated? What can be frustrated is the desire for expression. Such desire is of the mind. As with all things mental, frustration is inevitable.

Q: What is the place of sex in love?

M: Love is a state of being. Sex is energy. Love is wise, sex is blind. Once the true nature of love and sex is understood there will be no conflict or confusion.

Q: There is so much sex without love.

M: Without love all is evil. Life itself without love is evil.

Q: What can make me love?

M: You are love itself — when you are not afraid.   ●●●

29
Living is Life's only Purpose

Questioner: What does it mean to fail in Yoga? Who is a failure in Yoga *(yoga bhrashta)*?

Maharaj: It is only a question of incompletion. He who could not complete his Yoga for some reason is called failed in Yoga. Such failure is only temporary, for there can be no defeat in Yoga. This battle is always won, for it is a battle between the true and the false. The false has no chance.

Q: Who fails? The person *(vyakti)* or the self *(vyakta)*?

M: The question is wrongly put. There is no question of failure, neither in the short run nor in the long. It is like travelling a long and arduous road in an unknown country. Of all the innumerable steps there is only the last which brings you to your destination. Yet you will not consider all previous steps as failures. Each brought you nearer to your goal, even when you had to turn back to by-pass an obstacle. In reality each step brings you to your goal, because to be always on the move, learning, discovering, unfolding, is your eternal destiny. Living is life's only purpose. The self does not identify itself with success or failure — the very idea of becoming this or that is unthinkable. The self understands that success and failure are relative and related, that they are the very warp and weft of life. Learn from both and go beyond. If you have not learnt, repeat.

Q: What am I to learn?

M: To live without self-concern. For this you must know your own true being *(swarupa)* as indomitable, fearless, ever victorious. Once you know with absolute certainty that nothing can trouble you but your own imagination, you come to disregard your desires and fears, concepts and ideas and live by truth alone.

Q: What may be the reason that some people succeed and others fail in Yoga? Is it destiny or character, or just accident?

M: Nobody ever fails in Yoga. It is all a matter of the rate of progress. It is slow in the beginning and rapid in the end. When one is fully matured, realization is explosive. It takes place spontaneously, or at the slightest hint. The quick is not better than the slow. Slow ripening and rapid flowering alternate. Both are natural and right.

Yet, all this is so in the mind only. As I see it, there is really nothing of the kind. In the great mirror of consciousness images arise and disappear and only memory gives them continuity. And memory is material — destructible, perishable, transient. On such flimsy foundations we build a sense of personal existence — vague, intermittent, dreamlike. This vague persuasion: 'I-am-so-and-so' obscures the changeless state of pure awareness and makes us believe that we are born to suffer and to die.

Q: Just as a child cannot help growing, so does a man, compelled by nature, make progress. Why exert oneself? Where is the need of Yoga?

M: There is progress all the time. Everything contributes to progress. But this is the progress of ignorance. The circles of ignorance may be ever widening, yet it remains a bondage all the same. In due course a Guru appears to teach and inspire us to practise Yoga and a ripening takes place as a result of which the immemorial night of ignorance dissolves before the rising sun of wisdom. But in reality nothing happened. The sun is always there, there is no night to it; the mind blinded by the 'I-am-the-body' idea spins out endlessly its thread of illusion.

Q: If all is a part of a natural process, where is the need of effort?

M: Even effort is a part of it. When ignorance becomes obstinate and hard and the character gets perverted, effort and the pain of it become inevitable. In complete obedience to nature there is no effort. The seed of spiritual life grows in silence and in darkness until its appointed hour.

Q: We come across some great people, who, in their old age, become childish, petty, quarrelsome and spiteful. How could they deteriorate so much?

M: They were not perfect Yogis, having their bodies under complete control. Or, they might not have cared to protect their bodies from the natural decay. One must not draw conclusions without understanding all the factors. Above all, one must not make judgements of inferiority or superiority. Youthfulness is more a matter of vitality *(prana)* than of wisdom *(gnana)*.

Q: One may get old, but why should one lose all alertness and discrimination?

M: Consciousness and unconsciousness, while in the body, depend on the condition of the brain. But the self is beyond both, beyond the brain, beyond the mind. The fault of the instrument is no reflection on its user.

Q: I was told that a realized man will never do anything unseemly. He will always behave in an exemplary way.

M: Who sets the example? Why should a liberated man necessarily follow conventions? The moment he becomes predictable, he cannot be free. His freedom lies in his being free to fulfil the need of the moment, to obey the necessity of the situation. Freedom to do what one likes is really bondage, while being free to do what one must, what is right, is real freedom.

Q: Still there must be some way of making out who has realized and who has not. If one is indistinguishable from the other, of what use is he?

M: He who knows himself has no doubts about it. Nor does he care whether others recognize his state or not. Rare is the realized man who discloses his realization and fortunate are those who have met him, for he does it for their abiding welfare.

Q: When one looks round, one is appalled by the volume of unnecessary suffering that is going on. People who should be helped are not getting help. Imagine a big hospital ward full of incurables, tossing and moaning. Were you given the authority to kill them all and end their torture, would you not do so?

M: I would leave it to them to decide.

Q: But if their destiny is to suffer? How can you interfere with destiny?

M: Their destiny is what happens. There is no thwarting of destiny. You mean to say everybody's life is totally determined at his birth? What a strange idea! Were it so, the power that determines would see to it that nobody should suffer.

Q: What about cause and effect?

M: Each moment contains the whole of the past and creates the whole of the future.

Q: But past and future exist?

M: In the mind only. Time is in the mind, space is in the mind. The law of cause and effect is also a way of thinking. In reality all is here and now and all is one. Multiplicity and diversity are in the mind only.

Q: Still, you are in favour of relieving suffering, even through destruction of the incurably diseased body.

M: Again, you look from outside while I look from within. I do not see a sufferer, I am the sufferer. I know him from within and do what is right spontaneously and effortlessly. I follow no rules nor lay down rules. I flow with life — faithfully and irresistibly.

Q: Still you seem to be a very practical man in full control of your immediate surroundings.

M: What else do you expect me to be? A misfit?

Q: Yet you cannot help another much.

M: Surely, I can help. You too can help. Everybody can help. But the suffering is all the time recreated. Man alone can destroy in himself the roots of pain. Others can only help with the pain, but not with its cause, which is the abysmal stupidity of mankind.

Q: Will this stupidity ever come to an end?

M: In man — of course. Any moment. In humanity — as we know it — after very many years. In creation — never, for creation itself is rooted in ignorance; matter itself is ignorance. Not to know, and not to know that one does not know, is the cause of endless suffering.

Q: We are told of the great *avatars,* the saviours of the world.

M: Did they save? They have come and gone — and the world plods on. Of course, they did a lot and opened new dimensions in the human mind. But to talk of saving the world is an exaggeration.

Q: Is there no salvation for the world?

M: Which world do you want to save? The world of your own projection? Save it yourself. My world? Show me my world and I shall deal with it. I am not aware of any world separate from myself, which I am free to save or not to save. What business have you with saving the world, when all the world needs is to be saved from you? Get out of the picture and see whether there is anything left to save.

Q: You seem to stress the point that without you your world would not have existed and therefore the only thing you can do for it is to wind up the show. This is not a way out. Even if the world were of my own creation, this knowledge does not save it. It only explains it. The question remains: why did I create such a wretched world and what can I do to change it? You seem to say: forget it all and admire your own glory. Surely, you don't mean it. The description of a disease and its causes does not cure it. What we need is the right medicine.

M: The description and causation are the remedy for a disease caused by obtuseness and stupidity. Just like a deficiency disease is cured through the supply of the missing factor, so are the diseases of living cured by a good dose of intelligent detachment. *(viveka-vairagya).*

Q: You cannot save the world by preaching counsels of perfection. People are as they are. Must they suffer?

M: As long as they are as they are, there is no escape from suffering. Remove the sense of separateness and there will be no conflict.

Q: A message in print may be paper and ink only. It is the text that matters. By analyzing the world into elements and qualities we miss the most important — its meaning. Your reduction of everything to dream disregards the difference between the dream of an insect and the dream of a poet. All is dream, granted. But not all are equal.

M: The dreams are not equal, but the dreamer is one. I am the insect. I am the poet — in dream. But in reality I am neither. I am beyond all dreams. I am the light in which all dreams appear and disappear. I am both inside and outside the dream. Just as a man having headache knows the ache and also knows that he is not the ache, so do I know the dream, myself dreaming and myself not dreaming — all at the same time. I am what I am before, during and after the dream. But what I see in dream, I am not.

Q: It is all a matter of imagination. One imagines that one is dreaming, another imagines one is not dreaming. Are not both the same?

M: The same and not the same. Not dreaming, as an interval between two dreams, is of course, a part of dreaming. Not dreaming as a steady hold on, and timeless abidance in reality has nothing to do with dreaming. In that sense I never dream, nor ever shall.

Q: If both dream and escape from dream are imaginings, what is the way out?

M: There is no need of a way out! Don't you see that a way out is also a part of the dream? All you have to do is to see the dream as dream.

Q: If I start the practice of dismissing everything as a dream, where will it lead me?

M: Wherever it leads you, it will be a dream. The very idea of going beyond the dream is illusory. Why go anywhere? Just realize that you are dreaming a dream you call the world, and stop looking for ways out. The dream is not your problem. Your problem is that you like one part of your dream and not another. Love all, or none of it, and stop complaining. When you have seen the dream as a dream, you have done all that needs be done.

Q: Is dreaming caused by thinking?

M: Everything is a play of ideas. In the state free from ideation *(nirvikalpa samadhi)* nothing is perceived. The root idea is: 'I am'. It shatters the state of pure consciousness and is followed by the innumerable sensations and perceptions, feeling and ideas which in their totality constitute God and His world. The 'I am' remains as the witness, but it is by the will of God that everything happens.

Q: Why not by my will?

M: Again you have split yourself — into God and witness. Both are one.   ●●●

30

You are Free NOW

Questioner: There are so many theories about the nature of man and universe. The creation theory, the illusion theory, the dream theory — any number of them. Which is true?

Maharaj: All are true, all are false. You can pick up whichever you like best.

Q: You seem to favour the dream theory.

M: These are all ways of putting words together. Some favour one way, some favour another. Theories are neither right nor wrong. They are attempts at explaining the inexplicable. It is not the theory that matters, but the way it is being tested. It is the testing of the theory that makes it fruitful. Experiment with any theory you like — if you are truly earnest and honest, the attainment of reality will be yours. As a living being you are caught in an untenable and painful situation and you are seeking a way out. You are being offered several plans of your prison, none quite true. But they all are of some value, only if you are in dead earnest. It is the earnestness that liberates and not the theory.

Q: Theory may be misleading and earnestness — blind.

M: Your sincerity will guide you. Devotion to the goal of freedom and perfection will make you abandon all theories and systems and live by wisdom, intelligence and active love. Theories may be good as starting points, but must be abandoned, the sooner — the better.

Q: There is a Yogi who says that for realization the eightfold Yoga is not necessary; that will-power alone will do It is enough to concentrate on the goal with full confidence in the power of pure will to obtain effortlessly and quickly what others take decades to achieve.

M: Concentration, full confidence, pure will! With such assets no wonder one attains in no time. This Yoga of will is all right for the mature seeker, who has shed all desires but one. After all, what is will but steadiness of heart and mind. Given such steadfastness all can be achieved.

Q: I feel the Yogi did not mean mere steadiness of purpose, resulting in ceaseless pursuit and application. He meant that with will fixed on the goal no pursuit or application are needed. The mere fact of willing attracts its object.

M: Whatever name you give it: will, or steady purpose, or one-pointedness of the mind, you come back to earnestness, sincerity, honesty. When you are in dead earnest, you bend every incident, every second of your life to your purpose. You do not waste time and energy on other things. You are totally dedicated, call it will, or love, or plain honesty. We are complex beings, at war within and without. We contradict ourselves all the time, undoing today the work of yesterday. No wonder we are stuck. A little of integrity would make a lot of difference.

Q: What is more powerful, desire or destiny?

M: Desire shapes destiny.

Q: And destiny shapes desire. My desires are conditioned by

heredity and circumstances, by opportunities and accidents, by what we call destiny.

M: Yes, you may say so.

Q: At what point am I free to desire what I want to desire?

M: You are free now. What is it that you want to desire? Desire it.

Q: Of course I am free to desire, but I am not free to act on my desire. Other urges will lead me astray. My desire is not strong enough, even if it has my approval. Other desires, which I disapprove of, are stronger.

M: Maybe you are deceiving yourself. Maybe you are giving expression to your real desires and the ones you approve of are kept on the surface for the sake of respectability.

Q: It may be as you say, but this is another theory. The fact is that I do not feel free to desire what I think I should, and when I seem to desire rightly, I do not act accordingly.

M: It is all due to weakness of the mind and disintegration of the brain. Collect and strengthen your mind and you will find that your thoughts and feelings, words and actions will align themselves in the direction of your will.

Q: Again a counsel of perfection! To integrate and strengthen the mind is not an easy task! How does one begin?

M: You can start only from where you are. You are here and now, you cannot get out of here and now.

Q: But what *can* I do here and now?

M: You can be aware of your being — here and now.

Q: That is all?

M: That is all. There is nothing more to it.

Q: All my waking and dreaming I am conscious of myself. It does not help me much.

M: You were aware of thinking, feeling, doing. You were not aware of your *being*.

Q: What is the new factor you want me to bring in?

M: The attitude of pure witnessing, of watching the events without taking part in them.

Q: What will it do to me?

M: Weak-mindedness is due to lack of intelligence, of understanding, which again is the result of non-awareness. By striving for awareness you bring your mind together and strengthen it.

Q: I may be fully aware of what is going on, and yet quite unable to influence it in any way.

M: You are mistaken. What is going on is a projection of your mind. A weak mind cannot control its own projections. Be aware, therefore, of your mind and its projections. You cannot control what you do not know. On the other hand, knowledge gives power. In practice it is very simple. To control yourself — know yourself.

Q: Maybe, I can come to control myself, but shall I be able to deal with the chaos in the world?

M: There is no chaos in the world, except the chaos which your mind creates. It is self-created in the sense that at its very centre is the false idea of oneself as a thing different and separate from other things. In reality you are not a thing, nor separate. You are the infinite potentiality, the inexhaustible possibility. Because you *are,* all can be. The universe is but a partial manifestation of your limitless capacity to *become.*

Q: I find that I am totally motivated by desire for pleasure and fear of pain. However noble my desire and justified my fear, pleasure and pain are the two poles between which my life oscillates.

M: Go to the source of both pain and pleasure, of desire and fear. Observe, investigate, try to understand.

Q: Desire and fear both are feelings caused by physical or mental factors. They are there, easily observable. But why are they there? Why do I desire pleasure and fear pain?

M: Pleasure and pain are states of mind. As long as you think you are the mind, or rather, the body-mind, you are bound to raise such questions.

Q: And when I realize that I am not the body, shall I be free from desire and fear?

M: As long as there is a body and a mind to protect the body, attractions and repulsions will operate. They will be there, out in the field of events, but will not concern you. The focus of your attention will be elsewhere. You will not be distracted.

Q: Still they will be there. Will one never be completely free?

M: You are completely free even now. What you call destiny *(karma)* is but the result of your own will to live. How strong is this will you can judge by the universal horror of death.

Q: People die willingly quite often.

M: Only when the alternative is worse than death. But such readiness to die flows from the same source as the will to live, a source deeper even than life itself. To be a living being is not the ultimate state; there is something beyond, much more wonderful, which is neither being nor non-being, neither living nor not-living. It is a state of pure awareness, beyond the limitations of space and time. Once the illusion that the body-mind is oneself is abandoned, death loses its terror, it becomes a part of living.   ●●●

31

Do not Undervalue Attention

Questioner: As I look at you, you seem to be a poor man with very limited means, facing all the problems of poverty and old age, like everybody else.

Maharaj: Were I very rich, what difference would it make? I am what I am. What else can I be? I am neither rich nor poor, I am myself.

Q: Yet, you are experiencing pleasure and pain.

M: I am experiencing these in consciousness, but I am neither consciousness, nor its content.

Q: You say that in our real being we are all equal. How is it that your experience is so different from ours.

M: My actual experience is not different. It is my evaluation and attitude that differ. I see the same world as you do, but not the same way. There is nothing mysterious about it. Everybody sees the world through the idea he has of himself. As you think yourself to be, so you think the world to be. If you imagine yourself as separate from the world, the world will appear as separate from you and you will experience desire and fear. I do not see the world as separate from me and so there is nothing for me to desire, or fear.

Q: You are a point of light in the world. Not everybody is.

M: There is absolutely no difference between me and others, except in my knowing myself as I am. I am all. I know it for certain and you do not.

Q: So we differ all the same.

M: No, we do not. The difference is only in the mind and temporary. I was like you, you will be like me.

Q: God made a most diversified world.

M: The diversity is in you only. See yourself as you are and you will see the world as it is — a single block of reality, indivisible, indescribable. Your own creative power projects upon it a picture and all your questions refer to the picture.

Q: A Tibetan Yogi wrote that God creates the world for a purpose and runs it according to a plan. The purpose is good and the plan is most wise.

M: All this is temporary, while I am dealing with the eternal. Gods and their universes come and go, *avatars* follow each other in endless succession, and in the end we are back at the source. I talk only of the timeless source of all the gods with all their universes, past, present and future.

Q: Do you know them all? Do you remember them?

M: When a few boys stage a play for fun, what is there to see and to remember?

Q: Why is half humanity male and half female?

M: For their happiness. The impersonal *(avyakta)* becomes the personal *(vyakta)* for the sake of happiness in relationship. By the grace of my Guru I can look with equal eye on the impersonal as well as the personal. Both are one to me. In life the personal merges in the impersonal.

Q: How does the personal emerge from the impersonal?

M: The two are but aspects of one Reality. It is not correct to talk of one preceding the other. All these ideas belong to the waking state.

Q: What brings in the waking state?

M: At the root of all creation lies desire. Desire and imagination foster and reinforce each other. The fourth state *(turiya)* is a state of pure witnessing, detached awareness, passionless and wordless. It is like space, unaffected by whatever it contains. Bodily and mental troubles do not reach it — they are outside, 'there', while the witness is always 'here'.

Q: What is real, the subjective or the objective? I am inclined to believe that the objective universe is the real one and my subjective psyche is changeful and transient. You seem to claim reality for your inner, subjective states and deny all reality to the concrete, external world.

M: Both the subjective and the objective are changeful and transient. There is nothing real about them. Find the permanent in the fleeting, the one constant factor in every experience.

Q: What is this constant factor?

M: My giving it various names and pointing it out in many ways will not help you much, unless you have the capacity to see. A dim-sighted man will not see the parrot on the branch of a tree, however much you may prompt him to look. At best he will see your pointed finger. First purify your vision, learn to see instead of staring, and you will perceive the parrot. Also you must be eager to see. You need both clarity and earnestness for self-knowledge. You need maturity of heart and mind, which comes through earnest application in daily life of whatever little you have understood. There is no such thing as compromise in Yoga.

If you want to sin, sin wholeheartedly and openly. Sins too have their lessons to teach the earnest sinner, as virtues — the earnest saint. It is the mixing up the two that is so disastrous. Nothing can block you so effectively as compromise, for it shows lack of earnestness, without which nothing can be done.

Q: I approve of austerity, but in practice I am all for luxury. The habit of chasing pleasure and shunning pain is so ingrained in me, that all my good intentions, quite alive on the level of theory, find no roots in my day-to-day life. To tell me that I am not honest does not help me, for I just do not know how to make myself honest.

M: You are neither honest nor dishonest — giving names to mental states is good only for expressing your approval or disapproval. The problem is not yours — it is your mind's only. Begin by disassociating yourself from your mind. Resolutely remind yourself that you are not the mind and that its problems are not yours.

Q: I may go on telling myself: 'I am not the mind, I am not concerned with its problems,' but the mind remains and its problems remain just as they were. Now, please do not tell me that it is because I am not earnest enough and I should be more earnest! I know it and admit it and only ask you — how is it done?

M: At least you are asking! Good enough, for a start. Go on pondering, wondering, being anxious to find a way. Be conscious of yourself, watch your mind, give it your full attention. Don't look for quick results; there may be none within your noticing. Unknown to you, your psyche will undergo a change, there will be more clarity in your thinking, charity in your feeling, purity in your behaviour. You need not aim at these — you will witness the change all the same. For, what you are now is the result of inattention and what you become will be the fruit of attention.

Q: Why should mere attention make all the difference?

M: So far your life was dark and restless (tamas and rajas). Attention, alertness, awareness, clarity, liveliness, vitality, are all manifestations of integrity, oneness with your true nature (sattva). It is in the nature of sattva to reconcile and neutralize tamas and rajas and rebuild the personality in accordance with the true nature of the self. Sattva is the faithful servant of the self, ever attentive and obedient.

Q: And I shall come to it through mere attention?

M: Do not undervalue attention. It means interest and also love. To know, to do, to discover, or to create you must give your heart to it — which means attention. All the blessings flow from it.

Q: You advise us to concentrate on 'I am'. Is this too a form of attention?

M: What else? Give your undivided attention to the most important in your life — yourself. Of your personal universe you are the centre — without knowing the centre what else can you know?

Q: But how can I know myself? To know myself I must be away from myself. But what is away from myself cannot be myself. So, it looks that I cannot know myself, only what I take to be myself.

M: Quite right. As you cannot see your face, but only its reflection in the mirror, so you can know only your image reflected in the stainless mirror of pure awareness.

Q: How am I to get such stainless mirror?

M: Obviously, by removing stains. See the stains and remove them. The ancient teaching is fully valid.

Q: What is seeing and what is removing?

M: The nature of the perfect mirror is such that you cannot see it. Whatever you can see is bound to be a stain. Turn away from it, give it up, know it as unwanted.

Q: All perceivables, are they stains?

M: All are stains.

Q: The entire world is a stain.

M: Yes, it is.

Q: How awful! So, the universe is of no value?

M: It is of tremendous value. By going beyond it you realize yourself.

Q: But why did it come into being in the first instance?

M: You will know it when it ends

Q: Will it ever end?

M: Yes, for you.

Q: When did it begin?

M: Now.

Q: When will it end?

M: Now.

Q: It does not end now?

M: You don't let it.

Q: I want to let it.

M: You don't. All your life is connected with it. Your past and future, your desires and fears, all have their roots in the world. Without the world where are you, who are you?

Q: But that is exactly what I came to find out.

M: And I am telling you exactly this: find a foothold beyond and all will be clear and easy. ●●●

32

Life is the Supreme Guru

Questioner: We two came from far off countries; one of us is British, the other American. The world in which we were born is falling apart and, being young, we are concerned. The old people hope they will die their own death, but the young have no such hope. Some of us many refuse to kill, but none can refuse to be killed. Can we hope to set the world right within our lifetime?

Maharaj: What makes you think that the world is going to perish?

Q: The instruments of destruction have become unbelievably potent. Also, our very productivity has become destructive of nature and of our cultural and social values.

M: You are talking of the present times. It has been so everywhere and always? But the distressing situation may be temporary and local. Once over, it will be forgotten.

Q: The scale of the impending catastrophe is unbelievably big. We live in the midst of an explosion.

M: Each man suffers alone and dies alone. Numbers are irrelevant. There is as much death when a million die as when one perishes.

Q: Nature kills by the millions, but this does not frighten me. There may be tragedy or mystery in it, but no cruelty. What horrifies me is man-made suffering, destruction and desolation. Nature is magnificent in its doings and undoings. But there is meanness and madness in the acts of man.

M: Right. So, it is not suffering and death that are your problem, but the meanness and madness at their root. Is not meanness also a form of madness? And is not madness the misuse of the mind? Humanity's problem lies in this misuse of the mind only. All the treasures of nature and spirit are open to man who will use his mind rightly.

Q: What is the right use of mind?

M: Fear and greed cause the misuse of the mind. The right use of mind is in the service of love, of life, of truth, of beauty.

Q: Easier said than done. Love of truth, of man, goodwill — what luxury! We need plenty of it to set the world right, but who will provide?

M: You can spend an eternity looking elsewhere for truth and love, intelligence and goodwill, imploring God and man — all in vain. You must begin in yourself, with yourself — this is the inexorable law. You cannot change the image without changing the face. First realize that your world is only a reflection of yourself and stop finding fault with the reflection. Attend to yourself, set yourself right — mentally and emotionally. The physical will follow automatically. You talk so much of reforms: economic, social, political. Leave alone the reforms and mind the reformer. What kind of world can a man create who is stupid, greedy, heartless?

Q: If we have to wait for a change of heart, we shall have to wait indefinitely. Yours is a counsel of perfection, which is also a counsel of despair. When all are perfect, the world will be perfect. What useless truism!

M: I did not say it. I only said: You cannot change the world before changing yourself. I did not say — before changing everybody. It is neither necessary, nor possible to change others. But if you can change yourself you will find that no other change is needed. To change the picture you merely change the film, you do not attack the cinema screen!

Q: How can you be so sure of yourself? How do you know that what you say is true?

M: It is not of myself that I am sure, I am sure of you. All you need is to stop searching outside what can be found only within. Set your vision right before you operate. You are suffering from acute misapprehension. Clarify your mind, purify your heart, sanctify your life — this is the quickest way to a change of your world.

Q: So many saints and mystics lived and died. They did not change my world.

M: How could they? Your world is not theirs, nor is their yours.

Q: Surely there is a factual world common to all.

M: The world of things, of energy and matter? Even if there were such a common world of things and forces, it is not the world in which we live. Ours is a world of feelings and ideas, of attractions and repulsions, of scales of values, of motives and incentives; a mental world altogether. Biologically we need very little; our problems are of a different order. Problems created by desires and fears and wrong ideas can be solved only on the level of the mind. You must conquer your own mind and for this you must go beyond it.

Q: What does it mean to go beyond the mind?

M: You have gone beyond the body, haven't you? You do not

closely follow your digestion, circulation or elimination. These have become automatic. In the same way the mind should work automatically, without calling for attention. This will not happen unless the mind works faultlessly. We are, most of our time, mind and body-conscious, because they constantly call for help. Pain and suffering are only the body and the mind screaming for attention. To go beyond the body you must be healthy: to go beyond the mind, you must have your mind in perfect order. You cannot leave a mess behind and go beyond. The mess will bog you up. 'Pick up your rubbish' seems to be the universal law. And a just law too.

Q: Am I permitted to ask you how did you go beyond the mind?

M: By the grace of my Guru.

Q: What shape his grace took?

M: He told me what is true.

Q: What did he tell you?

M: He told me I am the Supreme Reality.

Q: What did you do about it?

M: I trusted him and remembered it.

Q: Is that all?

M: Yes, I remembered him; I remembered what he said.

Q: You mean to say that this was enough?

M: What more needs be done? It was quite a lot to remember the Guru and his words. My advice to you is even less difficult than this — just remember yourself. 'I am', is enough to heal your mind and take you beyond. Just have some trust. I don't mislead you. Why should I? Do I want anything from you? I wish you well — such is my nature. Why should I mislead you?

Commonsense too will tell you that to fulfil a desire you must keep your mind on it. If you want to know your true nature, you must have yourself in mind all the time, until the secret of your being stands revealed.

Q: Why should self-remembrance bring one to self-realization?

M: Because they are but two aspects of the same state. Self-remembrance is in the mind, self-realization is beyond the mind. The image in the mirror is of the face beyond the mirror.

Q: Fair enough. But what is the purpose?

M: To help others, one must be beyond the need of help.

Q: All I want is to be happy.

M: Be happy to make happy.

Q: Let others take care of themselves.

M: Sir, you are not separate. The happiness you cannot share is spurious. Only the shareable is truly desirable.

Q: Right. But do I need a Guru? What you tell me is simple and convincing. I shall remember it. This does not make you my Guru.

M: It is not the worship of a person that is crucial, but the steadiness and depth of your devotion to the task. Life itself is the Supreme Guru; be attentive to its lessons and obedient to its commands. When you personalize their source, you have an outer Guru; when you take them from life directly, the Guru is within. Remember, wonder, ponder, live with it, love it, grow into it, grow with it, make it your own — the word of your Guru, outer of inner. Put in all and you will get all. I was doing it. All my time I was giving to my Guru and to what he told me.

Q: I am a writer by profession. Can you give me some advice, for me specifically?

M: Writing is both a talent and a skill. Grow in talent and develop in skill. Desire what is worth desiring and desire it well. Just like you pick your way in a crowd, passing between people, so you find your way between events, without missing your general direction. It is easy, if you are earnest.

Q: So many times you mention the need of being earnest. But we are not men of single will We are congeries of desires and needs, instincts and promptings. They crawl over each other, sometimes one, sometimes another dominating, but never for long.

M: There are no needs, desires only.

Q: To eat, to drink, to shelter one's body; to live?

M: The desire to live is the one fundamental desire. All else depends on it.

Q: We live, because we must.

M: We live, because we crave sensory existence.

Q: A thing so universal cannot be wrong.

M: Not wrong, of course. In its own place and time nothing is wrong. But when you are concerned with truth, with reality, you must question every thing, your very life. By asserting the necessity of sensory and intellectual experience you narrow down your enquiry to search for comfort.

Q: I seek happiness, not comfort.

M: Beyond comfort of mind and body what happiness you know?

Q: Is there any other?

M: Find out for yourself. Question every urge, hold no desire legitimate. Empty of possession, physical and mental, free of all self-concern, be open for discovery.

Q: It is a part of Indian spiritual tradition that mere living in the proximity of a saint or sage is conducive to liberation and no other means are needed. Why don't you organize an Ashram so that people could live near you?

M: The moment I create an institution I become its prisoner. As a matter of fact I am available to all. Common roof and food will not make people more welcome. 'Living near' does not mean breathing the same air. It means trusting and obeying, not letting the good intentions of the teacher go to waste. Have your Guru always in your heart and remember his instructions — this is real abidance with the true. Physical proximity is least important. Make your entire life an expression of your faith and love for your teacher — this is real dwelling with the Guru.   ●●●

33

Everything Happens by Itself

Questioner: Does a *gnani* die?

Maharaj: He is beyond life and death. What we take to be inevitable — to be born and to die — appears to him but a way of expressing movement in the Immovable, change in the changeless, end in the endless. To the *gnani* it is obvious that nothing is born and nothing dies, nothing lasts and nothing changes, all is as it is — timelessly.

Q: You say the *gnani* is beyond. Beyond what? Beyond knowledge?

M: Knowledge has its rising and setting. Consciousness comes into being and goes out of being. It is a matter of daily occurrence and observation. We all know that sometimes we are conscious and sometimes not. When we are not conscious, it appears to us as a darkness or a blank. But a *gnani* is aware of himself as neither conscious nor unconscious, but purely aware, a witness to the three states of the mind and their contents.

Q: When does this witnessing begin?

M: To a *gnani* nothing has beginning or ending. As salt dissolves in water, so does everything dissolve into pure being. Wisdom is eternally negating the unreal. To see the unreal is wisdom. Beyond this lies the inexpressible.

Q: There is in me the conviction: 'I am the body' Granted, I am talking from unwisdom. But the state of feeling oneself the body, the body-mind, the mind-body, or even pure mind — when did it begin?

M: You cannot speak of a beginning of consciousness. The very ideas of beginning and time are within consciousness. To talk meaningfully of the beginning of anything, you must step out of it. And the moment you step out, you realize that there is no such thing and never was. There is only reality, in which no 'thing' has any being on its own. Like waves are inseparable from the ocean, so is all existence rooted in being.

Q: The fact is that here and now I am asking you: when did the feeling 'I am the body' arise? At my birth? or this morning?

M: Now.

Q: But I remember having it yesterday too!

M: The memory of yesterday is now only.

Q: But surely I exist in time. I have a past and a future.

M: That is how you imagine — now.

Q: There must have been a beginning.

M: Now.

Q: And what about ending?

M: What has no beginning cannot end.

Q: But I am conscious of my question.

M: A false question cannot be answered. It can only be seen as false.

Q: To me it is real.

M: When did it appear real to you? Now.

Q: Yes, it is quite real to me — now.

M: What is real about your question? It is a state of mind. No state of mind can be more real than the mind itself. Is the mind real? It is but a collection of states, each of them transitory. How can a succession of transitory states be considered real?

Q: Like beads on a string, events follow events — for ever.

M: They are all strung on the basic idea: 'I am the body'. But even this is a mental state and does not last. It comes and goes like all other states. The illusion of being the body-mind is there, only because it is not investigated. Non-investigation is the thread on which all the states of mind are strung. It is like darkness in a closed room. It is there — apparently. But when the room is opened, where does it go? It goes nowhere, because it was not there. All states of mind, all names and forms of existence are rooted in non-enquiry, non-investigation, in imagination and credulity. It is right to say 'I am', but to say 'I am this', 'I am that' is a sign of not enquiring, not examining, of mental weakness or lethargy.

Q: If all is light, how did darkness arise? How can there be darkness in the midst of light?

M: There is no darkness in the midst of light. Self-forgetfulness is the darkness. When we are absorbed in other things, in the not-self, we forget the self. There is nothing unnatural about it. But, why forget the self through excess of attachment? Wisdom lies in never forgetting the self as the ever-present source of both the experiencer and his experience.

Q: In my present state the 'I am the body' idea comes spontaneously, while the 'I am pure being' idea must be imposed on the mind as something true but not experienced.

M: Yes, sadhana (practice) consists in reminding oneself forcibly of one's pure 'being-ness', of not being anything in particular, nor a sum of particulars, not even the totality of all particulars, which make up a universe. All exists in the mind, even the body is an integration in the mind of a vast number of sensory perceptions, each perception also a mental state. If you say: 'I am the body', show it.

Q: Here it is.

M: Only when you think of it. Both mind and body are intermittent states. The sum total of these flashes creates the illusion of existence. Enquire what is permanent in the transient, real in the unreal. This is sadhana.

Q: The fact is that I am thinking of myself as the body.

M: Think of yourself by all means. Only don't bring the idea of a body into the picture. There is only a stream of sensations, perceptions, memories and ideations. The body is an abstraction, created by our tendency to seek unity in diversity — which again is not wrong.

Q: I am being told that to think 'I am the body' is a blemish in the mind.

M: Why talk like this? Such expressions create problems. The self is the source of all, and of all — the final destination. Nothing is external.

Q: When the body idea becomes obsessive, is it not altogether wrong?

M: There is nothing wrong in the idea of a body, nor even in the idea 'I am the body'. But limiting oneself to one body only is a mistake. In reality all existence, every form, is my own, within my consciousness. I cannot tell what I am because words can describe only what I am not. I am, and because I am, all is. But I am beyond consciousness and, therefore, in consciousness I cannot say what I am. Yet, I am. The question 'Who am I' has no answer. No experience can answer it, for the self is beyond experience.

Q: Still, the question 'Who am I' must be of some use.

M: It has no answer in consciousness and, therefore, helps to go beyond consciousness.

Q: Here I am — in the present moment. What is real in it, and what is not? Now, please don't tell me that my question is wrong. Questioning my questions leads me nowhere.

M: Your question is not wrong. It is unnecessary. You said: 'Here and now I am'. Stop there, this is real. Don't turn a fact into a question. There lies your mistake. You are neither knowing, nor not-knowing, neither mind nor matter; don't attempt to describe yourself in terms of mind and matter.

Q: Just now a boy came to you with a problem. You told him a few words and he went away. Did you help him?

M: Of course.

Q: How can you be so sure?

M: To help is my nature.

Q: How did you come to know it?

M: No need to know. It operates by itself.

Q: Still you have made a statement. On what is it based?

M: On what people tell me. But it is you who asks for proofs. do not need them. Setting things right lies in my very nature, which is *satyam, shivam, sundaram* (the true, the good, the beautiful).

Q: When a man comes to you for advice and you give him advice, wherefrom does it come and by what power does it help?

M: His own being affects his mind and induces a response.

Q: And what is your role?

M: In me the man and his self come together.

Q: Why does not the self help the man without you?

M: But I am the self! You imagine me as separate, hence your question. There is no 'my self' and 'his self'. There is the Self, the only Self of all. Misled by the diversity of names and shapes, minds and bodies, you imagine multiple selves. We both are the self, but you seem to be unconvinced. This talk of personal self and universal self is the learner's stage; go beyond, don't be stuck in duality.

Q: Let us come back to the man in need of help. He comes to you.

M: If he comes, he is sure to get help. Because he was destined to get help, he came. There is nothing fanciful about it. I cannot help some and refuse others. All who come are helped, for such is the law. Only the shape help takes varies according to the need.

Q: Why must he come here to get advice? Can't he get it from within?

M: He will not listen. His mind is turned outward. But in fact all experience is in the mind, and even his coming to me and getting help is all within himself. Instead of finding an answer within himself, he imagines an answer from without. To me there is no me, no man and no giving. All this is merely a flicker in the mind. I am infinite peace and silence in which nothing appears, for all that appears — disappears. Nobody comes for help, nobody offers help, nobody gets help. It is all but a display in consciousness.

Q: Yet the power to help is there and there is somebody or something that displays that power, call it God or Self or the Universal Mind. The name does not matter, but the fact does.

M: This is the stand the body-mind takes. The pure mind sees things as they are — bubbles in consciousness. These bubbles are appearing, disappearing and reappearing — without having real being. No particular cause can be ascribed to them, for each is caused by all and affects all. Each bubble is a body and all these bodies are mine.

Q: Do you mean to say, that you have the power to do everything rightly?

M: There is no power as separate from me. It is inherent in my very nature. Call it creativity. Out of a lump of gold you can make many ornaments — each will remain gold. Similarly, in whatever role I may appear and whatever function I may perform — I remain what I am: the 'I am' immovable, unshakable, independent. What you call the universe, nature, is my spontaneous creativity. Whatever happens — happens. But such is my nature that all ends in joy.

Q: I have a case of a boy gone blind because his stupid mother fed him methyl alcohol. I am requesting you to help him. You are full of compassion and, obviously, eager to help. By what power can you help him?

M: His case is registered in consciousness. It is there — indelibly. Consciousness will operate.

Q: Does it make any difference that I ask you to help?

M: Your asking is a part of the boy's blindness. Because he is blind, you ask. You have added nothing.

Q: But your help will be a new factor?

M: No, all is contained in the boy's blindness. All is in it — the mother, the boy, you and me and all else. It is one event.

Q: You mean to say that even our discussing the boy's case was predestined?

M: How else? All things contain their future. The boy appears in consciousness. I am beyond. I do not issue orders to consciousness. I know that it is in the nature of awareness to set things right. Let consciousness look after its creations! The boy's sorrow, your pity my listening and consciousness acting — all this is one single fact — don't split it into components and then ask questions.

Q: How strangely does your mind work?

M: You are strange, not me. I am normal. I am sane. I see things as they are, and therefore I am not afraid of them. But you are afraid of reality.

Q: Why should I?

M: It is ignorance of yourself that makes you afraid and also unaware that you are afraid. Don't try not to be afraid. Break down the wall of ignorance first.

People are afraid to die, because they do not know what is death. The *gnani* has died before his death, he saw that there was nothing to be afraid of. The moment you know your real being, you are afraid of nothing. Death gives freedom and power. To be free in the world, you must die to the world. Then the universe is your own, it becomes your body, an expression and a tool. The happiness of being absolutely free is beyond description. On the other hand, he who is afraid of freedom cannot die.

Q: You mean that one who cannot die, cannot live?

M: Put it as you like; attachment is bondage, detachment is freedom. To crave is to slave.

Q: Does it follow that if you are saved, the world is saved?

M: As a whole the world does not need saving. Man makes mistakes and creates sorrow; when it enters the field of awareness, the consciousness of a *gnani,* it is set right. Such is his nature.

Q: We can observe what may be called spiritual progress. A selfish man turns religious, controls himself, refines his thoughts and feelings, takes to spiritual practice, realizes his true being. Is such progress ruled by causality, or is it accidental?

M: From my point of view everything happens by itself, quite spontaneously. But man imagines that he works for an incentive, towards a goal. He has always a reward in mind and strives for it.

Q: A crude, unevolved man will not work without a reward. Is it not right to offer him incentives?

M: He will create for himself incentives anyhow. He does not know that to grow is in the nature of consciousness. He will progress from motive to motive and will chase Gurus for the fulfilment of his desires. When by the laws of his being he finds the way of return *(nivritti)* he abandons all motives, for his interest in the world is over. He wants nothing — neither from others nor from himself. He dies to all and becomes the All. To want nothing and do nothing — that is true creation! To watch the universe emerging and subsiding in one's heart is a wonder.

Q: The great obstacle to inner effort is boredom. The disciple gets bored.

M: Inertia and restlessness *(tamas* and *rajas)* work together and keep clarity and harmony *(sattva)* down. Tamas and Rajas must be conquered before Sattva can appear. It will all come in due course, quite spontaneously.

Q: Is there no need of effort then?

M: When effort is needed, effort will appear. When effortlessness becomes essential, it will assert itself. You need not push life about. Just flow with it and give yourself completely to the task of the present moment, which is the dying now to the now. For living is dying. Without death life cannot be.

Get hold of the main thing that the world and the self are one and perfect. Only your attitude is faulty and needs readjustment.

This process or readjustment is what you call *sadhana*. You come to it by putting an end to indolence and using all your energy to clear the way for clarity and charity. But in reality these all are signs of inevitable growth. Don't be afraid, don't resist, don't delay. Be what you are. There is nothing to be afraid of. Trust and try. Experiment honestly. Give your real being a chance to shape your life. You will not regret.   ●●●

34

Mind is Restlessness Itself

Questioner: I am a Swede by birth. Now I am teaching Hatha Yoga in Mexico and in the States.

Maharaj: Where did you learn it?

Q: I had a teacher in the States, an Indian Swami.

M: What did it give you?

Q: It gave me good health and a means of livelihood.

M: Good enough. Is it all you want?

Q: I seek peace of mind. I got disgusted with all the cruel things done by the so-called Christians in the name of Christ. For some time I was without religion. Then I got attracted to Yoga.

M: What did you gain?

Q: I studied the philosophy of Yoga and it did help me.

M: In what way did it help you? By what signs did you conclude that you have been helped?

Q: Good health is something quite tangible.

M: No doubt it is very pleasant to feel fit. Is pleasure all you expected from Yoga?

Q: The joy of well-being is the reward of Hatha Yoga. But Yoga in general yields more than that. It answers many questions.

M: What do you mean by Yoga?

Q: The whole teaching of India — evolution, re-incarnation, *karma* and so on.

M: All right, you got all the knowledge you wanted. But in what way are you benefitted by it?

Q: It gave me peace of mind.

M: Did it? Is your mind at peace? Is your search over?

Q: No, not yet.

M: Naturally. There will be no end to it, because there is no such thing as peace of mind. Mind means disturbance; restlessness itself is mind. Yoga is not an attribute of the mind, nor is it a state of mind.

Q: Some measure of peace I did derive from Yoga.

M: Examine closely and you will see that the mind is seething with thoughts. It may go blank occasionally, but it does it for a time and reverts to its usual restlessness. A becalmed mind is not peaceful mind.

You say you want to pacify your mind. Is he, who wants to pacify the mind, himself peaceful?

Q: No. I am not at peace, I take the help of Yoga.

M: Don't you see the contradiction? For many years you sought your peace of mind. You could not find it, for a thing essentially restless cannot be at peace.

Q: There is some improvement.

M: The peace you claim to have found is very brittle; any little thing can crack it. What you call peace is only absence of disturbance. It is hardly worth the name. The real peace cannot be disturbed. Can you claim a peace of mind that is unassailable?

Q: I am striving.

M: Striving too is a form of restlessness.

Q: So what remains?

M: The self does not need to be put to rest. It is peace itself, not at peace. Only the mind is restless. All it knows is restlessness, with its many modes and grades. The pleasant are considered superior and the painful are discounted. What we call progress is merely a change over from the unpleasant to the pleasant. But changes by themselves cannot bring us to the changeless, for whatever has a beginning must have an end. The real does not begin; it only reveals itself as beginningless and endless, all-pervading, all-powerful, immovable prime mover, timelessly changeless.

Q: So what has one to do?

M: Through Yoga you have accumulated knowledge and experience. This cannot be denied. But of what use is it all to you? Yoga means union, joining. What have you re-united, re-joined?

Q: I am trying to rejoin the personality back to the real self.

M: The personality *(vyakti)* is but a product of imagination. The self *(vyakta)* is the victim of this imagination. It is the taking yourself to be what you are not that binds you. The person cannot be said to exist on its own rights; it is the self that believes there is a person and is conscious of being it. Beyond the self *(vyakta)* lies the unmanifested *(avyakta)*, the causeless cause of everything. Even to talk of re-uniting the person with the self is not right, because there is no person, only a mental picture given a false reality by conviction. Nothing was divided and there is nothing to unite.

Q: Yoga helps in the search for and the finding of the self.

M: You can find what you have lost. But you cannot find what you have not lost.

Q: Had I never lost anything, I would have been enlightered. But I am not. I am searching. Is not my very search a proof of my having lost something?

M: It only shows that you believe you have lost. But who believes it? And what is believed to be lost? Have you lost a person like yourself? What is the self you are in search of? What exactly do you expect to find?

Q: The true knowledge of the self.

M: The true knowledge of the self is not a knowledge. It is not something that you find by searching, by looking everywhere. It is not to be found in space or time. Knowledge is but a memory, a pattern of thought, a mental habit. All these are motivated by pleasure and pain. It is because you are goaded by pleasure and pain that you are in search of knowledge. Being oneself is completely beyond all motivation. You cannot be yourself for some reason. You *are* yourself, and no reason is needed.

Q: By doing Yoga I shall find peace.

M: Can there be peace apart from yourself? Are you talking from your own experience or from books only? Your book knowledge is useful to begin with, but soon it must be given up for direct experience, which by its very nature is inexpressible

Words can be used for destruction also, of words images are built, by words they are destroyed. You got yourself into your present state through verbal thinking; you must get out of it the same way.

Q: I did attain a degree of inner peace. Am I to destroy it?

M: What has been attained may be lost again. Only when you realize the true peace, the peace you have never lost, that peace will remain with you, for it was never away. Instead of searching for what you do not have, find out what is it that you have never lost? That which is there before the beginning and after the ending of everything; that to which there is no birth, nor death. That immovable state, which is not affected by the birth and death of a body or a mind, that state you must perceive.

Q: What are the means to such perception?

M: In life nothing can be had without overcoming obstacles. The obstacles to the clear perception of one's true being are desire for pleasure and fear of pain. It is the pleasure-pain motivation that stands in the way. The very freedom from all motivation, the state in which no desire arises is the natural state.

Q: Such giving up of desires, does it need time?

M: If you leave it to time, millions of years will be needed. Giving up desire after desire is a lengthy process with the end never in sight. Leave alone your desires and fears, give your entire attention to the subject, to him who is behind the experience of desire and fear. Ask: who desires? Let each desire bring you back to yourself.

Q: The root of all desires and fears is the same — the longing for happiness.

M: The happiness you can think of and long for, is mere physical or mental satisfaction. Such sensory or mental pleasure is not the real, the absolute happiness.

Q: Even sensory and mental pleasures and the general sense of well-being which arises with physical and mental health, must have their roots in reality.

M: They have their roots in imagination. A man who is given a stone and assured that it is a priceless diamond will be mightily pleased until he realizes his mistake; in the same way pleasures lose their tang and pains their barb when the self is known. Both are seen as they are — conditional responses, mere reactions, plain attractions and repulsions, based on memories or pre-conceptions. Usually pleasure and pain are experienced when expected. It is all a matter of acquired habits and convictions.

Q: Well, pleasure may be imaginary. But pain is real.

M: Pain and pleasure go always together. Freedom from one means freedom from both. If you do not care for pleasure, you will not be afraid of pain. But there is happiness which is neither, which is completely beyond. The happiness you know is describable and measurable. It is objective, so to say. But the objective cannot be your own. It would be a grievous mistake to identify yourself with something external. This churning up of levels leads nowhere. Reality is beyond the subjective and objective, beyond all levels, beyond every distinction. Most definitely it is not their origin, source or root. These come from ignorance of reality, not from reality itself, which is indescribable, beyond being and not-being.

Q: Many teachers have I followed and studied many doctrines, yet none gave me what I wanted.

M: The desire to find the self will be surely fulfilled, provided you want nothing else. But you must be honest with yourself and really want nothing else. If in the meantime you want many other things and are engaged in their pursuit, your main purpose may be delayed until you grow wiser and cease being torn between contradictory urges. Go within, without swerving, without ever looking outward.

Q: But my desires and fears are still there.

M: Where are they but in your memory? Realize that their root is in expectation born of memory — and they will cease to obsess you.

Q: I have understood very well that social service is an endless task, because improvement and decay, progress and regress, go side by side. We can see it on all sides and on every level. What remains?

M: Whatever work you have undertaken — complete it. Do not take up new tasks, unless it is called for by a concrete situation of suffering and relief from suffering. Find yourself first, and end-less blessings will follow. Nothing profits the world as much as the abandoning of profits. A man who no longer thinks in terms of loss and gain is the truly non-violent man, for he is beyond all conflict.

Q: Yes, I was always attracted by the idea of *ahimsa* (non-violence).

M: Primarily, *ahimsa* means what it says: 'don't hurt'. It is not doing good that comes first, but ceasing to hurt, not adding to suffering. Pleasing others is not *ahimsa*.

Q: I am not talking of pleasing, but I am all for helping others.

M: The only help worth giving is freeing from the need for further help. Repeated help is no help at all. Do not talk of help-ing another, unless you can put him beyond all need of help.

Q: How does one go beyond the need of help? And can one help another to do so?

M: When you have understood that all existence, in separation and limitation, is painful, and when you are willing and able to live integrally, in oneness with all life, as pure being, you have gone beyond all need of help. You can help another by precept and example and, above all, by your being. You cannot give what you do not have and you don't have what you are not. You can only give what you are — and of that you can give limit-lessly.

Q: But, is it true that all existence is painful?

M: What else can be the cause of this universal search for pleasure? Does a happy man seek happiness? How restless people are, how constantly on the move! It is because they are in pain that they seek relief in pleasure. All the happiness they can imagine is in the assurance of repeated pleasure.

Q: If what I am, as I am, the person I take myself to be, cannot be happy, then what am I to do?

M: You can only cease to be — as you seem to be now. There is nothing cruel in what I say. To wake up a man from a night-mare is compassion. You came here because you are in pain, and all I say is: wake up, know yourself, be yourself. The end of pain lies not in pleasure. When you realize that you are beyond both pain and pleasure, aloof and unassailable, then the pursuit of happiness ceases and the resultant sorrow too. For pain aims at pleasure and pleasure ends in pain, relentlessly.

Q: In the ultimate state there can be no happiness?

M: Nor sorrow. Only freedom. Happiness depends on something or other and can be lost; freedom from everything depends on nothing and cannot be lost. Freedom from sorrow has no cause and, therefore, cannot be destroyed. Realize that freedom.

Q: Am I not born to suffer as a result of my past? Is freedom possible at all? Was I born of my own will? Am I not just a creature?

M: What is birth and death but the beginning and the ending of a stream of events in consciousness? Because of the idea of separation and limitation they are painful. Momentary relief from pain we call pleasure — and we build castles in the air hoping for endless pleasure which we call happiness. It is all misunderstanding and misuse. Wake up, go beyond, live really.

Q: My knowledge is, limited, my power negligible.

M: Being the source of both. the self is beyond both knowledge and power. The observable is in the mind. The nature of the self is pure awareness, pure witnessing, unaffected by the presence or absence of knowledge or liking.

Have your being outside this body of birth and death and all your problems will be solved. They exist because you believe yourself born to die. Undeceive yourself and be free. You are not a person.   ●●●

35

Greatest Guru is Your Inner Self

Questioner: On all sides I hear that freedom from desires and inclinations is the first condition of self-realization. But I find the condition impossible of fulfilment. Ignorance ot oneself causes desires and desires perpetuate ignorance. A truly vicious circlel

Maharaj: There are no conditions to fulfil. There is nothing to be done, nothing to be given up. Just look and remember, whatever you perceive is not you, nor yours. It is there in the field of consciousness, but you are not the field and its contents, nor even the knower of the field. It is your idea that you have to do things that entangle you in the results of your efforts — the motive, the desire, the failure to achieve, the sense of frustration — all this holds you back. Simply look at whatever happens and know that you are beyond it.

Q: Does it mean I should abstain from doing anything?

M: You cannot! What goes on must go on. If you stop suddenly, you will crash.

Q: Is it a matter of the known and the knower becoming one?

M: Both are ideas in the mind, and words that express them. There is no self in them. The self is neither, between nor beyond. To look for it on the mental level is futile. Stop searching, and see — it is here and now — it is that 'I am' you know so well. All you need to do is to cease taking yourself to be within the field of consciousness. Unless you have already considered these matters carefully, listening to me once will not do. Forget your past experiences and achievements, stand naked, exposed to the winds and rains of life and you will have a chance.

Q: Has devotion *(bhakti)* any place in your teaching?

M: When you are not well, you go to a physician who tells you what is wrong and what is the remedy. If you have confidence in him, it makes things simple: you take the medicine, follow the diet restrictions and get well. But if you do not trust him, you may still take a chance, or you may study medicine yourself! In all cases it is your desire for recovery that moves you, not the physician.

Without trust there is no peace. Somebody or other you always trust — it may be your mother, or your wife. Of all the people the knower of the self, the liberated man, is the most trustworthy. But merely to trust is not enough. You must also desire. Without desire for freedom of what use is the confidence that you can acquire freedom? Desire and confidence must go together. The stronger your desire, the easier comes the help. The greatest Guru is helpless as long as the disciple is not eager to learn. Eagerness and earnestness are all-important. Confidence will come with experience. Be devoted to your goal — and devotion to him who can guide you will follow. If your desire and confidence are strong, they will operate and take you to your goal, for you will not cause delay by hesitation and compromise.

The greatest Guru is your inner self. Truly, he is the supreme teacher. He alone can take you to your goal and he alone meets you at the end of the road. Confide in him and you need no outer Guru. But again you must have the strong desire to find him and do nothing that will create obstacles and delays. And do not waste energy and time on regrets. Learn from your mistakes and do not repeat them.

Q: If you do not mind my asking a personal question. . .?

M: Yes, go ahead.

Q: I see you sitting on an antelope skin. How does it tally with non-violence?

M: All my working life I was a cigarette-maker, helping people to spoil their health. And in front of my door the municipality has put up a public lavatory, spoiling my health. In this violent world how can one keep away from violence of some kind or other?

Q: Surely all avoidable violence should be avoided. And yet in

India every holy man has his tiger, lion, leopard or antelope skin to sit on.

M: Maybe because no plastics were available in ancient times and a skin was best to keep the damp away. Rheumatism has no charm, even for a saint! Thus the tradition arose that for lengthy meditations a skin is needed. Just like the drum-hide in a temple, so is the antelope skin of a Yogi. We hardly notice it.

Q: But the animal had to be killed.

M: I have never heard of a Yogi killing a tiger for his hide. The killers are not Yogis and the Yogis are not killers.

Q: Should you not express your disapproval by refusing to sit on a skin?

M: What an idea! I disapprove of the entire universe, why only a skin?

Q: What is wrong with the universe?

M: Forgetting your Self is the greatest injury; all the calamities flow from it. Take care of the most important, the lesser will take care of itself. You do not tidy up a dark room. You open the windows first. Letting in the light makes everything easy. So, let us wait with improving others until we have seen ourselves as we are — and have changed. There is no need to turn round and round in endless questioning; find yourself and everything will fall into its proper place.

Q: The urge to return to the source is very rare. Is it at all natural?

M: Outgoing is natural in the beginning, ingoing — in the end. But in reality the two are one, just like breathing in and out are one.

Q: In the same way are not the body and the dweller in the body one?

M: Events in time and space — birth and death, cause and effect — these may be taken as one; but the body and the embodied are not of the same order of reality. The body exists in time and space, transient and limited, while the dweller is timeless and spaceless, eternal and all-pervading. To identify the two is a grievous mistake and the cause of endless suffering.

You can speak of the mind and body as one, but the body-mind is not the underlying reality.

Q: Whoever he may be, the dweller is in control of the body and, therefore, responsible for it.

M: There is a universal power which is in control and is responsible.

Q: And so, I can do as I like and put the blame on some universal power? How easy!

M: Yes, very easy. Just realize the One Mover behind all that moves and leave all to Him. If you do not hesitate, or cheat, this is the shortest way to reality. Stand without desire and fear, relinquishing all control and all responsibility.

Q: What madness!

M: Yes, divine madness. What is wrong in letting go the illusion of personal control and personal responsibility? Both are in the mind only. Of course, as long as you imagine yourself to be in control, you should also imagine yourself to be responsible. One implies the other.

Q: How can the universal be responsible for the particular?

M: All life on earth depends on the sun. Yet you cannot blame the sun for all that happens, though it is the ultimate cause. Light causes the colour of the flower, but it neither controls, nor is responsible for it directly. It makes it possible, that is all.

Q: What I do not like in all this is taking refuge in some universal power.

M: You cannot quarrel with facts.

Q: Whose facts? Yours or mine?

M: Yours. You cannot deny my facts, for you do not know them. Could you know them, you would not deny them. Here lies the trouble. You take your imagining for facts and my facts for imagination. I know for certain that all is one. Differences do not separate. Either you are responsible for nothing, or for everything. To imagine that you are in control and responsible for one body only is the aberration of the body-mind.

Q: Still, you are limited by your body.

M: Only in matters pertaining to the body. This I do not mind It

is like enduring the seasons of the year. They come, they go —
they hardly affect me. In the same way body-minds come and
go — life is forever in search of new expressions.

Q: As long as you do not put all the burden of evil on God, I am
satisfied. There may be a God for all I know, but to me he is a
concept projected by the human mind. He may be a reality to
you, but to me society is more real than God, for I am both its
creature and its prisoner. Your values are wisdom and compassion: society's: sagacious selfishness. I live in a world quite different from yours.

M: None compels.

Q: None compels you, but I am compelled. My world is an evil
world, full of tears, toil and pain. To explain it away by the intel-
lectualizing, by putting forth theories of evolution and *karma* is
merely adding insult to injury. The God of an evil world is a cruel
God.

M: You are the god of your world and you are both stupid and
cruel. Let God be a concept — your own creation. Find out who
you are, how did you come to live, longing for truth, goodness
and beauty in a world full of evil. Of what use is your arguing for
or against God, when you just do not know who is God and what
are you talking about. The God born of fear and hope, shaped
by desire and imagination, cannot be the Power That Is, the
Mind and the Heart of the universe.

Q: I agree that the world I live in and the God I believe in are
both creatures of imagination. But in what way are they created
by desire? Why do I imagine a world so painful and a God so indifferent? What is wrong with me that I should torture myself so
cruelly? The enlightened man comes and tells me: 'it is but a
dream to put an end to', but is he not himself a part of the
dream? I find myself trapped and see no way out. You say you
are free. Of what are you free? For heaven's sake, don't feed me
on words, enlighten me, help me to wake up, since it is you who
sees me tossing in my sleep.

M: When I say I am free, I merely state a fact. If you are an
adult, you are free from infancy. I am free from all description
and identification. Whatever you may hear, see, or think of, I am
not that. I am free from being a percept, or a concept.

Q: Still, you have a body and you depend on it.

M: Again you assume that your point of view is the only correct one. I repeat: I was not, am not, shall not be a body. To me this is a fact. I too was under the illusion of having been born, but my Guru made me see that birth and death are mere ideas — birth is merely the idea: 'I have a body'. And death — 'I have lost my body'. Now, when I know I am not a body, the body may be there or may not — what difference does it make? The body-mind is like a room. It is there, but I need not live in it all the time.

Q: Yet, there is a body and you do take care of it.

M: The power that created the body takes care of it.

Q: We are jumping from level to level all the time.

M: There are two levels to consider — the physical — of facts, and mental — of ideas. I am beyond both. Neither your facts, nor ideas are mine. What I see is beyond. Cross-over to my side and see with me.

Q: What I want to say is very simple. As long as I believe: 'I am the body', I must not say: 'God will look after my body'. God will not. He will let it starve, sicken and die.

M: What else do you expect from a mere body? Why are you so anxious about it?

Because you think you are the body, you want it indestructible. You can extend its life considerably by appropriate practices, but for what ultimate good?

Q: It is better to live long and healthy. It gives us a chance to avoid the mistakes of childhood and youth, the frustrations of adulthood, the miseries and imbecility of old age.

M: By all means live long. But you are not the master. Can you decide the days of your birth and death? We are not speaking the same language. Yours is a make-believe talk, all hangs on suppositions and assumptions. You speak with assurance about things you are not sure of.

Q: Therefore, I am here.

M: You are not yet here. I am here. Come in! But you don't. You want me to live your life, feel your way, use your language. I cannot, and it will not help you. You must come to me. Words are of the mind and the mind obscures and distorts. Hence the absolute need to go beyond words and move over to my side.

Q: Take me over.

M: I am doing it, but you resist. You give reality to concepts, while concepts are distortions of reality. Abandon all concep- tualization and stay silent and attentive. Be earnest about it and all will be well with you.   ●●●

36

Killing Hurts the Killer, not the Killed

Questioner: A thousand years ago a man lived and died. His identity *(antahkarana)* re-appeared in a new body. Why does he not remember his previous life? And if he does, can the memory be brought into the conscious?

Maharaj: How do you know that the same person re-appeared in the new body? A new body may mean a new person al- together.

Q: Imagine a pot of ghee. (Indian clarified butter). When the pot breaks, the Ghee remains and can be transferred to another pot. The old pot had its own scent, the new — its own. The Ghee will carry the scents from pot to pot. In the same way the per- sonal identity is transferred from body to body.

M: It is all right. When there is the body, its peculiarities affect the person. Without the body we have the pure identity in the sense of 'I am'. But when you are reborn in a new body, where is the world formerly experienced?

Q: Every body experiences its own world.

M: In the present body the old body — is it merely an idea, or is it a memory?

Q: An idea, of course. How can a brain remember what it has not experienced?

M: You have answered your own question. Why play with ideas? Be content with what you are sure of. And the only thing you can be sure of is 'I am'. Stay with it, and reject everything else. This is Yoga.

Q: I can reject only verbally. At best I remember to repeat the formula: 'This is not me, this is not mine. I am beyond all this'.

M: Good enough. First verbally, then mentally and emotionally, then in action. Give attention to the reality within you and it will come to light. It is like churning the cream for butter. Do it correctly and assiduously and the result is sure to come.

Q: How can the absolute be the result of a process?

M: You are right, the relative cannot result in the absolute. But the relative can block the absolute, just as the non-churning of the cream may prevent the butter from separating. It is the real that creates the urge; the inner prompts the outer and the outer responds in interest and effort. But ultimately there is no inner, nor outer; the light of consciousness is both the creator and the creature, the experiencer and the experience, the body and the embodied. Take care of the power that projects all this and your problems will come to an end.

Q: Which is the projecting power?

M: It is imagination prompted by desire.

Q: I know all this, but have no power over it.

M: This is another illusion of yours, born from craving for results.

Q: What is wrong with purposeful action?

M: It does not apply. In these matters there is no question of purpose, nor of action. All you need is to listen, remember, ponder. It is like taking food. All you can do is to bite off, chew and

swallow. All else is unconscious and automatic. Listen, remember and understand — the mind is both the actor and the
stage. All is of the mind and you are not the mind. The mind is
born and reborn, not you. The mind creates the world and all the
wonderful variety of it. Just like in a good play you have all sorts
of characters and situations, so you need a little of everything to
make a world.

Q: Nobody suffers in a play.

M: Unless one identifies himself with it. Don't identify yourself
with the world and you will not suffer.

Q: Others will.

M: Then make your world perfect, by all means. If you believe in
God, work with Him. If you do not, become one. Either see the
world as a play or work at it with all your might. Or both.

Q: What about the identify of the dying man? What happens to
it when he is dead? Do you agree that it continues in another
body.

M: It continues and yet it does not. All depends how you look at
it. What is identity, after all? Continuity in memory? Can you talk
of identity without memory?

Q: Yes, I can. The child may not know its parents, yet the
hereditary characteristics will be there.

M: Who identifies them? Somebody with a memory to register
and compare. Don't you see that memory is the warp of your
mental life. And identity is merely a pattern of events in time and
space. Change the pattern and you have changed the man.

Q: The pattern is significant and important. It has its own value.
By saying that a woven design is merely coloured threads you
miss the most important — the beauty of it. Or by describing a
book as paper with ink stains on it, you miss the meaning. Identity is valuable because it is the basis of individuality; that which
makes us unique and irreplaceable. 'I am', is the intuition of uniqueness.

M: Yes and no. Identity, individuality, uniqueness — they are
the most valuable aspects of the mind, yet of the mind only. 'I
am all there is' too is an experience equally valid. The particular
and the universal are inseparable. They are the two aspects of

the nameless, as seen from without and from within. Unfortunately, words only mention, but don't convey. Try to go beyond the words.

Q: What dies with death?

M: The idea 'I am this body' dies; the witness does not.

Q: The Jains believe in a multiplicity of witnesses, forever separate.

M: That is their tradition based on the experience of some great people. The one witness reflects itself in the countless bodies as 'I am'. As long as the bodies, however subtle, last, the 'I am' appears as many. Beyond the body there is only the One.

Q: God?

M: The Creator is a person whose body is the world. The Nameless one is beyond all gods.

Q: Sri Ramana Maharshi died. What difference did it make to him?

M: None. What he was, he is — the Absolute Reality.

Q: But to the common man death makes a difference.

M: What he thinks himself to be before death he continues to be after death. His self-image survives.

Q: The other day there was a talk about the use by the *gnani* of animal skins for meditation etc. I was not convinced. It is easy to justify everything by referring to custom and tradition. Customs may be cruel and tradition corrupt. They explain, but do not justify.

M: I never meant to say that lawlessness follows self-realization. A liberated man is extremely law-abiding. But his laws are the laws of his real self, not of his society. These he observes, or breaks according to circumstances and necessity. But he will never be fanciful and disorderly.

Q: What I cannot accept is justification by custom and habit.

M: The difficulty lies in our differing points of view. You speak from the body-mind's. Mine is of the witness. The difference is basic.

Q: Still, cruelty is cruelty

M: None compels you to be cruel.

Q: Taking advantage of other people's cruelty is cruelty by proxy.

M: If you look into living process closely, you will find cruelty everywhere, for life feeds on life. This is a fact, but it does not make you feel guilty of being alive. You began a life of cruelty by giving your mother endless trouble. To the last day of your life you will compete for food, clothing, shelter, holding on to your body, fighting for its needs, wanting it to be secure, in a world of insecurity and death. From the animal's point of view being killed is not the worst form of dying; surely preferable to sickness and senile decay. The cruelty lies in the motive, not in the fact. Killing hurts the killer, not the killed.

Q: Agreed; then one must not accept the services of hunters and butchers.

M: Who wants you to accept?

Q: You accept.

M: That is how *you* see me! How quickly you accuse, condemn, sentence and execute! Why begin with me and not with yourself?

Q: A man like you should set an example.

M: Are you ready to follow my example? I am dead to the world, I want nothing, not even to live. Be as I am, do as I do. You are judging me by my clothes and food; while I only look at your motives; if you believe to be the body and the mind and act on it, you are guilty of the greatest cruelty — cruelty to your own real being. Compared to it all other cruelties do not count.

Q: You are taking refuge in the claim that you are not the body. But you are in control of the body and responsible for all it does. To allow the body full autonomy would be imbecility, madness!

M: Cool down. I am also against all killing of animals for flesh or fur, but I refuse to give it first place. Vegetarianism is a worthy cause, but not the most urgent; all causes are served best by the man who has returned to his source.

Q: When I was at Sri Ramanashram, I felt Bhagwan all over the place, all-pervading, all-perceiving.

M: You had the necessary faith. Those who have true faith in him will see him everywhere and at all times. All happens according to your faith and your faith is the shape of your desire.

Q: The faith you have in yourself, is not that too a shape of a desire?

M: When I say: 'I am', I do not mean a separate entity with a body as its nucleus. I mean the totality of being, the ocean of consciousness, the entire universe of all that is and knows. I have nothing to desire for I am complete forever.

Q: Can you touch the inner life of other people?

M: I am the people.

Q: I do not mean identity of essence or substance, nor similarity of form. I mean the actual entering into the minds and hearts of others and participating in their personal experiences Can you suffer and rejoice with me, or you only infer what I feel from observation and analogy?

M: All beings are in me. But bringing down into the brain the content of another brain requires special training. There is nothing that cannot be achieved by training.

Q: I am not your projection, nor are you mine. I am on my own right, not merely as your creation. This crude philosophy of imagination and projection does not appeal to me. You are depriving me of all reality. Who is the image of whom? You are my image or am I yours? Or am I an image in my own image! No, something is wrong somewhere.

M: Words betray their hollowness. The real cannot be described, it must be experienced. I cannot find better words for what I know. What I say may sound ridiculous. But what the words try to convey is the highest truth. All is one, however much we quibble. And all is done to please the one source and goal of every desire, whom we all know as the 'I am'.

Q: It is pain that is at the root of desire. The basic urge is to escape from pain.

M: What is the root of pain? Ignorance of yourself. What is the root of desire? The urge to find yourself. All creation toils for its self and will not rest until it returns to it.

Q: When will it return?

M: It can return whenever you want it.

Q: And the world?

M: You can take it with you.

Q: Must I wait with helping the world until I reach perfection?

M: By all means help the world. You will not help much, but the effort will make you grow. There is nothing wrong in trying to help the world.

Q: Surely there were people, common people, who helped greatly.

M: When the time comes for the world to be helped, some people are given the will, the wisdom and the power to cause great changes. ●●●

37

Beyond Pain and Pleasure there is Bliss

Maharaj: You must realize first of all that you are the proof of everything, including yourself. None can prove your existence, because his existence must be confirmed by you first. Your being and knowing you owe nobody. Remember, you are entirely on your own. You do not come from somewhere, you do not go anywhere. You are timeless being and awareness.

Questioner: There is a basic difference between us. You know the real while I know only the workings of my mind. Therefore, what you say is one thing, what I hear is another. What you say is true; what I understand is false, though the words are the same. There is a gap between us. How to close the gap?

M: Give up the idea of being what you think yourself to be and there will be no gap. By imagining yourself as separate you have created the gap. You need not cross it. Just don't create it. All is you and yours. There is nobody else. This is a fact.

Q: How strange! The very same words which to you are true, to me are false. 'There is nobody else'. How obviously untrue!

M: Let them be true or untrue. Words don't matter. What matters is the idea you have of yourself, for it blocks you. Give it up.

Q: From early childhood I was taught to think that I am limited to my name and shape. A mere statement to the contrary will not erase the mental groove. A regular brain-washing is needed — if at all it can be done.

M: You call it brain-washing, I call it Yoga — levelling up all the mental ruts. You must not be compelled to think the same thoughts again and again. Move on!

Q: Easier said than done.

M: Don't be childish! Easier to change, than to suffer. Grow out of your childishness, that is all.

Q: Such things are not done. They happen.

M: Everything happens all the time, but you must be ready for it. Readiness is ripeness. You do not see the real because your mind is not ready for it.

Q: If reality is my real nature, how can I ever be unready?

M: Unready means afraid. You are afraid of what you are. Your destination is the whole. But you are afraid that you will lose your identity. This is childishness, clinging to the toys, to your desires and fears, opinions and ideas. Give it all up and be ready for the real to assert itself. This self-assertion is best expressed in words: 'I am'. Nothing else has being. Of this you are absolutely certain.

Q: 'I am', of course, but 'I know' also. And I know that I am so and so, the owner of the body, in manifold relations with other owners.

M: It is all memory carried over into the *now*.

Q: I can be certain only of what is now. Past and future, memory and imagination, these are mental states, but they are all I know and they are now. You are telling me to abandon them. How does one abandon the now?

M: You are moving into the future all the time whether you like it or not.

Q: I am moving from now into now — I do not move at all. Everything else moves — not me.

M: Granted. But your mind does move. In the now you are both the movable and the immovable. So far you took yourself to be the movable and overlooked the immovable. Turn your mind inside out. Overlook the movable and you will find yourself to be the ever-present, changeless reality, inexpressible, but solid like a rock.

Q: If it is now, why am I not aware of it?

M: Because you hold on to the idea that you are not aware of it. Let go the idea.

Q: It does not make me aware.

M: Wait. You want to be on both sides of the wall at the same time. You can, but you must remove the wall. Or realize that the wall and both sides of it are one single space, to which no idea like 'here' or 'there' applies.

Q: Similies prove nothing. My only complaint is this: why do I not see what you see, why your words do not sound true in my mind. Let me know this much; all else can wait. You are wise and I am stupid; you see, I don't. Where and how shall I find my wisdom?

M: If you know yourself to be stupid, you are not stupid at all!

Q: Just as knowing myself sick does not make me well, so knowing myself foolish can not make me wise.

M: To know that you are ill must you not be well initially?

Q: Oh, no. I know by comparison. If I am blind from birth and you tell me that you know things without touching them, while I must touch to know, I am aware that I am blind without knowing what does it mean to see. Similarly, I know that I am lacking something when you assert things which I cannot grasp. You are telling me such wonderful things about myself; according to you I am eternal, omnipresent, omniscient, supremely happy, creator, preserver and destroyer of all there is, the source of all life, the heart of being, the lord and the beloved of every creature. You equate me with the Ultimate Reality, the source and the goal of all existence. I just blink, for I know myself to be a tiny little bundle of desires and fears, a bubble of suffering, a transient flash of consciousness in an ocean of darkness.

M: Before pain was, you were. After pain had gone, you remained. Pain is transient, you are not.

Q: I am sorry, but I do not see what you see. From the day I was born till the day I die, pain and pleasure will weave the pattern of my life. Of being before birth and after death I know nothing. I neither accept nor deny you. I hear what you say, but I do not *know* it.

M: Now you are conscious, are you not?

Q: Please do not ask me about before and after. I just know only what is now.

M: Good enough. You are conscious. Hold on to it. There are states when you are not conscious. Call it unconscious being.

Q: Being unconscious?

M: Consciousness and unconsciousness do not apply here. Existence is in consciousness, essence is independent of consciousness.

Q: It is void? Is it silence?.

M: Why elaborate? Being pervades and transcends consciousness. Objective consciousness is a part of pure consciousness, not beyond it.

Q: How do you come to know a state of pure being which is neither conscious nor unconscious? All knowledge is in consciousness only. There may be such a state as the abeyance of the mind. Does consciousness then appear as the witness?

M: The witness only registers events. In the abeyance of the mind even the sense 'I am' dissolves. There is no 'I am' without the mind.

Q: Without the mind means without thoughts. 'I am' as a thought subsides. 'I am' as the sense of being remains.

M: All experience subsides with the mind. Without the mind there can be no experiencer nor experience.

Q: Does not the witness remain?

M: The witness merely registers the presence or absence of experience. It is not an experience by itself, but it becomes an experience when the thought: 'I am the witness' arises.

Q: All I know is that sometimes the mind works and sometimes it stops. The experience of mental silence I call the abeyance of the mind.

M: Call it silence, or void, or abeyance, the fact is that the three — experiencer, experiencing, experience — are not. In witnessing, in awareness, self-consciousness, the sense of being this or that, is not. Unidentified being remains.

Q: As a state of unconsciousness?

M: With reference to anything, it is the opposite. It is also between and beyond all opposites. It is neither consciousness nor unconsciousness, nor midway, nor beyond the two. It is by itself, not with reference to anything which may be called experience or its absence.

Q: How strange! You speak of it as if it were an experience.

M: When I think of it — it becomes an experience.

Q: Like the invisible light, intercepted by a flower, becoming colour?

M: Yes, you may say so. It is in the colour but not the colour.

Q: The same old four-fold negation of Nagarjuna: neither this nor that, nor both, nor either. My mind reels!

M: Your difficulty stems from the idea that reality is a state of consciousness, one among many. You tend to say: "This is real. That is not real. And this is partly real, partly unreal", as if reality were an attribute or quality to have in varying measures.

Q: Let me put it differently. After all, consciousness becomes a problem only when it is painful. An ever-blissful state does not give rise to questions. We find all consciousness to be a mixture of the pleasant and the painful. Why?

M: All consciousness is limited and therefore painful. At the root of consciousness lies desire, the urge to experience.

Q: Do you mean to say that without desire there can be no consciousness? And what is the advantage of being unconscious? If I have to forego pleasure for the freedom from pain, I better keep both.

M: Beyond pain and pleasure there is bliss.

Q: Unconscious bliss, of what use is it?

M: Neither conscious nor unconscious. Real.

Q: What is your objection to consciousness?

M: It is a burden. Body means burden. Sensations, desires, thoughts — these are all burdens. All consciousness is of conflict.

Q: Reality is described as true being, pure consciousness, infinite bliss. What has pain to do with it?

M: Pain and pleasure happen, but pain is the price of pleasure, pleasure is the reward of pain. In life too you often please by hurting and hurt by pleasing. To know that pain and pleasure are one is peace.

Q: All this is very interesting, no doubt, but my goal is more simple. I want more pleasure and less pain in life. What am I to do?

M: As long as there is consciousness, there must be pleasure and pain. It is in the nature of the 'I am', of consciousness, to identify itself with the opposites.

Q: Then of what use is all this to me? It does not satisfy.

M: Who are you, who is unsatisfied?

Q: I am, the pain-pleasure man.

M: Pain and pleasure are both *ananda* (bliss). Here I am sitting in front of you and telling you — from my own immediate and unchanging experience — pain and pleasure are the crests and valleys of the waves in the ocean of bliss. Deep down there is utter fulness.

Q: Is your experience constant?

M: It is timeless and changeless.

Q: All I know is desire for pleasure and fear of pain.

M: That is what you think about yourself. Stop it. If you cannot break a habit all at once, consider the familiar way of thinking and see its falseness. Questioning the habitual is the duty of the mind. What the mind created, the mind must destroy. Or realize that there is no desire outside the mind and stay out.

Q: Honestly, I distrust this explaining everything as mind-made. The mind is only an instrument, as the eye is an instrument. Can you say that perception is creation? I see the world through the window, not in the window. All you say holds well together because of the common foundation, but I do not know whether your foundation is in reality, or only in the mind. I can have only a mental picture of it. What it means to you I do not know.

M: As long as you take your stand in the mind, you will see me in the mind.

Q: How inadequate are words for understanding!

M: Without words, what is there to understand? The need for understanding arises from mis-understanding. What I say is true, but to you it is only a theory. How will you come to know that it is true? Listen, remember, ponder, visualize, experience. Also apply it in your daily life. Have patience with me and, above all. have patience with yourself, for you are your only obstacle. The way leads through yourself beyond yourself. As long as you believe only the particular to be real, conscious and happy and reject the non-dual reality as something imagined, an abstract concept, you will find me doling out concepts and abstractions. But once you have touched the real within your own being, you will find me describing what for you is the nearest and the dearest.   ●●●

38

Spiritual Practice is Will Asserted and Re-asserted

Questioner: The Westerners who occasionally come to see you are faced with a peculiar difficulty. The very notion of a liberated man, a realized man, a self-knower, a God-knower, a man beyond the world, is unknown to them. All they have in their Christian culture is the idea of a saint: a pious man, law-abiding, God-fearing, fellow-loving, prayerful, sometimes prone to ecstasies and confirmed by a few miracles. The very idea of a *gnani* is foreign to Western culture, something exotic and rather unbelievable. Even when his existence is accepted, he is looked at with suspicion, as a case of self-induced euphoria caused by strange physical postures and mental attitudes. The very idea of a new dimension in consciousness seems to them implausible and improbable.

What will help them is the opportunity of hearing a *gnani* relate his own experience of realization, its causes and beginnings, its progress and attainments and its actual practice in daily life. Much of what he says may remain strange, even meaningless, yet there will remain a feeling of reality, an atmosphere of actual experiencing, ineffable, yet very real, a centre from which an exemplary life can be lived.

Maharaj: The experience may be incommunicable. Can one communicate an experience?

Q: Yes, if one is an artist. The essence of art is communication of feeling, of experience.

M: To receive communication, you must be receptive.

Q: Of course. There must be a receiver. But if the transmitter does not transmit, of what use is the receiver?

M: The *gnani* belongs to all. He gives himself tirelessly and completely to whoever comes to him. If he is not a giver, he is not a *gnani*. Whatever he has, he shares.

Q: But can he share what he *is*?

M: You mean, can he make others into *gnanis*? Yes and no. No, since *gnanis* are not made, they realize themselves as such, when they return to their source, their real nature. I cannot make you into what you already are. All I can tell you is the way I travelled and invite you to take it.

Q: This does not answer my question. I have in mind the critical and sceptical Westerner who denies the very possibility of higher states of consciousness. Recently drugs have made a breach in his disbelief, without affecting his materialistic outlook. Drugs or no drugs, the body remains the primary fact and the mind is secondary. Beyond the mind, they see nothing. From Buddha onwards the state of self-realization was described in negative terms, as 'not this, not that'. Is it inevitable? Is it not possible to illustrate it, if not describe. I admit, no verbal description will do, when the state described is beyond words. Yet it is also within words. Poetry is the art of putting into words the inexpressible.

M: There is no lack of religious poets. Turn to them for what you want. As far as I am concerned, my teaching is simple: trust me for a while and do what I tell you. If you persevere, you will find that your trust was justified.

Q: And what to do with people who are interested, but cannot trust?

M: If they could stay with me, they would come to trust me. Once they trust me, they will follow my advice and discover for themselves.

Q: It is not for the training that I am asking just now, but for its results. You had both. You are willing to tell us all about the training, but when it comes to results, you refuse to share. Either you tell us that your state is beyond words, or that there is no difference; that where we see a difference, you see none. In both cases we are left without any insight into your state.

M: How can you have insight into my state when you are without insight into your own? When the very instrument of insight is lacking, is it not important to find it first? It is like a blind man wanting to learn painting before he regains his eyesight. You want to know my state — but do you know the state of your wife or servant?

Q: I am asking for some hints only.

M: Well, I gave you a very significant clue — where you see differences, I don't. To me it is enough. If you think it is not enough, I can only repeat; it is enough. Think it out deeply and you will come to see what I see.

You seem to want instant insight, forgetting that the instant is always preceded by a long preparation. The fruit falls suddenly, but the ripening takes time.

After all, when I talk of trusting me, it is only for a short time, just enough time to start you moving. The more earnest you are, the less belief you need, for soon you will find your faith in me justified. You want me to prove to you that I am trustworthy! How can I and why should I? After all, what I am offering you is the operational approach, so current in Western science. When a scientist describes an experiment and its results, usually you accept his statements on trust and repeat his experiment as he describes it. Once you get the same or similar results, you need not trust him any more; you trust your own experience. Encouraged, you proceed and arrive in the end at substantially identical results.

Q: The Indian mind was made ready for metaphysical experiments by culture and nurture. To the Indian words like 'direct perception of the Supreme Reality' make sense and bring out responses from the very depths of his being. They mean little to a Westerner; even when brought up in his own variety of Christianity, he does not think beyond conformity with God's commandments and Christ's injunctions. First-hand knowledge of reality is not only beyond ambition, but also beyond conceiving. Some Indians tell me: 'Hopeless. The Westerner will not, for he cannot. Tell him nothing about self-realization; let him live a useful life and earn a rebirth in India. Then only will he have a chance'. Some say: 'Reality is for all equally, but not all are equally endowed with the capacity to grasp it. The capacity come with desire, which will grow into devotion and ultimately into total self-dedication. With integrity and earnestness and iron determination to overcome all obstacles, the Westerner has the same chance as the Oriental man. All he needs is the rousing of interest'. To rouse his interest in self-knowledge he needs to be convinced about its advantages.

M: You believe it is possible to transmit a personal experience?

Q: I do not know. You speak of unity, identity of the seer with the seen. When all is one, communication should be feasible.

M: To have the direct experience of a country one must go and live there. Don't ask for the impossible. A man's spiritual victory no doubt benefits mankind, but to benefit another individual, a close personal relation is required. Such relation is not accidental and not everybody can claim it. On the other hand, the scientific approach is for all. 'Trust-test-taste'. What more do you need? Why push the Truth down unwilling throats? It cannot be done, anyhow. Without a receiver what can the giver do?

Q: The essence of art is to use the outer form to convey an inner experience. Of course, one must be sensitive to the inner, before the outer can be meaningful. How does one grow in sensitivity?

M: Whichever way you put it, it comes to the same. Givers there are many; where are the takers?

Q: Can you not share your own sensitivity?

M: Yes, I can, but sharing is a two-way street. Two are needed in sharing. Who is willing to take what I am willing to give?

Q: You say we are one. Is this not enough?

M: I am one with you. Are you one with me? If you are, you will not ask questions. If you are not, if you do not see what I see, what can I do beyond showing you the way to improve your vision?

Q: What you cannot give is not your own.

M: I claim nothing as my own. When the 'I' is not, where is the 'mine'?. Two people look at a tree. One sees the fruit hidden among the leaves and the other does not. Otherwise there is no difference between the two. The one that sees knows that with a little attention the other will also see, but the question of sharing does not arise. Believe me, I am not close-fisted, holding back your share of reality. On the contrary, I am all yours, eat me and drink me. But while you repeat verbally: 'give, give', you do nothing to take what is offered. I am showing you a short and easy way to being able to see what I see, but you cling to your old habits of thought, feeling and action and put all the blame on me. I have nothing which you do not have. Self-knowledge is not a piece of property to be offered and accepted. It is a new dimension altogether, where there is nothing to give or take.

Q: Give us at least some insight into the content of your mind while you live your daily life. To eat, to drink, to talk, to sleep — how does it feel at your end?

M: The common things of life: I experience them just as you do. The difference lies in what I do not experience. I do not experience fear or greed, hate or anger. I ask nothing, refuse nothing, keep nothing. In these matters I do not compromise. Maybe this is the outstanding difference between us. I will not compromise, I am true to myself, while you are afraid of reality.

Q: From the Westerner's point of view there is something disturbing in your ways. To sit in a corner all by oneself and keep on repeating: 'I am God, God I am', appears to be plain madness. How to convince a Westerner that such practices lead to supreme sanity?

M: The man who claims to be God and the man who doubts it — both are deluded. They talk in their dream.

Q: If all is dreaming, what is waking?

M: How to describe the waking state in dreamland language? Words do not describe, they are only symbols.

Q: Again the same excuse that words cannot convey reality.

M: If you want words, I shall give you some of the ancient words of power. Repeat any of them ceaselessly; they can work wonders.

Q: Are you serious? Would you tell a Westerner to repeat 'Om' or 'Ram' or 'Hare Krishna' ceaselessly, though he lacks completely the faith and conviction born of the right cultural and religious background. Without confidence and fervour, repeating mechanically the same sounds, will he ever achieve anything?

M: Why not? It is the urge, the hidden motive that matters, not the shape it takes. Whatever he does, if he does it for the sake of finding his own real self, will surely bring him to himself.

Q: No need of faith in the efficacy of the means?

M: No need of faith which is but expectation of results. Here the action only counts. Whatever you do for the sake of truth, will take you to truth. Only be earnest and honest. The shape it takes hardly matters.

Q: Then where is the need of giving expression to one's longing?

M: No need. Doing nothing is as good. Mere longing, undiluted by thought and action, pure, concentrated longing, will take you speedily to your goal. It is the true motive that matters, not the manner.

Q: Unbelievable! How can dull repetition in boredom verging on despair, be effective?

M: The very facts of repetition, of struggling on and on and of endurance and perseverance, in spite of boredom and despair and complete lack of conviction are really crucial. They are not important by themselves, but the sincerity behind them is all-important. There must be a push from within and pull from without.

Q: My questions are typical of the West. There people think in terms of cause and effect, means and goals. They do not see what causal connection can there be between a particular word and the Absolute Reality.

M: None whatsoever. But there is a connection between the word and its meaning, between the action and its motive. Spiritual practice is will asserted and re-asserted. Who has not the daring will not accept the real even when offered. Unwillingness born out of fear is the only obstacle.

Q: What is there to be afraid of?

M: The unknown. The not-being, not-knowing, not-doing. The beyond.

Q: You mean to say that while you can share the manner of your achievement, you cannot share the fruits?

M: Of course I can share the fruits and I am doing so all the time. But mine is a silent language. Learn to listen and understand.

Q: I do not see how one can begin without conviction.

M: Stay with me for some time, or give your mind to what I say and do and conviction will dawn.

Q: Not everybody has the chance of meeting you.

M: Meet your own self. Be with your own self, listen to it, obey it, cherish it, keep it in mind ceaselessly. You need no other guide. As long as your urge for truth affects your daily life, all is well with you. Live your life without hurting anybody. Harmlessness is a most powerful form of Yoga and it will take you speedily to your goal. This is what I call *nisarga yoga,* the Natural yoga. It is the art of living in peace and harmony, in friendliness and love. The fruit of it is happiness, uncaused and endless.

Q: Still, all this presupposes some faith.

M: Turn within and you will come to trust yourself. In everything else confidence comes with experience.

Q: When a man tells me that he knows something I do not know, I have the right to ask: 'what is it that you know, that I do not know?'

M: And if he tells you that it cannot be conveyed in words?

Q: Then I watch him closely and try to make out.

M: And this is exactly what I want you to do! Be interested, give attention, until a current of mutual understanding is established. Then the sharing will be easy. As a matter of fact, all realization is only sharing. You enter a wider consciousness and share in it. Unwillingness to enter and to share is the only hindrance. I never talk of differences, for to me there are none. You do, so it is up to you to show them to me. By all means, show me the differences. For this you will have to understand me, but then you will no longer talk of differences. Understand one thing well, and you have arrived. What prevents you from knowing is not the lack of opportunity, but the lack of ability to focus in your mind what you want to understand. If you could but keep in mind what you do not know, it would reveal to you its secrets. But if you are shallow and impatient, not earnest enough to look and wait, you are like a child crying for the moon.   ●●●

39

By Itself Nothing has Existence

Questioner: As I listen to you I find that it is useless to ask you questions. Whatever the question, you invariably turn it upon itself and bring me to the basic fact that I am living in an illusion of my own making and that reality is inexpressible in words. Words merely add to the confusion and the only wise course is the silent search within.

Maharaj: After all, it is the mind that creates illusion and it is the mind that gets free of it. Words may aggravate illusion, words may also help dispel it. There is nothing wrong in repeating the same truth again and again until it becomes reality. Mother's work is not over with the birth of the child. She feeds it day after day, year after year until it needs her no longer. People need hearing words, until facts speak to them louder than words.

Q: So we are children to be fed on words?

M: As long as you give importance to words, you are children.

Q: All right, then be our mother.

M: Where was the child before it was born? Was it not with the mother? Because it was already with the mother it could be born.

Q: Surely, the mother did not carry the child when she was a child herself.

M: Potentially, she was the mother. Go beyond the illusion of time.

Q: Your answer is always the same. A kind of clockwork which strikes the same hours again and again.

M: It cannot be helped. Just like the one sun is reflected in a billion dew drops, so is the timeless endlessly repeated. When I repeat: 'I am, I am', I merely assert and re-assert an ever-present fact. You get tired of my words because you do not see the living truth behind them. Contact it and you will find the full meaning of words and of silence — both.

Q: You say that the little girl is already the mother of her future child. Potentially — yes. Actually — no.

M: The potential becomes actual by thinking. The body and its affairs exist in the mind.

Q: And the mind is consciousness in motion and consciousness is the conditioned *(saguna)* aspect of the Self. The unconditioned *(nirguna)* is another aspect and beyond lies the abyss of the absolute *(paramartha)*.

M: Quite right — you have put it beautifully.

Q: But these are mere words to me. Hearing and repeating them is not enough, they must be experienced.

M: Nothing stops you but preoccupation with the outer which prevents you from focussing the inner. It cannot be helped, you cannot skip your *sadhana.* You have to turn away from the world and go within, until the inner and the outer merge and you can go beyond the conditioned, whether inner or outer.

Q: Surely, the unconditioned is merely an idea in the conditioned mind. By itself it has no existence.

M: By itself nothing has existence. Everything needs its own absence. To be, is to be distinguishable, to be here and not there, to be now and not then, to be thus and not otherwise. Like water is shaped by the container, so is everything determined by conditions *(gunas).* As water remains water regardless of the vessels, as light remains itself regardless of the colours it brings out, so does the real remain real, regardless of conditions in which it is reflected. Why keep the reflection only in the focus of consciousness? Why not the real itself?

Q: Consciousness itself is a reflection. How can it hold the real?

M: To know that consciousness and its content are but reflections, changeful and transient, is the focussing of the real. The refusal to see the snake in the rope is the necessary condition for seeing the rope.

Q: Only necessary, or also sufficient?

M: One must also know that a rope exists and looks like a snake. Similarly, one must know that the real exists and is of the nature of witness-consciousness. Of course it is beyond the witness, but to enter it one must first realize the state of pure witnessing. The awareness of conditions brings one to the unconditioned.

Q: Can the unconditioned be experienced?

M: To know the conditioned as conditioned is all that can be said about the unconditioned. Positive terms are mere hints and misleading.

Q: Can we talk of witnessing the real?

M: How can we? We can talk only of the unreal, the illusory, the transient, the conditioned. To go beyond, we must pass through total negation of everything as having independent existence. All things depend.

Q: On what do they depend?

M: On consciousness. And consciousness depends on the witness.

Q: And the witness depends on the real?

M: The witness is the reflection of the real in all its purity. It depends on the condition of the mind. Where clarity and detachment predominate, the witness-consciousness comes into being. It is just like saying that where the water is clear and quiet, the image of the moon appears. Or like daylight that appears as sparkle in the diamond.

Q: Can there be consciousness without the witness?

M: Without the witness it becomes unconsciousness, just living. The witness is latent in every state of consciousness, just like light in every colour. There can be no knowledge without the knower and no knower without his witness. Not only you know, but you know that you know.

Q: If the unconditioned cannot be experienced, for all experience is conditioned, then why talk of it at all?

M: How can there be knowledge of the conditioned without the unconditioned? There must be a source from which all this flows, a foundation on which all stands. Self-realization is primarily the knowledge of one's conditioning and the awareness that the infinite variety of conditions depends on our infinite ability to be conditioned and to give rise to variety. To the conditioned mind the unconditioned appears as the totality as well as the absence of everything. Neither can be directly experienced, but this does not make it non-existent.

Q: Is it not a feeling?

M: A feeling too is a state of mind. Just like a healthy body does not call for attention, so is the unconditioned free from experience. Take the experience of death. The ordinary man is afraid to die, because he is afraid of change. The *gnani* is not afraid because his mind is dead already. He does not think: 'I live'. He knows: 'There is life'. There is no change in it and no death. Death appears to be a change in time and space. Where there is neither time nor space, how can there be death? The *gnani* is already dead to name and shape. How can their loss affect him? The man in the train travels from place to place, but the man off the train goes nowhere, for he is not bound for a destination. He has nowhere to go, nothing to do, nothing to become. Those who make plans will be born to carry them out. Those who make no plans need not be born.

Q: What is the purpose of pain and pleasure?

M: Do they exist by themselves, or only in the mind?

Q: Still, they exist. Never mind the mind.

M: Pain and pleasure are merely symptoms, the results of wrong knowledge and wrong feeling. A result cannot have a purpose of its own.

Q: In God's economy everything must have a purpose.

M: Do you know God that you talk of him so freely? What is God to you? A sound, a word on paper, an idea in the mind?

Q: By his power I am born and kept alive.

M: And suffer, and die. Are you glad?

Q: It may be my own fault that I suffer and die. I was created unto life eternal.

M: Why eternal in the future and not in the past. What has a beginning must have an end. Only the beginningless is endless.

Q: God may be a mere concept, a working theory. A very useful concept all the same!

M: For this it must be free of inner contradictions, which is not the case. Why not work on the theory that you are your own creation and creator. At least there will be no external God to battle with.

Q: The world is so rich and complex — how could I create it?

M: Do you know yourself enough to know what you can do and what you cannot? You do not know your own powers. You never investigated. Begin with yourself now.

Q: Everybody believes in God.

M: To me you are your own God. But if you think otherwise, think to the end. If there be God, then all is God's and all is for the best. Welcome all that comes with a glad and thankful heart. And love all creatures. This too will take you to your Self.   ●●●

40

Only the Self is Real

Maharaj: The world is but a show, glittering and empty. It is, and yet is not. It is there as long as I want to see it and take part in it. When I cease caring, it dissolves. It has no cause and serves no purpose. It just happens when we are absent-minded. It appears exactly as it looks, but there is no depth in it, nor meaning. Only the onlooker is real, call him Self or *Atma.* To the Self the world is but a colourful show, which he enjoys as long as it lasts and forgets when it is over. Whatever happens on the stage makes him shudder in terror or roll with laughter, yet all the time he is aware that it is but a show. Without desire or fear he enjoys it, as it happens.

Questioner: The person immersed in the world has a life of many flavours. He weeps, he laughs, loves and hates, desires and fears, suffers and rejoices. The desireless and fearless *gnani,* what life has he? Is he not left high and dry in his aloofness?

M: His state is not so desolate. It tastes of the pure, uncaused, undiluted bliss. He is happy and fully aware that happiness is his very nature and that he need not do anything, nor strive for anything to secure it. It follows him, more real than the body, nearer than the mind itself. You imagine that without cause there can be no happiness. To me dependence on anything for happiness is utter misery. Pleasure and pain have causes, while my state is my own, totally uncaused. independent, unassailable.

Q: Like a play on the stage?

M: The play was written, planned and rehearsed. The world just spouts into being out of nothing and returns to nothing.

Q: Is there no creator? Was not the world in the mind of *Brahma,* before it was created?

M: As long as you are outside my state, you will have Creators, Preservers and Destroyers, but once with me you will know the Self only and see yourself in all.

Q: You function nevertheless.

M: When you are giddy, you see the world running circles round you. Obsessed with the idea of means and end, of work and purpose, you see me apparently functioning. In reality I only look. Whatever is done, is done on the stage. Joy and sorrow, life and death, they all are real to the man in bondage; to me they are all in the show, as unreal as the show itself.

I may perceive the world just like you. but you believe to be in it, while I see it as an iridescent drop in the vast expanse of consciousness.

Q: We are all getting old. Old age is not pleasant — all aches and pains, weakness and the approaching end. How does a *gnani* feel as an old man? How does his inner self look at his own senility.

M: As he gets older he grows more and more happy and peaceful. After all, he is going home. Like a traveller nearing his destination and collecting his luggage, he leaves the train without regret.

Q: Surely there is a contradiction. We are told the *gnani* is beyond all change. His happiness neither grows nor wanes. How can he grow happier because older, and that in spite of physical weakness and so on?

M: There is no contradiction. The reel of destiny is coming to its end — the mind is happy. The mist of bodily existence is lifting — the burden of the body is growing less from day to day.

Q: Let us say, the *gnani* is ill. He has caught some flu and every joint aches and burns. What is his state of mind?

M: Every sensation is contemplated in perfect equanimity. There is no desire for it, nor refusal. It is as it is and the he looks at it with a smile of affectionate detachment.

Q: He may be detached from his own suffering, but still it is there.

M: 't is there, but it does not matter. Whatever state I am in, I see it as a state of mind to be accepted as it is.

Q: Pain is pain. You experience it all the same.

M: He who experiences the body, experiences its pains and pleasures. I am neither the body, nor the experiencer of the body.

Q: Let us say you are twenty-five years old. Your marriage is arranged and performed, and the household duties crowd upon you. How would you feel?

M: Just as I feel now. You keep on insisting that my inner state is moulded by outer events. It is just not so. Whatever happens, I remain. At the root of my being is pure awareness, a speck of intense light. This speck, by its very nature, radiates and creates pictures in space and events in time — effortlessly and spontaneously. As long as it is merely aware there are no problems. But when the discriminative mind comes into being and creates distinctions, pleasure and pain arise. During sleep the mind is in abeyance and so are pain and pleasure. The process of creation continues, but no notice is taken. The mind is a form of consciousness, and consciousness is an aspect of life. Life creates everything, but the Supreme is beyond all.

Q: The Supreme is the master and consciousness — his servant.

M: The master is in consciousness, not beyond it. In terms of consciousness the Supreme is both creation and dissolution, concretion and abstraction, the focal and the universal. It is also neither. Words do not reach there, nor mind.

Q: The *gnani* seems to be a very lonely being, all by himself.

M: He is alone, but he is all. He is not even a being. He is the beingness of all beings. Not even that. No words apply. He is what he is, the ground from which all grows.

Q: Are you not afraid to die?

M: I shall tell you how my Guru's Guru died. After announcing that his end was nearing, he stopped eating, without changing the routine of his daily life. On the eleventh day, at prayer time he was singing and clapping vigorously and suddenly died! Just like that, between two movements, like a blown out candle. Everybody dies as he lives. I am not afraid of death, because I am not afraid of life. I live a happy life and shall die a happy death. Misery is to be born, not to die. All depends how you look at it.

Q: There can be no evidence of your state. All I know about it is what you say. All I see is a very interesting old man.

M: You are the interesting old man, not me! I was never born. How can I grow old? What I appear to be to you exists only in your mind. I am not concerned with it.

Q: Even as a dream you are a most unusual dream.

M: I am a dream that can wake you up. You will have the proof of it in your very waking up.

Q: Imagine, news reach you that I have died. Somebody tells you: 'You know so-and-so? He died'. What would be your reaction?

M: I would be very happy to have you back home. Really glad to see you out of this foolishness.

Q: Which foolishness?

M: Of thinking that you were born and will die, that you are a body displaying a mind and all such nonsense. In my world nobody is born and nobody dies. Some people go on a journey and come back, some never leave. What difference does it make since they travel in dreamlands, each wrapped up in his own dream. Only the waking up is important. It is enough to know the 'I am' as reality and also love.

Q: My approach is not so absolute, hence my question. Throughout the West people are in search of something real. They turn to science, which tells them a lot about matter, a little about the mind. and nothing about the nature and purpose of consciousness. To them reality is objective, outside the observable and describable, directly or by inference; about the subjective aspect of reality they know nothing. It is extremely important to let them know that there is reality and it is to be found in the freedom of consciousness from matter and its limitations and distortions. Most of the people in the world just do not know that there is reality which can be found and experienced in consciousness. It seems very important that they should hear the good news from somebody who has actually experienced. Such witnesses have always existed and their testimony is precious.

M: Of course. The gospel of self-realization, once heard, will never be forgotten. Like a seed left in the ground, it will wait for the right season and sprout and grow into a mighty tree.   ●●●

41

Develop the Witness Attitude

Questioner: What is the daily and hourly state of mind of a realized man? How does he see, hear, eat, drink, wake and sleep, work and rest? What proof is there of his state as different from ours? Apart from the verbal testimony of the so-called realized people, is there no way of verifying their state objectively. Are there not some observable differences in their physiological and nervous responses, in their metabolism, or brain waves, or in their psychosomatic structure?

Maharaj: You may find differences, or you may not. All depends on your capacity of observation. The objective differences are however, the least important. What matters is their outlook, their attitude, which is that of total detachment, aloofness, standing apart.

Q: Does not a *gnani* feel sorrow when his child dies, does he not suffer?

M: He suffers with those who suffer. The event itself is of little importance, but he is full of compassion for the suffering being, whether alive or dead, in the body or out of it. After all, love and compassion are his very nature. He is one with all that lives and love is that oneness in action.

Q: People are very much afraid of death.

M: The *gnani* is afraid of nothing. But he pities the man who is afraid. After all, to be born, to live and to die is natural. To be afraid is not. To the event, of course, attention is given.

Q: Imagine you are ill — high fever, aches, shivers. The doctor tells you the condition is serious, there are only a few days to live. What would be your first reaction?

M: No reaction. As it is natural for the incense stick to burn out, so it is natural for the body to die. Really, it is a matter of very little importance. What matters is that I am neither the body nor the mind. *I am.*

Q: Your family will be desperate, of course. What would you tell them?

M: The usual stuff: fear not, life goes on, God will protect you, we shall be soon together again and so on. But to me the entire commotion is meaningless, for I am not the entity that imagines itself alive or dead. I am neither born nor can I die. I have nothing to remember or to forget.

Q: What about the prayers for the dead?

M: By all means pray for the dead. It pleases them very much. They are flattered. The *gnani* does not need your prayers. He is himself the answer to your prayers.

Q: How does the *gnani* fare after death?

M: The *gnani* is dead already. Do you expect him to die again?

Q: Surely, the dissolution of the body is an important event even to a *gnani.*

M: There are no important events for a *gnani,* except when somebody reaches the highest goal. Then only his heart rejoices. All else is of no concern. The entire universe is his body, all life is his life. As in a city of lights, when one bulb burns out, it does not affect the network, so the death of a body does not affect the whole

Q: The particular may not matter to the whole, but it does matter to the particular. The whole is an abstraction, the particular, the concrete, is real.

M: That is what you say. To me it may be the other way — the whole is real, the part comes and goes. The particular is born and reborn, changing name and shape, the *gnani* is the Changeless Reality, which makes the changeful possible. But he cannot give you the conviction. It must come with your own experience. With me all is one, all is equal.

Q: Are sin and virtue one and the same?

M: These are all man-made values! What are they to me? What ends in happiness is virtue, what ends in sorrow is sin. Both are states of mind. Mine is not a state of mind.

Q: We are like the blind people at a loss to understand what does it mean to see.

M: You can put it as you like.

Q: Is the practice of silence as a *sadhana* effective?

M: Anything you do for the sake of enlightenment takes you nearer. Anything you do without remembering enlightenment puts you off. But why complicate? Just know that you are above and beyond all things and thoughts. What you want to be, you are it already. Just keep it in mind.

Q: I hear you saying it, but I cannot believe.

M: I was in the same position myself. But I trusted my Guru and he proved right. Trust me, if you can. Keep in mind what I tell you: desire nothing, for you lack nothing. The very seeking prevents you from finding.

Q: You seem to be so very indifferent to everything!

M: I am not indifferent, I am impartial. I give no preference to the me and the mine. A basket of earth and a basket of jewels are both unwanted. Life and death are all the same to me.

Q: Impartiality makes you indifferent.

M: On the contrary, compassion and love are my very core. Void of all predilections, I am free to love.

Q: Buddha said that the idea of enlightenment is extremely important. Most people go through their lives not even knowing that there is such a thing as enlightenment, leave alone the striving for it. Once they have heard of it, a seed was sown which cannot die. Therefore, he would send his *bhikhus* to preach ceaselessly for eight months every year.

M: 'One can give food, clothes, shelter, knowledge, affection, but the highest gift is the gospel of enlightenment', my Guru used to say. You are right, enlightenment is the highest good. Once you have it, nobody can take it away from you.

Q: If you would talk like this in the West, people would take you for mad.

M: Of course, they would! To the ignorant all that they can not understand is madness. What of it? Let them be as they are. I am as I am, for no merit of mine and they are as they are, for no fault of theirs. The Supreme Reality manifests itself in innumerable ways. Infinite in number are its names and shapes. All arise, all merge in the same ocean, the source of all is one. Looking for causes and results is but the pastime of the mind. What *is*, is lovable. Love is not a result, it is the very ground of being. Wherever you go, you will find being, consciousness and love. Why and what for make preferences?

Q: When by natural causes thousands and millions of lives are extinguished (as it happens in floods and earthquakes), I do not grieve. But when one man dies at the hand of man, I grieve extremely. The inevitable has its own majesty, but killing is avoidable and, therefore, ugly and altogether horrible.

M: All happens as it happens. Calamities, whether natural or man-made, happen, and there is no need to feel horrified.

Q: How can anything be without cause?

M: In every event the entire universe is reflected. The ultimate cause is untraceable. The very idea of causation is only a way of thinking and speaking. We cannot imagine, uncaused emergence. This, however, does not prove the existence of causation.

Q: Nature is mindless, hence irresponsible. But man has a mind. Why is it so perverse?

M: The causes of perversity are also natural — heredity, environment and so on. You are too quick to condemn. Do not worry about others. Deal with your own mind first. When you realize that your mind too is a part of nature, the duality will cease.

Q: There is some mystery in it which I cannot fathom. How can the mind be a part of nature?

M: Because nature is in the mind; without the mind where is nature?

Q: If nature is in the mind and the mind is my own, I should be able to control nature, which is not really the case. Forces beyond my control determine my behaviour.

M: Develop the witness attitude and you will find in your own experience that detachment brings control. The state of witnessing is full of power, there is nothing passive about it.   ●●●

42

Reality can not be Expressed

Questioner: I have noticed a new self emerging in me, independent of the old self. They somehow co-exist. The old self goes on its habitual ways; the new lets the old be, but does not identify itself with it.

Maharaj: What is the main difference between the old self and the new?

Q: The old self wants everything defined and explained. It wants things to fit each other verbally. The new does not care for verbal explanations — it accepts things as they are and does not seek to relate them to things remembered.

M: Are you fully and constantly aware of the difference between the habitual and the spiritual? What is the attitude of the new self to the old?

Q: The new just looks at the old. It is neither friendly nor inimical. It just accepts the old self along with everything else. It does not deny its being, but does not accept its value and validity.

M: The new is the total denial of the old. The permissive new is not really new. It is but a new attitude of the old. The really new obliterates the old completely. The two cannot be together. Is there a process of self-denudation, a constant refusal to accept the old ideas and values, or is there just a mutual tolerance? What is their relation?

Q: There is no particular relation. They co-exist.

M: When you talk of the old self and new, whom do you have in mind? As there is continuity in memory between the two, each remembering the other, how can you speak of two selves?

Q: One is a slave to habits, the other is not. One conceptualizes, the other is free from all ideas.

M: Why two selves? Between the bound and the free there can be no relationship. The very fact of co-existence proves their basic unity. There is but one self — it is always *now*. What you call the other self — old or new — is but a modality, another aspect of the one self. The self is single. You are that self and you have ideas of what you have been or will be. But an idea is not the self. Just now, as you are sitting in front of me, which self are you? The old or the new?

Q: The two are in conflict.

M: How can there be conflict between what is and what is not? Conflict is the characteristic of the old. When the new emerges, the old is no longer. You cannot speak of the new and the conflict in the same breath. Even the effort of striving for the new self is of the old. Wherever there is conflict, effort, struggle, striving, longing for a change, the new is not. To what extent are you free from the habitual tendency to create and perpetuate conflicts?

Q: I cannot say that I am now a different man. But I did discover new things about myself, states so unlike what I knew before, that I feel justified in calling them new.

M: The old self is your own self. The state which sprouts suddenly and without cause, carries no stain of self; you may call it 'god'. What is seedless and rootless, what does not sprout and grow, flower and fruit, what comes into being suddenly and in full glory, mysteriously and marvellously, you may call that 'god'. It is entirely unexpected yet inevitable, infinitely familiar yet most surprising, beyond all hope yet absolutely certain. Because it is without cause, it is without hindrance. It obeys one law only; the law of freedom. Anything that implies a continuity, a sequence, a passing from stage to stage cannot be the real. There is no progress in reality, it is final, perfect, unrelated.

Q: How can I bring it about?

M: You can do nothing to bring it about, but you can avoid creating obstacles. Watch your mind, how it comes into being, how it operates. As you watch your mind, you discover your self as the watcher. When you stand motionless, only watching, you discover your self as the light behind the watcher. The source of light is dark, unknown is the source of knowledge. That source alone is. Go back to that source and abide there. It is not

in the sky nor in the all-pervading ether. God is all that is great
and wonderful; I am nothing, have nothing, can do nothing. Yet
all comes out of me — the source is me; the root, the origin is
me.

When reality explodes in you, you may call it experience of
God. Or, rather, it is God experiencing you. God knows you
when you know yourself. Reality is not the result of a process; it
is an explosion. It is definitely beyond the mind, but all you can
do is to know your mind well. Not that the mind will help you, but
by knowing your mind you may avoid your mind disabling you.
You have to be very alert, or else your mind will play false with
you. It is like watching a thief — not that you expect anything
from a thief, but you do not want to be robbed. In the same way
you give a lot of attention to the mind without expecting anything
from it.

Or, take another example. We wake and we sleep. After a
day's work sleep comes. Now, do I go to sleep or does inadvertence — characteristic of the sleeping state — come to me? In
other words — we are awake because we are asleep. We do not
wake up into a really waking state. In the waking state the world
emerges due to ignorance and takes one into a waking-dream
state. Both sleep and waking are misnomers. We are only
dreaming. True waking and true sleeping only the *gnani* knows.
We dream that we are awake, we dream that we are asleep. The
three states are only varieties of the dream state. Treating everything as a dream liberates. As long as you give reality to
dreams, you are their slave. By imagining that you are born as
so-and-so, you become a slave to the so-and-so. The essence
of slavery is to imagine yourself to be a process, to have past
and future, to have history. In fact, we have no history, we are
not a process, we do not develop, nor decay; also see all as a
dream and stay out of it.

Q: What benefit do I derive from listening to you?

M: I am calling you back to yourself. All I ask you is to look at
yourself, towards yourself, into yourself.

Q: To what purpose?

M: You live, you feel, you think. By giving attention to your living, feeling and thinking, you free yourself from them and go

beyond them. Your personality dissolves and only the witness remains. Then you go beyond the witness. Do not ask how it happens. Just search within yourself.

Q: What makes the difference between the person and the witness?

M: Both are modes of consciousness. In one you desire and fear, in the other you are unaffected by pleasure and pain and are not ruffled by events. You let them come and go.

Q: How does one get established in the higher state, the state of pure witnessing?

M: Consciousness does not shine by itself. It shines by a light beyond it. Having seen the dreamlike quality of consciousness, look for the light in which it appears, which gives it being. There is the content of consciousness as well as the awareness of it.

Q: I know and I know that I know.

M: Quite so, provided the second knowledge is unconditional and timeless. Forget the known, but remember that you are the knower. Don't be all the time immersed in your experiences. Remember that you are beyond the experiencer ever unborn and deathless. In remembering it, the quality of pure knowledge will emerge, the light of unconditional awareness.

Q: At what point does one experience reality?

M: Experience is of change, it comes and goes. Reality is not an event, it cannot be experienced. It is not perceivable in the same way as an event is perceivable. If you wait for an event to take place, for the coming of reality, you will wait for ever, for reality neither comes nor goes. It is to be perceived, not expected. It is not to be prepared for and anticipated. But the very longing and search for reality is the movement, operation, action of reality. All you can do is to grasp the central point, that reality is not an event and does not happen and whatever happens, whatever comes and goes, is not reality. See the event as event only, the transient as transient, experience as mere experience and you have done all you can. Then you are vulnerable to reality, no longer armoured against it, as you were when you gave reality to events and experiences. But as soon as there is some like or dislike, you have drawn a screen.

Q: Would you say that reality expresses itself in action rather than in knowledge? Or, is it a feeling of sorts?

M: Neither action, nor feeling, nor thought express reality. There is no such thing as an expression of reality. You are introducing a duality where there is none. Only reality *is*, there is nothing else. The three states of waking, dreaming and sleeping are not me and I am not in them. When I die, the world will say — 'Oh, Maharaj is dead!' But to me these are words without content; they have no meaning. When the worship is done before the image of the Guru, all takes place as if he wakes and bathes and eats and rests, and goes for a stroll and returns, blesses all and goes to sleep. All is attended to in minutest details and yet there is a sense of unreality about it all. So is the case with me. All happens as it needs, yet nothing happens. I do what seems to be necessary, but at the same time I know that nothing is necessary, that life itself is only a make-belief.

Q: Why then live at all? Why all this unnecessary coming and going, waking and sleeping, eating and digesting?

M: Nothing is done by me, everything just happens I do not expect, I do not plan, I just watch events happening, knowing them to be unreal.

Q: Were you always like this from the first moment of enlightenment?

M: The three states rotate as usual — there is waking and sleeping and waking again, but they do not happen to me. They just happen. To me nothing ever happens. There is something changeless, motionless, immovable, rock-like, unassailable; a solid mass of pure being-consciousness-bliss. I am never out of it. Nothing can take me out of it, no torture, no calamity.

Q: Yet, you are conscious!

M: Yes and no. There is peace — deep, immense, unshakeable. Events are registered in memory, but are of no importance. I am hardly aware of them.

Q: If I understand you rightly, this state did not come by cultivation.

M: There was no coming. It was so — always. There was discovery and it was sudden. Just as at birth you discover the world suddenly, as suddenly I discovered my real being.

Q: Was it clouded over and your *sadhana* dissolved the mist? When your true state became clear to you, did it remain clear, or did it get obscured again? Is your condition permanent or intermittent?

M: Absolutely steady. Whatever I may do, it stays like a rock — motionless. Once you have awakened into reality, you stay in it. A child does not return to the womb! It is a simple state, smaller than the smallest, bigger than the biggest. It is self-evident and yet beyond description.

Q: Is there a way to it?

M: Everything can become a way, provided you are interested. Just puzzling over my words and trying to grasp their full meaning is a *sadhana* quite sufficient for breaking down the wall. Nothing troubles me. I offer no resistance to trouble — therefore it does not stay with me. On your side there is so much trouble. On mine there is no trouble at all. Come to my side. You are trouble-prone. I am immune. Anything may happen — what is needed is sincere interest. Earnestness does it.

Q: Can I do it?

M: Of course. You are quite capable of crossing over. Only be sincere.   ●●●

43

Ignorance can be
Recognized, not *Gnana*

Questioner: From year to year your teaching remains the same. There seems to be no progress in what you tell us.

Maharaj: In a hospital the sick are treated and get well. The treatment is routine, with hardly any change, but there is nothing monotonous about health. My teaching may be routine, but the fruit of it is new from man to man.

Q: What is realization? Who is a realized man? By what is the *gnani* recognized?

M: There are no distinctive marks of *gnana*. Only ignorance can be recognized, not *gnana*. Nor does a *gnani* claim to be something special. All those who proclaim their own greatness and uniqueness are not *gnanis*. They are mistaking some unusual development for realization. The *gnani* shows no tendency to proclaim himself to be a *gnani*. He considers himself to be perfectly normal, true to his real nature. Proclaiming oneself to be an omnipotent, omniscient and omnipotent deity is a clear sign of ignorance.

Q: Can the *gnani* convey his experience to the ignorant? Can *gnana* be transmitted from one man to another?

M: Yes, it can. The words of a *gnani* have the power of dispelling ignorance and darkness in the mind. It is not the words that matter, but the power behind them.

Q: What is that power?

M: The power of conviction, based on personal realization, on one's own direct experience.

Q: Some realized people say that knowledge must be won, not got. Another can only teach, but the learning is one's own.

M: It comes to the same.

Q: There are many who have practised Yoga for years and years without any result. What may be the cause of their failure?

M: Some are addicted to trances, with their consciousness in abeyance. Without full consciousness what progress can there be?

Q: Many are practising *samadhis* (states of rapturous absorption). In *samadhis* consciousness is quite intense, yet they do not result in anything.

M: What results do you expect? And why should *gnana* be the result of anything? One thing leads to another, but *gnana* is not a thing to be bound by causes and results. It is beyond causality altogether. It is abidance in the self. The Yogi comes to know many wonders, but of the self he remains ignorant. The *gnani* may look and feel quite ordinary, but the self he knows well.

Q: There are many who strive for self-knowledge earnestly, but with scant results. What may be the cause of it?

M: They have not investigated the sources of knowledge sufficiently, their sensations, feelings and thoughts they do not know well enough. This may be one cause of delay. The other: some desires may still be alive.

Q: Ups and downs in *sadhana* are inevitable. Yet the earnest seeker plods on in spite of all. What can the *gnani* do for such a seeker?

M: If the seeker is earnest, the light can be given. The light is for all and always there, but the seekers are few, and among those few, those who are ready are very rare. Ripeness of heart and mind is indispensable.

Q: Did you get your own realization through effort or by the grace of your Guru?

M: His was the teaching and mine was the trust. My confidence in him made me accept his words as true, go deep into them, live them, and that is how I came to realize what I am. The Guru's person and words made me trust him and my trust made them fruitful.

Q: But can a Guru give realization without words, without trust, just like this, without any preparation?

M: Yes, one can, but where is the taker? You see, I was so attuned to my Guru, so completely trusting him, there was so little of resistance in me, that it all happened easily and quickly. But not everybody is so fortunate. Laziness and restlessness often stand in the way and until they are seen and removed, the progress is slow. All those who have realized on the spot, by mere touch, look or thought, have been ripe for it. But such are very few. The majority needs some time for ripening. *Sadhana* is accelerated ripening.

Q: What makes one ripe? What is the ripening factor?

M: Earnestness of course, one must be really anxious. After all, the realized man is the most earnest man. Whatever he does, he does it completely, without limitations and reservations. Integrity will take you to reality.

Q: Do you love the world?

M: When you are hurt, you cry. Why? Because you love yourself. Don't bottle up your love by limiting it to the body, keep it open. It will be then the love for all. When all the false self-identifications are thrown away, what remains is all-embracing love. Get rid of all ideas about yourself, even of the idea that you are God. No self-definition is valid.

Q: I am tired of promises. I am tired of *sadhanas,* which take all my time and energy and bring nothing. I want reality here and now. Can I have it?

M: Of course you can, provided you are really fed up with everything, including your *sadhanas.* When you demand nothing of the world, nor of God, when you want nothing, seek nothing, expect nothing then the Supreme State will come to you uninvited and unexpected!

Q: If a man engrossed in family life and in the affairs of the world does his *sadhana* strictly as prescribed by his scriptures, will he get results?

M: Results he will get, but he will be wrapped up in them like in a cocoon.

Q: So many saints say that when you are ripe and ready, you

will realize. Their words may be true, but they are of little use.
There must be a way out, independent of ripening which needs
time, of *sadhana* which needs effort.

M: Don't call it a way; it is more a kind of skill. It is not even that.
Stay open and quiet, that is all. What you seek is so near you,
that there is no place for a way.

Q: There are so many ignorant people in the world and so few
gnanis. What may be the cause of it?

M: Don't concern yourself with others, take care of yourself.
You know that you *are*. Don't burden yourself with names, just
be. Any name or shape you give yourself obscures your real nature.

Q: Why should seeking end before one can realize?

M: The desire for truth is the highest of all desires, yet, it is still a
desire. All desires must be given up for the real to *be*.
Remember that you *are*. This is your working capital. Rotate it
and there will be much profit.

Q: Why should there be seeking at all.

M: Life is seeking, one cannot help seeking. When all search
ceases, it is the Supreme State.

Q: Why does the Supreme State come and go?

M: It neither comes nor goes. It *is*.

Q: Do you speak from your own experience?

M: Of course. It is a timeless state, ever present.

Q: With me it comes and goes, with you it does not. Why this
difference?

M: Maybe because I have no desires. Or you do not desire the
Supreme strongly enough. You must feel desperate when your
mind is out of touch.

Q: All my life I was striving and achieved so little. I was reading,
I was listening — all in vain.

M: Listening and reading became a habit with you.

Q: I gave it up too. I do not read nowadays.

M: What you gave up is of no importance now. What have you
not given up? Find that out and give up that. *Sadhana* is a

search for what to give up. Empty yourself completely.

Q: How can a fool desire wisdom? One needs to know the object of desire, to desire it. When the Supreme is not known, how can it be desired?

M: Man naturally ripens and becomes ready for realization.

Q: But what is the ripening factor?

M: Self-remembrance, awareness of 'I am' ripens him powerfully and speedily. Give up all ideas about yourself and simply *be*.

Q: I am tired of all the ways and means and skills and tricks, of all these mental acrobatics. Is there a way to perceive reality directly and immediately?

M: Stop making use of your mind and see what happens. Do this one thing thoroughly. That is all.

Q: When I was younger, I had strange experiences, short but memorable, of being nothing, just nothing, yet fully conscious. But the danger is that one has the desire to recreate from memory the moments that have passed.

M: This is all imagination. In the light of consciousness all sorts of things happen and one need not give special importance to any. The sight of a flower is as marvellous as the vision of God. Let them be. Why remember them and then make memory into a problem? Be bland about them; do not divide them into high and low, inner and outer, lasting and transient. Go beyond, go back to the source, go to the self that is the same whatever happens. Your weakness is due to your conviction that you were born into the world. In reality the world is ever recreated in you and by you. See everything as emanating from the light which is the source of your own being. You will find that in that light there is love and infinite energy.

Q: If I am that light, why do I not know it?

M: To know, you need a knowing mind, a mind capable of knowing. But your mind is ever on the run, never still, never fully reflecting. How can you see the moon in all her glory when the eye is clouded with disease?

Q: Can we say that while the sun is the cause of the shadow, one cannot see the sun in the shadow. One must turn round.

M: Again you have introduced the trinity of the sun, the body and shadow. There is no such division in reality. What I am talking about has nothing to do with dualities and trinities. Don't mentalize and verbalize. Just see and be.

Q: Must I see, to be?

M: See what you are. Don't ask others, don't let others tell you about yourself. Look within and see. All the teacher can tell you is only this. There is no need of going from one to another. The same water is in all the wells. You just draw from the nearest. In my case the water is within me and I am the water.   ●ↄↄ

44

'I am' is True, all else is Inference

Maharaj: The perceiver of the world, is he prior to the world, or does he come into being along with the world?

Questioner: What a strange question! Why do you ask such questions?

M: Unless you know the correct answer, you will not find peace.

Q: When I wake up in the morning, the world is already there, waiting for me. Surely the world comes into being first. I do, but much later, at the earliest at my birth. The body mediates between me and the world. Without the body there would be neither me nor the world.

M: The body appears in your mind, your mind is the content of your consciousness; you are the motionless witness of the river of consciousness which changes eternally without changing you in any way. Your own changelessness is so obvious that you do not notice it. Have a good look at yourself and all these misapprehensions and misconceptions will dissolve. Just as all the little watery lives are in water and cannot be without water, so all the universe is in you and cannot be without you.

Q: We call it God.

M: God is only an idea in your mind. The fact is you. The only thing you know for sure is: 'here and now I am'. Remove, the 'here and now' the 'I am' remains, unassailable. The word exists in memory, memory comes into consciousness; consciousness exists in awareness and awareness is the reflection of the light on the waters of existence.

Q: Still I do not see how can the world be in me when the opposite 'I am in the world' is so obvious.

M: Even to say 'I am the world, the world is me', is a sign of ignorance. But when I keep in mind and confirm in life my identity with the world, a power arises in me which destroys the ignorance, burns it up completely.

Q: Is the witness of ignorance separate from ignorance? Is not to say: 'I am ignorant' a part of ignorance?

M: Of course. All I can say truly is: 'I am', all else is inference. But the inference has become a habit. Destroy all habits of thinking and seeing. The sense 'I am' is the manifestation of a deeper cause, which you may call self, God. Reality or by any other name. The 'I am' is in the world; but it is the key which can open the door out of the world. The moon dancing on the water is seen in the water, but it is caused by the moon in the sky and not by the water.

Q: Still the main point seems to escape me. I can admit that the world in which I live and move and have my being is of my own creation, a projection of myself, of my imagination, on the unknown world, the world as it is, the world of 'absolute matter', whatever this matter may be. The world of my own creation may be quite unlike the ultimate, the real world, just like the cinema screen is quite unlike the pictures projected onto it. Nevertheless, this absolute world exists, quite independent of myself.

M: Quite so, the world of Absolute Reality, onto which your mind has projected a world of relative unreality is independent of yourself, for the very simple reason that it is yourself.

Q: Is there no contradiction in terms? How can independence prove identity?

M: Examine the motion of change and you will see. What can change while you do not change, can be said to be independent of you. But what is changeless must be one with whatever else is changeless. For, duality implies interaction and interaction means change. In other words, the absolutely material and the absolutely spiritual, the totally objective and the totally subjective are identical, both in substance and essence.

Q: Like in a tri-dimensional picture, the light forms its own screen.

M: Any comparison will do. The main point to grasp is that you have projected onto yourself a world of your own imagination, based on memories, on desires and fears, and that you have imprisoned yourself in it. Break the spell and be free.

Q: How does one break the spell?

M: Assert your independence in thought and action. After all, all hangs on your faith in yourself, on the conviction that what you see and hear, think and feel is real. Why not question your faith? No doubt, this world is painted by you on the screen of consciousness and is entirely your own private world. Only your sense 'I am', though in the world, is not of the world. By no effort of logic or imagination can you change the 'I am' into 'I am not'. In the very denial of your being you assert it. Once you realize that the world is your own projection, you are free of it. You need not free yourself of a world that does not exist, except in your own imagination! However is the picture, beautiful or ugly, you are painting it and you are not bound by it. Realize that there is nobody to force it on you, that it is due to the habit of taking the imaginary to be real. See the imaginary as imaginary and be free of fear.

Just as the colours in this carpet are brought out by light but light is not the colour, so is the world caused by you but you are not the world.

That which creates and sustains the world, you may call it God or providence, but ultimately you are the proof that God exists, not the other way round. For, before any question about God can be put, you must be there to put it.

Q: God is an experience in time, but the experiencer is timeless.

M: Even the experiencer is secondary. Primary is the infinite expanse of consciousness, the eternal possibility, the immeasurable potential of all that was, is, and will be. When you look at anything, it is the ultimate you see, but you imagine that you see a cloud or a tree.

Learn to look without imagination, to listen without distortion: that is all. Stop attributing names and shapes to the essentially nameless and formless, realize that every mode of perception is subjective, that what is seen or heard, touched or smelt, felt or thought, expected or imagined, is in the mind and not in reality, and you will experience peace and freedom from fear.

Even the sense of 'I am' is composed of the pure light and the sense of being. The 'I' is there even without the 'am'. So is the pure light there whether you say 'I' or not. Become aware of that pure light and you will never lose it. The beingness in being, the awareness in consciousness, the interest in every experience — that is not describable, yet perfectly accessible, for there is nothing else.

Q: You talk of reality directly — as the all-pervading, everpresent, eternal, all-knowing, all-energizing first cause. There are other teachers, who refuse to discuss reality at all. They say reality is beyond the mind while all discussions are within the realm of the mind, which is the home of the unreal. Their approach is negative; they pinpoint the unreal and thus go beyond it into the real.

M: The difference lies in the words only. After all, when I talk of the real, I describe it as not-unreal, space-less, time-less, cause-less, beginning-less and end-less. It comes to the same. As long as it leads to enlightenment, what does the wording matter? Does it matter whether you pull the cart or push it, as long as it is kept rolling? You may feel attracted to reality at one time and repelled from the false at another; these are only moods which alternate; both are needed for perfect freedom. You may go one way or another — but each time it will be the right way at the moment; just go whole-heartedly, don't waste time on doubting or hesitating. Many kinds of food are needed to make the child grow, but the act of eating is the same. Theoretically — all approaches are good. In practice, and at a given moment, you proceed by one road only. Sooner or later you are bound to discover that if you really want to find, you must dig at one place only — within.

Neither your body nor mind can give you what you seek — the being and knowing your self and the great peace that comes with it.

Q: Surely there is something valid and valuable in every approach.

M: In each case the value lies in bringing you to the need of seeking within. Playing with various approaches may be due to resistance to going within, to the fear of having to abandon the illusion of being something or somebody in particular. To find water you do not dig small pits all over the place, but drill deep in one place only. Similarly, to find your self you have to explore yourself. When you realize that you are the light of the world, you will also realize that you are the love of it; that to know is to love and to love is to know.

Of all the affections the love of oneself comes first. Your love of the world is the reflection of your love of yourself, for your world is of your own creation. Light and love are impersonal, but they are reflected in your mind as knowing and wishing oneself well. We are always friendly towards ourselves, but not always wise. A Yogi is a man whose goodwill is allied to wisdom.　　●●●

45

What Comes and Goes has no Being

Questioner: I have come to be with you, rather than to listen. Little can be said in words, much more can be conveyed in silence.

Maharaj: First words, then silence. One must be ripe for silence.

Q: Can I live in silence?

M: Unselfish work leads to silence, for when you work selflessly, you don't need to ask for help. Indifferent to results, you are willing to work with the most inadequate means. You do not care to be much gifted and well equipped. Nor do you ask for recognition and assistance. You just do what needs be done, leaving success and failure to the unknown. For everything is caused by innumerable factors, of which your personal endeavour is but one. Yet such is the magic of man's mind and heart that the most improbable happens when human will and love pull together.

Q: What is wrong with asking for help when the work is worthy?

M: Where is the need of asking? It merely shows weakness and anxiety. Work on, and the universe will work with you. After all the very idea of doing the right thing comes to you from the unknown. Leave it to the unknown as far as the results go, just go through the necessary movements. You are merely one of the links in the long chain of causation. Fundamentally, all happens in the mind only. When you work for something whole-heartedly and steadily, it happens, for it is the function of the mind to make things happen. In reality nothing is lacking and nothing is needed, all work is on the surface only. In the depths there is perfect peace. All your problems arise because you have defined and therefore limited yourself. When you do not think yourself to be this or that, all conflict ceases. Any attempt to do something about your problems is bound to fail, for what is caused by desire can be undone only in freedom from desire. You have enclosed yourself in time and space, squeezed yourself into the span of a lifetime and the volume of a body and thus created the innumerable conflicts of life and death, pleasure and pain, hope and fear. You cannot be rid of problems without abandoning illusions.

Q: A person is naturally limited.

M: There is no such thing as a person. There are only restrictions and limitations. The sum total of these defines the person. You think you know yourself when you know *what* you are. But you never know *who* you are. The person merely appears to be, like the space within the pot appears to have the shape and volume and smell of the pot. See that you are not what you believe yourself to be. Fight with all the strength at your disposal against the idea that you are nameable and describable. You are not. Refuse to think of yourself in terms of this or that. There is no other way out of misery, which you have created for yourself through blind acceptance without investigation. Suffering is a call for enquiry, all pain needs investigation. Don't be lazy to think.

Q: Activity is the essence of reality. There is no virtue in not working. Along with thinking something must be done.

M: To work in the world is hard, to refrain from all unnecessary work is even harder.

Q: For the person I am all this seems impossible.

M: What do you know about yourself? You can only be what you are in reality; you can only appear what you are not. You have never moved away from perfection. All idea of self-improvement is conventional and verbal. As the sun knows not darkness, so does the self know not the non-self. It is the mind, which by knowing the other, becomes the other. Yet the mind is nothing else but the self. It is the self that becomes the other, the not-self, and yet remains the self. All else is an assumption. Just as a cloud obscures the sun without in any way affecting it, so does assumption obscure reality without destroying it. The very idea of destruction of reality is ridiculous; the destroyer is always more real than the destroyed. Reality is the ultimate destroyer. All separation, every kind of estrangement and alienation is false. All is one — this is the ultimate solution of every conflict.

Q: How is it that in spite of so much instruction and assistance we make no progress?

M: As long as we imagine ourselves to be separate personalities, one quite apart from another, we cannot grasp reality which is essentially impersonal. First we must know ourselves as witnesses only, dimensionless and timeless centres of observation, and then realize that immense ocean of pure awareness, which is both mind and matter and beyond both.

Q: Whatever I may be in reality, yet I feel myself to be a small and separate person, one amongst many.

M: Your being a person is due to the illusion of space and time; you imagine yourself to be at a certain point occupying a certain volume; your personality is due to your self-identification with the body. Your thoughts and feelings exist in succession, they have their span in time and make you imagine yourself, because of memory, as having duration. In reality time and space exist in you; you do not exist in them. They are modes of perception, but they are not the only ones. Time and space are like words written on paper; the paper is real, the words merely a convention. How old are you?

Q: Forty-eight!

M: What makes you say forty-eight? What makes you say: I am here? Verbal habits born from assumptions. The mind creates time and space and takes its own creations for reality. All is here and now, but we do not see it. Truly, all is in me and by me. There is nothing else. The very idea of 'else' is a disaster and a calamity.

Q: What is the cause of personification, of self-limitation in time and space?

M: That which does not exist cannot have a cause. There is no such thing as a separate person. Even taking the empirical point of view, it is obvious that everything is the cause of everything, that everything is as it is, because the entire universe is as it is.

Q: Yet personality must have a cause.

M: How does personality come into being? By memory. By identifying the present with the past and projecting it into the future. Think of yourself as momentary, without past and future and your personality dissolves.

Q: Does not 'I am' remain?

M: The word 'remain' does not apply. 'I am' is ever afresh. You do not need to remember in order to be. As a matter of fact, before you can experience anything, there must be the sense of being. At present your being is mixed up with experiencing. All you need is to unravel being from the tangle of experiences. Once you have known pure being, without being this or that, you will discern it among experiences and you will no longer be misled by names and forms.

Self-limitation is the very essence of personality.

Q: How can I become universal?

M: But you are universal. You need not and you cannot become what you are already. Only cease imagining yourself to be the particular. What comes and goes has no being. It owes its very appearance to reality. You know that there is a world, but does the world know you? All knowledge flows from you, as all being and all joy. Realize that you are the eternal source and accept all as your own. Such acceptance is true love.

Q: All you say sounds very beautiful. But how has one to make it into a way of living?

M: Having never left the house you are asking for the way home. Get rid of wrong ideas, that is all. Collecting right ideas also will take you nowhere. Just cease imagining.

Q: It is not a matter of achievement, but of understanding.

M: Don't try to understand! Enough if you do not misunderstand. Don't rely on your mind for liberation. It is the mind that brought you into bondage. Go beyond it altogether.

What is beginningless cannot have a cause. It is not that you knew what you are and then you have forgotten. Once you know, you cannot forget. Ignorance has no beginning, but can have an end. Enquire: who is ignorant and ignorance will dissolve like a dream. The world is full of contradictions, hence your search for harmony and peace. These you cannot find in the world, for the world is the child of chaos. To find order you must search within. The world comes into being only when you are born in a body. No body — no world. First enquire whether you are the body. The understanding of the world will come later.

Q: What you say sounds convincing, but of what use is it to the private person, who knows itself to be in the world and of the world?

M: Millions eat bread, but few know all about wheat. And only those who know can improve the bread. Similarly, only those who know the self, who have seen beyond the world, can improve the world. Their value to private persons is immense, for they are their only hope of salvation. What is in the world cannot save the world; if you really care to help the world, you must step out of it.

Q: But can one step out of the world?

M: Who was born first, you or the world? As long as you give first place to the world, you are bound by it; once you realize, beyond all trace of doubt that the world is in you and not you in the world, you are out of it. Of course your body remains in the world and of the world, but you are not deluded by it. All scriptures say that before the world was, the Creator was. Who knows the Creator? He alone who was before the Creator, your own real being, the source of all the worlds with their creators.

Q: All you say is held together by your assumption that the world is your own projection. You admit that you mean your personal, subjective world, the world given you through your senses and your mind. In that sense each one of us lives in a world of his own projection. These private worlds hardly touch each other and they arise from and merge into the 'I am' at their centre. But surely behind these private worlds there must be a common objective world, of which the private worlds are mere shadows. Do you deny the existence of such objective world, common to all?

M: Reality is neither subjective nor objective, neither mind nor matter, neither time nor space. These divisions need somebody to whom to happen, a conscious separate centre. But reality is all and nothing, the totality and the exclusion, the fullness and the emptiness, fully consistent, absolutely paradoxical. You cannot speak about it, you can only lose your self in it. When you deny reality to anything, you come to a residue which cannot be denied.

All talk of *gnana* is a sign of ignorance. It is the mind that imagines that it does not know and then comes to know. Reality knows nothing of these contortions. Even the idea of God as the Creator is false. Do I owe my being to any other being? Because I *am,* all *is.*

Q: How can it be? A child is born into the world, not the world into the child. The world is old and the child is new.

M: The child is born into your world. Now, were you born into your world, or did your world appear to you? To be born means to create a world round yourself as the centre. But do you ever create yourself? Or did anyone create you? Everyone creates a world for himself and lives in it, imprisoned by one's ignorance. All we have to do is to deny reality to our prison.

Q: Just as the waking state exists in seed form during sleep, so does the world the child creates on being born exist before its birth. With whom does the seed lie?

M: With him who is the witness of birth and death, but is neither born nor dies. He alone is the seed of creation as well as its residue. Don't ask the mind to confirm what is beyond the mind. Direct experience is the only valid confirmation.   •••

46

Awareness of Being is Bliss

Questioner: By profession I am a physician. I began with surgery, continued with psychiatry and also wrote some books on mental health and healing by faith. I came to you to learn the laws of spiritual health.

Maharaj: When you are trying to cure a patient, what exactly are you trying to cure? What is cure? When can you say that a man is cured?

Q: I seek to cure the body as well as improve the link between the body and the mind. I also seek to set right the mind.

M: Did you investigate the connection between the mind and the body? At what point are they connected?

Q: Between the body and the indwelling consciousness lies the mind.

M: Is not the body made of food? And can there be a mind without food?

Q: The body is built and maintained by food. Without food the mind usually goes weak. But the mind is not mere food. There is a transforming factor which creates a mind in the body. What is that transforming factor?

M: Just like the wood produces fire which is not wood, so does the body produces the mind which is not the body. But to whom does the mind appear? Who is the perceiver of the thoughts and feelings which you call the mind? There is wood, there is fire and there is the enjoyer of the fire. Who enjoys the mind? Is the enjoyer also a result of food, or is it independent?

Q: The perceiver is independent.

M: How do you know? Speak from your own experience. You are not the body nor the mind. You say so. How do you know?

Q: I really do not know. I guess so.

M: Truth is permanent. The real is changeless. What changes is not real, what is real does not change. Now, what is it in you that does not change? As long as there is food, there is body and mind. When the food is stopped, the body dies and the mind dissolves. But does the observer perish?

Q: I guess it does not. But I have no proof.

M: You yourself are the proof. You have not, nor can you have any other proof. You are yourself, you know yourself, you love yourself. Whatever the mind does, it does for the love of its own self. The very nature of the self is love. It is loved, loving and lovable. It is the self that makes the body and the mind so interesting, so very dear. The very attention given to them comes from the self.

Q: If the self is not the body nor the mind, can it exist without the body and the mind?

M: Yes, it can. It is a matter of actual experience that the self has being independent of mind and body. It is being — awareness — bliss. Awareness of being is bliss.

Q: It may be a matter of actual experience to you, but it is not my case. How can I come to the same experience? What practices to follow, what exercises to take up?

M: To know that you are neither body nor mind, watch yourself steadily and live unaffected by your body and mind, completely aloof, as if you were dead. It means you have no vested interests, either in the body or in the mind.

Q: Dangerous!

M: I am not asking you to commit suicide. Nor can you. You can only kill the body, you cannot stop the mental process, nor can you put an end to the person you think you are. Just remain unaffected. This complete aloofness, unconcern with mind and body is the best proof that at the core of your being you are neither mind nor body. What happens to the body and the mind may not be within your power to change, but you can always put an end to your imagining yourself to be body and mind. Whatever happens, remind yourself that only your body and mind are affected, not yourself. The more earnest you are at remembering what needs to be remembered, the sooner will you be aware of yourself as you are, for memory will become experience. Earnestness reveals being. What is imagined and willed becomes actuality — here lies the danger as well as the way out.

Tell me, what steps have you taken to separate your real self, that in you which is changeless, from your body and mind?

Q: I am a medical man, I have studied a lot, I imposed on myself a strict discipline in the way of exercises and periodical fasts and I am a vegetarian.

M: But in the depth of your heart what is it that you want?

Q: I want to find reality.

M: What price are you willing to pay for reality? Any price?

Q: While in theory I am ready to pay any price, in actual life again and again I am being prompted to behave in ways which come in between me and reality. Desire carries me away.

M: Increase and widen your desires till nothing but reality can fulfil them. It is not desire that is wrong, but its narrowness and smallness. Desire is devotion. By all means be devoted to the real, the infinite, the eternal heart of being. Transform desire into love. All you want is to be happy. All your desires, whatever they may be, are expressions of your longing for happiness. Basically, you wish yourself well.

Q: I know that I should not. . .

M: Wait! Who told you that you should not? What is wrong with wanting to be happy?

Q: The self must go, I know.

M: But the self is there. Your desires are there. Your longing to be happy is there. Why? Because you love yourself. By all means love yourself — wisely. What is wrong is to love yourself stupidly, so as to make yourself suffer. Love yourself wisely. Both indulgence and austerity have the same purpose in view — to make you happy. Indulgence is the stupid way, austerity is the wise way.

Q: What is austerity?

M: Once you have gone through an experience, not to go through it again is austerity. To eschew the unnecessary is austerity. Not to anticipate pleasure or pain is austerity. Having things under control at all times is austerity. Desire by itself is not wrong. It is life itself, the urge to grow in knowledge and experience.

It is the choices you make that are wrong. To imagine that some little thing — food, sex, power, fame — will make you happy is to deceive yourself. Only something as vast and deep as your real self can make you truly and lastingly happy.

Q: Since there is nothing basically wrong in desire as an expression of love of self, how should desire be managed?

M: Live your life intelligently, with the interests of your deepest self always in mind. After all, what do you really want? Not perfection; you are already perfect. What you seek is to express in action what you are. For this you have a body and a mind. Take them in hand and make them serve you.

Q: Who is the operator here? Who is to take the body-mind in hand?

M: The purified mind is the faithful servant of the self. It takes charge of the instruments, inner and outer, and makes them serve their purpose.

Q: And what is their purpose?

M: The self is universal and its aims are universal. There is nothing personal about the self. Live an orderly life, but don't make it a goal by itself. It should be the starting point for high adventure.

Q: Do you advise me to come to India repeatedly?

M: If you are earnest, you don't need moving about. You are yourself wherever you are and you create your own climate. Locomotion and transportation will not give you salvation. You are not the body and dragging the body from place to place will take you nowhere. Your mind is free to roam the three worlds — make full use of it.

Q: If I am free, why am I in a body?

M: You are not in the body, the body is in you! The mind is in you. They happen to you. They are there because you find them interesting. Your very nature has the infinite capacity to enjoy. It is full of zest and affection. It sheds its radiance on all that comes within its focus of awareness and nothing is excluded. It does not know evil nor ugliness, it hopes, it trusts, it loves. You people do not know how much you miss by not knowing your own true self. You are neither the body nor the mind, neither the fuel nor the fire. They appear and disappear according to their own laws.

That which you are, your true self, you love it, and whatever you do, you do for your own happiness. To find it, to know it, to cherish it is your basic urge. Since time immemorial you loved yourself, but never wisely. Use your body and mind wisely in the service of the self, that is all. Be true to your own self, love your self absolutely. Do not pretend that you love others as yourself. Unless you have realized them as one with yourself, you cannot love them. Don't pretend to be what you are not, don't refuse to be what you are. Your love of others is the result of self-knowledge, not its cause. Without self-realization, no virtue is genuine. When you know beyond all doubting that the same life flows through all that is and you are that life, you will love all naturally and spontaneously. When you realize the depth and fullness of your love of yourself, you know that every living being and the entire universe are included in your affection. But when you look at anything as separate from you, you cannot love it for you are afraid of it. Alienation causes fear and fear deepens alienation. It is a vicious circle. Only self-realization can break it. Go for it resolutely.   ●●●

47

Watch your Mind

Questioner: In one's search for the essential, one soon realizes one's inadequacy and the need for a guide or a teacher. This implies a certain discipline for you are expected to trust your guide and follow implicitly his advice and instruction. Yet the social urgencies and pressures are so great, personal desires and fears so powerful, that the simplicity of mind and will, essential in obedience, are not forthcoming. How to strike a balance between the need for a Guru and the difficulty in obeying him implicitly?

Maharaj: What is done under pressure of society and circumstances does not matter much, for it is mostly mechanical, mere reacting to impacts. It is enough to watch oneself dispassionately to isolate oneself completely from what is going on. What has been done without minding, blindly, may add to one's *karma* (destiny), otherwise it hardly matters. The Guru demands one thing only; clarity and intensity of purpose, a sense of responsibility for oneself. The very reality of the world must be questioned. Who is the Guru, after all? He who knows the state in which there is neither the world nor the thought of it, he is the Supreme Teacher. To find him means to reach the state in which imagination is no longer taken for reality. Please, understand that the Guru stands for reality, for truth, for what *is*. He is a realist in the highest sense of the term. He cannot and shall not come to terms with the mind and its delusions. He comes to take you to the real; don't expect him to do anything else.

The Guru you have in mind, one who gives you information and instructions, is not the real Guru. The real Guru is he who knows the real, beyond the glamour of appearances. To him your questions about obedience and discipline do not make sense, for in his eyes the person you take yourself to be does not exist. Your questions are about a non-existing person. What exists for you does not exist for him. What you take for granted, he denies absolutely. He wants you to see yourself as he sees you. Then you will not need a Guru to obey and follow, for you will obey and follow your own reality. Realize that whatever you think yourself to be is just a stream of events; that while all happens, comes and goes, you alone are, the changeless among the changeful, the self-evident among the inferred. Separate the observed from the observer and abandon false identifications.

Q: In order to find the reality, one should discard all that stands in the way. On the other hand, the need to survive within a given society compels one to do and endure many things. Does one need to abandon one's profession and one's social standing in order to find reality?

M: Do your work. When you have a moment free, look within. What is important is not to miss the opportunity when it presents itself. If you are earnest you will use your leisure fully. That is enough.

Q: In my search for the essential and discarding the unessential, is there any scope for creative living? For instance, I love painting. Will it help me if I give my leisure hours to painting?

M: Whatever you may have to do, watch your mind. Also you must have moments of complete inner peace and quiet, when your mind is absolutely still. If you miss it, you miss the entire thing. If you do not, the silence of the mind will dissolve and absorb all else.

Your difficulty lies in your wanting reality and being afraid of it at the same time. You are afraid of it because you do not know it. The familiar things are known, you feel secure with them. The unknown is uncertain and therefore dangerous. But to know reality is to be in harmony with it. And in harmony there is no place for fear.

An infant knows its body, but not the body-based distinctions. It is just conscious and happy. After all, that was the purpose for which it was born. The pleasure to be is the simplest form of self-love, which later grows into love of the self. Be like an infant with nothing standing between the body and the self. The constant noise of the psychic life is absent. In deep silence the self contemplates the body. It is like the white paper on which nothing is written yet. Be like that infant, instead of trying to be this or that, be happy to *be*. You will be a fully awakened witness of the field of consciousness. But there should be no feelings and ideas to stand between you and the field.

Q: To be content with mere being seems to be a most selfish way of passing time.

M: A most worthy way of being selfish! By all means be selfish by foregoing everything but the Self. When you love the Self and nothing else, you go beyond the selfish and the unselfish. All distinctions lose their meaning. Love of one and love of all merge together in love, pure and simple, addressed to none, denied to none. Stay in that love, go deeper and deeper into it, investigate yourself and love the investigation and you will solve not only your own problems but also the problems of humanity. You will know what to do. Do not ask superficial questions; apply yourself to fundamentals, to the very roots of your being.

Q: Is there a way for me to speed up my self-realization?

M: Of course there is.

Q: Who will do this speeding up? Will you do it for me?

M: Neither you will do it, nor me. It will just happen.

Q: My very coming here has proved it. Is this speeding up due to holy company? When I left last time, I hoped to come back. And I did! Now I am desperate that so soon I have to leave for England.

M: You are like a newly born child. It was there before, but not conscious of its being. At its birth a world arose in it, and with it the consciousness of being. Now you have just to grow in consciousness, that is all. The child is the king of the world — when it grows up, it takes charge of its kingdom. Imagine that in its infancy it fell seriously ill and the physician cured it. Does it mean that the young king owes his kingdom to the physician? Only, perhaps as one of the contributing factors. There were so many others; all contributed. But the main factor, the most crucial, was the fact of being born the son of a king. Similarly, the Guru may help. But the main thing that helps is to have reality within. It will assert itself. Your coming here definitely helped you. It is not the only thing that is going to help you. The main thing is your own being. Your very earnestness testifies to it.

Q: Does my pursuing a vocation deny my earnestness?

M: I told you already. As long as you allow yourself an abundance of moments of peace, you can safely practise your most honourable profession. These moments of inner quiet will burn out all obstacles without fail. Don't doubt its efficacy. Try it.

Q: But, I did try!

M: Never faithfully, never steadily. Otherwise you would not be asking such questions. You are asking because you are not sure of yourself. And you are not sure of yourself because you never paid attention to yourself, only to your experiences. Be interested in yourself beyond all experience, be with yourself, love yourself; the ultimate security is found only in self-knowledge. The main thing is earnestness. Be honest with yourself and nothing will betray you. Virtues and powers are mere tokens for children to play with. They are useful in the world, but do not take you out of it. To go beyond, you need alert immobility, quiet attention.

Q: What then becomes of one's physical being?

M: As long as you are healthy, you live on.

Q: This life of inner immobility, will it not affect one's health?

M: Your body is food transformed. As your food, gross and subtle, so will be your health.

Q: And what happens to the sex instinct? How can it be controlled?

M: Sex is an acquired habit. Go beyond. As long as your focus is on the body, you will remain in the clutches of food and sex fear and death. Find yourself and be free.   ●●●

48

Awareness is Free

Questioner: I have just arrived from Sri Ramanashram. I have spent seven months there.

Maharaj: What practice were you following at the Ashram?

Q: As far as I could, I concentrated on the 'Who am I'?

M: Which way were you doing it? Verbally?

Q: In my free moments during the course of the day. Sometimes I was murmuring to myself 'Who am I?' 'I am, but who am I?' Or, I did it mentally. Occasionally I would have some nice feeling, or get into moods of quiet happiness. On the whole I was trying to be quiet and receptive, rather than labouring for experiences.

M: What were you actually experiencing when you were in the right mood?

Q: A sense of inner stillness, peace and silence.

M: Did you notice yourself becoming unconscious?

Q: Yes, occasionally and for a very short time. Otherwise I was just quiet, inwardly and outwardly.

M: What kind of quiet was it? Something akin to deep sleep, yet conscious all the same. A sort of wakeful sleep?

Q: Yes. Alertly asleep. *(jagrit-sushupti).*

M: The main thing is to be free of negative emotions — desire, fear etc., the 'six enemies' of the mind. Once the mind is free of them, the rest will come easily. Just as cloth kept in soap water will become clean, so will the mind get purified in the stream of pure feeling.

When you sit quiet and watch yourself, all kinds of things may come to the surface. Do nothing about them, don't react to them; as they have come so will they go, by themselves. All that matters is mindfulness, total awareness of oneself or rather, of one's mind.

Q: By 'oneself' do you mean the daily self?

M: Yes, the person, which alone is objectively observable. The observer is beyond observation. What is observable is not the real self.

Q: I can always observe the observer, in endless recession.

M: You can observe the observation, but not the observer. You know you are the ultimate observer by direct insight, not by a logical process based on observation. You are what you are, but you know what you are not. The self is known as being, the not-self is known as transient. But in reality all is in the mind. The observed, observation and observer are mental constructs. The self alone *is*.

Q: Why does the mind create all these divisions?

M: To divide and particularize is in the mind's very nature. There is no harm in dividing. But separation goes against fact. Things and people are different, but they are not separate. Nature is one, reality is one. There are opposites, but no opposition.

Q: I find that by nature I am very active. Here I am advised to avoid activity. The more I try to remain inactive, the greater the urge to do something. This makes me not only active outwardly, but also struggling inwardly to be what by nature I am not. Is there a remedy against longing for work?

M: There is a difference between work and mere activity. All nature works. Work is nature, nature is work. On the other hand, activity is based on desire and fear, on longing to possess and enjoy, on fear of pain and annihilation. Work is by the whole for the whole, activity is by oneself for oneself.

Q: Is there a remedy against activity?

M: Watch it, and it shall cease. Use every opportunity to remind yourself that you are in bondage, that whatever happens to you is due to the fact of your bodily existence. Desire, fear, trouble, joy, they cannot appear unless you are there to appear to. Yet, whatever happens, points to your existence as a perceiving centre. Disregard the pointers and be aware of what they are pointing to. It is quite simple, but it needs be done. What matters is the persistence with which you keep on returning to yourself.

Q: I do get into peculiar states of deep absorption into myself, but unpredictably and momentarily. I do not feel myself to be in control of such states.

M: The body is a material thing and needs time to change. The mind is but a set of mental habits, of ways of thinking and feeling, and to change they must be brought to the surface and examined. This also takes time. Just resolve and persevere, the rest will take care of itself.

Q: I seem to have a clear idea of what needs be done, but I find myself getting tired and depressed and seeking human company and thus wasting time that should be given to solitude and meditation.

M: Do what you feel like doing. Don't bully yourself. Violence will make you hard and rigid. Do not fight with what you take to be obstacles on your way. Just be interested in them, watch them, observe, enquire. Let anything happen — good or bad. But don't let yourself be submerged by what happens.

Q: What is the purpose in reminding oneself all the time that one is the watcher?

M: The mind must learn that beyond the moving mind there is the background of awareness, which does not change. The mind must come to know the true self and respect it and cease covering it up, like the moon which obscures the sun during solar eclipse. Just realize that nothing observable, or experienceable is you, or binds you. Take no notice of what is not yourself.

Q: To do what you tell me I must be ceaselessly aware.

M: To be aware is to be awake. Unaware means asleep. You are aware anyhow, you need not try to be. What you need is to be aware of being aware. Be aware deliberately and consciously, broaden and deepen the field of awareness. You are always conscious of the mind, but you are not aware of yourself as being conscious.

Q: As I can make out, you give distinct meanings to the words 'mind', 'consciousness', and 'awareness'.

M: Look at it this way. The mind produces thoughts ceaselessly, even when you do not look at them. When you know what is going on in your mind, you call it consciousness. This is your waking state — your consciousness shifts from sensation to sensation, from perception to perception, from idea to idea, in endless succession. Then comes awareness, the direct insight into the whole of consciousness, the totality of the mind. The mind is like a river, flowing ceaselessly in the bed of the body; you identify yourself for a moment with some particular ripple and call it: 'my thought'. All you are conscious of is your mind; awareness is the cognizance of consciousness as a whole.

Q: Everybody is conscious, but not everybody is aware.

M: Don't say: 'everybody is conscious'. Say: 'there is consciousness', in which everything appears and disappears. Our minds are just waves on the ocean of consciousness. As waves they come and go. As ocean they are infinite and eternal. Know yourself as the ocean of being, the womb of all existence. These are all metaphors of course; the reality is beyond description. You can know it only by being it.

Q: Is the search for it worth the trouble?

M: Without it all is trouble. If you want to live sanely, creatively and happily and have infinite riches to share, search for what you are.

While the mind is centred in the body and consciousness is centred in the mind, awareness is free. The body has its urges and mind its pains and pleasures. Awareness is unattached and unshaken. It is lucid, silent, peaceful, alert and unafraid, without desire and fear. Meditate on it as your true being and try to be it in your daily life, and you shall realize it in its fullness.

Mind is interested in what happens, while awareness is interested in the mind itself. The child is after the toy, but the mother watches the child, not the toy.

By looking tirelessly, I became quite empty and with that emptiness all came back to me except the mind. I find I have lost the mind irretrievably.

Q: As you talk to us just now, are you unconscious?

M: I am neither conscious nor unconscious, I am beyond the mind and its various states and conditions. Distinctions are created by the mind and apply to the mind only. I am pure Consciousness itself, un-broken awareness of all that is. I am in a more real state than yours. I am undistracted by the distinctions and separations which constitute a person. As long as the body lasts, it has its needs like any other, but my mental process has come to an end.

Q: You behave like a person who thinks.

M: Why not? But my thinking, like my digestion, is unconscious and purposeful.

Q: If your thinking is unconscious, how do you know that it is right?

M: There is no desire, nor fear to thwart it. What can make it wrong? Once I know myself and what I stand for, I do not need to check on myself all the time. When you know that your watch shows correct time, you do not hesitate each time you consult it.

Q: At this very moment who talks, if not the mind?

M: That which hears the question, answers it.

Q: But who is it?

M: Not who, but what. I am not a person in your sense of the word, though I may appear a person to you. I am that infinite ocean of consciousness in which all happens. I am also beyond all existence and cognition, pure bliss of being. There is nothing I feel separate from, hence I am all. No thing is me, so I am nothing.

The same power that makes the fire burn and the water flow, the seeds sprout and the trees grow, makes me answer your questions. There is nothing personal about me, though the language and the style may appear personal. A person is a set pattern of desires and thoughts and resulting actions; there is no such pattern in my case. There is nothing I desire or fear — how can there be a pattern?

Q: Surely, you will die.

M: Life will escape, the body will die, but it will not affect me in the least. Beyond space and time I am, uncaused, uncausing, yet the very matrix of existence.

Q: May I be permitted to ask how did you arrive at your present condition?

M: My teacher told me to hold on to the sense 'I am' tenaciously and not to swerve from it even for a moment. I did my best to follow his advice and in a comparatively short time I realized within myself the truth of his teaching. All I did was to remember his teaching, his face, his words constantly. This brought an end to the mind; in the stillness of the mind I saw myself as I am — unbound.

Q: Was your realization sudden or gradual.

M: Neither. One is what one is timelessly. It is the mind that realizes as and when it get cleared of desires and fears.

Q: Even the desire for realization?

M: The desire to put an end to all desires is a most peculiar desire, just like the fear of being afraid is a most peculiar fear. One stops you from grabbing and the other from running. You may use the same words, but the states are not the same. The man who seeks realization is not addicted to desires; he is a seeker who goes against desire, not with it. A general longing for liberation is only the beginning; to find the proper means and use them is the next step. The seeker has only one goal in view: to find his own true being. Of all desires it is the most ambitious, for nothing and nobody can satisfy it; the seeker and the sought are one and the search alone matters.

Q: The search will come to an end. The seeker will remain.

M: No, the seeker will dissolve, the search will remain. The search is the ultimate and timeless reality.

Q: Search means lacking, wanting, incompleteness and imperfection.

M: No, it means refusal and rejection of the incomplete and the imperfect. The search for reality is itself the movement of reality. In a way all search is for the real bliss, or the bliss of the real. But here we mean by search the search for oneself as the root of being conscious, as the light beyond the mind. This search will never end, while the restless craving for all else must end, for real progress to take place.

One has to understand that the search for reality, or God, or

Guru and the search for the self are the same; when one is found, all are found. When 'I am' and 'God is' become in your mind indistinguishable, than something will happen and you will know without a trace of doubt that God is because you are, you are because God is. The two are one.

Q: Since all is pre-ordained, is our self-realization also preordained? Or are we free there at least?

M: Destiny refers only to name and shape. Since you are neither body nor mind, destiny has no control over you. You are completely free. The cup is conditioned by its shape, material, use and so on. But the space within the cup is free. It happens to be in the cup only when viewed in connection with the cup. Otherwise it is just space. As long as there is a body, you appear to be embodied. Without the body you are not disembodied — you just are.

Even destiny is but an idea. Words can be put together in so many ways! Statements can differ, but do they make any change in the actual? There are so many theories devised for explaining things — all are plausible, none is true. When you drive a car, you are subjected to the laws of mechanics and chemistry: step out of the car and you are under the laws of physiology and biochemistry.

Q: What is meditation and what are its uses?

M: As long as you are a beginner certain formalized meditations, or prayers may be good for you. But for a seeker for reality there is only one meditation — the rigorous refusal to harbour thoughts. To be free from thoughts is itself meditation.

Q: How is it done?

M: You begin by letting thoughts flow and watching them. The very observation slows down the mind till it stops altogether. Once the mind is quiet, keep it quiet. Don't get bored with peace, be in it, go deeper into it.

Q: I heard of holding on to one thought in order to keep other thoughts away. But how to keep all thoughts away? The very idea is also a thought.

M: Experiment anew, don't go by past experience. Watch your thoughts and watch yourself watching the thoughts. The state of freedom from all thoughts will happen suddenly and by the bliss of it you shall recognize it.

Q: Are you not at all concerned about the state of the world? Look at the horrors in East Pakistan.* Do they not touch you at all?

M: I am reading newspapers, I know what is going on! But my reaction is not like yours. You are looking for a cure, while I am concerned with prevention. As long as there are causes, there must also be results. As long as people are bent on dividing and separating, as long as they are selfish and aggressive, such things will happen. If you want peace and harmony in the world, you must have peace and harmony in your hearts and minds. Such change cannot be imposed; it must come from within. Those who abhor war must get war out of their system. Without peaceful people how can you have peace in the world? As long as people are as they are, the world must be as it is. I am doing my part in trying to help people to know themselves as the only cause of their own misery. In that sense I am a useful man. But what I am in myself, what is my normal state cannot be expressed in terms of social consciousness and usefulness.

I may talk about it, use metaphors or parables, but I am acutely aware that it is just not so. Not that it cannot be experienced. It is experiencing itself! But it cannot be described in the terms of a mind that must separate and oppose in order to know.

The world is like a sheet of paper on which something is typed. The reading and the meaning will vary with the reader, but the paper is the common factor, always present, rarely perceived. When the ribbon is removed, typing leaves no trace on the paper. So is my mind — the impressions keep on coming, but no trace is left.

Q: Why do you sit here talking to people? What is your real motive?

M: No motive. You say I must have a motive. I am not sitting here, nor talking: no need to search for motives. Don't confuse me with the body. I have no work to do, no duties to perform.

* This conversation and a few more in the following pages took place in 1971, when a war was on in East Pakistan, now known as Bangla Desh.

That part of me which you may call God will look after the world. This world of yours, that so much needs looking after, lives and moves in your mind. Delve into it, you will find your answers there and there only. Where else do you expect them to come from? Outside your consciousness does anything exist?

Q: It may exist without my ever knowing it.

M: What kind of existence would it be? Can being be divorced from knowing? All being, like all knowing, relates to you. A thing is because you know it to be either in your experience or in your being. Your body and your mind exist as long as you believe so. Cease to think that they are yours and they will just dissolve. By all means let your body and mind function, but do not let them limit you. If you notice imperfections, just keep on noticing; your very giving attention to them will set your heart and mind and body right.

Q: Can I cure myself of a serious illness by merely taking cognizance of it?

M: Take cognizance of the whole of it, not only of the outer symptoms. All illness begins in the mind. Take care of the mind first, by tracing and eliminating all wrong ideas and emotions. Then live and work disregarding illness and think no more of it. With the removal of causes the effect is bound to depart.

Man becomes what he believes himself to be. Abandon all ideas about yourself and you will find yourself to be the pure witness, beyond all that can happen to the body or the mind.

Q: If I become anything I think myself to be, and I start thinking that I am the Supreme Reality, will not my Supreme Reality remain a mere idea?

M: First reach that state and then ask the question.   ●●●

49

Mind Causes Insecurity

Questioner: People come to you for advice. How do you know what to answer?

Maharaj: As I hear the question, so do I hear the answer.

Q: And how do you know that your answer is right?

M: Once I know the true source of the answers, I need not doubt them. From a pure source only pure water will flow. I am not concerned with people's desires and fears. I am in tune with facts, not with opinions. Man takes his name and shape to be himself, while I take nothing to be myself. Were I to think myself to be a body known by its name, I would not have been able to answer your questions. Were I to take you to be a mere body, there would be no benefit to you from my answers. No true teacher indulges in opinions. He sees things as they are and shows them as they are. If you take people to be what they think themselves to be, you will only hurt them, as they hurt themselves so grievously all the time. But if you see them as they are in reality, it will do them enormous good. If they ask you what to do, what practices to adopt, which way of life to follow, answer: 'Do nothing, just *be*. In being all happens naturally.'

Q: It seems to me that in your talks you use the words 'naturally' and 'accidentally' indiscriminately. I feel there is a deep difference in the meaning of the two words. The natural is orderly, subject to law; one can trust nature; the accidental is chaotic, unexpected, unpredictable. One could plead that everything is natural, subject to nature's laws; to maintain that everything is accidental, without any cause, is surely an exaggeration.

M: Would you like it better if I use the word 'spontaneous' instead of 'accidental'?

Q: You may use the word 'spontanous' or 'natural' as opposed
to 'accidental'. In the accidental there is the element of disorder,
of chaos. An accident is always a breach of rules, an exception,
a surprise.

M: Is not life itself a stream of surprises?

Q: There is harmony in nature. The accidental is a disturbance.

M: You speak as a person, limited in time and space, reduced
to the contents of a body and a mind. What you like, you call
'natural' and what you dislike, you call 'accidental'.

Q: I like the natural, and the law-abiding, the expected and I
fear the law-breaking, the disorderly, the unexpected, the meaningless. The accidental is always monstrous. There may be so-
called 'lucky accidents', but they only prove the rule that in an
accident-prone universe life would be impossible.

M: I feel there is a misunderstanding. By 'accidental' I mean
something to which no known law applies. When I say everything is accidental, uncaused, I only mean that the causes and
the laws according to which they operate are beyond our knowing, or even imagining. If you call what you take to be orderly,
harmonious, predictable, to be natural, then what obeys higher
laws and is moved by higher powers may be called spontaneous. Thus, we shall have two natural orders: the personal and
predictable and the impersonal, or super-personal, and unpredictable. Call it lower nature and higher nature and drop the
word accidental. As you grow in knowledge and insight, the
borderline between lower and higher nature keeps on receding,
but the two remain until they are seen as one. For, in fact, everything is most wonderfully inexplicable!

Q: Science explains a lot.

M: Science deals with names and shapes, quantities and qualities, patterns and laws; it is all right in its own place. But life is to
be lived; there is no time for analysis. The response must be instantaneous — hence the importance of the spontaneous, the
timeless. It is in the unknown that we live and move. The known
is the past.

Q: I can take my stand on what I feel I am. I am an individual, a
person among persons. Some people are integrated and har-

monized, and some are not.—Some live effortlessly, respond spontaneously to every situation correctly, doing full justice to the need of the moment, while others fumble, err and generally make a nuisance of themselves. The harmonized people may be called natural, ruled by law, while the disintegrated are chaotic and subject to accidents.

M: The very idea of chaos presupposes the sense of the orderly, the organic, the inter-related. Chaos and cosmos: are they not two aspects of the same state?

Q: But you seem to say that all is chaos, accidental, unpredictable.

M: Yes, in the sense that not all the laws of being are known and not all events are predictable. The more you are able to understand, the more the universe becomes satisfactory, emotionally and mentally. Reality is good and beautiful; we create the chaos.

Q: If you mean to say that it is the free will of man that causes accidents, I would agree. But we have not yet discussed free will.

M: Your order is what gives you pleasure and disorder is what gives you pain.

Q: You may put it that way, but do not tell me that the two are one. Talk to me in my own language — the language of an individual in search of happiness. I do not want to be misled by non-dualistic talks.

M: What makes you believe that you are a separate individual?

Q: I behave as an individual. I function on my own. I consider myself primarily; and others only in relation to myself. In short, I am busy with myself.

M: Well, go on being busy with yourself. On what business have you come here?

Q: On my old business of making myself safe and happy. I confess I have not been too successful. I am neither safe nor happy. Therefore, you find me here. This place is new to me, but my reason for coming here is old: the search for safe happiness, happy safety. So far I did not find it. Can you help me?

M: What was never lost can never be found. Your very search

for safety and joy keeps you away from them. Stop searching, cease losing. The disease is simple and the remedy equally simple. It is your mind only that makes you insecure and unhappy. Anticipation makes you insecure, memory — unhappy. Stop misusing your mind and all will be well with you. You need not set it right — it will set itself right, as soon as you give up all concern with the past and the future and live entirely in the *now*.

Q: But the now has no dimension. I shall become a nobody, a nothing!

M: Exactly. As nothing and nobody you are safe and happy. You can have the experience for the asking. Just try.

But let us go back to what is accidental and what is spontaneous, or natural. You said nature is orderly while accident is a sign of chaos. I denied the difference and said that we call an event accidental when its causes are untraceable. There is no place for chaos in nature. Only in the mind of man there is chaos. The mind does not grasp the whole — its focus is very narrow. It sees fragments only and fails to perceive the picture. Just as a man who hears sounds, but does not understand the language, may accuse the speaker of meaningless jabbering, and be altogether wrong. What to one is a chaotic stream of sounds is a beautiful poem to another.

King Janaka once dreamt that he was a beggar. On waking up he asked his Guru — Vasishta: Am I a king dreaming of being a beggar, or a beggar dreaming of being a king? The Guru answered: You are neither, you are both. You are, and yet you are not what you think yourself to be. You are because you behave accordingly; you are not because it does not last. Can you be a king or a beggar for ever? All must change. You are what does not change. What are you? Janaka said: Yes, I am neither king nor beggar, I am the dispassionate witness. The Guru said. This is your last illusion that you are a *gnani,* that you are different from, and superior to, the common man. Again you identify yourself with your mind, in this case a well-behaved and in every way an exemplary mind. As long as you see the least difference, you are a stranger to reality. You are on the level of the mind. When the 'I am myself' goes, the 'I am all' comes. When the 'I am all' goes, 'I am' comes. When even 'I am' goes, reality alone *is* and in it every 'I am' is preserved and glorified.

Diversity without separateness is the Ultimate that the mind can touch. Beyond that all activity ceases, because in it all goals are reached and all purposes fulfilled.

Q: Once the Supreme State is reached, can it be shared with others?

M: The Supreme State is universal, here and now; everybody already shares in it. It is the state of being — knowing and liking. Who does not like to be, or does not know his own existence? But we take no advantage of this joy of being conscious, we do not go into it and purify it of all that is foreign to it. This work of mental self-purification, the cleansing of the psyche, is essential. Just as a speck in the eye, by causing inflammation, may wipe out the world, so the mistaken idea: 'I am the body-mind' causes the self-concern, which obscures the universe. It is useless to fight the sense of being a limited and separate person unless the roots of it are laid bare. Selfishness is rooted in the mistaken ideas of oneself. Clarification of the mind is Yoga. ●●●

50
Self-awareness is the Witness

Questioner: You told me that I can be considered under three aspects: the personal *(vyakti),* the super-personal *(vyakta)* and the impersonal *(avyakta).* The Avyakta is the universal and real pure 'I'; the Vyakta is its reflection in consciousness as 'I am'; the Vyakti is the totality of physical and vital processes. Within the narrow confines of the present moment, the super-personal is aware of the person, both in space and time; not only one person, but the long series of persons strung together on the thread of *karma*. It is essentially the witness as well as the residue of the accumulated experiences, the seat of memory, the connecting link *(sutratma)*. It is man's character which life builds and shapes from birth to birth. The universal is beyond all name and shape, beyond consciousness and character, pure unselfconscious *being*. Did I put down your views rightly?

Maharaj: On the level of the mind — yes. Beyond the mental level not a word applies.

Q: I can understand that the person is a mental construct, a collective noun for a set of memories and habits. But, he to whom the person happens, the witnessing centre, is it mental too?

M: The personal needs a base, a body to identify oneself with, just as a colour needs a surface to appear on. The seeing of the colour is independent of the colour — it is the same whatever the colour. One needs an eye to see a colour. The colours are many, the eye is single. The personal is like the light in the colour and also in the eye, yet simple, single, indivisible and unperceivable, except in its manifestations. Not unknowable, but unperceivable, un-objectival, inseparable. Neither material nor mental, neither objective nor subjective, it is the root of matter and the source of consciousness. Beyond mere living and dying, it is the all-inclusive, all-exclusive Life, in which birth is death and death is birth.

Q: The Absolute or Life you talk about, is it real, or a mere theory to cover up our ignorance?

M: Both. To the mind, a theory; in itself — a reality. It is reality in its spontaneous and total rejection of the false. Just as light destroys darkness by its very presence, so does the absolute destroy imagination. To see that all knowledge is a form of ignorance is itself a movement of reality. The witness is not a person. The person comes into being when there is a basis for it, an organism, a body. In it the absolute is reflected as awareness. Pure awareness becomes self-awareness. When there is a self, self-awareness is the witness. When there is no self to witness, there is no witnessing either. It is all very simple; it is the presence of the person that complicates. See that there is no such thing as a permanently separate person and all becomes clear. Awareness — mind — matter — they are one reality in its two aspects as immovable and movable, and the three attributes of inertia, energy and harmony.

Q: What comes first: consciousness or awareness?

M: Awareness becomes consciousness when it has an object. The object changes all the time. In consciousness there is movement; awareness by itself is motionless and timeless, here and now.

Q: There is suffering and bloodshed in East Pakistan at the present moment. How do you look at it? How does it appear to you, how do you react to it?

M: In pure consciousness nothing ever happens.

Q: Please come down from these metaphysical heights! Of what use is it to a suffering man to be told that nobody is aware of his suffering but himself? To relegate everything to illusion is insult added to injury. The Bengali of East Pakistan is a fact and his suffering is a fact. Please, do not analyze them out of existence! You are reading newspapers, you hear people talking about it. You cannot plead ignorance. Now, what is your attitude to what is happening?

M: No attitude. Nothing is happening.

Q: Any day there may be a riot right in front of you, perhaps people killing each other. Surely you cannot say: nothing is happening and remain aloof.

M: I never talked of remaining aloof. You could as well see me jumping into the fray to save somebody and getting killed. Yet to me nothing happened.

Imagine a big building collapsing. Some rooms are in ruins, some are intact. But can you speak of the space as ruined or intact? It is only the structure that suffered and the people who happened to live in it. Nothing happened to space itself. Similarly, nothing happens to life when forms break down and names are wiped out. The goldsmith melts down old ornaments to make new. Sometimes a good piece goes with the bad. He takes it in his stride, for he knows that no gold is lost.

Q: It is not death that I rebel against. It is the manner of dying.

M: Death is natural, the manner of dying is man-made. Separateness causes fear and aggression, which again cause violence. Do away with man-made separations and all this horror of people killing each other will surely end. But in reality there is no killing and no dying. The real does not die, the unreal never lived. Set your mind right and all will be right. When you know that the world is one, that humanity is one, you will act accordingly. But first of all you must attend to the way you feel, think and live. Unless there is order in yourself, there can be no order in the world.

In reality nothing happens. Onto the screen of the mind destiny forever projects its pictures, memories of former projections and thus illusion constantly renews itself. The pictures come and go — light intercepted by ignorance. See the light and disregard the picture.

Q: What a callous way of looking at things! People are killing and getting killed and here you talk of pictures.

M: By all means go and get killed yourself — if that is what you think you should do. Or even go and kill, if you take it to be your duty. But that is not the way to end the evil. Evil is the stench of a mind that is diseased. Heal your mind and it will cease to project distorted, ugly pictures.

Q: What you say I understand, but emotionally I cannot accept it. This merely idealistic view of life repels me deeply. I just cannot think myself to be permanently in a state of dream.

M: How can you be permanently in a state caused by an impermanent body? The misunderstanding is based on your idea that you are the body. Examine the idea, see its inherent contradictions, realize that your present existence is like a shower of sparks, each spark lasting a second and the shower itself — a minute or two. Surely a thing of which the beginning is the end, can have no middle. Respect your terms. Reality cannot be momentary. It is timeless, but timelessness is not duration.

Q: I admit that the world in which I live is not the real world. But there is a real world, of which I see a distorted picture. The distortion may be due to some blemish in my body or mind. But when you say there is no real world, only a dream world in my mind, I just cannot take it. I wish I could believe that all the horrors of existence are due to my having a body. Suicide would be the way out.

M: As long as you pay attention to ideas, your own or of others, you will be in trouble. But if you disregard all teachings, all books, anything put into words and dive deeply within yourself and find yourself, this alone will solve all your problems and leave you in full mastery of every situation, because you will not be dominated by your ideas about the situation. Take an example. You are in the company of an attractive woman. You get ideas about her and this creates a sexual situation. A problem is created and you start looking for books on continence, or enjoyment. Were you a baby, both of you could be naked and together without any problem arising. Just stop thinking you are bodies and the problems of love and sex will lose their meaning. With all sense of limitation gone, fear, pain and the search for pleasure — all cease. Only awareness remains.   ●●●

51

Be Indifferent to Pain and Pleasure

Questioner: I am a Frenchman by birth and domicil and since about ten years I have been practicing Yoga.

Maharaj: After ten years of work are you anywhere nearer your goal?

Q: A little nearer, maybe. It is hard work, you know.

M: The Self is near and the way to it is easy. All you need doing is doing nothing.

Q: Yet I found my *sadhana* very difficult.

M: Your *sadhana* is to *be*. The doing happens. Just be watchful. Where is the difficulty in remembering that you are? You *are* all the time.

Q: The sense of being is there all the time — no doubt. But the field of attention is often overrun by all sorts of mental events — emotions, images, ideas. The pure sense of being is usually crowded out.

M: What is your procedure for clearing the mind of the unnecessary? What are your means, your tools for the purification of the mind?

Q: Basically, man is afraid. He is afraid of himself most. I feel I am like a man who is carrying a bomb that is going to explode. He cannot defuse it, he cannot throw it away. He is terribly frightened and is searching frantically for a solution, which he cannot find. To me liberation is getting rid of this bomb. I do not know much about the bomb. I only know that it comes from early childhood. I feel like the frightened child protesting passionately against not being loved. The child is craving for love and because he does not get it, he is afraid and angry. Sometimes I feel like killing somebody, or myself. This desire is so strong that I am constantly afraid. And I do not know how to get free from fear.

You see there is a difference between a Hindu mind and a European mind. The Hindu mind is comparatively simple. The European is a much more complex being. The Hindu is basically *sattvic*. He does not understand the European's restlessness, his tireless pursuit of what he thinks needs be done; his greater general knowledge.

M: His reasoning capacity is so great, that he will reason himself out of all reason! His self-assertiveness is due to his reliance on logic.

Q: But thinking, reasoning is the mind's normal state. The mind just cannot stop working.

M: It may be the habitual state, but it need not be the normal state. A normal state cannot be painful, while wrong habit often leads to chronic pain.

Q: If it is not the natural, or normal state of the mind, then how to stop it? There must be a way to quieten the mind. How often I tell myself: enough, please stop, enough of this endless chatter of sentences repeated round and round! But my mind would not stop. I feel that one can stop it for a while, but not for long. Even the so-called 'spiritual' people use tricks to keep their mind quiet. They repeat formulas, they sing, pray, breathe forcibly or gently, shake, rotate, concentrate, meditate, chase trances, cultivate virtues, — working all the time, in order to cease working, cease chasing, cease moving. Were it not so tragic, it would be ridiculous.

M: The mind exists in two states: as water and as honey. The water vibrates at the least disturbance, while the honey, however disturbed, returns quickly to immobility.

Q: By its very nature the mind is restless. It can perhaps be made quiet, but it is not quiet by itself.

M: You may have chronic fever and shiver all the time. It is desires and fears that make the mind restless. Free from all negative emotions it is quiet.

Q: You cannot protect the child from negative emotions. As soon as it is born it learns pain and fear. Hunger is a cruel master and teaches dependence and hate. The child loves the mother because she feeds it and hates her because she' is late with food. Our unconscious mind is full of conflicts, which overflow into the conscious. We live on a volcano; we are always in danger. I agree that the company of people whose mind is peaceful has a very soothing effect, but as soon as I am away from them, the old trouble starts. This is why I come periodically to India to seek the company of my Guru.

M: You think you are coming and going, passing through various states and moods. I see things as they are, momentary events, presenting themselves to me in rapid succession, deriving their being from me, yet definitely neither me nor mine. Among phenomena I am not one, nor subject to any. I am independent so simply and totally, that your mind, accustomed to opposition and denial, cannot grasp it. I mean literally what I say: ı do not need oppose, or deny, because it is clear to me that I cannot be the opposite or denial of anything. I am just beyond, in a different dimension altogether. Do not look for me in identification with, or opposition to something: I am where desire,and fear are not. Now, what is your experience? Do you also feel that you stand totally aloof from all transient things?

Q: Yes, I do — occasionally. But at once a sense of danger sets in, I feel isolated, outside all relationship with others. You see, here lies the difference in our mentalities. With the Hindu, the emotion follows the thought. Give a Hindu an idea and his emotions are roused. With the Westerner it is the opposite: give him an emotion and he will produce an idea. Your ideas are very attractive — intellectually, but emotionally I do not respond.

M: Set your intellect aside. Don't use it in these matters.

Q: Of what use is an advice which I cannot carry out? These are all ideas and you want me to respond feelingly to ideas, ıor without feelings there can be no action.

M: Why do you talk of action? Are you acting ever? Some unknown power acts and you imagine that you are acting. You are merely watching what happens, without being able to influence it in any way.

Q: Why is there such a tremendous resistance in me against accepting that I just can do nothing?

M: But what can you do? You are like a patient under anaesthetics on whom a surgeon performs an operation. When you wake up you find the operation over; can you say you have done something?

Q: But it is me who has chosen to submit to an operation.

M: Certainly not. It is your illness on one side and the pressure of your physician and family on the other that have made you decide. You have no choice, only the illusion of it.

Q: Yet I feel I am not as helpless as you make me appear. I feel I can do everything I can think of, only I do not know how. It is not the power I lack, but the knowledge.

M: Not knowing the means is admittedly as bad as not having the power! But let us drop the subject for the moment; after all it is not important why we feel helpless, as long as we see clearly that for the time being we are helpless.

I am now 74 years old. And yet I feel that I am an infant. I feel clearly that in spite of all the changes I am a child. My Guru told me: that child, which is you even now, is your real self *(swarupa)*. Go back to that state of pure being, where the 'I am' is still in its purity before it got contaminated with 'this I am' or 'that I am'. Your burden is of false self-identifications — abandon them all. My Guru told me — 'Trust me. I tell you; you are divine. Take it as the absolute truth. Your joy is divine, your suffering is divine too. All comes from God. Remember it always. You are God, your will alone is done'. I did believe him and soon realized how wonderfully true and accurate were his words. I did not condition my mind by thinking: 'I am God, I am wonderful, I am beyond'. I simply followed his instruction which was to focus the mind on pure being 'I am', and stay in it. I used to sit for hours together, with, nothing but the 'I am' in my mind and soon peace and joy and a deep all-embracing love became my normal state. In it all disappeared — myself, my Guru, the life I lived, the world around me. Only peace remained and unfathomable silence.

Q: It all looks very simple and easy, but it is just not so. Sometimes the wonderful state of joyful peace dawns on me and I look and wonder: how easily it comes and how intimate it seems, how totally my own. Where was the need to strive so hard for a state so near at hand? This time, surely, it has come to stay. Yet how soon it all dissolves and leaves me wondering — was it a taste of reality or another aberration. If it was reality, why did it go? Maybe some unique experience is needed to fix me for good in the new state and until the crucial experience comes, this game of hide and seek must continue.

M: Your expectation of something unique and dramatic, of some wonderful explosion, is merely hindering and delaying your self-realization. You are not to expect an explosion, for the explosion has already happened — at the moment when you were born, when you realized yourself as being-knowing-feeling. There is only one mistake you are making: you take the inner for the outer and the outer for the inner. What is in you, you take to be outside you and what is outside, you take to be in you. The mind and feelings are external, but you take them to be intimate. You believe the world to be objective, while it is entirely a projection of your psyche. That is the basic confusion and no new explosion will set it right. You have to think yourself out of it. There is no other way.

Q: How am I to think myself out when my thoughts come and go as they like. Their endless chatter distracts and exhausts me.

M: Watch your thoughts as you watch the street traffic. People come and go; you register without response. It may not be easy in the beginning, but with some practice you will find that your mind can function on many levels at the same time and you can be aware of them all. It is only when you have a vested interest in any particular level, that your attention gets caught in it and you black out on other levels. Even then the work on the blacked out levels goes on, outside the field of consciousness. Do not struggle with your memories and thoughts; try only to include in your field of attention the other, more important questions, like 'Who am I?' 'How did I happen to be born?' 'Whence this universe around me?'. 'What is real and what is momentary?' No memory will persist, if you lose interest in it; it is the emotional link that perpetuates the bondage. You are always seeking pleasure, avoiding pain, always after happiness and peace. Don't you see that it is your very search for happiness that makes you feel miserable? Try the other way: indifferent to pain and pleasure, neither asking, nor refusing, give all your attention to the level on which 'I am' is timelessly present. Soon you will realize that peace and happiness are in your very nature and it is only seeking them through some particular channels, that disturbs. Avoid the disturbance, that is all. To seek there is no need; you would not seek what you already have. You yourself are God, the Supreme Reality. To begin with, trust me, trust the Teacher. It enables you to make the first step — and then your trust is justified by your own experience. In every walk of life initial trust is essential; without it little can be done. Every undertaking is an act of faith. Even your daily bread you eat on trust! By remembering what I told you you will achieve everything. I am telling you again: You are the all-pervading, all transcending reality. Behave accordingly: think, feel and act in harmony with the whole and the actual experience of what I say will dawn upon you in no time. No effort is needed. Have faith and act on it.

Please see that I want nothing from you. It is in your own interest that–I speak, because above all you· love yourself, you want yourself secure and happy. Don't be ashamed of it, don't deny it. It is natural and good to love oneself. Only you should know what exactly do you love. It is not the body that you love, it is Life — perceiving, feeling, thinking, doing, loving, striving, creating. It is that Life you love, which is you, which is all. Realize it in its totality, beyond all divisions and limitations, and all your desires will merge in it, for the greater contains the smaller. Therefore find yourself, for in finding that you find all.

Everybody is glad to be. But few know the fulness of it. You come to know by dwelling in your mind on 'I am', 'I know', 'I love' — with the will of reaching the deepest meaning of these words.

Q: Can I think 'I am God'?

M: Don't identify yourself with an idea. If you mean by God the Unknown, then you merely say: 'I do not know what I am'. If you know God as you know your self, you need not say it. Best is the simple feeling 'I am'. Dwell on it patiently. Here patience is wisdom; don't think of failure. There can be no failure in this undertaking.

Q: My thoughts will not let me.

M: Pay no attention. Don't fight them. Just do nothing about them, let them be, whatever they are. Your very fighting them gives them life. Just disregard. Look through. Remember to remember: 'whatever happens — happens because I am . All reminds you that you *are*. Take full advantage of the fact that to experience you must *be*. You need not stop thinking. Just cease being interested. It is disinterestedness that liberates. Don't hold on, that is all. The world is made of rings. The hooks are all yours. Make straight your hooks and nothing can hold you: Give up your addictions. There is nothing else to give up. Stop your routine of acquisitiveness, your habit of looking for results and the freedom of the universe is yours. Be effortless.

Q: Life is effort. There are so many things to do.

M: What needs doing, do it. Don't resist. Your balance must be dynamic, based on doing just the right thing, from moment to moment. Don't be a child unwilling to grow up. Stereotyped gestures and postures will not help you. Rely entirely on your clarity of thought, purity of motive and integrity of action. You cannot possibly go wrong. Go beyond and leave all behind.

Q: But can anything be left for good?

M: You want something like a round-the-clock ecstasy. Ecstasies come and go, necessarily, for the human brain cannot stand the tension for a long time. A prolonged ecstasy will burn out your brain, unless it is extremely pure and subtle. In nature nothing is at stand-still, everything pulsates, appears and disappears. Heart, breath, digestion, sleep and waking — birth and death everything comes and goes in waves. Rhythm, periodicity, harmonious alternation of extremes is the rule. No use rebelling against the very pattern of life. If you seek the Immutable, go beyond experience. When I say: remember 'I am' all the time, I mean: come back to it repeatedly'. No particular thought can be mind's natural state, only silence. Not the idea of silence, but silence itself. When the mind is in its natural state, it reverts to silence spontaneously after every experience or, rather, every experience happens against the background of silence.

Now, what you have learnt here becomes the seed. You may forget it — apparently. But it will live and in due season sprout and grow and bring forth flowers and fruits. All will happen by itself. You need not do anything, only don't prevent it.   ●●●

52

Being Happy, Making Happy is the Rhythm of Life

Questioner: I came from Europe a few months ago on one of my periodical visits to my Guru near Calcutta. Now I am on my way back home. I was invited by a friend to meet you and I am glad I came.

Maharaj: What did you learn from your Guru and what practice did you follow?

Q: He is a venerable old man of about eighty. Philosophically he is a Vedantin and the practice he teaches has much to do with rousing the unconscious energies of the mind and bringing the hidden obstacles and blockages into the conscious. My personal *sadhana* was related to my peculiar problem of early infancy and childhood. My mother could not give me the feeling of being secure and loved, so important to the child's normal development. She was a woman not fit to be a mother; ridden with anxieties and neuroses, unsure of herself, she felt me to be a responsibility and a burden beyond her capacity to bear. She never watned me to be born. She did not want me to grow and to develop, she wanted me back in her womb, unborn, non-existent. Any movement of life in me she resisted, any attempt to go beyond the narrow circle of her habitual existence she fought fiercely. As a child I was both sensitive and affectionate. I craved for love above everything else and love, the simple, in-stinctive love of a mother for her child was denied me. The child's search for its mother became the leading motive of my life and I never grew out of it. A happy child, a happy childhood became an obsession with me. Pregnancy, birth, infancy in-terested me passionately. I became an obstetrician of some re-

nown and contributed to the development of the method of painless childbirth. A happy child of a happy mother — that was my
ideal all my life. But my mother was always there — unhappy
herself, unwilling and incapable to see me happy. It manifested
itself in strange ways. Whenever I was unwell, she felt better;
when I was in good shape, she was down again, cursing herself
and me too. As if she never forgave me my crime of having been
born, she made me feel guilty of being alive. 'You live because
you hate me. If you love me — die', was her constant, though
silent message. And so I spent my life, being offered death instead of love. Imprisoned, as I was, in my mother, the perennial
infant, I could not develop a meaningful relation with a woman;
the image of the mother would stand between, unforgiving, un-
forgiven. I sought solace in my work and found much; but I could
not move from the pit of infancy. Finally, I turned to spiritual
search and I am on this line steadily for many years. But, in a
way it is the same old search for mother's love, call it God or
Atma or Supreme Reality. Basically I want to love and be loved;
unfortunately the so-called religious people are against life and
all for the mind. When faced with life's needs and urges, they
begin by classifying, abstracting and conceptualizing and then
make the classification more important than life itself. They ask
to concentrate on and impersonate a concept. Instead of the
spontaneous integration through love they recommend a deliberate and laborious concentration on a formula. Whether it is
God or Atma, the me or the other, it comes to the same! Something to think about, not somebody to love. It is not theories and
systems that I need; there are many equally attractive or plausible. I need a stirring of the heart, a renewal of life, and not a new
way of thinking. There are no new ways of thinking, but feelings
can be ever fresh. When I love somebody, I meditate on him
spontaneously and powerfully, with warmth and vigour, which
my mind cannot command.

Words are good for shaping feelings; words without feeling
are like clothes with no body inside — cold and limp. This
mother of mine — she drained me of all feelings — my sources
have run dry. Can I find here the richness and abundance of
emotions, which I needed in such ample measure as a child?

M: Where is your childhood now? And what is your future?

Q: I was born, I have grown, I shall die.

M: You mean your body, of course. And your mind. I am not talking of your physiology and psychology. They are a part of nature and are governed by nature's laws. I am talking of your search for love. Had it a beginning? Will it have an end?

Q: I really cannot say. It is there — from the earliest to the last moment of my life. This yearning for love — how constant and how hopeless!

M: In your search for love what exactly are you searching for?

Q: Simply this: to love and to be loved.

M: You mean a woman?

Q: Not necessarily. A friend, a teacher, a guide — as long as the feeling is bright and clear. Of course, a woman is the usual answer. But it need not be the only one.

M: Of the two what would you prefer, to love or to be loved?

Q: I would rather have both! But I can see that to love is greater, nobler, deeper. To be loved is sweet, but it does not make one grow.

M: Can you love on your own, or must you be made to love?

Q: One must meet somebody lovable, of course. My mother was not only not loving, she was also not lovable.

M: What makes a person lovable? Is it not the being loved? First you love and then you look for reasons.

Q: It can be the other way round. You love what makes you happy.

M: But what makes you happy?

Q: There is no rule about it. The entire subject is highly individual and unpredictable.

M: Right. Whichever way you put it, unless you love there is no happiness. But, does love make you always happy? Is not the association of love with happiness a rather early, infantile stage? When the beloved suffers, don't you suffer too? And do you cease to love, because you suffer? Must love and happiness come and go together? Is love merely the expectation of pleasure?

Q: Of course not. There can be much suffering in love.

M: Then what is love? Is it not a state of being rather than a state of mind? Must you know that you love in order to love? Did you not love your mother unknowingly? Your craving for her love, for an opportunity to love her, is it not the movement of love? Is not love as much a part of you, as consciousness of being? You sought the love of your mother, because you loved her.

Q: But she would not let me!

M: She could not stop you.

Q: Then, why was I unhappy all my life?

M: Because you did not go down to the very roots of your being. It is your complete ignorance of yourself, that covered up your love and happiness and made you seek for what you had never lost. Love is will, the will to share your happiness with all. Being happy — making happy — this is the rhythm of love. ●●●

53

Desires Fulfilled, Breed More Desires

Questioner: I must confess I came today in a rebellious mood. I got a raw deal at the airlines office. When faced with such situations everything seems doubtful, everything seems useless.

Maharaj: This is a very useful mood. Doubting all, refusing all, unwilling to learn through another. It is the fruit of your long *sadhana*. After all one does not study for ever.

Q: Enough of it. It took me nowhere.

M: Don't say 'nowhere'. It took you where you are — now.

Q: It is again the child and its tantrums. I have not moved an inch from where I was.

M: You began as a child and you will end as a child. Whatever you have acquired in the meantime you must lose and start at the beginning.

Q: But the child kicks. When it is unhappy or denied anything it kicks.

M: Let it kick. Just look at the kicking. And if you are too afraid of the society to kick convincingly look at that too. I know it is a painful business. But there is no remedy — except one — the search for remedies must cease.

If you are angry or in pain, separate yourself from anger and pain and watch them. Externalization is the first step to liberation. Step away and look. The physical events will go on happening, but by themselves they have no importance. It is the mind alone that matters. Whatever happens, you cannot kick and scream in an airline office or in a Bank. Society does not allow it. If you do not like their ways, or are not prepared to endure them, don't fly or carry money. Walk, and if you cannot walk, don't travel. If you deal with society you must accept its ways, for its ways are your ways. Your needs and demands have created them. Your desires are so complex and contradictory — no wonder the society you create is also complex and contradictory.

Q: I do see and admit that the outer chaos is merely a reflection of my own inner disharmony. But what is the remedy?

M: Don't seek remedies.

Q: Sometimes one is in a 'state of grace' and life is happy and harmonious. But such a state does not last! The mood changes and all goes wrong.

M: If you could only keep quiet, clear of memories and expectations, you would be able to discern the beautiful pattern of events. It is your restlessness that causes chaos.

Q: For full three hours that I spent in the airline office I was practising patience and forbearance. It did not speed up matters.

M: At least it did not slow them down, as your kicking would have surely done! You want immediate results! We do not dispense magic here. Everybody does the same mistake: refusing the means, but wanting the ends. You want peace and harmony in the world, but refuse to have them in yourself. Follow my advice implicitly and you will not be disappointed. I cannot solve your problem by mere words. You have to act on what I told you and persevere. It is not the right advice that liberates, but the action based on it. Just like a doctor, after giving the patient an injection, tells him: 'Now, keep quiet. Do nothing more, just keep quiet,' I am telling you: you have got your 'injection', now keep quiet, just keep quiet. You have nothing else to do. My Guru did the same. He would tell me something and then said: 'Now keep quiet. Don't go on ruminating all the time. Stop. Be silent'.

Q: I can keep quiet for an hour in the morning. But the day is long and many things happen that throw me out of balance. It is easy to say 'be silent', but to be silent when all is screaming in me and round me — please tell me how it is done.

M: All that needs doing can be done in peace and silence. There is no need to get upset.

Q: It is all theory which does not fit the facts. I am returning to Europe with nothing to do there. My life is completely empty.

M: If you just try to keep quiet, all will come — the work, the strength for work, the right motive. Must you know everything beforehand? Don't be anxious about your future — be quiet now and all will fall in place. The unexpected is bound to happen, while the anticipated may never come. Don't tell me you cannot control your nature. You need not control it. Throw it overboard. Have no nature to fight, or to submit to. No experience will hurt you, provided you don't make it into a habit. Of the entire universe you are the subtle cause. All is because you are. Grasp this point firmly and deeply and dwell on it repeatedly. To realize this as absolutely true, is liberation.

Q: If I am the seed of my universe, then a rotten seed I am! By the fruit the seed is known.

M: What is wrong with your world that you swear at it?

Q: It is full of pain.

M: Nature is neither pleasant nor painful. It is all intelligence and beauty. Pain and pleasure are in the mind. Change your scale of values and all will change. Pleasure and pain are mere disturbances of the senses; treat them equally and there will be only bliss. And the world is, what you make it; by all means make it happy. Only contentment can make you happy — desires fulfilled breed more desires. Keeping away from all desires and contentment in what comes by itself is a very fruitful state — a precondition to the state of fulness. Don't distrust its apparent sterility and emptiness. Believe me, it is the satisfaction of desires that breeds misery. Freedom from desires is bliss.

Q: There are things we need.

M: What you need will come to you, if you do not ask for what you do not need. Yet only few people reach this state of complete dispassion and detachment. It is a very high state, the very threshold of liberation.

Q: I have been barren for the last two years, desolate and empty and often was I praying for death to come.

M: Well, with your coming here events have started rolling. Let things happen as they happen — they will sort themselves out nicely in the end. You need not strain towards the future — the future will come to you on its own. For some time longer you will remain sleep-walking, as you do now, bereft of meaning and assurance; but this period will end and you will find your work both fruitful and easy. There are always moments when one feels empty and estranged. Such moments are most desirable for it means the soul had cast its moorings and is sailing for distant places. This is detachment — when the old is over and the new has not yet come. If you are afraid, the state may be distressing; but there is really nothing to be afraid of. Remember the instruction: whatever you come across — go beyond.

Q: The Buddhas rule: to remember what needs to be remembered. But I find it so difficult to remember the right thing at the right moment. With me forgetting seems to be the rule!

M: It is not easy to remember when every situation brings up a storm of desires and fears. Craving born of memory is also the destroyer of memory.

Q: How am I to fight desire? There is nothing stronger.

M: The waters of life are thundering over the rocks of objects — desirable or hateful. Remove the rocks by insight and detachment and the same waters will flow deep and silent and swift, in greater volume and with greater power. Don't be theoretical about it, give time to thought and consideration; if you desire to be free, neglect not the nearest step to freedom. It is like climbing a mountain: not a step can be missed. One step less — and the summit is not reached.   ●●●

54

Body and Mind are Symptoms of Ignorance

Questioner: We were discussing one day the person — the witness — the absolute *(vyakti-vyakta-avyakta).* As far as I remember, you said that the absolute alone is real and the witness is absolute only at a given point of space and time. The person is the organism, gross and subtle, illumined by the presence of the witness. I do not seem to grasp the matter clearly; could we discuss it again? You also use the terms *mahadakash, chidakash* and *paramakash.* How are they related to person, witness, and the absolute?

Maharaj: *Mahadakash* is nature, the ocean of existences, the physical space with all that can be contacted through the senses. *Chidakash* is the expanse of awareness, the mental space of time, perception and cognition. *Paramakash* is the timeless and spaceless reality, mindless, undifferenciated, the infinite potentiality, the source and origin, the substance and the essence, both matter and consciousness, — yet beyond both. It cannot be perceived, but can be experienced as ever witnessing the witness, perceiving the perceiver, the origin and the end of all manifestation, the root of time and space, the prime cause in every chain of causation.

Q: What is the difference between *vyakta* and *avyakta*?

M: There is no difference. It is like light and daylight. The universe is full of light which you do not see; but the same light you see as daylight. And what the daylight reveals is the *vyakti*. The person is always the object, the witness is the subject and their relation of mutual dependence is the reflection of their absolute identity. You imagine that they are distinct and separate states. They are not. They are the same consciousness at rest and in movement, each state conscious of the other. In *chit* man knows God and God knows man. In *chit* the man shapes the world and the world shapes man. *Chit* is the link, the bridge between extremes, the balancing and uniting factor in every experience. The totality of the perceived is what you call matter. The totality of all perceivers is what you call the universal mind. The identity of the two, manifesting itself as perceptibility and perceiving, harmony and intelligence, loveliness and loving, reasserts itself eternally.

Q: The three gunas, *sattva — rajas — tamas,* are they only in matter, or also in the mind?

M: In both, of course, because the two are not separate. It is only the absolute that is beyond *gunas*. In fact, these are but points of view, ways of looking. They exist only in the mind. Beyond the mind all distinctions cease.

Q: Is the universe a product of the senses?

M: Just as you recreate your world on waking up, so is the universe unrolled. The mind with its five organs of perception, five organs of action, and five vehicles of consciousness appears as memory, thought, reason and selfhood.

Q: The sciences have made much progress. We know the

body and the mind much better than our ancestors. Your traditional way, describing and analyzing mind and matter, is no longer valid.

M: But where are your scientists with their sciences? Are they not again images in your own mind?

Q: Here lies the basic difference! To me they are not my own projections. They were before I was born and shall be there when I am dead.

M: Of course. Once you accept time and space as real, you will consider yourself minute and short-lived. But are they real? Do they depend on you, or you on them? As body, you are in space. As mind, you are in time. But are you mere body with a mind in it? Have you ever investigated?

Q: I had neither the motive nor the method.

M: I am suggesting both. But the actual work of insight and detachment (viveka–vairagya) is yours.

Q: The only motive I can perceive is my own causeless and timeless happiness. And what is the method?

M: Happiness is incidental. The true and effective motive is love. You see people suffer and you seek the best way of helping them. The answer is obvious — first put yourself beyond the need of help. Be sure your attitude is of pure goodwill, free of expectation of any kind.

Those who seek mere happiness may end up in sublime indifference, while love will never rest.

As to method, there is only one — you must come to know yourself — both what you appear to be and what you are. Clarity and charity go together — each needs and strengthens the other.

Q: Compassion implies the existence of an objective world, full of avoidable sorrow.

M: The world is not objective and the sorrow of it is not avoidable. Compassion is but another word for the refusal to suffer for imaginary reasons.

Q: If the reasons are imaginary, why should the suffering be inevitable?

M: It is always the false that makes you suffer, the false desires

and fears, the false values and ideas, the false relationships between people. Abandon the false and you are free of pain; truth
makes happy — truth liberates.

Q: The truth is that I am a mind imprisoned in a body and this is
a very unhappy truth.

M: You are neither the body nor in the body — there is no such
thing as body. You have grievously misunderstood yourself; to
understand rightly — investigate.

Q: But I was born as a body, in a body and shall die with the
body, as a body.

M: This is your misconception. Enquire, investigate, doubt
yourself and others. To find truth, you must not cling to your
convictions; if you are sure of the immediate, you will never
reach the ultimate. Your idea that you were born and that you
will die is absurd: both logic and experience contradict it.

Q: All right, I shall not insist that I am the body. You have a point
here. But here and now, as I talk to you, I am in my body — obviously. The body may not be me, but it is mine.

M: The entire universe contributes incessantly to your existence. Hence the entire universe is your body. In that sense — I
agree.

Q: My body influences me deeply. In more than one way my
body is my destiny. My character, my moods, the nature of my
reactions, my desires and fears — inborn or acquired — they
are all based on the body. A little alcohol, some drug or other
and all changes. Until the drug wears off I become another man.

M: All this happens because you think yourself to be the body.
Realize your real self and even drugs will have no power over
you.

Q: You smoke?

M: My body kept a few habits which may as well continue till it
dies. There is no harm in them.

Q: You eat meat?

M: I was born among meat-eating people and my children are
eating meat. I eat very little — and make no fuss.

Q: Meat-eating implies killing.

M: Obviously. I make no claims of consistency. You think absolute consistency is possible; prove it by example. Don't preach
what you do not practise.

Coming back to the idea of having been born. You are stuck
with what your parents told you: all about conception, pregnancy and birth, infant, child, youngster, teenager, and so on.
Now, divest yourself of the idea that you are the body with the
help of the contrary idea that you are not the body. It is also an
idea, no doubt; treat it like something to be abandoned when its
work is done. The idea that I am not the body gives reality to the
body, when in fact, there is no such thing as body; it is but a
state of mind. You can have as many bodies and as diverse as
you like; just remember steadily what you want and reject the
incompatibles.

Q: I am like a box within box, within box, the outer box acting as
the body and the one next to it — as the indwelling soul. Abstract the outer box and the next becomes the body and the one
next to it the soul. It is an infinite series, an endless opening of
boxes, is the last one the ultimate soul?

M: If you have a body, you must have a soul; here your simile of
a nest of boxes applies. But here and now, through all your
bodies and souls shines awareness, the pure light of *chit*. Hold
on to it unswervingly. Without awareness, the body would not
last a second. There is in the body a current of energy, affection
and intelligence, which guides, maintains and energizes the
body. Discover that current and stay with it.

Of course, all these are manners of speaking. Words are as
much a barrier, as a bridge. Find the spark of life that weaves
the tissues of your body and be with it. It is the only reality the
body has.

Q: What happens to that spark of life after death?

M: It is beyond time. Birth and death are but points in time. Life
weaves eternally its many webs. The weaving is in time, but life
itself is timeless. Whatever name and shape you give to its expressions, it is like the ocean — never changing, ever changing.

Q: All you say sounds beautifully convincing, yet my feeling of
being just a person in a world strange and alien, often inimical
and dangerous, does not cease. Being a person, limited in

space and time, how can I possibly realize myself as the opposite; a de-personalized, universalized awareness of nothing in particular?

M: You assert yourself to be what you are not and deny yourself to be what you are. You omit the element of pure cognition, of awareness free from all personal distortions. Unless you admit the reality of *chit*, you will never know yourself.

Q: What am I to do? I do not see myself as you see me. Maybe you are right and I am wrong, but how can I cease to be what I feel I am?

M: A prince who believes himself to be a beggar can be convinced conclusively in one way only: he must behave as a prince and see what happens. Behave as if what I say is true and judge by what actually happens. All I ask is the little faith needed for making the first step. With experience will come confidence and you will not need me any more. I know what you are and I am telling you. Trust me for a while.

Q: To be here and now, I need my body and its senses. To understand, I need a mind.

M: The body and the mind are only symptoms of ignorance, of misapprehension. Behave as if you were pure awareness, bodiless and mindless, spaceless and timeless, beyond 'where' and 'when' and 'how'. Dwell on it, think of it, learn to accept its reality. Don't oppose it and deny it all the time. Keep an open mind at least. Yoga is bending the outer to the inner. Make your mind and body express the real which is all and beyond all. By doing you succeed, not by arguing.

Q: Kindly allow me to come back to my first question. How does the error of being a person originate?

M: The absolute precedes time. Awareness comes first. A bundle of memories and mental habits attracts attention, awareness gets focalized and a person suddenly appears. Remove the light of awareness, go to sleep or swoon away — and the person disappears. The person *(vyakti)* flickers, awareness *(vyakta)* contains all space and time, the absolute *(avyakta)* — Is.   ●●●

55

Give up All and You Gain All

Qustioner: What is your state at the present moment?

Maharaj: A state of non-experiencing. In it all experience is included.

Q: Can you enter into the mind and heart of another man and share his experience?

M: No. Such things require special training. I am like a dealer in wheat. I know little about breads and cakes. Even the taste of a wheat-gruel I may not know. But about the wheat grain I know all and well. I know the source of all experience. But the innumerable particular forms experience can take I do not know. Nor do I need to know. From moment to moment, the little I need to know to live my life, I somehow happen to know.

Q: Your particular existence and my particular existence, do they both exist in the mind of *Brahma*?

M: The universal is not aware of the particular. The existence as a person is a personal matter. A person exists in time and space, has name and shape, beginning and end; the universal includes all persons and the absolute is at the root of and beyond all.

Q: I am not concerned with the totality. My personal consciousness and your personal consciousness — what is the link between the two?

M: Between two dreamers what can be the link?

Q: They may dream of each other.

M: That is what people are doing. Everyone imagines 'others' and seeks a link with them. The seeker is the link, there is none other.

Q: Surely there must be something in common between the many points of consciousness we are.

M: Where are the many points? In your mind. You insist that your world is independent of your mind. How can it be? Your desire to know other people's minds is due to your not knowing your own mind. First know your own mind and you will find that the question of other minds does not arise at all, for there are no other people. You are the common factor, the only link between the minds. Being is consciousness; 'I am' applies to all.

Q: The Supreme Reality *(Parabrahman)* may be present in all of us. But of what use is it to us?

M: You are like a man who says: 'I need a place where to keep my things, but of what use is space to me?' or 'I need milk, tea, coffee or soda, but for water I have no use'. Don't you see that the Supreme Reality is what makes everything possible? But if you ask of what use is it to you, I must answer: 'None'. In matters of daily life the knower of the real has no advantage: he may be at a disadvantage rather: being free from greed and fear, he does not protect himself. The very idea of profit is foreign to him; he abhors accretions; his life is constant divesting oneself, sharing, giving.

Q: If there is no advantage in gaining the Supreme, then why take the trouble?

M: There is trouble only when you cling to something. When you hold on to nothing, no trouble arises. The relinquishing of the lesser is the gaining of the greater. Give up all and you gain all. Then life becomes what it was meant to be: pure radiation from an inexhaustible source. In that light the world appears dimly like a dream.

Q: If my world is merely a dream and you are a part of it, what can you do for me? If the dream is not real, having no being, how can reality affect it?

M: While it lasts, the dream has temporary being. It is your desire to hold on to it, that creates the problem. Let go. Stop imagining that the dream is yours.

Q: You seem to take for granted that there can be a dream without a dreamer and that I identify myself with the dream of my

own sweet will. But I am the dreamer and the dream too. Who is
to stop dreaming?

M: Let the dream unroll itself to its very end. You cannot help it.
But you can look at the dream as a dream, refuse it the stamp of
reality.

Q: Here am I, sitting before you. I am dreaming and you are
watching me talking in my dream. What is the link between us?

M: My intention to wake you up is the link. My heart wants you
awake. I see you suffer in your dream and I know that you must
wake up to end your woes. When you see your dream as dream,
you wake up. But in your dream itself I am not interested.
Enough for me to know that you must wake up. You need not
bring your dream to a definite conclusion, or make it noble, or
happy, or beautiful; all you need is to realize that you are dreaming. Stop imagining, stop believing. See the contradictions, the
incongruities, the falsehood and the sorrow of the human state,
the need to go beyond. Within the immensity of space floats a
tiny atom of consciousness and in it the entire universe is contained.

Q: There are affections in the dream which seem real and everlasting. Do they disappear on waking up?

M: In dream you love some and not others. On waking up you
find you are love itself, embracing all. Personal love, however intense and genuine, invariably binds; love in freedom is love of
all.

Q: People come and go. One loves whom one meets, one cannot love all.

M: When you are love itself, you are beyond time and numbers.
In loving one you love all, in loving all, you love each. One and
all are not exclusive.

Q: You say you are in a timeless state. Does it mean that past
and future are open to you? Did you meet Vashishta Muni,
Rama's Guru?

M: The question is in time and about time. Again you are asking
me about the contents of a dream. Timelessness is beyond the
illusion of time, it is not an extension in time. He who called himself Vashishta knew Vashishta. I am beyond all names and

shapes. Vashishta is a dream in your dream. How can I know him? You are too much concerned with past and future. It is all due to your longing to continue, to protect yourself against extinction. And as you want to continue, you want others to keep you company, hence your concern with their survival. But what you call survival is but the survival of a dream. Death is preferable to it. There is a chance of waking up.

Q: You are aware of eternity, therefore you are not concerned with survival.

M: It is the other way round. Freedom from all desire is eternity. All attachment implies fear, for all things are transient. And fear makes one a slave. This freedom from attachment does not come with practice; it is natural, when one knows one's true being. Love does not cling; clinging is not love.

Q: So there is no way to gain detachment?

M: There is nothing to gain. Abandon all imaginings and know yourself as you are. Self-knowledge is detachment. All craving is due to a sense of insufficiency. When you know that you lack nothing, that all there is, is you and yours, desire ceases.

Q: To know myself must I practise awareness?

M: There is nothing to practise. To know yourself, be yourself. To be yourself, stop imagining yourself to be this or that. Just be. Let your true nature emerge. Don't distrub your mind with seeking.

Q: It will take much time if I just wait for self-realization.

M: What have you to wait for when it is already here and now? You have only to look and see. Look at your self, at your own being. You know that you are and you like it. Abandon all imagining, that is all. Do not rely on time. Time is death. Who waits — dies. Life is now only. Do not talk to me about past and future — they exist only in your mind.

Q: You too will die.

M: I am dead already. Physical death will make no difference in my case. I am timeless being. I am free of desire or fear, because I do not remember the past, or imagine the future. Where there are no names and shapes, how can there be desire and fear? With desirelessness comes timelessness. I am safe, because what is not, cannot touch what is. You feel unsafe, because you imagine danger. Of course, your body as such is complex and vulnerable and needs protection. But not you. Once you realize your own unassailable being, you will be at peace.

Q: How can I find peace when the world suffers?

M: The world suffers for very valid reasons. If you want to help the world, you must be beyond the need of help. Then all your doing as well as not doing will help the world most effectively.

Q: How can non-action be of use where action is needed?

M: Where action is needed, action happens. Man is not the actor. His is to be aware of what is going on. His very presence is action. The window is the absence of the wall and it gives air and light because it is empty. Be empty of all mental content, of all imagination and effort, and the very absence of obstacles will cause reality to rush in. If you really want to help a person, keep away. If you are emotionally committed to helping, you will fail to help. You may be very busy and be very pleased with your charitable nature, but not much will be done. A man is really helped when he is no longer in need of help. All else is just futility.

Q: There is not enough time to sit and wait for help to happen. One must do something.

M: By all means — do. But what you can do is limited; the self alone is unlimited. Give limitlessly — of yourself. All else you can give in small measures only. You alone are immeasurable. To help is your very nature. Even when you eat and drink you help your body. For yourself you need nothing. You are pure giving, beginning-less, endless, inexhaustible. When you see sorrow and suffering, be with it. Do not rush into activity. Neither learning nor action can really help. Be with sorrow and lay bare its roots — helping to understand is real help.

Q: My death is nearing.

M: Your body is short of time, not you. Time and space are in the mind only. You are not bound. Just understand yourself — that itself is eternity.   ●●●

56

Consciousness Arising, World Arises

Questioner: When an ordinary man dies, what happens to him?

Maharaj: According to his belief it happens, As life before death is but imagination, so is life after. The dream continues.

Q: And what about the *gnani?*

M: The *gnani* does not die because he was never born.

Q: He appears so to others.

M: But not to himself. In himself he is free of things — physical and mental.

Q: Still you must know the state of the man who died. At least from your own past lives.

M: Until I met my Guru I knew so many things. Now I know nothing, for all knowledge is in dream only and not valid. I know myself and I find no life nor death in me, only pure being — not being this or that, but just *being.* But the moment the mind, drawing on its stock of memories, begins to imagine, it fills the space with objects and time with events. As I do not know even this birth, how can I know past births? It is the mind that, itself in movement, sees everything moving, and having created time, worries about the past and future. All the universe is cradled in consciousness *(maha tattva),* which arises where there is perfect order and harmony *(maha sattva).* As all waves are in the ocean, so are all things physical and mental in awareness. Hence awareness itself is all important, not the content of it. Deepen and broaden your awareness of yourself and all the blessings will flow. You need not seek anything, all will come to you most naturally and effortlessly. The five senses and the four functions of the mind — memory, thought, understanding and selfhood; the five elements — earth, water, fire, air and ether; the two aspects of creation — matter and spirit, all are contained in awareness.

Q: Yet, you must believe in having lived before.

M: The scriptures say so, but I know nothing about it. I know myself as I am; as I appeared or will appear is not within my experience. It is not that I do not remember. In fact there is nothing to remember. Reincarnation implies a reincarnating self. There is no such thing. The bundle of memories and hopes, called the 'I', imagines itself existing everlastingly and creates time to accommodate its false eternity: To be, I need no past or future. All experience is born of imagination; I do not imagine, so no birth or death happens to me. Only those who think themselves born can think themselves re-born. You are accusing me of having been born — I plead not guilty!

All exists in awareness and awareness neither dies nor is reborn. It is the changeless reality itself.

All the universe of experience is born with the body and dies with the body; it has its beginning and end in awareness, but awareness knows no beginning, nor end. If you think it out carefully and brood over it for a long time, you will come to see the light of awareness in all its clarity and the world will fade out of your vision. It is like looking at a burning incense stick; you see the stick and the smoke first; when you notice the fiery point, you realize that it has the power to consume mountains of sticks and fill the universe with smoke. Timelessly the self actualizes itself, without exhausting its infinite possibilities. In the incense stick simile the stick is the body and the smoke is the mind. As long as the mind is busy with its contortions, it does not perceive its own source. The Guru comes and turns your attention to the spark within. By its very nature the mind is outward turned; it always tends to seek for the source of things among the things themselves; to be told to look for the source within, is, in a way, the beginning of a new life. Awareness takes the place of consciousness; in consciousness there is the 'I', who is conscious, while awareness is undivided; awareness is aware of itself. The 'I am' is a thought, while awareness is not a thought; there is no 'I am aware' in awareness. Consciousness is an attribute while awareness is not; one can be aware of being conscious, but not conscious of awareness. God is the totality of consciousness, but awareness is beyond all — being as well as not-being.

Q: I had started with the question about the condition of a man after death. When his body is destroyed, what happens to his consciousness? Does he carry his senses of seeing, hearing etc. along with him or does he leave them behind? And, if he loses his senses, what becomes to his consciousness?

M: Senses are mere modes of perception. As the grosser modes disappear, finer states of consciousness emerge.

Q: Is there no transition to awareness after death?

M: There can be no transition from consciousness to awareness, for awareness is not a form of consciousness. Consciousness can only become more subtle and refined and that is what happens after death. As the various vehicles of man die off, the modes of consciousness induced by them also fade away.

Q: Until only unconsciousness remains?

M: Look at yourself talking of unconsciousness as something that comes and goes! Who is there to be conscious of unconsciousness? As long as the window is open, there is sunlight in the room. With the windows shut, the sun remains, but does it see the darkness in the room? Is there anything like darkness to the sun? There is no such thing as unconsciousness, for unconsciousness is not experienceable. We infer unconsciousness when there is a lapse in memory or communication. If I stop reacting, you will say that I am unconscious. In reality I may be most acutely conscious, only unable to communicate or remember.

Q: I am asking a simple question: there are about four billion people in the world and they are all bound to die. What will be their condition after death — not physically, but psychologically? Will their consciousness continue? And if it does, in what form? Do not tell me that I am not asking the right question, or that you do not know the answer, or that in your world my question is meaningless; the moment you start talking about your world and my world as different and incompatible, you build a wall between us. Either we live in one world or your experience is of no use to us.

M: Of course we live in one world. Only I see it as it is, while you don't. You see yourself in the world, while I see the world in myself. To you, you get born and die, while to me, the world appears and disappears. Our world is real, but your view of it is not. There is no wall between us, except the one built by you. There is nothing wrong with the senses, it is your imagination that misleads you. It covers up the world as it is, with what you imagine it to be — something existing independently of you and yet closely following your inherited, or acquired patterns. There is a deep contradiction in your attitude, which you do not see and which is the cause of sorrow. You cling to the idea that you were born into a world of pain and sorrow; I know that the world is a child of love, having its beginning, growth and fulfilment in love. But I am beyond love even.

Q: If you have created the world out of love, why is it so full of pain?

M: You are right — from the body's point of view. But you are not the body. You are the immensity and infinity of consciousness. Don't assume what is not true and you will see things as I see them. Pain and pleasure, good and bad, right and wrong: these are relative terms and must not be taken absolutely. They are limited and temporary.

Q: In the Buddhist tradition it is stated that a Nirvani, an enlightened Buddha, has the freedom of the universe. He can know and experience for himself all that exists. He can command, interfere with nature, with the chain of causation, change the sequence of events, even undo the past! The world is still with him, but he is free in it.

M: What you describe is God. Of course, where there is a universe, there will also be its counterpart, which is God. But I am beyond both. There was a kingdom in search of a king. They found the right man and made him king. In no way had he changed. He was merely given the title, the rights and the duties of a king. His nature was not affected, only his actions. Similarly, with the enlightened man; the content of his consciousness undergoes a radical transformation. But he is not misled. He knows the changeless.

Q: The changeless cannot be conscious. Consciousness is always of change. The changeless leaves no trace in consciousness.

M: Yes and no. The paper is not the writing, yet it carries the writing. The ink is not the message, nor is the reader's mind the message — but they all make the message possible.

Q: Does consciousness come down from reality or is it an attribute of matter?

M: Consciousness as such is the subtle counterpart of matter. Just as inertia *(tamas)* and energy *(rajas)* are attributes of matter, so does harmony *(sattva)* manifest itself as consciousness. You may consider it in a way as a form of very subtle energy. Wherever matter organizes itself into a stable organism, consciousness appears spontaneously. With the destruction of the organism consciousness disappears.

Q: Then what survives?

M: That, of which matter and consciousness are but aspects, which is neither born nor dies.

Q: If it is beyond matter and consciousness, how can it be experienced?

M: It can be known by its effects on both; look for it in beauty and in bliss. But you will understand neither body nor consciousness, unless you go beyond both.

Q: Please tell us squarely: are you conscious or unconscious?

M: The enlightened *(gnani)* is neither. But in his enlightenment *(gnana)* all is contained. Awareness contains every experience. But he who is aware is beyond every experience. He is beyond awareness itself.

Q: There is the background of experience, call it matter. There is the experiencer, call it mind. What makes the bridge between the two?

M: The very gap between is the bridge. That, which at one end looks like matter and at the other as mind, is in itself the bridge. Don't separate reality into mind and body and there will be no need of bridges.

Consciousness arising, the world arises. When you consider the wisdom and the beauty of the world, you call it God. Know the source of it all, which is in yourself, and you will find all your questions answered.

Q: The seer and the seen: are they one or two?

M: There is only seeing; both the seer and the seen are contained in it. Don't create differences where there are none.

Q: I began with the question about the man who died. You said that his experiences will shape themselves according to his expectations and beliefs.

M: Before you were born you expected to live according to a plan, which you yourself had laid down. Your own will was the backbone of your destiny.

Q: Surely, *karma* interfered.

M: *Karma* shapes the circumstances: the attitudes are your own. Ultimately your character shapes your life and you alone can shape your character.

Q: How does one shape one's character?

M: By seeing it as it is, and being sincerely sorry. This integral seeing-feeling can work miracles. It is like casting a bronze image; metal alone, or fire alone will not do; nor will the mould be of any use; you have to melt down the metal in the heat of the fire and cast it in the mould.   ●●●

57

Beyond Mind, there is no Suffering

Questioner: I see you sitting in your son's house waiting for lunch to be served. And I wonder whether the content of your consciousness is similar to mine, or partly different, or totally different. Are you hungry and thirsty as I am, waiting rather impatiently for the meals to be served, or are you in an altogether different state of mind?

Maharaj: There is not much difference on the surface, but very much of it in depth. You know yourself only through the senses and the mind. You take yourself to be what they suggest; having no direct knowledge of yourself, you have mere ideas; all mediocre, second-hand, by hearsay. Whatever you think you are you take it to be true; the habit of imagining yourself perceivable and describable is very strong with you.

I see as you see, hear as you hear, taste as you taste, eat as you eat. I also feel thirst and hunger and expect my food to be served on time. When starved or sick, my body and mind go weak. All this I perceive quite clearly, but somehow I am not in it, I feel myself as if floating over it, aloof and detached. Even not aloof and detached. There is aloofness and detachment as there is thirst and hunger; there is also the awareness of it all and a sense of immense distance, as if the body and the mind and all that happens to them were somewhere far out on the horizon. I am like a cinema screen — clear and empty — the pictures pass over it and disappear, leaving it as clear and empty as before. In no way is the screen affected by the pictures, nor are the pictures affected by the screen. The screen intercepts and reflects the pictures, it does not shape them. It has nothing to do with the rolls of films. These are as they are, lumps of destiny *(prarabdha)*, but not my destiny; the destinies of the people on the screen.

Q: You do not mean to say that the people in a picture have destinies! They belong to the story, the story is not theirs.

M: And what about you? Do you shape your life or are you shaped by it?

Q: Yes, you are right. A life-story unrolls itself of which I am one of the actors. I have no being outside it, as it has no being without me. I am merely a character, not a person.

M: The character will become a person, when he begins to shape his life instead of accepting it as it comes, and identifying himself with it.

Q: When I ask a question and you answer, what exactly happens?

M: The question and the answer — both appear on the screen. The lips move, the body speaks — and again the screen is clear and empty.

Q: When you say: clear and empty, what do you mean?

M: I mean free of all contents. To myself I am neither perceivable nor conceivable; there is nothing I can point out and say: 'this I am'. You identify yourself with everything so easily; I find it impossible. The feeling: 'I am not this or that, nor is anything mine' is so strong in me that as soon as a thing or a thought appears, there comes at once the sense 'this I am not'.

Q: Do you mean to say that you spend your time repeating 'this I am not, that I am not'?

M: Of course not. I am merely verbalizing for your sake. By the grace of my Guru I have realized once and for good that I am neither object nor subject and I do not need to remind myself all the time.

Q: I find it hard to grasp what exactly do you mean by saying that you are neither the object nor the subject. At this very moment, as we talk, am I not the object of your experience, and you the subject?

M: Look, my thumb touches my forefinger. Both touch and are touched. When my attention' is on the thumb, the thumb is the feeler and the forefinger — the self. Shift the focus of attention and the relationship is reversed. I find that somehow, by shifting the focus of attention, I become the very thing I look at and experience the kind of consciousness it has; I become the inner witness of the thing. I call this capacity of entering other focal points of consciousness — love; you may give it any name you like. Love says: 'I am everything'. Wisdom says: 'I am nothing' Between the two my life flows. Since at any point of time and space I can be both the subject and the object of experience, I express it by saying that I am both, and neither, and beyond both.

Q: You make all these extraordinary statements about yourself. What makes you say those things? What do you mean by saying that you are beyond space and time?

M: You ask and the answer comes. I watch myself — I watch the answer and see no contradiction. It is clear to me that I am telling you the truth. It is all very simple. Only you must trust me that I mean what I say, that I am quite serious. As I told you already, my Guru showed me my true nature — and the true nature of the world. Having realized that I am one with, and yet beyond the world, I became free from all desire and fear. I did not reason out that I should be free — I found myself free — unexpectedly, without the least effort. This freedom from desire and fear remained. with me since then. Another thing I noticed was that I do not need to make an effort; the deed follows the thought, without delay and friction. I have also found that thoughts become self-fulfilling; things would fall in place smoothly and rightly. The main change was in the mind; it became motionless and silent, responding quickly, but not perpetuating the response. Spontaneity became a way of life, the real became natural and the natural became real. And above all, infinite affection, love, dark and quiet, radiating in all directions, embracing all, making all interesting and beautiful, significant and auspicious.

Q: We are told that various Yogic powers arise spontaneously in a man who has realized his own true being. What is your experience in these matters?

M: Man's fivefold body (physical etc.) has potential powers beyond our wildest dreams. Not only is the entire universe reflected in man, but also the power to control the universe is waiting to be used by him. The wise man is not anxious to use such powers, except when the situation calls for them. He finds the abilities and skills of the human personality quite adequate for the business of daily living. Some of the powers can be developed by specialized training, but the man who flaunts such powers is still in bondage. The wise man counts nothing as his own. When at some time and place some miracle is attributed to some person, he will not establish any causal link between events and people, nor will he allow any conclusions to be drawn. All happened as it happened because it had to happen; everything happens as it does, because the universe is as it is.

Q: The universe does not seem a happy place to live in. Why is there so much suffering?

M: Pain is physical; suffering is mental. Beyond the mind there is no suffering. Pain is merely a signal that the body is in danger and requires attention. Similarly, suffering warns us that the structure of memories and habits, which we call the person *(vyakti),* is threatened by loss or change. Pain is essential for the survival of the body, but none compels you to suffer. Suffering is due entirely to clinging or resisting; it is a sign of our unwillingness to move on, to flow with life.

As a sane life is free of pain, so is a saintly life free from suffering.

Q: Nobody has suffered more than saints.

M: Did they tell you, or do you say so on your own? The essence of saintliness is total acceptance of the present moment, harmony with things as they happen. A saint does not want things to be different from what they are; he knows that, considering all factors, they are unavoidable. He is friendly with the inevitable and, therefore, does not suffer. Pain he may know, but it does not shatter him. If he can, he does the needful to restore the lost balance — or he lets things take their course.

Q: He may die.

M: So what? What does he gain by living on and what does he lose by dying? What was born, must die; what was never born cannot die. It all depends on what he takes himself to be.

Q: Imagine you fall mortally ill. Would you not regret and resent?

M: But I am dead already, or, rather, neither alive nor dead. You see my body behaving the habitual way and draw your own conclusions. You will not admit that your conclusions bind nobody but you. Do see that the image you have of me may be altogether wrong. Your image of yourself is wrong too, but that is your problem. But you need not create problems for me and then ask me to solve them. I am neither creating problems nor solving them.   •••

58
Perfection, Destiny of All

Questioner: When asked about the means for self-realization, you invariably stress the importance of the mind dwelling on the sense 'I am'. Where is the causal factor? Why should this particular thought result in self-realization? How does the contemplation of 'I am' affect me?

Maharaj: The very fact of observation alters the observer and the observed. After all, what prevents the insight into one's true nature is the weakness and obtuseness of the mind and its tendency to skip the subtle and focus the gross only. When you follow my advice and try to keep your mind on the notion of 'I am' only, you become fully aware of your mind and its vagaries. Awareness, being lucid harmony (sattva) in action, dissolves dullness and quietens the restlessness of the mind and gently, but steadily changes its very substance. This change need not be spectacular; it may be hardly noticeable; yet it is a deep and fundamental shift from darkness to light, from inadvertence to awareness.

Q: Must it be the 'I am' formula? Will not any other sentence do? If I concentrate on 'there is a table', will it not serve the same purpose?

M: As an exercise in concentration — yes. But it will not take you beyond the idea of a table. You are not interested in tables, you want to know yourself. For this keep steadily in the focus of consciousness the only clue you have: your certainty of being. Be with it, play with it, ponder over it, delve deeply into it, till the shell of ignorance breaks open and you emerge into the realm of reality.

Q: Is there any causal link between my focussing the 'I am' and the breaking of the shell?

M: The urge to find oneself is a sign that you are getting ready. The impulse always comes from within. Unless your time has come, you will have neither the desire nor the strength to go for self-enquiry whole-heartedly.

Q: Is not the grace of the Guru responsible for the desire and its fulfilment? Is not the Guru's radiant face the bait on which we are caught and pulled out of this mire of sorrow?

M: It is the Inner Guru (sadguru) who takes you to the Outer Guru, as a mother takes her child to a teacher. Trust and obey your Guru, for he is the messenger of your Real Self.

Q: How do I find a Guru whom I can trust?

M: Your own heart will tell you. There is no difficulty in finding a Guru, because the Guru is in search of you. The Guru is always ready; you are not ready. You have to be ready to learn; or you may meet your Guru and waste your chance by sheer inattentiveness and obstinacy. Take my example; there was nothing in me of much promise, but when I met my Guru, I listened, trusted and obeyed.

Q: Must I not examine the teacher before I put myself entirely into his hands?

M: By all means examine! But what can you find out? Only as he appears to you on your own level.

Q: I shall watch whether he is consistent, whether there is harmony between his life and his teaching.

M: You may find plenty of disharmony — so what? It proves nothing. Only motives matter. How will you know his motives?

Q: I should at least expect him to be a man of self-control who lives a righteous life.

M: Such you will find many — and of no use to you. A Guru can show the way back home, to your real self. What has this to do with the character, or temperament of the person he appears to be? Does he not clearly tell you that he is not the person? The only way you can judge is by the change in yourself when you are in his company. If you feel more at peace and happy, if you understand yourself with more than usual clarity and depth, it means you have met the right man. Take your time, but once you have made up your mind to trust him, trust him absolutely and follow every instruction fully and faithfully. It does not matter much if you do not accept him as your Guru and are satisfied with his company only. *Satsang* alone can also take you to your goal, provided it is unmixed and undisturbed. But once you accept somebody as your Guru, listen, remember and obey. Half-heartedness is a serious drawback and the cause of much self-created sorrow. The mistake is never the Guru's; it is always the obtuseness and cussedness of the discipline that is at fault.

Q: Does the Guru then dismiss, or disqualify a disciple?

M: He would not be a Guru if he did! He bides his time and waits till the disciple, chastened and sobered, comes back to him in a more receptive mood.

Q: What is the motive? Why does the Guru take so much trouble?

M: Sorrow and the ending of sorrow. He sees people suffering in their dreams and he wants them to wake up. Love is intolerant of pain and suffering. The patience of a Guru has no limits and, therefore, it cannot be defeated. The Guru never fails.

Q: Is my first Guru also my last, or do I have to pass from Guru to Guru?

M: The entire universe is your Guru. You learn from everything, if you are alert and intelligent. Were your mind clear and your heart clean, you would learn from every passerby. It is because you are indolent or restless, that your inner Self manifests as the outer Guru and makes you trust him and obey.

Q: Is a Guru inevitable?

M: It is like asking 'Is a mother inevitable?' To rise in consciousness from one dimension to another, you need help. The help may not always be in the shape of a human person, it may be a subtle presence, or a spark of intuition, but help must come. The inner Self is watching and waiting for the son to return to his father. At the right time he arranges everything affectionately and effectively. Where a messenger is needed, or a guide, he sends the Guru to do the needful.

Q: There is one thing I cannot grasp. You speak of the inner self as wise and good and beautiful and in every way perfect, and of the person as mere reflection without a being of its own. On the other hand you take so much trouble in helping the person to realize itself. If the person is so unimportant, why be so concerned with its welfare? Who cares for a shadow?,

M: You have brought in duality where there is none. There is the body and there is the Self. Between them is the mind, in which the Self is reflected as 'I am'. Because of the imperfections of the mind, its crudity and restlessness, lack of discernment and insight, it takes itself to be the body, not the Self. All that is needed is to purify the mind so that it can realize its identity with the Self. When the mind merges in the Self, the body presents no problems. It remains what it is, an instrument of cognition and action, the tool and the expression of the creative fire within. The ultimate value of the body is that it serves to discover the cosmic body, which is the universe in its entirety. As you realize yourself in manifestation, you keep on discovering that you are ever more than what you have imagined.

Q: Is there no end to self-discovery?

M: As there is no beginning, there is no end. But what I have discovered by the grace of my Guru is; I am nothing that can be pointed at I am neither a 'this' nor a 'that'. This holds absolutely.

Q: Then, where comes in the never-ending discovery, the end-less transcending oneself into new dimensions?

M: All this belongs to the realm of manifestation; it is in the very structure of the universe, that the higher can be had only through the freedom from the lower.

Q: What is lower and what is higher?

M: Look at it in terms of awareness. Wider and deeper consciousness is higher. All that lives, works for protecting, perpetuating and expanding consciousness. This is the world's sole meaning and purpose. It is the very essence of Yoga — ever raising the level of consciousness, discovery of new dimensions, with their properties, qualities and powers. In that sense the entire universe becomes a school of Yoga (yogakshetra).

Q: Is perfection the destiny of all human beings?

M: Of all living beings — ultimately. The possibility becomes a certainty when the notion of enlightenment appears in the mind. Once a living being has heard and understood that deliverance is within his reach, he will never forget, for it is the first message from within. It will take roots and grow and in due course take the blessed shape of the Guru.

Q: So all we are concerned with is the redemption of the mind?

M: What else? The mind goes astray, the mind returns home. Even the word 'astray' is not proper. The mind must know itself in every mood. Nothing is a mistake unless repeated.   ●●●

59

Desire and Fear: Self-centred States

Questioner: I would like to go again into the question of plea- sure and pain, desire and fear. I understand fear which is mem- ory and anticipation of pain. It is essential for the preservation of the organism and its living pattern. Needs, when felt, are painful and their anticipation is full of fear; we are rightly afraid of not being able to meet our basic needs. The relief experienced when a need is met, or an anxiety allayed is entirely due to the ending of pain. We may give it positive names like pleasure, or joy, or happiness, but essentially it is relief from pain. It is this fear of pain that holds together our social, economic and politi- cal institutions.

What puzzles me is that we derive pleasure from things and states of mind, which have nothing to do with survival. On the contrary, our pleasures are usually destructive. They damage or destroy the object, the instrument and also the subject of plea- sure. Otherwise, pleasure and pursuit of pleasure would be no problem. This brings me to the core of my question: why is pleasure destructive? Why, in spite of its destructiveness, is it wanted?

I may add, I do not have in mind the pleasure-pain pattern by which nature compels us to go her way. I think of the man-made pleasures, both sensory and subtle, ranging from the grossest, like overeating, to the most refined. Addiction to pleasure, at whatever cost, is so universal that there must be something sig- nificant at the root of it.

Of course, not every activity of man must be utilitarian, de- signed to meet a need. Play, for example, is natural and man is the most playful animal in existence. Play fulfils the need for self-discovery and self-development. But even on his play man becomes destructive of nature, others and himself.

Maharaj: In short, you do not object to pleasure, but only to its price in pain and sorrow.

Q: If reality itself is bliss, then pleasure in some way must be related to it.

M: Let us not proceed by verbal logic. The bliss of reality does not exclude suffering. Besides, you know only pleasure, not the bliss of pure being. So let us examine pleasure at its own level.

If you look at yourself in your moments of pleasure or pain, you will invariably find that it is not the thing in itself that is pleasant or painful, but the situation of which it is a part. Pleasure lies in the relationship between the enjoyer and the enjoyed. And the essence of it is acceptance. Whatever may be the situation, if it is acceptable, it is pleasant. If it is not acceptable, it is painful. What makes it acceptable is not important; the cause may be physical, or psychological, or untraceable; acceptance is the decisive factor. Obversely, suffering is due to non-acceptance.

Q: Pain is not acceptable.

M: Why not? Did you ever try? Do try and you will find in pain a joy which pleasure cannot yield, for the simple reason that acceptance of pain takes you much deeper than pleasure does. The personal self by its very nature is constantly pursuing pleasure and avoiding pain. The ending of this pattern is the ending of the self. The ending of the self with its desires and fears enables you to return to your real nature, the source of all happiness and peace. The perennial desire for pleasure is the reflection of the timeless harmony within. It is an observable fact that one becomes self-conscious only when caught in the conflict between pleasure and pain, which demands choice and decision. It is this clash between desire and fear that causes anger, which is the great destroyer of sanity in life. When pain is accepted for what it is, a lesson and a warning, and deeply looked into and heeded, the separation between pain and pleasure breaks down, both become experience — painful when resisted, joyful when accepted.

Q: Do you advise shunning pleasure and pursuing pain?

M: No, nor pursuing pleasure and shunning pain. Accept both as they come, enjoy both while they last, let them go, as they must.

Q: How can I possibly enjoy pain? Physical pain calls for action.

M: Of course. And so does mental. The bliss is in the awareness of it, in not shrinking, or in any way turning away from it. All happiness comes from awareness. The more we are conscious, the deeper the joy. Acceptance of pain, non-resistance, courage and endurance — these open deep and perennial sources of real happiness, true bliss.

Q: Why should pain be more effective than pleasure?

M: Pleasure is readily accepted, while all the powers of the self reject pain. As the acceptance of pain is the denial of the self, and the self stands in the way of true happiness, the wholehearted acceptance of pain releases the springs of happiness.

Q: Does the acceptance of suffering act the same way?

M: The fact of pain is easily brought within the focus of awareness. With suffering it is not that simple. To focus suffering is not enough, for mental life, as we know it, is one continuous stream of suffering. To reach the deeper layers of suffering you must go to its roots and uncover their vast underground network, where fear and desire are closely interwoven and the currents of life's energy oppose, obstruct and destroy each other.

Q: How can I set right a tangle which is entirely below the level of my consciousness?

M: By being with yourself, the 'I am'; by watching yourself in your daily life with alert interest, with the intention to understand rather than to judge, in full acceptance of whatever may emerge, because it is there, you encourage the deep to come to the surface and enrich your life and consciousness with its captive energies. This is the great work of awareness; it removes obstacles and releases energies by understanding the nature of life and mind. Intelligence is the door to freedom and alert attention is the mother of intelligence.

Q: One more question. Why does pleasure end in pain?

M: Everything has a beginning and an end and so does pleasure. Don't anticipate and don't regret, and there will be no pain. it is memory and imagination that cause suffering.

Of course pain after pleasure may be due to the misuse of the body or the mind. The body knows its measure, but the mind does not. Its appetites are numberless and limitless. Watch your mind with great diligence; for there lies your bondage and also the key to freedom.

Q: My question is not yet fully answered: Why are man's pleasures destructive? Why does he find so much pleasure in destruction? Life's concern lies in protection, perpetuation and expansion of itself. In this it is guided by pain and pleasure. At what point do they become destructive?

M: When the mind takes over, remembers and anticipates, it exaggerates, it distorts, it overlooks. The past is projected into future and the future betrays the expectations. The organs ol sensation and action are stimulated beyond capacity and they inevitably break down. The objects of pleasure cannot yield what is expected of them and get worn out, or destroyed, by misuse. It results in excess of pain where pleasure was looked for.

Q: We destroy not only ourselves, but others too!

M: Naturally, selfishness is always destructive. Desire and fear, both are self-centered states. Between desire and fear anger arises, with anger hatred, with hatred passion for destruction. War is hatred in action, organized and equipped with all the instruments of death.

Q: Is there a way to end these horrors?

M: When more people come to know their real nature, their influence, however subtle, will prevail and the world's emotional atmosphere will sweeten up. People follow their leaders and when among the leaders appear some, great in heart and mind, and absolutely free from self-seeking, their impact will be enough to make the crudities and crimes of the present age impossible. A new golden age may come and last for a time and succumb to its own perfection. For, ebb begins when the tide is at its highest.

Q: Is there no such thing as permanent perfection?

M: Yes, there is, but it includes all imperfection. It is the perfection of our self-nature which makes everything possible, perceivable, interesting. It knows no suffering, for it neither likes nor dislikes; neither accepts nor rejects. Creation and destruction are the two poles between which it weaves its ever-changing pattern. Be free from predilections and preferences and the mind with its burden of sorrow will be no more.

Q: But I am not alone to suffer. There are others.

M: When you go to them with your desires and fears, you merely add to their sorrows. First be free of suffering yourself and then only hope of helping others. You do not even need to hope — your very existence will be the greatest help a rnan can give his fellowmen.   ●●●

60

Live Facts, not Fancies

Questioner: You say that whatever you see is yourself. You also admit that you see the world as we see it. Here is today's newspaper with all the horrors going on. Since the world is yourself, how can you explain such misbehaviour?

Maharaj: Which world do you have in mind?

Q: Our common world, in which we live.

M: Are you sure we live in the same world? I do not mean nature, the sea and the land, plants and animals. They are not the problem, nor the endless space, the infinite time, the inexhaustible power. Do not be misled by my eating and smoking, reading and talking. My mind is not here, my life is not here. Your world, of desires and their fulfilments, of fears and their escapes, is definitely not my world. I do not even perceive it, except through what you tell me about it. It is your private dream-world and my only reaction to it is to ask you to stop dreaming.

Q: Surely, wars and revolutions are not dreams. Sick mothers and starving children are not dreams. Wealth, ill-gotten and misused, is not a dream.

M: What else?

Q: A dream cannot be shared.

M: Nor can the waking state. All the three states — of waking, dreaming and sleeping — are subjective, personal, intimate. They all happen to and are contained within the little bubble in consciousness, called 'I'. The real world lies beyond the self.

Q: Self or no self, facts are real.

M: Of course facts are real! I live among them. But you live with fancies, not with facts. Facts never clash, while your life and world are full of contradictions. Contradiction is the mark of the false; the real never contradicts itself.

For instance, you complain that people are abjectly poor. Yet you do not share your riches with them. You mind the war next door, but you hardly give it a thought when it is in some far off country. The shifting fortunes of your ego determine your values; 'I think', 'I want', 'I must' are made into absolutes.

Q: Nevertheless, the evil is real.

M: Not more real than you are. Evil is in the wrong approach to problems created by mis-understanding and mis-use. It is a vicious circle.

Q: Can the circle be broken?

M: A false circle need not be broken. It is enough to see it as it is — non-existent.

Q: But, real enough to make us submit to and inflict indignities and atrocities.

M: Insanity is universal. Sanity is rare. Yet there is hope, because the moment we perceive our insanity, we are on the way to sanity. This is the function of the Guru — to make us see the madness of our daily living. Life makes you conscious, but the teacher makes you aware.

Q: Sir, you are neither the first nor the last. Since immemorial times people were breaking into reality. Yet how little it affected our lives! The Ramas and the Krishnas, the Buddhas and the Christs have come and gone and we are as we were; wallowing in sweat and tears. What have the great ones done, whose lives we witnessed? What have you done, Sir, to alleviate the world's thrall?

M: You alone can undo the evil you have created. Your own callous selfishness is at the root of it. Put first your own house in order and you will see that your work is done.

Q: The men of wisdom and of love, who came before us, did set themselves right, often at a tremendous cost. What was the outcome? A shooting star, however bright, does not make the night less dark.

M: To judge them and their work you must become one of them. A frog in a well knows nothing about the birds in the sky.

Q: Do you mean to say that between good and evil there is no wall?

M: There is no wall, because there is no good and no evil. In every concrete situation there is only the necessary and the unnecessary. The needful is right, the needless is wrong.

Q: Who decides?

M: The situation decides. Every situation is a challenge which demands the right response. When the response is right, the challenge is met and the problem ceases. If the response is wrong, the challenge is not met and the problem remains unsolved. Your unsolved problems — that is what constitutes your *karma*. Solve them rightly and be free.

Q: You seem to drive me always back into myself. Is there no objective solution to the world's problems?

M: The world problems were created by numberless people like you, each full of his own desires and fears. Who can free you of your past, personal and social, except yourself? And how will you do it unless you see the urgent need of your being first free of cravings born of illusion? How can you truly help, as long as you need help yourself?

Q: In what way did the ancient sages help? In what way do you help? A few individuals profit, no doubt; your guidance and example may mean a lot to them; but in what way do you affect humanity, the totality of life and consciousness? You say that you are the world and the world is you; what impact have you made on it?

M: What kind of impact do you expect?

Q: Man is stupid, selfish, cruel.

M: Man is also wise, affectionate and kind.

Q: Why does not goodness prevail?

M: It does — in my real world. In my world even what you call evil is the servant of the good and therefore necessary. It is like boils and fevers that clear the body of impurities. Disease is painful, even dangerous, but if dealt with rightly, it heals.

Q: Or kills.

M: In some cases death is the best cure. A life may be worse than death, which is but rarely an unpleasant experience, whatever the appearances. Therefore, pity the living, never the dead. This problem of things, good and evil in themselves, does not exist in my world. The needful is good and the needless is evil. In your world the pleasant is good and the painful is evil.

Q: What is necessary?

M: To grow is necessary. To outgrow is necessary. To leave behind the good for the sake of the better is necessary.

Q: To what end?

M: The end is in the beginning. You end where you start — in the Absolute.

Q: Why all this trouble then? To come back to where I started?

M: Whose trouble? Which trouble? Do you pity the seed that is to grow and multiply till it becomes a mightly forest? Do you kill an infant to save him from the bother of living? What is wrong with life, ever more life? Remove the obstacles to growing and all your personal, social, economic and political problems will just dissolve. The universe is perfect as a whole and the part's striving for perfection is a way of joy. Willingly sacrifice the imperfect to the perfect and there will be no more talk about good and evil.

Q: Yet we are afraid of the better and cling to the worse.

M: This is our stupidity, verging on insanity.   ●●●

61

Matter is Consciousness Itself

Questioner: I was lucky to have holy company all my life. Is it enough for self-realization?

Maharaj: It depends what you make of it.

Q: I was told that the liberating action of *satsang* is automatic. Just like a river carries one to the estuary, so the subtle and silent influence of good people will take me to reality.

M: It will take you to the river, but the crossing is your own. Freedom cannot be gained nor kept without will-to-freedom. You must strive for liberation; the least you can do is uncover and remove the obstacles diligently. If you want peace you must strive for it. You will not get peace just by keeping quiet.

Q: A child just grows. He does not make plans for growth, nor has he a pattern; nor does he grow by fragments, a hand here a leg there; he grows integrally and unconsciously.

M: Because he is free of imagination. You can also grow like this, but you must not indulge in forecasts and plans, born of memory and anticipation. It is one of the peculiarities of a *gnani* that he is not concerned with the future. Your concern with future is due to fear of pain and desire for pleasure, to the *gnani* all is bliss: he is happy with whatever comes.

Q: Surely, there are many things that would make even a *gnani* miserable.

M: A *gnani* may meet with difficulties, but they do not make him suffer. Bringing up a child from birth to maturity may seem a hard task, but to a mother the memories of hardships are a joy. There is nothing wrong with the world. What is wrong is in the way you look at it. It is your own imagination that misleads you. Without imagination there is no world. Your conviction that you are conscious of a world is the world. The world you perceive is made of consciousness; what you call matter is consciousness itself. You are the space *(akash)* in which it moves, the time in which it lasts, the love that gives it life. Cut off imagination and attachment and what remains?

Q: The world remains. I remain.

M: Yes. but how different it is when you can see it as it is, not through the screen of desire and fear.

Q: What for are all these distinctions — reality and illusion, wisdom and ignorance, saint and sinner? Everyone is in search of happiness, everyone strives desperately; everyone is a Yogi and his life a school of wisdom. Each learns his own way the lessons he needs. Society approves of some, disapproves of others; there are no rules that apply everywhere and for all time.

M: In my world love is the only law. I do not ask for love, I give it. Such is my nature.

Q: I see you living your life according to a pattern. You run a meditation class in the morning, lecture and have discussions regularly; twice daily there is worship *(puja)* and religious singing *(bhajan)* in the evening. You seem to adhere to the routine scrupulously.

M: The worship and the singing are as I found them and I saw no reason to interfere. The general routine is according to the wishes of the people with whom I happen to live or who come to listen. They are working people, with many obligations and the timings are for their convenience. Some repetitive routine is inevitable. Even animals and plants have their time-tables.

Q: Yes, we see a regular sequence in all life. Who maintains the order? Is there an inner ruler, who lays down laws and enforces order?

M: Everything moves according to its nature. Where is the need of a policeman? Every action creates a reaction, which balances and neutralizes the action. Everything happens, but there is a continuous cancelling out, and in the end it is as if nothing happened.

Q: Do not console me with final harmonies. The accounts tally, but the loss is mine.

M: Wait and see. You may end up with a profit good enough to justify the outlays.

Q: There is a long life behind me and I often wonder whether its many events took place by accident, or there was a plan. Was there a pattern laid down before I was born by which I had to live my life? If yes, who made the plans and who enforced them? Could there be deviations and mistakes? Some say destiny is immutable and every second of life is pre-determined; others say that pure accident decides everything.

M: You can have it as you like. You can distinguish in your life a pattern or see merely a chain of accidents. Explanations are meant to please the mind. They need not be true. Reality is indefinable and indescribable.

Q: Sir, you are escaping my question! I want to know how *you* look at it. Wherever we look we find structure of unbelievable intelligence and beauty. How can I believe that the universe is formless and chaotic? Your world, the world in which you live, may be formless, but it need not be chaotic.

M: The objective universe has structure, is orderly and beautiful. Nobody can deny it. But structure and pattern, imply constraint and compulsion. My world is absolutely free; everything in it is self-determined. Therefore I keep on saying that all happens by itself. There is order in my world too, but it is not imposed from outside. It comes spontaneously and immediately, because of its timelessness. Perfection is not in the future. It is *now*.

Q: Does your world affect mine?

M: At one point only — at the point of the *now*. It gives it momentary being, a fleeting sense of reality. In full awareness the contact is established. It needs effortless, un-self-conscious attention.

Q: Is not attention an attitude of mind?

M: Yes, when the mind is eager for reality, it gives attention. There is nothing wrong with your world, it is your thinking yourself to be separate from it that creates disorder. Selfishness is the source of all evil.

Q: I am coming back to my question. Before I was born, did my inner self decide the details of my life, or was it entirely accidental and at the mercy of heredity and circumstances?

M: Those who claim to have selected their father and mother and decided how they are going to live their next life may know for themselves. I know for myself. I was never born.

Q: I see you sitting in front of me and replying my questions.

M: You see the body only which, of course, was born and will die.

Q: It is the life-story of this body-mind that I am interested in. Was it laid down by you or somebody else, or did it happen accidentally?

M: There is a catch in your very question. I make no distinction between the body and the universe. Each is the cause of the other; each is the other, in truth. But I am out of it all. When I am telling you that I was never born, why go on asking me what were my preparations for the next birth? The moment you allow your imagination to spin, it at once spins out a universe. It is not at all as you imagine and I am not bound by your imaginings.

Q: It requires intelligence and energy to build and maintain a living body. Where do they come from?

M: There is only imagination. The intelligence and power are all used up in your imagination. It has absorbed you so completely that you just cannot grasp how far from reality you have wandered. No doubt imagination is richly creative. Universe within universe are built on it. Yet they are all in space and time, past and future, which just do not exist.

Q: I have read recently a report about a little girl who was very cruelly handled in her early childhood. She was badly mutilated and disfigured and grew up in an orphanage, completely estranged from its surroundings. This little girl was quiet and obedient, but completely indifferent. One of the nuns who were looking after the children, was convinced that the girl was not mentally retarded, but merely withdrawn, irresponsive. A psychoanalyst was asked to take up the case and for full two years he would see the child once a week and try to break the wall of isolation. She was docile and well-behaved, but would give no attention to her doctor. He brought her a toy house, with rooms and movable furniture and dolls representing father, mother and their children. It brought out a response, the girl got interested. One day the old hurts revived and came to the surface. Gradually she recovered, a number of operations brought back her face and body to normal and she grew into an efficient and attractive young woman. It took the doctor more than five years, but the work was done. He was a real Guru! He did not put down conditions nor talk about readiness and eligibility. Without faith, without hope, out of love only he tried and tried again.

M: Yes, that is the nature of a Guru. He will never give up. But, to succeed, he must not be met with too much resistance. Doubt and disobedience necessarily delay. Given confidence and pliability, he can bring about a radical change in the disciple speedily. Deep insight in the Guru and earnestness in the disciple, both are needed. Whatever was her condition, the girl in your story suffered for lack of earnestness in people. The most difficult are the intellectuals. They talk a lot, but are not serious.

What you call realization is a natural thing. When you are ready, your Guru will be waiting. Sadhana is effortless. When the relationship with your teacher is right you grow. Above all, trust him. He cannot mislead you.

Q: Even when he asks me to do something patently wrong?

M: Do it. A Sanyasi had been asked by his Guru to marry. He obeyed and suffered bitterly. But his four children were all saints and seers, the greatest in Maharashtra. Be happy with whatever comes from your Guru and you will grow to perfection without striving.

Q: Sir, have you any wants or wishes. Can I do anything for you?

M: What can you give me that I do not have? Material things are needed for contentment. But I am contented with myself. What else do I need?

Q: Surely, when you are hungry you need food and when sick you need medicine.

M: Hunger brings the food and illness brings the medicine. It is all nature's work.

Q: If I bring something I believe you need, will you accept it?

M: The love that made you offer will make me accept.

Q: If somebody offers to build you a beautiful Ashram?

M: Let him, by all means. Let him spend a fortune, employ hundreds, feed thousands.

Q: Is it not a desire?

M: Not at all. I am only asking him to do it properly, not stingily, half-heartedly. He is fulfilling his own desire, not mine. Let him do it well and be famous among men and gods.

Q: But do you want it?

M: I do not want it.

Q: Will you accept it?

M: I don't need it.

Q: Will you stay in it?

M: If I am compelled.

Q: What can compel you?

M: Love of those who are in search of light.

Q: Yes, I see your point. Now, how am I to go into *samadhi?*

M: If you are in the right state, whatever you see will put you into *samadhi.* After all, *samadhi* is nothing unusual. When the mind is intensely interested, it becomes one with the object of interest — the seer and the seen become one in seeing, the hearer and the heard become one in hearing, the lover and the loved become one in loving. Every experience can be the ground for *samadhi.*

Q: Are you always in a state of *samadhi?*

M: Of course not *Samadhi* is a state of mind, after all. I am beyond all experience, even of *samadhi.* I am the great devourer and destroyer: whatever I touch dissolves into void *(akash).*

Q: I need *samadhis* for self-realization.

M: You have all the self-realization you need, but you do not trust it. Have courage, trust yourself, go, talk, act; give it a chance to prove itself. With some realization comes imperceptibly, but somehow they need convincing. They have changed, but they do not notice it. Such non-spectacular cases are often the most reliable.

Q: Can one believe himself to be realized and be mistaken?

M: Of course. The very idea 'I am self-realized' is a mistake. There is no 'I am this', 'I am that' in the Natural State.   ●●●

62

In the Supreme the Witness Appears

Questioner: Some forty years ago J. Krishnamurti said that there is life only and all talk of personalities and individualities has no foundation in reality. He did not attempt to describe life — he merely said that while life need not and cannot be described, it can be fully experienced, if the obstacles to its being experienced are removed. The main hindrance lies in our idea of, and addiction to, time, in our habit of anticipating a future in the light of the past. The sum total of the past becomes the 'I was', the hoped for future becomes the 'I shall be' and life is a constant effort of crossing over from what 'I was' to what 'I shall be'. The present moment, the 'now' is lost sight of. Maharaj speaks of 'I am'. Is it an illusion, like 'I was' and 'I shall be', or is there something real about it? And if the 'I am' too is an illusion, how does one free oneself from it? The very notion of I am free of 'I am' is an absurdity. Is there something real, something lasting, about the 'I am' in distinction from the 'I was', or 'I shall be', which change with time, as added memories create new expectations?

Maharaj: The present 'I am' is as false as the 'I was' and 'I shall be'. It is merely an idea in the mind, an impression left by memory, and the separate identity it creates is false. This habit of referring to a false centre must be done away with; the notion: 'I see', 'I feel', 'I think', 'I do', must disappear from the field of consciousness; what remains when the false is no more, is real.

Q: What is this big talk about elimination of the self? How can the self eliminate itself? What kind of metaphysical acrobatics can lead to the disappearance of the acrobat? In the end he will reappear, mightily proud of his disappearing.

M: You need not chase the 'I am' to kill it. You cannot. All you need is a sincere longing for reality. We call it *atma-bhakti,* the love of the Supreme: or *moksha-sankalpa,* the determination to be free from the false. Without love, and will inspired by love, nothing can be done. Merely talking about Reality without doing anything about it is self-defeating. There must be love in the relation between the person who says 'I am' and the observer of that 'I am'. As long as the observer, the inner self, the 'higher' self, considers himself apart from the observed, the 'lower' self, despises it and condemns it, the situation is hopeless. It is only when the observer *(vyakta)* accepts the person *(vyakti)* as a projection or manifestation of himself, and, so to say, takes the self into the Self, the duality of 'I' and 'this' goes and in the identity of the outer and the inner the Supreme Reality manifests itself.

This union of the seer and the seen happens when the seer becomes conscious of himself as the seer; he is not merely interested in the seen, which he is anyhow, but also interested in being interested, giving attention to attention, aware of being aware. Affectionate awareness is the crucial factor that brings Reality into focus.

Q: According to the Theosophists and allied occultists, man consists of three aspects: personality, individuality and spirituality. Beyond spirituality lies divinity. The personality is strictly temporary and valid for one birth only. It begins with the birth of the body and ends with the birth of the next body. Once over, it is over for good; nothing remains of it except a few sweet or bitter lessons.

The individuality begins with the animal-man and ends with the fully human. The split between the personality and individuality is characteristic of our present-day humanity. On one side the individuality with its longing for the true, the good and the beautiful; on the other side an ugly struggle between habit and ambition, fear and greed, passivity and violence.

The spirituality aspect is still in abeyance. It cannot manifest itself in an atmosphere of duality. Only when the personality is re-united with the individuality and becomes a limited, perhaps, but true expression of it, that the light and love and beauty of the spiritual come into their own.

You teach of the *vyakti, vyakta, avyakta* (observer, observed and ground of observation). Does it tally with the other view?

M: Yes, when the *vyakti* realizes its non-existence in separation from the *vyakta,* and the *vyakta* sees the *vyakti* as his own expression, then the peace and silence of the *avyakta* state come into being. In reality, the three are one: the *vyakta* and the *avyakta* are inseparable, while the *vyakti* is the sensing-feeling-thinking process, based on the body made of and fed by the five elements.

Q: What is the relation between the *vyakta* and the *avyakta?*

M: How can there be relation when they are one? All talk of separation and relation is due to the distorting and corrupting influence of 'I-am-the-body' idea. The outer self *(vyakti)* is merely a projection on the body-mind of the inner self *(vyakta),* which again is only an expression of the Supreme Self *(avyakta)* which is all and none.

Q: There are teachers who will not talk of the higher self and lower self. They address the man as if only the lower self existed. Neither Buddha nor Christ ever mentioned a higher self. J. Krishnamurti too fights shy of any mention of the higher self. Why is it so?

M: How can there be two selves in one body? The 'I am' is one. There is no 'higher I-am' and 'lower I-am'. All kinds of states of mind are presented to awareness and there is self-identification with them. The objects of observation are not what they appear to be and the attitudes they are met with are not what they need be. If you think that Buddha, Christ or Krishnamurti speak to the person, you are mistaken. They know well that the *vyakti,* the outer self, is but a shadow of the *vyakta,* the inner self, and they address and admonish the *vyakta* only. They tell him to give attention to the outer self, to guide and help it, to feel responsible for it; in short, to be fully aware of it. Awareness comes from the Supreme and pervades the inner self; the so-called outer self is only that part of one's being of which one is not aware. One may be conscious, for every being is conscious, but one is not aware. What is included in awareness becomes the inner and partakes of the inner. You may put it differently: the body defines the outer self, consciousness the inner, and in pure awareness the Supreme is contacted.

Q: You said the body defines the outer self. Since you have a body, do you have also an outer self?

M: I would, were I attached to the body and take it to be myself.

Q: But you are aware of it and attend to its needs.

M: The contrary is nearer to truth — the body knows me and is aware of my needs. But neither is really so. This body appears in your mind; in my mind nothing is.

Q: Do you mean to say you are quite unconscious of having a body?

M: On the contrary, I am conscious of not having a body.

Q: I see you smoking!

M: Exactly so. You see me smoking. Find out for yourself how did you come to see me smoking, and you will easily realize that it is your 'I-am-the-body' state of mind that is responsible for this 'I-see-you-smoking' idea.

Q: There is the body and there is myself. I know the body. Apart from it, what am I?

M: There is no 'I' apart from the body, nor the world. The three appear and disappear together. At the root is the sense 'I am'. Go beyond it. The idea: 'I-am-not-the-body' is merely an antidote to the idea 'I-am-the-body' which is false. What is that 'I am'? Unless you know yourself, what else can you know?

Q: From what you say I conclude that without the body there can be no liberation. If the idea: 'I-am-not-the-body' leads to liberation, the presence of the body is essential.

M: Quite right. 'Without the body, how can the idea: 'I-am-not-the-body' come into being? The idea 'I-am-free' is as false as the idea 'I-am-in-bondage'. Find out the 'I am' common to both and go beyond.

Q: All is a dream only.

M: All are mere words, of what use are they to you? You are entangled in the web of verbal definitions and formulations. Go beyond your concepts and ideas; in the silence of desire and thought the truth is found.

Q: One has to remember not to remember. What a task!

M: It cannot be done, of course. It must happen. But it does happen when you truly see the need of it. Again, earnestness is the golden key.

Q: At the back of my mind there is a hum going on all the time. Numerous weak thoughts swarm and buzz and this shapeless cloud is always with me. Is it the same with you? What is at the back of your mind?

M: Where there is no mind, there no back to it. I am all front, no back! The void speaks, the void remains.

Q: Is there no memory left?

M: No memory of past pleasure or pain is left. Each moment is newly born.

Q: Without memory you cannot be conscious.

M: Of course I am conscious, and fully aware of it. I am not a block of wood! Compare consciousness and its content to a cloud. You are inside the cloud, while I look at. You are lost in it, hardly able to see the tips of your fingers, while I see the cloud and many other clouds and the blue sky too and the sun, the moon, the stars. Reality is one for both of us, but for you it is a prison and for me it is a home.

Q: You spoke of the person *(vyakti)*, the witness *(vyakta)* and the Supreme *(avyakta)*. Which comes first?

M: In the Supreme the witness appears. The witness creates the person and thinks itself as separate from it. The witness sees that the person appears in consciousness, which again appears in the witness. This realization of the basic unity is the working of the Supreme. It is the power behind the witness, the source from which all flows. It cannot be contacted, unless there is unity and love and mutual help between the person and the witness, unless the doing is in harmony with the being and the knowing. The Supreme is both the source and the fruit of such harmony. As I talk to you, I am in the state of detached but affectionate awareness *(turiya)*. When this awareness turns upon itself, you may call it the Supreme State, *(turiyatita)*. But the fundamental reality is beyond awareness, beyond the three states of becoming, being and not-being.

Q: How is it that here my mind is engaged in high topics and finds dwelling on them easy and pleasant. When I return home I find myself forgetting all I have learnt here, worrying and fretting, unable to remember my real nature even for a moment. What may be the cause?

M: It is your childishness you are returning to. You are not fully grown up; there are levels left undeveloped because unattended. Just give full attention to what in you is crude and primitive, unreasonable and unkind, altogether childish, and you will ripen. It is the maturity of heart and mind that is essential. It comes effortlessly when the main obstacle is removed — inattention, unawareness. In awareness you grow.   ●●●

63

Notion of Doership is Bondage

Questioner: We have been staying at the Satya Sai Baba Ashram for some time. We have also spent two months at Sri Ramanashram at Tiruvannamalai. Now we are on our way back to the United States.

Maharaj: Did India cause any change in you?

Q: We feel we have shed our burden. Sri Satya Sai Baba told us to leave everything to him and just live from day to day as righteously as possible. 'Be good and leave the rest to me', he used to tell us.

M: What were you doing at the Sri Ramanashram?

Q: We were going on with the *mantra* given to us by the Guru. We also did some meditation. There was not much of thinking or study; we were just trying to keep quiet. We are on the *bhakti* path and rather poor in philosophy. We have not much to think about — just trust our Guru and live our lives.

M: Most of the *bhaktas* trust their Guru only as long as all is well with them. When troubles come, they feel let down and go out in search of another Guru.

Q: Yes, we were warned against this danger. We are trying to take the hard along with the soft. The feeling: 'All is Grace' must be very strong. A *sadhu* was walking eastwards, from where a strong wind started blowing. The *sadhu* just turned round and walked west. We hope to live just like that — adjusting ourselves to circumstances as sent us by our Guru.

M: There is only life. There is nobody who lives a life.

Q: That we understand, yet constantly we make attempts to live our lives instead of just living. Making plans for the future seems to be an inveterate habit with us.

M: Whether you plan or don't, life goes on. But in life itself a little whorl arises in the mind, which indulges in fantasies and imagines itself dominating and controlling life.

Life itself is desireless. But the false self wants to continue — pleasantly. Therefore it is always engaged in ensuring one's continuity. Life is unafraid and free. As long as you have the idea of influencing events, liberation is not for you: The very notion of doership, of being a cause, is bondage.

Q: How can we overcome the duality of the doer and the done?

M: Contemplate life as infinite, undivided, ever present, ever active, until you realize yourself as one with it. It is not even very difficult, for you will be returning only to your own natural condition.

Once you realize that all comes from within, that the world in which you live has not been projected onto you but by you, your fear comes to an end. Without this realization you identify yourself with the externals, like the body, mind, society, nation, humanity, even God or the Absolute. But these are all escapes from fear. It is only when you fully accept your responsibility for the little world in which you live and watch the process of its creation, preservation and destruction, that you may be free from your imaginary bondage.

Q: Why should I imagine myself so wretched?

M: You do it by habit only. Change your ways of feeling and thinking, take stock of them and examine them closely. You are in bondage by inadvertence. Attention liberates. You are taking so many things for granted. Begin to question. The most obvious things are the most doubtful. Ask yourself such questions as: 'Was I really born?' 'Am I really so-and-so? 'How do I know that I exist? 'Who are my parents?' 'Have they created me, or have I created them?' 'Must I believe all I am told about myself?' 'Who am I, anyhow?' You have put so much energy into building a prison for yourself. Now spend as much on demolishing it. In fact, demolition is easy, for the false dissolves when it is discovered. All hangs on the idea 'I am'. Examine it very thoroughly. It lies at the root of every trouble. It is a sort of skin that separates you from the reality. The real is both within and without the skin, but the skin itself is not real. This 'I am' idea was not born with you. You could have lived very well without it. It came later due to your self-identification with the body. It created an illusion of separation where there was none. It made you a stranger in your own world and made the world alien and inimical. Without the sense of 'I am' life goes on. There are moments when we are without the sense of 'I am', at peace and happy. With the return of the 'I am' trouble starts.

Q: How is one to be free from the 'I'-sense?

M: You must deal with the 'I'-sense if you want to be free of it. Watch it in operation and at peace, how it starts and when it ceases, what it wants and how it gets it, till you see clearly and understand fully. After all, all the Yogas, whatever their source and character, have only one aim: to save you from the calamity of separate existence, of being a meaningless dot in a vast and beautiful picture.

You suffer because you have alienated yourself from reality and now you seek an escape from this alienation. You cannot escape from your own obsessions. You can only cease nursing them.

It is because the 'I am' is false that it wants to continue. Reality need not continue — knowing itself indestructible, it is indifferent to the destruction of forms and expressions. To strengthen, and stabilize the 'I am' we do all sorts of things — all in vain, for the 'I am' is being rebuilt from moment to moment. It is unceasing work and the only radical solution is to dissolve the separative sense of 'I am such-and-such, person' once and for good. Being remains, but not self-being.

Q: I have definite spiritual ambitions. Must I not work for their fulfilment?

M: No ambition is spiritual. All ambitions are for the sake of the 'I am'. If you want to make real progress you must give up all idea of personal attainment. The ambitions of the so-called Yogis are preposterous. A man's desire for a woman is innocence itself compared to the lusting for an everlasting personal bliss. The mind is a cheat. The more pious it seems, the worse the betrayal.

Q: People come to you very often with their worldly troubles and ask for help. How do you know what to tell them?

M: I just tell them what comes to my mind at the moment. I have no standardized procedure in dealing with people.

Q: You are sure of yourself. But when people come to me for advice, how am I to be sure that my advice is right?

M: Watch in what state you are, from what level you talk. If you talk from the mind, you may be wrong. If you talk from full insight into the situation, with your own mental habits in abeyance your advice may be a true response. The main point is to be fully aware that neither you nor the man in front of you are mere bodies; if your awareness is clear and full, a mistake is less probable. ●●●

64
Whatever Pleases you, Keeps you Back

Questioner: I am a retired chartered accountant and my wife is engaged in social work for poor women. Our son is leaving for the United States and we came to see him off. We are Panjabis, but we live in Delhi. We have a Guru of the Radha-Soami faith and we value *satsang* highly. We feel very fortunate to be brought here. We have met many holy people and we are glad to meet one more.

Maharaj: You have met many anchorites and ascetics, but a fully realized man conscious of his divinity *(swarupa)* is hard to find. The saints and Yogis, by immense efforts and sacrifices, acquire many miraculous powers and can do much good in the way of helping people and inspiring faith, yet it does not make them perfect. It is not a way to reality, but merely an enrichment of the false. All effort leads to more effort; whatever was built up must be maintained, whatever was acquired must be protected against decay or loss. Whatever can be lost is not really one's own; and what is not your own of what use can it be to you? In my world nothing is pushed about, all happens by itself. All existence is in space and time, limited and temporary. He who experiences existence is also limited and temporary. I am not concerned either with 'what exists' or with 'who exists'. I take my stand beyond, where I am both and neither.

The persons who, after much effort and penance, have fulfilled their ambitions and secured higher levels of experience and action, are usually acutely conscious of their standing; they grade people into hierarchies, ranging from the lowest non-achiever to the highest achiever. To me all are equal. Differences in appearance and expression are there, but they do not matter. Just as the shape of a gold ornament does not affect the gold, so does man's essence remain unaffected. Where this sense of equality is lacking it means that reality had not been touched.

Mere knowledge is not enough; the knower must be known. The Pandits and the Yogis may know many things, but of what use is mere knowledge when the self is not known? It will be certainly misused. Without the knowledge of the knower there can be no peace.

Q: How does one come to know the knower?

M: I can only tell you what I know from my own experience. When I met my Guru, he told me: 'You are not what you take yourself to be. Find out what you are. Watch the sense 'I am', find your real self'. I obeyed him, because I trusted him. I did as he told me. All my spare time I would spend looking at myself in silence. And what a difference it made, and how soon! It took me only three years to realize my true nature. My Guru died soon after I met him, but it made no difference. I remembered what he told me and persevered. The fruit of it is here, with me.

Q: What is it?

M: I know myself as I am in reality. I am neither the body, nor the mind, nor the mental faculties. I am beyond all these.

Q: Are you just nothing?

M: Come on, be reasonable. Of course I am, most tangibly. Only I am not what you may think me to be. This tells you all.

Q: It tells me nothing.

M: Because it cannot be told. You must gain your own experience. You are accustomed to deal with things, physical and mental. I am not a thing, nor are you. We are neither matter nor energy, neither body nor mind. Once you have a glimpse of your own being, you will not find me difficult to understand.

We believe in so many things on hearsay. We believe in distant lands and people, in heavens and hells, in gods and goddesses, because we were told. Similarly, we were told about ourselves, our parents, name, position, duties and so on. We never cared to verify. The way to truth lies through the destruction of the false. To destroy the false, you must question your most inveterate beliefs. Of these the idea that you are the body is the worst. With the body comes the world, with the world — God, who is supposed to have created the world and thus it starts — fears, religions, prayers, sacrifices, all sorts of systems — all to protect and support the child-man, frightened out of his wits by monsters of his own making. Realize that what you are cannot be born nor die and with the fear gone all suffering ends.

What the mind invents, the mind destroys. But the real is not invented and cannot be destroyed. Hold on to that over which the mind has no power. What I am telling you about is neither in the past nor in the future. Nor is it in the daily life as it flows in the now. It is timeless and the total timelessness of it is beyond the mind. My Guru and his words: 'You are myself' are timelessly with me. In the beginning I had to fix my mind on them, but now it has become natural and easy. The point when the mind accepts the words of the Guru as true and lives by them spontaneously and in every detail of daily life is the threshold of realization. In a way it is salvation by faith, but the faith must be intense and lasting.

However, you must not think that faith itself is enough. Faith expressed in action is a sure means to realization. Of all the means it is the most effective. There are teachers who deny faith and trust reason only. Actually it is not faith they deny, but blind beliefs. Faith is not blind. It is the willingness to try.

Q: We were told that of all forms of spiritual practices the practice of the attitude of a mere witness is the most efficatious. How does it compare with faith?

M: The witness attitude is also faith; it is faith in oneself. You believe that you are not what you experience and you look at everything as from a distance. There is no effort in witnessing. You understand that you are the witness only and the understanding acts. You need nothing more, just remember that you are the witness only. If in the state of witnessing you ask yourself: 'Who am I?', the answer comes at once, though it is wordless and silent. Cease to be the object and become the subject of all that happens; once having turned within, you will find yourself beyond the subject. When you have found yourself, you will find that you are also beyond the object, that both the subject and the object exist in you, but you are neither.

Q: You speak of the mind, of the witnessing consciousness beyond the mind and of the Supreme, which is beyond awareness. Do you mean to say that even awareness is not real?

M: As long as you deal in terms: real — unreal, awareness is the only reality that can be. But the Supreme is beyond all distinctions and to it the term 'real' does not apply, for in it all is real and, therefore, need not be labelled as such. It is the very source of reality, it imparts reality to whatever it touches. It just cannot be understood through words. Even a direct experience, however sublime, merely bears testimony, nothing more.

Q: But who creates the world?

M: The Universal Mind *(chidakash)* makes and unmakes everything. The Supreme *(paramakash)* imparts reality to whatever comes into being. To say that it is the universal love may be the nearest we can come to it in words. Just like love it makes everything real, beautiful, desirable.

Q: Why desirable?

M: Why not? Wherefrom come all the powerful attractions that make all created things respond to each other, that bring people together, if not from the Supreme? Shun not desire; see only that it flows into the right channels. Without desire you are dead. But with low desires you are a ghost.

Q: What is the experience which comes nearest to the Supreme?

M: Immense peace and boundless love. Realize that whatever there is true, noble and beautiful in the universe, it all comes from you, that you yourself are at the source of it. The gods and goddesses that supervise the world may be most wonderful and glorious beings; yet they are like the gorgeously dressed servants who proclaim the power and the riches of their master.

Q: How does one reach the Supreme State?

M: By renouncing all lesser desires. As long as you are pleased with the lesser, you cannot have the highest. Whatever pleases you, keeps you back. Until you realize the unsatisfactoriness of everything, its transiency and limitation, and collect your energies in one great longing, even the first step is not made. On the other hand, the integrity of the desire for the Supreme is by itself a call from the Supreme. Nothing, physical or mental, can give you freedom. You are free once you understand that your bondage is of your own making and you cease forging the chains that bind you.

Q: How does one find the faith in a Guru?

M: To find the Guru and also the trust in him is rare luck. It does not happen often.

Q: Is it destiny that ordains?

M: Calling it destiny explains little. When it happens, you cannot say why it happens and you merely cover up your ignorance by calling it *karma* or Grace, or the Will of God.

Q: Krishnamurti says that Guru is not needed.

M: Somebody must tell you about the Supreme Reality and the way that leads to it. Krishnamurti is doing nothing else. In a way he is right — most of the so-called disciples do not trust their Gurus; they disobey them and finally abandon them. For such disciples it would have been infinitely better if they had no Guru at all and just looked within for guidance. To find a living Guru is a rare opportunity and a great responsibility. One should not treat these matters lightly. You people are out to buy yourself the heaven and you imagine that the Guru will supply it for a price. You seek to strike a bargain by offering little but asking much. You cheat nobody except yourselves.

Q: You were told by your Guru that you are the Supreme and you trusted him and acted on it. What gave you this trust?

M: Say, I was just reasonable. It would have been foolish to distrust him. What interest could he possibly have in misleading me?

Q: You told a questioner that we are the same, that we are equals. I cannot believe it. Since I do not believe it, of what use is your statement to me?

M: Your disbelief does not matter. My words are true and they will do their work. This is the beauty of noble company *(satsang)*.

Q: Just sitting near you can it be considered spiritual practice?

M: Of course. The river of life is flowing. Some of its water is here, but so much of it has already reached its goal. You know only the present. I see much further into the past and future, into what you are and what you can be. I cannot but see you as myself. It is in the very nature of love to see no difference.

Q: How can I come to see myself as you see me?

M: It is enough if you do not imagine yourself to be the body. It is the 'I-am-the body' idea that is so calamitous. It blinds you completely to your real nature. Even for a moment do not think that you are the body. Give yourself no name, no shape. In the darkness and the silence reality is found.

Q: Must not I think with some conviction that I am not the body? Where am I to find such conviction?

M: Behave as if you were fully convinced and the confidence will come. What is the use of mere words? A formula, a mental pattern will not help you. But unselfish action, free from all concern with the body and its interests will carry you into the very heart of Reality.

Q: Where am I to get the courage to act without conviction?

M: Love will give you the courage. When you meet somebody wholly admirable, love-worthy, sublime, your love and admiration will give you the urge to act nobly.

Q: Not everybody knows to admire the admirable. Most of the people are totally insensitive.

M: Life will make them appreciate. The very weight of accumulated experience will give them eyes to see. When you meet a worthy man, you will love and trust him and follow his advice. This is the role of the realized people — to set an example of perfection for others to admire and love. Beauty of life and character is a tremendous contribution to the common good.

Q: Must we not suffer to grow?

M: It is enough to know that there is suffering, that the world suffers. By themselves neither pleasure nor pain enlighten. Only understanding does. Once you have grasped the truth that the world is full of suffering, that to be born is a calamity, you will find the urge and the energy to go beyond it. Pleasure puts you to sleep and pain wakes you up. If you do not want to suffer, don't go to sleep. You cannot know yourself through bliss alone, for bliss is your very nature. You must face the opposite, what you are not, to find enlightenment.   ●●●

65

A Quiet Mind is All You Need

Questioner: I am not well. I feel rather weak. What am I to do?

Maharaj: Who is unwell, you or the body?

Q: My body, of course.

M: Yesterday you felt well. What felt well?

Q: The body.

M: You were glad when the body was well and you are sad when the body is unwell. Who is glad one day and sad the next?

Q: The mind.

M: And who knows the variable mind?

Q: The mind.

M: The mind is the knower. Who knows the knower?

Q: Does not the knower know itself?

M: The mind is discontinuous. Again and again it blanks out, like in sleep or swoon, or distraction. There must be something continuous to register discontinuity.

Q: The mind remembers. This stands for continuity.

M: Memory is always partial, unreliable and evanescent. It does not explain the strong sense of identity pervading consciousness, the sense 'I am'. Find out what is at the root of it.

Q: However deeply I look, I find only the mind. Your words 'beyond the mind' give me no clue.

M: While looking with the mind, you cannot go beyond it. To go beyond, you must look away from the mind and its contents.

Q: In what direction am I to look?

M: All directions are within the mind! I am not asking you to look in any particular direction. Just look away from all that happens in your mind and bring it to the feeling 'I am'. The 'I am' is not a direction. It is the negation of all direction. Ultimately even the 'I am' will have to go, for you need not keep on asserting what is obvious. Bringing the mind to the feeling 'I am' merely helps in turning the mind away from everything else.

Q: Where does it all lead me?

M: When the mind is kept away from its preoccupations, it becomes quiet. If you do not disturb this quiet and stay in it, you find that it is permeated with a light and a love you have never known; and yet you recognize it at once as your own nature. Once you have passed through this experience, you will never be the same man again; the unruly mind may break its peace and obliterate its vision; but it is bound to return, provided the effort is sustained; until the day when all bonds are broken, delusions and attachments end and life becomes supremely concentrated in the present.

Q: What difference does it make?

M: The mind is no more. There is only love in action.

Q: How shall I recognize this state when I reach it?

M: There will be no fear.

Q: Surrounded by a world full of mysteries and dangers, how can I remain unafraid?

M: Your own little body too is full of mysteries and dangers, yet you are not afraid of it, for you take it as your own. What you do not know is that the entire universe is your body and you need not be afraid of it. You may say you have two bodies; the personal and the universal. The personal comes and goes, the universal is always with you. The entire creation is your universal body. You are so blinded by what is personal, that you do not see the universal. This blindness will not end by itself — it must be undone skilfully and deliberately. When all illusions are understood and abandoned, you reach the error-free and perfect state in which all distinctions between the personal and the universal are no more.

Q: I am a person and therefore limited in space and time. I occupy little space and last but a few moments; I cannot even conceive myself to be eternal and all-pervading.

M: Nevertheless you *are*. As you dive deep into yourself in search of your true nature, you will discover that only your body is small and only your memory is short; while the vast ocean of life is yours.

Q: The very words 'I' and 'universal' are contradictory. One excludes the other.

M: They don't. The sense of identity pervades the universal. Search and you shall discover the Universal Person, who is yourself and infinitely more.

Anyhow, begin by realizing that the world is in you, not you in the world.

Q: How can it be? I am only a part of the world. How can the whole world be contained in the part, except by reflection, mirror like?

M: What you say is true. Your personal body is a part in which the whole is wonderfully reflected. But you have also a universal body. You cannot even say that you do not know it, because you see and experience it all the time. Only you call it 'the world' and are afraid of it.

Q: I feel I know my little body, while the other I do not know, except through science.

M: Your little body is full of mysteries and wonders which you do not know. There also science is your only guide. Both anatomy and astronomy describe you.

Q: Even If I accept your doctrine of the universal body as a working theory, in what way can I test it and of what use is it to me?

M: Knowing yourself as the dweller in both the bodies you will disown nothing. All the universe will be your concern; every living thing you will love and help most tenderly and wisely. There will be no clash of interests between you and others. All exploitation will cease absolutely. Your every action will be beneficial, every movement will be a blessing.

Q: It is all very tempting, but how am I to proceed to realize my universal being?

M: You have two ways: you can give your heart and mind to self-discovery, or you accept my words on trust and act accordingly. In other words, either you become totally self-concerned, or totally un-self-concerned. It is the word 'totally' that is important. You must be extreme to reach the Supreme.

Q: How can I aspire to such heights, small and limited as I am?

M: Realize yourself as the ocean of consciousness in which all happens. This is not difficult. A little of attentiveness, of close observation of oneself, and you will see that no event is outside your consciousness.

Q: The world is full of events which do not appear in my consciousness.

M: Even your body is full of events which do not appear in your consciousness. This does not prevent you from claiming your body to be your own. You know the world exactly as you know your body — through your senses. It is your mind that has separated the world outside your skin from the world inside and put them in opposition. This created fear and hatred and all the miseries of living.

Q: What I do not follow is what you say about going beyond consciousness. I understand the words, but I cannot visualize he experience. After all, you yourself have said that all experience is in consciousness.

M: You are right, there can be no experience beyond consciousness. Yet there is the experience of just *being*. There is a state beyond consciousness, which is not unconscious. Some call it super-consciousness, or pure consciousness, or supreme consciousness. It is pure awareness free from the subject-object nexus.

Q: I have studied Theosophy and I find nothing familiar in what you say. I admit Theosophy deals with manifestation only. It describes the universe and its inhabitants in great details. It admits many levels of matter and corresponding levels of experience, but it does not seem to go beyond. What you say goes beyond all experience. If it is not experienceable, why at all talk about it?

M: Consciousness is intermittent, full of gaps. Yet there is the continuity of identity. What is this sense of identity due to, if not to something beyond consciousness?

Q: If I am beyond the mind, how can I change myself?

M: Where is the need of changing anything? The mind is changing anyhow all the time. Look at your mind dispassionately; this is enough to calm it. When it is quiet, you can go beyond it. Do not keep it busy all the time. Stop it — and just *be*. If you give it rest, it will settle down and recover its purity and strength. Constant thinking makes it decay.

Q: If my true being is always with me, how is it that I am ignorant of it?

M: Because it is very subtle and your mind is gross, full of gross thoughts and feelings. Calm and clarify your mind and you will know yourself as you are.

Q: Do I need the mind to know myself?

M: You are beyond the mind, but you know with your mind. It is obvious that the extent, depth and character of knowledge depend on what instrument you use. Improve your instrument and your knowledge will improve.

Q: To know perfectly I need a perfect mind.

M: A quiet mind is all you need. All else will happen rightly, once your mind is quiet. As the sun on rising makes the world active, so does self-awareness affect changes in the mind. In the light of calm and steady self-awareness inner energies wake up and work miracles without any effort on your part.

Q: You mean to say that the greatest work is done by not working?

M: Exactly. Do understand that you are destined for enlightenment. Co-operate with your destiny, don't go against it, dont thwart it. Allow it to fulfil itself. All you have to do is to give attention to the obstacles created by the foolish mind.   ●●●

66

All Search for Happiness is Misery

Questioner: I have come from England and I am on my way to Madras. There I shall meet my father and we shall go by car overland to London. I am to study psychology, but I do not yet know what I shall do when I get my degree. I may try industrial psychology, or psychotherapy. My father is a general physician, I may follow the same line.

But this does not exhaust my interests. There are certain questions which do not change with time. I understand you have some answers to such questions and this made me come to see you.

Maharaj: I wonder whether I am the right man to answer your questions. I know little about things and people. I know only that I am, and that much you also know. We are equals.

Q: Of course I know that I am. But I do not know what it means.

M: What you take to be the 'I' in the 'I am' is not you. To know that you *are* is natural, to know what you are is the result of much investigation. You will have to explore the entire field of consciousness and go beyond it. For this you must find the right teacher and create the conditions needed for discovery. Generally speaking, there are two ways: external and internal. Either you live with somebody who knows the Truth and submit yourself entirely to his guiding and moulding influence, or you seek the inner guide and follow the inner light wherever it takes you. In both cases your personal desires and fears must be disregarded. You learn either by proximity or by investigation, the passive or the active way. You either let yourself be carried by the river of life and love represented by your Guru, or you make your own efforts, guided by your inner star. In both cases you must move on, you must be earnest. Rare are the people who are lucky to find somebody worthy of trust and love. Most of them must take the hard way, the way of intelligence and understanding, of discrimination and detachment *(viveka-vairagya)*. This is the way open to all.

Q: I am lucky to have come here: though I am leaving tomorrow, one talk with you may affect my entire life.

M: Yes, once you say 'I want to find Truth', all your life will be deeply affected by it. All your mental and physical habits, feelings and emotions, desires and fears, plans and decisions will undergo a most radical transformation.

Q: Once I have made up my mind to find The Reality, what do I do next?

M: It depends on your temperament. If you are earnest, whatever way you choose will take you to your goal. It is the earnestness that is the decisive factor.

Q: What is the source of earnestness?

M: It is the homing instinct, which makes the bird return to its nest and the fish to the mountain stream where it was born. The seed returns to the earth, when the fruit is ripe. Ripeness is all.

Q: And what will ripen me? Do I need experience?

M: You already have all the experience you need, otherwise you would not have come here. You need not gather any more, rather you must go beyond experience. Whatever effort you make, whatever method *(sadhana)* you follow, will merely generate more experience, but will not take you beyond. Nor will reading books help you. They will enrich your mind, but the person you are will remain intact. If you expect any benefits from your search, material, mental or spiritual, you have missed the point. Truth gives no advantage. It gives you no higher status, no power over others; all you get is truth and the freedom from the false.

Q: Surely truth gives you the power to help others.

M: This is mere imagination, however noble! In truth you do not help others, because there are no others. You divide people into noble and ignoble and you ask the noble to help the ignoble.

You separate, you evaluate, you judge and condemn — in the name of truth you destroy it. Your very desire to formulate truth denies it, because it cannot be contained in words. Truth can be expressed only by the denial of the false — in action. For this you must see the false as false *(viveka)* and reject it *(vairagya)*. Renunciation of the false is liberating and energizing. It lays open the road to perfection.

Q: When do I know that I have discovered truth?

M: When the idea 'this is true', 'that is true' does not arise. Truth does not assert itself, it is in the seeing of the false as false and rejecting it. It is useless to search for truth, when the mind is blind to the false. It must be purged of the false completely before truth can dawn on it.

Q: But what is false?

M: Surely, what has no being is false.

Q: What do you mean by having no being? The false is there, hard as a nail.

M: What contradicts itself, has no being. Or it has only momentary being, which comes to the same. For, what has a beginning and an end has no middle. It is hollow. It has only the name and shape given to it by the mind, but it has neither substance nor essence.

Q: If all that passes has no being, then the universe has no being either.

M: Who ever denies it? Of course the universe has no being.

Q: What has?

M: That which does not depend for its existence, which does not arise with the universe arising, nor set with the universe setting, which does not need any proof, but imparts reality to all it touches. It is the nature of the false that it appears real for a moment. One could say that the true becomes the father of the false. But the false is limited in time and space and is produced by circumstances.

Q· How am I to get rid of the false and secure the real?

M: To what purpose?

Q: In order to live a better, a more satisfactory life, integrated and happy.

M: Whatever is conceived by the mind must be false, for it is bound to be relative and limited. The real is inconceivable and cannot be harnessed to a purpose. It must be wanted for its own sake.

Q: How can I want the inconceivable?

M: What else is there worth wanting? Granted, the real cannot be wanted, as a thing is wanted. But you can see the unreal as unreal and discard it. It is the discarding the false that opens the way to the true.

Q: I understand, but how does it look in actual daily life?

M: Self-interest and self-concern are the focal points of the false. Your daily life vibrates between desire and fear. Watch it intently and you will see how the mind assumes innumerable names and shapes, like a river foaming between the boulders. Trace every action to its selfish motive and look at the motive intently till it dissolves.

Q: To live, one must look after oneself, one must earn money for oneself.

M: You need not earn for yourself, but you may have to — for a woman and a child. You may have to keep on working for the sake of others. Even just to keep alive can be a sacrifice. There is no need whatsoever to be selfish. Discard every self-seeking motive as soon as it is seen and you need not search for truth; truth will find you.

Q: There is a minimum of needs.

M: Were they not supplied since you were conceived? Give up the bondage of self-concern and be what you are — intelligence and love in action.

Q: But one must survive!

M: You can't help surviving! The real you is timeless and beyond birth and death. And the body will survive as long as it is needed. It is not important that it should live long. A full life is better than a long life.

Q: Who is to say what is a full life? It depends on my cultural background.

M: If you seek reality you must set yourself free of all back-grounds, of all cultures, of all patterns of thinking and feeling. Even the idea of being man or woman, or even human, should be discarded. The ocean of life contains all, not only humans. So, first of all abandon all self-identification, stop thinking of yourself as such-and-such, so-and-so, this or that. Abandon all self-concern, worry not about your welfare, material or spiritual, abandon every desire, gross or subtle, stop thinking of achievement of any kind. You are complete here and now, you need absolutely nothing.

It does not mean that you must be brainless and foolhardy, improvident or indifferent; only the basic anxiety for oneself must go. You need some food, clothing and shelter for you and yours, but this will not create problems as long as greed is not taken for a need. Live in tune with things as they are and not as they are imagined.

Q: What am I if not human?

M: That which makes you think that you are a human is not human. It is but a dimensionless point of consciousness, a con-scious nothing; all you can say about yourself is: 'I am.' You are pure being — awareness — bliss. To realize that is the end of all seeking. You come to it when you see all you think yourself to be as mere imagination and stand aloof in pure awareness of the transient as transient, imaginary as imaginary, unreal as unreal. It is not at all difficult, but detachment is needed. It is the cling-ing to the false that makes the true so difficult to see. Once you understand that the false needs time and what needs time is false, you are nearer the Reality, which is timeless, ever in the *now*. Eternity in time is mere repetitiveness, like the movement of a clock. It flows from the past into the future endlessly, an empty perpetuity. Reality is what makes the present so vital, so different from the past and future, which are merely mental. If you need time to achieve something, it must be false. The real is always with you; you need not wait to be what you *are*. Only you must not allow your mind to go out of yourself in search. When you want something, ask yourself: do I really need it? and if the answer is no, then just drop it.

Q: Must I not be happy? I may not need a thing, yet if it can make me happy, should I not grasp it?

M: Nothing can make you happier than you are. All search for happiness is misery and leads to more misery. The only happiness worth the name is the natural happiness of conscious being.

Q: Don't I need a lot of experience before I can reach such high level of awareness?

M: Experience leaves only memories behind and adds to the burden which is heavy enough. You need no more experiences. The past ones are sufficient. And if you feel you need more, look into the hearts of people around you. You will find a variety of experiences which you would not be able to go through in a thousand years. Learn from the sorrows of others and save yourself your own. It is not experience that you need, but the freedom from all experience. Don't be greedy for experience; you need none.

Q: Don't you pass through experiences yourself?

M: Things happen round me, but I take no part in them. An event becomes an experience only when I am emotionally involved. I am in a state which is complete, which seeks not to improve on itself. Of what use is experience to me?

Q: One needs knowledge, education.

M: To deal with things knowledge of things is needed. To deal with people, you need insight, sympathy. To deal with yourself you need nothing. Be what you are: conscious being and don't stray away from yourself.

Q: University education is most useful.

M: No doubt, it helps you to earn a living. But it does not teach you how to live. You are a student of psychology. It may help you in certain situations. But can you live by psychology? Life is worthy of the name only when it reflects Reality in action. No university will teach you how to live so that when the time of dying comes, you can say: I lived well, I do not need to live again. Most of us die wishing we could live again. So many mistakes committed, so much left undone. Most of the people vegetate, but do not live. They merely gather experience and enrich their memory But experience is the denial of Reality, which is neither sensory nor conceptual, neither of the body, nor of the mind, though it includes and transcends both.

Q: But experience is most useful. By experience you learn not to touch a flame.

M: I have told you already that knowledge is most useful in dealing with things. But it does not tell you how to deal with people and yourself, how to live a life. We are not talking of driving a car, or earning money. For this you need experience. But for being a light unto yourself material knowledge will not help you. You need something much more intimate and deeper than mediate knowledge, to be your self in the true sense of the word. Your outer life is unimportant. You can become a night watchman and live happily. It is what you are inwardly that matters. Your inner peace and joy you have to earn. It is much more difficult than earning money. No university can teach you to be yourself. The only way to learn is by practice. Right away begin to be yourself. Discard all you are not and go ever deeper. Just as a man digging a well discards what is not water, until he reaches the water-bearing strata, so must you discard what is not your own, till nothing is left which you can disown. You will find that what is left is nothing which the mind can hook on to You are not even a human being. You just *are* — a point of awareness, co-extensive with time and space and beyond both, the ultimate cause, itself uncaused. If you ask me: 'Who are you?' My answer would be: 'Nothing in particular. Yet, I am.'

Q: If you are nothing in particular, then you must be the universal.

M: What is to be universal — not as a concept, but as a way of life? Not to separate, not to oppose, but to understand and love whatever contacts you, is living universally. To be able to say truly: I am the world, the world is me, I am at home in the world, the world is my own. Every existence is my existence, every consciousness is my consciousness, every sorrow is my sorrow and every joy is my joy — this is universal life. Yet, my real being, and yours too, is beyond the universe and, therefore, beyond the categories of the particular and the universal. It is what it is, totally self-contained and independent.

Q: I find it hard to understand.

M: You must give yourself time to brood over these things. The old grooves must be erased in your brain, without forming new ones. You must realize yourself as the immovable, behind and beyond the movable, the silent witness of all that happens.

Q: Does it mean that I must give up all idea of an active life?

M: Not at all. There will be marriage, there will be children, there will be earning money to maintain a family; all this will happen in the natural course of events, for destiny must fulfil itself; you will go through it without resistance, facing tasks as they come, attentive and thorough, both in small things and big. But the general attitude will be of affectionate detachment, enormous goodwill, without expectation of return, constant giving without asking. In marriage you are neither the husband nor the wife; you are the love between the two. You are the clarity and kindness that makes everything orderly and happy. It may seem vague to you, but if you think a little, you will find that the mystical is most practical, for it makes your life creatively happy. Your consciousness is raised to a higher dimension, from which you see everything much clearer and with greater intensity. You realize that the person you became at birth and will cease to be at death is temporary and false. You are not the sensual, emotional and intellectual person, gripped by desires and fears. Find out your real being. What am I? is the fundamental question of all philosophy and psychology. Go into it deeply.   ●●●

67

Experience is not the Real Thing

Maharaj: The seeker is he who is in search of himself. Soon he discovers that his own body he cannot be. Once the conviction: 'I am not the body' becomes so well grounded that he can no longer feel, think and act for and on behalf of the body, he will easily discover that he is the universal being, knowing, acting, that in him and through him the entire universe is real, conscious and active. This is the heart of the problem. Either you are body-conscious and a slave of circumstances, or you are the universal consciousness itself — and in full control of every event.

Yet consciousness, individual or universal, is not my true abode; I am not in it, it is not mine, there is no 'me' in it. I am beyond, though it is not easy to explain how one can be neither conscious, nor unconscious, but just beyond. I cannot say that I am in God or I am God; God is the universal light and love, the universal witness: I am beyond the universal even.

Questioner: In that case you are without name and shape. What kind of being have you?

M: I am what I am, neither with form nor formless, neither conscious nor unconscious. I am outside all these categories.

Q: You are taking the *neti-neti* (not this, not this) approach.

M: You cannot find me by mere denial. I am as well everything, as nothing. Nor both, nor either. These definitions apply to the Lord of the Universe, not to me.

Q: Do you intend to convey that you are just nothing.

M: Oh, no! I am complete and perfect. I am the beingness of being, the knowingness of knowing, the fulness of happiness. You cannot reduce me to emptiness!

Q: If you are beyond words, what shall we talk about? Metaphysically speaking, what you say holds together; there is no inner contradiction. But there is no food for me in what you say. It is so completely beyond my urgent needs. When I ask for bread, you are giving jewels. They are beautiful, no doubt, but I am hungry.

M: It is not so. I am offering you exactly what you need — awakening. You are not hungry and you need no bread. You need cessation, relinquishing, disentanglement. What you believe you need is not what you need. Your real need I know, not you. You need to return to the state in which I am — your natural state. Anything else you may think of is an illusion and an obstacle. Believe me, you need nothing except to be what you are. You imagine you will increase your value by acquisition. It is like gold imagining that an addition of copper will improve it. Elimination and purification, renunciation of all that is foreign to your nature is enough. All else is vanity.

Q: It is easier said than done. A man comes to you with stomach-ache and you advise him to disgorge his stomach. Of course, without the mind there will be no problems. But the mind is there — most tangibly.

M: It is the mind that tells you that the mind is there. Don't be deceived. All the endless arguments about the mind are produced by the mind itself, for its own protection, continuation and expansion. It is the blank refusal to consider the convolutions and convulsions of the mind that can take you beyond it.

Q: Sir, I am an humble seeker. while you are the Supreme Reality itself. Now the seeker approaches the Supreme in order to be enlightened. What does the Supreme do?

M: Listen to what I keep on telling you and do not move away from it. Think of it all the time and of nothing else. Having reached that far, abandon all thoughts, not only of the world, but of yourself also. Stay beyond all thoughts, in silent being-awareness. It is not progress, for what you come to is already there in you, waiting for you.

Q: So you say I should try to stop thinking and stay steady in the idea: 'I am'.

M: Yes, and whatever thoughts come to you in connection with the 'I am', empty them of all meaning, pay them no attention.

Q: I happen to meet many young people coming from the West and I find that there is a basic difference when I compare them to the Indians. It looks as if their psyche *(antahkarana)* is different. Concepts like Self, Reality, pure mind, universal consciousness the Indian mind grasps easily. They ring familiar, they taste sweet. The Western mind does not respond, or just rejects them. It concretizes and wants to utilize at once in the service of accepted values. These values are often personal: health, well-being, prosperity; sometimes they are social — a better society, a happier life for all; all are connected with worldly problems, personal or impersonal. Another difficulty one comes across quite often in talking with the Westerners is that to them everything is experience — as they want to experience food, drink and women, art and travels, so do they want to experience Yoga, realization and liberation. To them it is just another experience, to be had for a price. They imagine such experience can be purchased and they bargain about the cost. When one Guru quotes too high, in terms of time and effort, they go to another, who offers instalment terms, apparently very easy, but beset with unfulfillable conditions. It is the old story of not thinking of the grey monkey when taking the medicine! In this case it is not thinking of the world, 'abandoning all self-hood', 'extinguishing every desire', 'becoming perfect celibates' etc. Naturally there is vast cheating going on all levels and the results are nil. Some Gurus in sheer desperation abandon all discipline, prescribe no conditions, advise effortlessness, naturalness, simply living in passive awareness, without any pattern of 'must' and 'must not'. And there are many disciples whose past experiences brought them to dislike themselves so badly that they just do not want to look at themselves. If they are not disgusted, they are bored. They have surfeit of self-knowledge, they want something else.

M: Let them not think of themselves, if they do not like it. Let them stay with a Guru, watch him, think of him. Soon they will experience a kind of bliss, quite new, never experienced before, except, maybe, in childhood. The experience is so unmistakably new, that it will attract their attention and create interest; once the interest is roused, orderly application will follow.

Q: These people are very critical and suspicious. They cannot be otherwise, having passed through much learning and much disappointment. On one hand they want experience, on the other they mistrust it. How to reach them, God alone knows!

M: True insight and love will reach them.

Q: When they have some spiritual experience, another difficulty arises. They complain that the experience does not last, that it comes and goes in a haphazard way. Having got hold of the lollypop, they want to suck it all the time.

M: Experience, however sublime, is not the real thing. By its very nature it comes and goes. Self-realization is not an acquisition. It is more of the nature of understanding. Once arrived at, it cannot be lost. On the other hand, consciousness is changeful, flowing, undergoing transformation from moment to moment. Do not hold on to consciousness and its contents. Consciousness held, ceases. To try to perpetuate a flash of insight, or a burst of happiness is destructive of what it wants to preserve. What comes must go. The permanent is beyond all comings and goings. Go to the root of all experience, to the sense of being. Beyond being and not-being lies the immensity of the real. Try and try again.

Q: To try one needs faith.

M: There must be the desire first. When the desire is strong, the willingness to try will come. You do not need assurance of success, when the desire is strong. You are ready to gamble.

Q: Strong desire, strong faith — it comes to the same. These people do not trust either their parents or the society, or even themselves. All they touched turned to ashes. Give them one experience absolutely genuine, indubitable, beyond the argumentations of the mind and they will follow you to the world's end.

M: But I am doing nothing else! Tirelessly I draw their attention to the one incontrovertible factor — that of being. Being needs no proofs — it proves all else. If only they go deeply into the fact of being and discover the vastness and the glory to which the 'I am' is the door, and cross the door and go beyond, their life will be full of happiness and light. Believe me, the effort needed is as nothing when compared with the discoveries arrived at.

Q: What you say is right. But these people have neither confidence nor patience. Even a short effort tires them. It is really pathetic to see them groping blindly and yet unable to hold on to the helping hand. They are such nice people fundamentally, but totally bewildered. I tell them: you cannot have truth on your own terms. You must accept the conditions. To this they answer: Some will accept the conditions and some will not. Acceptance or non-acceptance are superficial and accidental; reality is in all; there must be a way for all to tread — with no conditions attached.

M: There is such a way, open to all, on every level, in every walk of life. Everybody is aware of himself. The deepening and broadening of self-awareness is the royal way. Call it mindfulness, or witnessing, or just attention — it is for all. None is unripe for it and none can fail.

But, of course, you must not be merely alert. Your mindfulness must include the mind also. Witnessing is primarily awareness of consciousness and its movements.   ●●●

68

Seek the Source of Consciousness

Questioner: We were talking the other day about the ways of the modern Western mind and the difficulty it finds in submitting to the moral and intellectual discipline of the Vedanta. One of the obstacles lies in the young European's or American's pre-occupation with the disastrous condition of the world and the urgent need of setting it right.

They have no patience with people like you who preach personal improvement as a pre-condition for the betterment of the world. They say it is neither possible nor necessary. Humanity is ready for a change of systems — social, economic, political. A world-government, world-police, world-planning and the abolition of all physical and ideological barriers: this is enough, no personal transformation is needed. No doubt, people shape society, but society shapes people too. In a humane society people will be humane; besides, science provides the answer to many questions which formerly were in the domain of religion.

Maharaj: No doubt, striving for the improvement of the world is a most praiseworthy occupation. Done selflessly, it clarifies the mind and purifies the heart. But soon man will realize that he pursues a mirage. Local and temporary improvement is always possible and was achieved again and again under the influence of a great king or teacher; but it would soon come to an end, leaving humanity in a new cycle of misery. It is in the nature of all manifestation that the good and the bad follow each other and in equal measure. The true refuge is only in the unmanifested.

Q: Are you not advising escape?

M: On the contrary. The only way to renewal lies through destruction. You must melt down the old jewellery into formless gold before you can mould a new one. Only the people who have gone beyond the world can change the world. It never happened otherwise. The few whose impact was long lasting were all knowers of reality. Reach their level and then only talk of helping the world.

Q: It is not the rivers and mountains that we want to help, but the people.

M: There is nothing wrong with the world, but for the people who make it bad. Go and ask them to behave.

Q: Desire and fear make them behave as they do.

M: Exactly. As long as human behaviour is dominated by desire and fear, there is not much hope. And to know how to approach the people effectively, you must yourself be free of all desire and fear.

Q: Certain basic desires and fears are inevitable, such as are connected with food, sex and death.

M: These are needs and, as needs, they are easy to meet.

Q: Even death is a need?

M: Having lived a long and fruitful life you feel the need to die. Only when wrongly applied, desire and fear are destructive. By all means desire the right and fear the wrong. But when people desire what is wrong and fear what is right, they create chaos and despair.

Q: What is right and what is wrong?

M: Relatively, what causes suffering is wrong, what alleviates it is right. Absolutely, what brings you back to reality is right and what dims reality is wrong.

Q: When we talk of helping humanity, we mean a struggle against disorder and suffering.

M: You merely talk of helping. Have you ever helped, really helped, a single man? Have you ever put one soul beyond the need of further help? Can you give a man character, based on full realization of his duties and opportunities at least, if not on the insight into his true being? When you do not know what is good for yourself, how can you know what is good for others?

Q: The adequate supply of means of livelihood is good for all. You may be God himself, but you need a well-fed body to talk to us.

M: It is you that need my body to talk to you. I am not my body, nor do I need it. I am the witness only. I have no shape of my own.

You are so accustomed to think of yourselves as bodies having consciousness that you just cannot imagine consciousness as having bodies. Once you realize that bodily existence is but a state of mind, a movement in consciousness, that the ocean of consciousness is infinite and eternal, and that, when in touch with consciousness, you are the witness only, you will be able to withdraw beyond consciousness altogether.

Q: We are told there are many levels of existence. Do you exist and function on all the levels? While you are on earth, are you also in heaven *(swarga)*?

M: I am nowhere to be found! I am not a thing to be given a place among other things. All things are in me, but I am not among things. You are telling me about the superstructure while I am concerned with the foundations. The superstructures rise and fall, but the foundations last. I am not interested in the transient, while you talk of nothing else.

Q: Forgive me a strange question. If somebody with a razor-sharp sword would suddenly severe your head, what difference would it make to you?

M: None whatsoever. The body will lose its head, certain lines of communication will be cut, that is all. Two people talk to each other on the phone and the wire is cut. Nothing happens to the people, only they must look for some other means of communication. The Bhagavad Gita says: "the sword does not cut it". It is literally so. It is in the nature of consciousness to survive its vehicles. It is like fire. It burns up the fuel, but not itself. Just like a fire can outlast a mountain of fuel, so does consciousness survive innumerable bodies.

Q: The fuel affects the flame.

M: As long as it lasts. Change the nature of the fuel and the colour and appearance of the flame will change.

Now we are talking to each other. For this presence is
needed; unless we are present, we cannot talk. But presence
by itself is not enough. There must also be the desire to talk.

Above all, we want to remain conscious. We shall bear every
suffering and humiliation, but we shall rather remain conscious.
Unless we revolt against this craving for experience and let go
the manifested altogether, there can be no relief. We shall remain trapped.

Q: You say you are the silent witness and also you are beyond
consciousness. Is there no contradiction in it? If you are beyond
consciousness, what are you witnessing to?

M: I am conscious and unconscious, both conscious and unconscious, neither conscious nor unconscious — to all this I am
witness — but really there is no witness, because there is nothing to be a witness to. I am perfectly empty of all mental formations, void of mind — yet fully aware. This I try to express by saying that I am beyond the mind.

Q: How can I reach you then?

M: Be aware of being conscious and seek the source of consciousness. That is all. Very little can be conveyed in words. It is
the doing as I tell you that will bring light, not my telling you. The
means do not matter much; it is the desire, the urge, the earnestness that count.   ●●●

69

Transiency is Proof of Unreality

Questioner: My friend is a German and I was born in England from French parents. I am in India since over a year wandering from Ashram to Ashram.

Maharaj: Any spiritual practices *(sadhanas)*?

Q: Studies and meditation.

M: What did you meditate on?

Q: On what I read.

M: Good.

Q: What are you doing, sir?

M: Sitting.

Q: And what else?

M: Talking.

Q: What are you talking about?

M: Do you want a lecture? Better ask something that really touches you, so that you feel strongly about it. Unless you are emotionally involved, you may argue with me, but there will be no real understanding between us. If you say: 'nothing worries me, I have no problems', it is all right with me, we can keep quiet. But if something really touches you, then there is purpose in talking.

Shall I ask you? What is the purpose of your moving from place to place?

Q: To meet people, to try to understand them.

M: What people are you trying to understand? What exactly are you after?

Q: Integration.

M: If you want integration, you must know whom you want to integrate.

Q: By meeting people and watching them, one comes to know oneself also. It goes together.

M: It does not necessarily go together.

Q: One improves the other.

M: It does not work that way. The mirror reflects the image, but the image does not improve the mirror. You are neither the mirror nor the image in the mirror. Having perfected the mirror so that it reflects correctly, truly, you can turn the mirror round and see in it a true reflection of yourself — true as far as the mirror can reflect. But the reflection is not yourself — you are the seer of the reflection. Do understand it clearly — whatever you may perceive you are not what you perceive.

Q: I am the mirror and the world is the image?

M: You can see both the image and the mirror. You are neither. Who are you? Don't go by formulas. The answer is not in words. The nearest you can say in words is: I am what makes perception possible, the life beyond the experiencer and his experience.

Now, can you separate yourself both from the mirror and the image in the mirror and stand completely alone, all by yourself?

Q: No, I cannot.

M: How do you know that you cannot? There are so many things you are doing without knowing how to do it. You digest, you circulate your blood and lymph, you move your muscles — all without knowing how. In the same way, you perceive, you feel, you think without knowing the why and how of it. Similarly, you are yourself without knowing it. There is nothing wrong with you as the Self. It is what it is to perfection. It is the mirror that is not clear and true and, therefore, gives you false images. You need not correct yourself — only set right your idea of yourself. Learn to separate yourself from the image and the mirror, keep on remembering: I am neither the mind nor its ideas: do it patiently and with conviction and you will surely come to the direct vision of yourself as the source of being — knowing — loving, eternal, all-embracing all-pervading. You are the infinite focussed in a body. Now you see the body only. Try earnestly and you will come to see the infinite only.

Q: The experience of reality, when it comes, does it last?

M: All experience is necessarily transient. But the ground of all experience is immovable. Nothing that may be called an event will last. But some events purify the mind and some stain it. Moments of deep insight and all-embracing love purify the mind, while desires and tears, envies and anger, blind beliefs and intellectual arrogance pollute and dull the psyche.

Q: Is self-realization so important?

M: Without it you will be consumed by desires and fears, repeating themselves meaninglessly in endless suffering. Most of the people do not know that there can be an end to pain. But once they have heard the good news, obviously going beyond all strife and struggle is the most urgent task that can be. You know that you can be free and now it is up to you. Either you remain forever hungry and thirsty, longing, searching, grabbing, holding, ever losing and sorrowing, or go out wholeheartedly in search of the state of timeless perfection to which nothing can be added, from which nothing — taken away. In it all desires and fears are absent, not because they were given up, but because they have lost their meaning.

Q: So far I have been following you. Now, what am I expected to do?

M: There is nothing to do. Just *be*. Do nothing. *Be*. No climbing mountains and sitting in caves. I do not even say: 'be yourself', since you do not know yourself. Just *be*. Having seen that you are neither the 'outer' world of perceivables, nor the 'inner' world of thinkables, that you are neither body nor mind — just *be*.

Q: Surely, there are degrees of realization.

M: There are no steps to self-realization. There is nothing gradual about it. It happens suddenly and is irreversible. You rotate into a new dimension, seen from which the previous ones are mere abstractions. Just like on sunrise you see things as they are, so on self-realization you see everything as it is. The world of illusions is left behind.

Q: In the state of realization do things change? They become colourful and full of meaning?

M: The experience is quite right, but it is not the experience of reality *(sadanubhav)*, but of harmony *(satvanubhav)* of the universe.

Q: Nevertheless, there is progress.

M: There can be progress only in the preparation *(sadhana)*. Realization is sudden. The fruit ripens slowly, but falls suddenly and without return.

Q: I am physically and mentally at peace. What more do I need?

M: Yours may not be the ultimate state. You will recognize that you have returned to your natural state by a complete absence of all desire and fear. After all, at the root of all desire and fear is the feeling of not being what you are. Just as a dislocated joint pains only as long as it is out of shape, and is forgotten as soon as it is set right, so is all self-concern a symptom of mental distortion which disappears as soon as one is in the normal state.

Q: Yes, but what is the *sadhana* for achieving the natural state?

M: Hold on to the sense 'I am' to the exclusion of everything else. When thus the mind becomes completely silent, it shines with a new light and vibrates with new knowledge. It all comes spontaneously, you need only hold on to the 'I am'. Just like emerging from sleep or a state of rapture you feel rested and yet you cannot explain why and how you come to feel so well, in the same way on realization you feel complete, fulfilled, free from the pleasure-pain complex, and yet not always able to explain what happened, why and how. You can put it only in negative terms: 'Nothing is wrong with me any longer.' It is only by comparison with the past that you know that you are out of it. Otherwise — you are just yourself. Don't try to convey it to others. If you can, it is not the real thing. Be silent and watch it expressing itself in action.

Q: If you could tell me what I shall become, it may help me to watch over my development.

M: How can anybody tell you what you shall become when there is no becoming? You merely discover what you are. All moulding oneself to a pattern is a grievous waste of time. Think neither of the past nor of the future, just *be*.

Q: How can I just be? Changes are inevitable.

M: Changes are inevitable in the changeful, but you are not subject to them. You are the changeless background, against which changes are perceived.

Q: Everything changes, the background also changes. There is no need of a changeless background to notice changes. The self is momentary — it is merely the point where the past meets the future.

M: Of course the self based on memory is momentary. But such self demands unbroken continuity behind it. You know from experience that there are gaps when your self is forgotten. What brings it back to life? What wakes you up in the morning? There must be some constant factor bridging the gaps in consciousness. If you watch carefully you will find that even your daily consciousness is in flashes, with gaps intervening all the time. What is in the gaps? What can there be but your real being, that is timeless; mind and mindlessness are one to it.

Q: Is there any particular place you would advise me to go to for spiritual attainment?

M: The only proper place is within. The outer world neither can help nor hinder. No system, no pattern of action will take you to your goal. Give up all working for a future, concentrate totally on the *now*, be concerned only with your response to every movement of life as it happens.

Q: What is the cause of the urge to roam about?

M: There is no cause. You merely dream that you roam about. In a few years your stay in India will appear as a dream to you. You will dream some other dream at that time. Do realize that it is not you who moves from dream to dream, but the dreams flow before you and you are the immutable witness. No happening affects your real being — this is the absolute truth.

Q: Cannot I move about physically and keep steady inwardly?

M: You can, but what purpose does it serve? If you are earnest. you will find that in the end you will get fed up with roaming and regret the waste of energy and time. To find your self you need not take a single step.

Q: Is there any difference between the experience of the Self *(atman)* and of the Absolute *(brahman)*?

M: There can be no experience of the Absolute as it is beyond all experience. On the other hand, the self is the experiencing factor in every experience and thus, in a way, validates the multiplicity of experiences. The world may be full of things of great value, but if there is nobody to buy them, they have no price. The Absolute contains everything experienceable, but without the experiencer they are as nothing. That which makes the experience possible is the Absolute. That which makes it actual is the Self.

Q: Don't we reach the Absolute through a gradation of experiences? Beginning with the grossest, we end with the most sublime.

M: There can be no experience without desire for it. There can be gradation between desires, but between the most sublime desire and the freedom from all desire there is an abyss which must be crossed. The unreal may look real, but it is transient. The real is not afraid of time.

Q: Is not the unreal the expression of the real?

M: How can it be? It is like saying that truth expresses itself in dreams. To the real the unreal is not. It appears to be real only because you believe in it. Doubt it, and it ceases. When you are in love with somebody, you give it reality — you imagine your love to be all-powerful and everlasting. When it comes to an end, you say: 'I thought it was real, but it wasn't'. Transiency is the best proof of unreality. What is limited in time, and space and applicable to one person only, is not real. The real is for all and forever.

Above everything else you cherish yourself. You would accept nothing in exchange for your existence. The desire to *be* is the strongest of all desires and will go only on the realization of your true nature.

Q: Even in the unreal there is a touch of reality.

M: Yes, the reality you impart to it by taking it to be real. Having convinced yourself, you are bound by your conviction. When the sun shines, colours appear. When it sets, they disappear. Where are the colours without the light?

Q: This is thinking in terms of duality.

M: All thinking is in duality. In identity no thought survives. ●●●

70

God is the End of All Desire and Knowledge

Maharaj: Where are you coming from? What have you come for?

Questioner: I come from America and my friend is from the Republic of Ireland. I came about six months ago and I was travelling from Ashram to Ashram. My friend came on his own.

M: What have you seen?

Q: I have been at Sri Ramanashram and also I have visited Rishikesh. Can I ask you what is your opinion of Sri Ramana Maharshi?

M: We are both in the same ancient state. But what do you know of Maharshi? You take yourself to be a name and a body, so all you perceive are names and bodies.

Q: Were you to meet the Maharshi, what would happen?

M: Probably we would feel quite happy. We may even exchange a few words.

Q: But would he recognize you as a liberated man?

M: Of course. As a man recognizes a man, so a *gnani* recognizes a *gnani*. You cannot appreciate what you have not experienced. You are what you think yourself to be, but you cannot think yourself to be what you have not experienced.

Q: To become an engineer I must learn engineering. To become God, what must I learn?

M: You must unlearn everything. God is the end of all desire and knowledge.

Q: You mean to say that I become God merely by giving up the desire to become God?

M: All desires must be given up, because by desiring you take the shape of your desires. When no desires remain, you revert to your natural state.

Q: How do I come to know that I have achieved perfection?

M: You can not know perfection, you can know only imperfection. For knowledge to be, there must be separation and disharmony. You can know what you are not, but you can not know your real being. You can be only what you are. The entire approach is through understanding, which is in the seeing of the false as false. But to understand, you must observe from outside.

Q: The Vedantic concept of Maya, illusion, applies to the manifested. Therefore our knowledge of the manifested is unreliable. But we should be able to trust our knowledge of the unmanifested.

M: There can be no knowledge of the unmanifested. The potential is unknowable. Only the actual can be known.

Q: Why should the knower remain unknown?

M: The knower knows the known. Do you know the knower? Who is the knower of the knower? You want to know the unmanifested. Can you say you know the manifested?

Q: I know things and ideas and their relations. It is the sum total of all my experiences.

M: All?

Q: Well, all actual experiences. I admit I cannot know what did not happen.

M: If the manifested is the sum total of all actual experiences, including their experiencers, how much of the total do you know? A very small part indeed. And what is the little you know?

Q: Some sensory experiences as related to myself.

M: Not even that. You only know that you react. Who reacts and to what, you do not know. You know on contact that you exist — 'I am'. The 'I am this', 'I am that' are imaginary.

Q: I know the manifested because I participate in it. I admit, my part in it is very small, yet it is as real as the totality of it. And what is more important, I give it meaning. Without me the world is dark and silent.

M: A firefly illumining the world! You don't give meaning to the world, you find it. Dive deep into yourself and find the source from where all meaning flows. Surely it is not the superficial mind that can give meaning.

Q: What makes me limited and superficial?

M: The total is open and available, but you will not take it. You are attached to the little person you think yourself to be. Your desires are narrow, your ambitions — petty. After all, without a centre of perception where would be the manifested? Unperceived, the manifested is as good as the unmanifested. And you are the perceiving point, the non-dimensional source of all dimensions. Know yourself as the total.

Q: How can a point contain a universe?

M: There is enough space in a point for an infinity of universes. There is no lack of capacity. Self-limitation is the only problem. But you cannot run away from yourself. However far you go, you come back to yourself and to the need of understanding this point, which is as nothing and yet the source of everything.

Q: I came to India in search of a Yoga teacher. I am still in search.

M: What kind of Yoga do you want to practise, the Yoga of getting, or the Yoga of giving up?

Q: Don't they come to the same in the end?

M: How can they? One enslaves, the other liberates. The motive matters supremely. Freedom comes through renunciation. All possession is bondage.

Q: What I have the strength and the courage to hold on to, why should I give up? And if I have not the strength, how can I give up? I do not understand this need of giving up. When I want something, why should I not pursue it? Renunciation is for the weak.

M: If you do not have the wisdom and the strength to give up, just look at your possessions. Your mere looking will burn them up. If you can stand outside your mind, you will soon find that total renunciation of possessions and desires is the most obviously reasonable thing to do.

You create the world and then worry about it. Becoming selfish makes you weak. If you think you have the strength and courage to desire, it is because you are young and inexperienced. Invariably the object of desire destroys the means of acquiring it and then itself withers away. It is all for the best, because it teaches you to shun desire like poison.

Q: How am I to practise desirelessness?

M: No need of practice. No need of any acts of renunciation. Just turn your mind away, that is all. Desire is merely the fixation of the mind on an idea. Get it out of its groove by denying it attention.

Q: That is all?

M: Yes, that is all. Whatever may be the desire or fear, don't dwell upon it. Try and see for yourself. Here and there you may forget, it does not matter. Go back to your attempts till the brushing away of every desire and fear, of every reaction becomes automatic.

Q: How can one live without emotions?

M: You can have all the emotions you want, but beware of reactions, of induced emotions. Be entirely self-determined and ruled from within, not from without.

Merely giving up a thing to secure a better one is not true relinquishment. Give it up because you see its valuelessness. As you keep on giving up, you will find that you grow spontaneously in intelligence and power and inexhaustible love and joy,

Q: Why so much insistence on relinquishing all desires and fears? Are they not natural?

M: They are not. They are entirely mind-made. You have to give up everything to know that you need nothing, not even your body. Your needs are unreal and your efforts are meaningless. You imagine that your possessions protect you. In reality they make you vulnerable. Realize yourself as away from all that can be pointed at as 'this' or 'that'. You are unreachable by any sensory experience or verbal construction. Turn away from them. Refuse to impersonate.

Q: After I have heard you, what am I to do?

M: Only hearing will not help you much. You must keep it in mind and ponder over it and try to understand the state of mind which makes me say what I say. I speak from truth; stretch your hand and take it. You are not what you think yourself to be, I assure you. The image you have of yourself is made up from memories and is purely accidental.

Q: What I am is the result of my *karma*.

M: What you appear to be, you are not. *Karma* is only a word you have learnt to repeat. You have never been, nor shall ever be a person. Refuse to consider yourself as one. But as long as you do not even doubt yourself to be a Mr. So-and-so, there is little hope. When you refuse to open your eyes, what can you be shown?

Q: I imagine *karma* to be a mysterious power that urges me towards perfection.

M: That's what people told you. You are already perfect, here and now. The perfectible is not you. You imagine yourself to be what you are not — stop it. It is the cessation that is important, not what you are going to stop.

Q: Did not *karma* compel me to become what I am?

M: Nothing compels. You are as you believe yourself to be. Stop believing.

Q: Here you are sitting on your seat and talking to me. What compels you is your *karma*.

M: Nothing compels me. I do what needs doing. But you do so many unnecessary things. It is your refusal to examine that creates *karma*. It is the indifference to your own suffering that perpetuates it.

Q: Yes, it is true. What can put an end to this indifference?

M: The urge must come from within as a wave of detachment, or compassion.

Q: Could I meet this urge half way?

M: Of course. See your own condition, see the condition of the world.

Q: We were told about *karma* and reincarnation, evolution and Yoga, masters and disciples. What are we to do with all this knowledge?

M: Leave it all behind you. Forget it. Go forth, unburdened with ideas and beliefs. Abandon all verbal structures, all relative truth, all tangible objectives. The Absolute can be reached by absolute devotion only. Don't be half-hearted.

Q: I must begin with some absolute truth. Is there any?

M: Yes, there is, the feeling: 'I am'. Begin with that.

Q: Nothing else is true?

M: All else is neither true nor false. It seems real when it appears, it disappears when it is denied. A transient thing is a mystery.

Q: I thought the real is the mystery.

M: How can it be? The real is simple, open, clear and kind, beautiful and joyous. It is completely free of contradictions. It is ever new, ever fresh, endlessly creative. Being and non-being, life and death, all distinctions merge in it.

Q: I can admit that all is false. But, does it make my mind non-existent?

M: The mind is what it thinks. To make it true, think true.

Q: If the shape of things is mere appearance, what are they in reality?

M: In reality there is only perception. The perceiver and the perceived are conceptual, the fact of perceiving is actual.

Q: Where does the Absolute come in?

M: The Absolute is the birthplace of perceiving. It makes perception possible.

But too much analysis leads you nowhere. There is in you the core of being which is beyond analysis, beyond the mind. You can know it in action only. Express it in daily life and its light will grow ever brighter.

The legitimate function of the mind is to tell you what is not. But if you want positive knowledge, you must go beyond the mind.

Q: In all the universe is there one single thing of value?

M: Yes, the power of love.   ●●●

71

In Self-awareness you Learn about Yourself

Questioner: It is our repeated experience that the disciples do much harm to their Gurus. They make plans and carry them out, without considering the Guru's wishes. In the end there is only endless worry for the Guru and bitterness for his disciples.

Maharaj: Yes, it does happen.

Q: Who compels the Guru to submit to these indignities?

M: The Guru is basically without desire. He sees what happens, but feels no urge to interfere. He makes no choices, takes no decisions. As pure witness, he watches what is going on and remains unaffected.

Q: But his work suffers.

M: Victory is always his — in the end. He knows that if the disciples do not learn from his words, they will learn from their own mistakes. Inwardly he remains quiet and silent. He has no sense of being a separate person. The entire universe is his own, including his disciples with their petty plans. Nothing in particular affects him, or, which comes to the same, the entire universe affects him in equal measure.

Q: Is there no such thing as the Guru's grace?

M: His grace is constant and universal. It is not given to one and denied to another.

Q: How does it affect me personally?

M: It is by The Guru's grace that your mind is engaged in search for truth and it is by his grace that you will find it. It works unwaringly towards your ultimate good. And it is for all.

Q: Some disciples are ready, mature, and some are not. Must not the Guru exercise choice and make decisions?

M: The Guru knows the Ultimate and relentlessly propels the disciple towards it. The disciple is full of obstacles, which he himself must overcome. The Guru is not very much concerned with the superficialities of the disciple's life. It is like gravitation The fruit must fall — when no longer held back.

Q: If the disciple does not know the goal, how can he make out the obstacles?

M: The goal is shown by the Guru, obstacles are discovered by the disciple. The Guru has no preferences, but those who have obstacles to overcome seem to be lagging behind.

In reality the disciple is not different from the Guru. He is the same dimensionless centre of perception and love in action. It is only his imagination and self-identification with the imagined, that encloses him and converts him into a person. The Guru is concerned little with the person. His attention is on the inner watcher. It is the task of the watcher to understand and thereby eliminate the person. While there is grace on one side, there must be dedication to the task on the other.

Q: But the person does not want to be eliminated.

M: The person is merely the result of a misunderstanding. In reality, there is no such thing. Feelings, thoughts and actions race before the watcher in endless succession, leaving traces in the brain and creating an illusion of continuity. A reflection of the watcher in the mind creates the sense of 'I' and the person acquires an apparently independent existence. In reality there is no person, only the watcher identifying himself with the 'I' and the 'mine'. The teacher tells the watcher: you are not this, there is nothing of yours in this, except the little point of 'I am', which is the bridge between the watcher and his dream. 'I am this, I am that' is dream, while pure 'I am' has the stamp of reality on it. You have tasted so many things — all came to naught. Only the sense 'I am' persisted — unchanged. Stay with the changeless among the changeful, until you are able to go beyond.

Q: When will it happen?

M: It will happen as soon as you remove the obstacles.

Q: Which obstacles?

M: Desire for the false and fear of the true. You, as the person, imagine that the Guru is interested in you as a person. Not at all. To him you are a nuisance and a hindrance to be done away with. He actually aims at your elimination as a factor in consciousness.

Q: If I am eliminated, what will remain?

M: Nothing will remain, all will remain. The sense of identity will remain, but no longer identification with a particular body. Being — awareness — love will shine in full splendour. Liberation is never of the person, it is always from the person.

Q: And no trace remains of the person?

M: A vague memory remains, like the memory of a dream, or early childhood. After all, what is there to remember? A flow of events, mostly accidental and meaningless. A sequence of desires and fears and inane blunders. Is there anything worth remembering? The person is but a shell imprisoning you. Break the shell.

Q: Whom are you asking to break the shell? Who is to break the shell?

M: Break the bonds of memory and self-identification and the shell will break by itself. There is a centre that imparts reality to whatever it perceives. All you need is to understand that you are the source of reality, that you give reality instead of getting it, that you need no support and no confirmation. Things are as they are, because you accept them as they are. Stop accepting them and they will dissolve. Whatever you think about with desire or fear appears before you as real. Look at it without desire or fear and it does lose substance. Pleasure and pain are momentary. It is simpler and easier to disregard them than to act on them.

Q: If all things come to an end, why did they appear at all?

M: Creation is in the very nature of consciousness. Consciousness causes appearances. Reality is beyond consciousness.

Q: While we are conscious of appearances, how is it that we are not conscious that these are mere appearances?

M: The mind covers up reality, without knowing it. To know the nature of the mind, you need intelligence, the capacity to look at the mind in silent and dispassionate awareness.

Q: If I am of the nature of all-pervading consciousness, how could ignorance and illusion happen to me?

M: Neither ignorance nor illusion ever happened to you. Find the self to which you ascribe ignorance and illusion and your question will be answered. You talk as if you know the self and see it to be under the sway of ignorance and illusion. But, in fact, you do not know the self, nor are you aware of ignorance. By all means become aware — this will bring you to the self and you will realize that there is neither ignorance nor delusion in it. It is like saying: if there is sun, how can darkness be? As under a stone there will be darkness, however strong the sunlight, so in the shadow of the 'I-am-the-body' consciousness there must be ignorance and illusion.

Q: But why did the body consciousness come into being?

M: Don't ask 'why', ask 'how'. It is in the nature of creative imagination to identify itself with its creations. You can stop it any moment by switching off attention. Or through investigation.

Q: Does creation come before investigation?

M: First you create a world, then the 'I am' becomes a person, who is not happy for various reasons. He goes out in search of happiness, meets a Guru who tells him: 'You are not a person, find who you are'. He does it and goes beyond.

Q: Why did he not do it at the very start?

M: It did not occur to him. He needed somebody to tell him.

Q: Was that enough?

M: It was enough.

Q: Why does it not work in my case?

M: You do not trust me.

Q: Why is my faith weak?

M: Desires and fears have dulled your mind. It needs some scrubbing.

Q. How can I clear my mind?

M: By watching it relentlessly. Inattention obscures, attention clarifies.

Q: Why do the Indian teachers advocate inactivity?

M: Most of people's activities are valueless, if not outright destructive. Dominated by desire and fear, they can do nothing good. Ceasing to do evil precedes beginning to do good. Hence the need for stopping all activities for a time, to investigate one's urges and their motives, see all that is false in one's life, purge the mind of all evil and then only restart work, beginning with one's obvious duties. Of course, if you have a chance to help somebody, by all means do it and promptly too, don't keep him waiting till you are perfect. But do not become a professional do-gooder.

Q: I do not feel there are too many do-gooders among disciples. Most of those I met are too absorbed in their own petty conflicts. They have no heart for others.

M: Such self-centeredness is temporary. Be patient with such people. For so many years they gave attention to everything but themselves. Let them turn to themselves for a change.

Q: What are the fruits of self-awareness?

M: You grow more intelligent. In awareness you learn. In self-awareness you learn about yourself. Of course, you can only learn what you are not. To know what you are, you must go beyond the mind.

Q: Is not awareness beyond the mind?

M: Awareness is the point at which the mind reaches out beyond itself into reality. In awareness you seek not what pleases, but what is true.

Q: I find that awareness brings about a state of inner silence, a state of psychic void.

M: It is all right as it goes, but it is not enough. Have you felt the all-embracing emptiness in which the universe swims like a cloud in the blue sky?

Q: Sir, let me first come to know well my own inner space.

M: Destroy the wall that separates, the 'I-am-the-body' idea, and the inner and the outer will become one.

Q: Am I to die?

M: Physical destruction is meaningless. It is the clinging to sensate life that binds you. If you could experience the inner void fully, the explosion into the totality would be near.

Q: My own spiritual experience has its seasons. Sometimes I feel glorious, then again I am down. I am like a lift boy — going up, going down, going up, going down.

M: All changes in consciousness are due to the 'I-am-the-body' idea. Divested of this idea the mind becomes steady. There is pure being, free of experiencing anything in particular. But to realize it you must do what your teacher tells you. Mere listening, even memorizing, is not enough. If you do not struggle hard to apply every word of it in your daily life, don't complain that you made no progress. All real progress is irreversible. Ups and downs merely show that the teaching has not been taken to heart and translated into action fully.

Q: The other day you told us that there is no such thing as *karma*. Yet we see that every thing has a cause and the sum total of all the causes may be called *karma*.

M: As long as you believe yourself to be a body, you will ascribe causes to everything. I do not say things have no causes.

Each thing has innumerable causes. It is as it is, because the world is as it is. Every cause in its ramifications covers the universe.

When you realize that you are absolutely free to be what you consent to be, that you are what you appear to be because of ignorance or indifference, you are free to revolt and change. You allow yourself to be what you are not. You are looking for the causes of being what you are not! It is a futile search. There are no causes, but your ignorance of your real being, which is perfect and beyond all causation. For whatever happens, all the universe is responsible and you are the source of the universe.

Q: I know nothing about being the cause of the universe.

M: Because you do not investigate. Enquire, search within and you will know.

Q: How can a speck like me create the vast universe?

M: When you are infected with the 'I-am-the body' virus, a whole universe springs into being. But when you have had enough of it, you cherish some fanciful ideas about liberation and pursue lines of action totally futile. You concentrate, you meditate, you torture your mind and body, you do all sorts of unnecessary things, but you miss the essential which is the elimination of the person.

Q: In the beginning we may have to pray and meditate for some time before we are ready for self-enquiry.

M: If you believe so, go on. To me, all delay is a waste of time. You can skip all the preparation and go directly for the ultimate search within. Of all the Yogas it is the simplest and the shortest.   ●●●

72

What is Pure, Unalloyed, Unattached is Real

Maharaj: You are back in India! Where have you been, what have you seen?

Questioner: I come from Switzerland. I stayed there with a remarkable man who claims to have realized. He has done many Yogas in his past and had many experiences that passed away. Now he claims no special abilities, nor knowledge; the only unusual thing about him is connected with sensations; he is unable to separate the seer from the seen. For instance, when he sees a car rushing at him, he does not know whether the car is rushing at him, or he at a car. He seems to be both at the same time, the seer and the seen. They become one. Whatever he sees, he sees himself. When I asked him some Vedantic questions he said: 'I really cannot answer. I do not know. All I know is this strange identity with whatever I perceive. You know, I expected anything but this.'

He is on the whole a humble man; he makes no disciples and in no way puts himself on a pedestal. He is willing to talk about his strange condition, but that is all.

M: Now he knows what he knows. All else is over. At least he still talks. Soon he may cease talking.

Q: What will he do then?

M: Immobility and silence are not inactive. The flower fills the space with perfume, the candle — with light. They do nothing yet they change everything by their mere presence. You can photograph the candle, but not its light. You can know the man, his name and appearance, but not his influence. His very presence is action.

Q: Is it not natural to be active?

M: Everybody wants to be active, but where do his actions originate? There is no central point: each action begets another, meaninglessly and painfully, in endless succession. The alternation of work and pause is not there. First find the immutable centre where all movement takes birth. Just like a wheel turns round an axle, so must you be always at the axle in the centre and not whirling at the periphery.

Q: How do I go about it in practice?

M: Whenever a thought or emotion of desire or fear comes to your mind, just turn away from it.

Q: By suppressing my thoughts and feelings I shall provoke a reaction.

M: I am not talking of suppression. Just refuse attention.

Q: Must I not use effort to arrest the movements of the mind?

M: It has nothing to do with effort. Just turn away, look between the thoughts, rather than at the thoughts. When you happen to walk in a crowd, you do not fight every man you meet — you just find your way between.

Q: If I use my will to control the mind, it only strengthens the ego.

M: Of course. When you fight, you invite a fight. But when you do not resist, you meet with no resistance. When you refuse to play the game, you are out of it.

Q: How long will it take me to get free of the mind?

M: It may take a thousand years, but really no time is required. All you need is to be in dead earnest. Here the will is the deed. If you are sincere, you have it. After all, it is a matter of attitude. Nothing stops you from being a gnani here and now, except fear. You are afraid of being impersonal, of impersonal being. It is all quite simple. Turn away from your desires and fears and from the thoughts they create and you are at once in your natural state.

Q: No question of reconditioning, changing, or eliminating the mind?

M: Absolutely none. Leave your mind alone, that is all. Don't go along with it. After all, there is no such thing as mind apart from thoughts which come and go obeying their own laws, not yours. They dominate you only because you are interested in them. It is exactly as Christ said 'Resist not evil'. By resisting evil you merely strengthen it.

Q: Yes, I see now. All I have to do is to deny existence to evil. Then it fades away. But does it not boil down to some kind of auto-suggestion?

M: The auto-suggestion is in full swing now, when you think yourself to be a person, caught between good and evil. What I am asking you to do is to put an end to it, to wake up and see things as they are.

About your stay in Switzerland with that strange friend of yours: what did you gain in his company?

Q: Nothing absolutely. His experience did not affect me at all. One thing I have understood: there is nothing to search for. Wherever I may go, nothing waits for me at the end of the journey. Discovery is not the result of transportation.

M: Yes, you are quite apart from anything that can be gained or lost.

Q: Do you call it *vairagya*, relinquishment, renunciation?

M: There is nothing to renounce. Enough if you stop acquiring. To give you must have, and to have you must take. Better don't take. It is simpler than to practise renunciation, which leads to a dangerous form of 'spiritual' pride.

All this weighing, selecting, choosing, exchanging — it is all shopping in some 'spiritual' market. What is your business there? What deal are you out to strike? When you are not out for business, what is the use of this endless anxiety of choice? Restlessness takes you nowhere. Something prevents you from seeing that there is nothing you need. Find it out and see its falseness. It is like having swallowed some poison and suffering from unquenchable craving for water. Instead of drinking beyond all measure, why not eliminate the poison and be free of this burning thirst?

Q: I shall have to eliminate the ego!

M: The sense 'I am a person in time and space' is the poison. In a way, time itself is the poison. In time all things come to an end and new are born, to be devoured in their turn. Do not identify yourself with time, do not ask anxiously: 'what next, what next?' Step out of time and see it devour the world. Say: 'Well, it is in the nature of time to put an end to everything. Let it be. It does not concern me. I am not combustible, nor do I need to collect fuel'.

Q: Can the witness be without the things to witness?

M: There is always something to witness. If not a thing, then its absence. Witnessing is natural and no problem. The problem is excessive interest, leading to self-identification. Whatever you are engrossed in you take to be real.

Q: Is the 'I am' real or unreal? Is the 'I am' the witness? Is the witness real or unreal?

M: What is pure, unalloyed, unattached, is real. What is tainted, mixed up, dependent and transient is unreal. Do not be misled by words — one word may convey several and even contradictory meanings. The 'I am' that pursues the pleasant and shuns the unpleasant is false; the 'I am' that sees pleasure and pain as inseparable sees rightly. The witness that is enmeshed in what he perceives is the person; the witness who stands aloof, unmoved and untouched, is the watch-tower of the real, the point at which awareness, inherent in the unmanifested, contacts the manifested. There can be no universe without the witness, there can be no witness without the universe.

Q: Time consumes the world. Who is the witness of time?

M: He who is beyond time — the Un-nameable. A glowing ember, moved round and round quickly enough, appears as a glowing circle. When the movement ceases, the ember remains. Similarly, the 'I am' in movement creates the world. The 'I am' at peace becomes the Absolute. You are like a man with an electric torch walking through a gallery. You can see only what is within the beam. The rest is in darkness.

Q: If I project the world, I should be able to change it.

M: Of course, you can. But you must cease identifying yourself with it and go beyond. Then you have the power to destroy and re-create.

Q: All I want is to be free.

M: You must know two things: What are you to be free from and what keeps you bound.

Q: Why do you want to annihilate the universe?

M: I am not concerned with the universe. Let it be or not be. It is enough if I know myself.

Q: If you are beyond the world, then you are of no use to the world.

M: Pity the self that is, not the world that is not! Engrossed in a dream you have forgotten your true self.

Q: Without the world there is no place for love.

M: Quite so. All these attributes; being, consciousness, love and beauty are reflections of the real in the world. No real — no reflection.

Q: The world is full of desirable things and people. How can I imagine it non-existent?

M: Leave the desirables to those who desire. Change the current of your desire from taking to giving. The passion for giving, for sharing, will naturally wash the idea of an external world out of your mind, and of giving as well. Only the pure radiance of love will remain, beyond giving and receiving.

Q: In love there must be duality, the lover and the beloved.

M: In love there is not the one even, how can there be two? Love is the refusal to separate, to make distinctions. Before you can think of unity, you must first create duality. When you truly love, you do not say: 'I love you'; where there is mentation, there is duality.

Q: What is it that brings me again and again to India? It cannot be only the comparative cheapness of life here? Nor the colourfulness and variety of impressions. There must be some more important factor.

M: There is also the spiritual aspect. The division between the outer and the inner is less in India. It is easier here to express the inner in the outer. Integration is easier. Society is not so oppressive.

Q: Yes, in the West it is all *tamas* and *rajas*. In India there is more of *sattva,* of harmony and balance.

M: Can't you go beyond the *gunas?* Why chose the *sattva?* Be what you are, wherever you are and worry not about *gunas.*

Q: I have not the strength.

M: It merely shows that you have gained little in India. What you truly have you cannot lose. Were you well-grounded in your self, change of place would not affect it.

Q: In India spiritual life is easy. It is not so in the West. One has to conform to environment to a much greater extent.

M: Why don't you create your own environment? The world has only as much power over you as you give it. Rebel. Go beyond duality, make no difference between east and west.

Q: What can one do when one finds oneself in a very unspiritual environment?

M: Do nothing. Be yourself. Stay out. Look beyond.

Q: There may be clashes at home. Parents rarely understand.

M: When you know your true being, you have no problems. You may please your parents or not, marry or not, make a lot of money or not; it is all the same to you. Just act according to circumstances, yet in close touch with the facts, with the reality in every situation.

Q: Is it not a very high state?

M: Oh no, it is the normal state. You call it high because you are afraid of it. First be free from fear. See that there is nothing to be afraid of. Fearlessness is the door to the Supreme.

Q: No amount of effort can make me fearless.

M: Fearlessness comes by itself, when you see that there is nothing to be afraid of. When you walk in a crowded street, you just bypass people. Some you see, some you just glance at, but you do not stop. It is the stopping that creates the bottleneck. Keep moving! Disregard names and shapes, don't be attached to them; your attachment is your bondage.

Q: What should I do when a man slaps me on my face?

M: You will react according to your character, inborn or acquired.

Q: Is it inevitable? Am I, is the world, condemned to remain as we are?

M: A jeweller who wants to re-fashion an ornament, first melts it down to shapeless gold. Similarly, one must return to one's original state before a new name and form can emerge. Death is essential for renewal.

Q: You are always stressing the need of going beyond, of aloofness, of solitude. You hardly ever use the words 'right' and wrong'. Why is it so?

M: It is right to be oneself, it is wrong not to be. All else is conditional. You are eager to separate right from wrong, because you need some basis for action. You are always after doing something or other. But, personally motivated action, based on some scale of values, aiming at some result is worse than inaction, for its fruits are always bitter.

Q: Are awareness and love one and the same?

M: Of course. Awareness is dynamic, love is being. Awareness is love in action. By itself the mind can actualize any number of possibilities, but unless they are prompted by love, they are valueless. Love precedes creation. Without it there is only chaos.

Q: Where is the action in awareness?

M: You are so incurably operational! Unless there is movement, restlessness, turmoil, you do not call it action. Chaos is movement for movement's sake. True action does not displace; it transforms. A change of place is mere transportation; a change of heart is action. Just remember, nothing perceivable is real. Activity is not action. Action is hidden, unknown, unknowable. You can only know the fruit.

Q: Is not God the all-doer?

M: Why do you bring in an outer doer? The world recreates itself out of itself. It is an endless process, the transitory begetting the transitory. It is your ego that makes you think that there must be a doer. You create a God to your own image, however dismal the image. Through the film of your mind you project a world and also a God to give it cause and purpose. It is all imagination — step out of it.

Q: How difficult it is to see the world as purely mental! The tangible reality of it seems so very convincing.

M: This is the mystery of imagination, that it seems to be so real. You may be celibate or married, a monk or a family man; that is not the point. Are you a slave of your imagination, or are you not? Whatever decision you take, whatever work you do, it will be invariably based on imagination, on assumptions parading as facts.

Q: Here I am sitting in front of you. What part of it is imagination?

M: The whole of it. Even space and time are imagined.

Q: Does it mean that I don't exist?

M: I too do not exist. All existence is imaginary.

Q: Is *being* too imaginary?

M: Pure being, filling all and beyond all, is not existence which is limited. All limitation is imaginary, only the unlimited is real.

Q: When you look at me, what do you see?

M: I see you imagining yourself to be.

Q: There are many like me. Yet each is different.

M: The totality of all projections is what is called *maha-maya,* the Great Illusion.

Q: But when you look at yourself, what do you see?

M: It depends how I look. When I look through the mind, I see numberless people. When I look beyond the mind, I see the witness. Beyond the witness there is the infinite intensity of emptiness and silence.

Q: How to deal with people?

M: Why make plans and what for? Such questions show anxiety. Relationship is a living thing. Be at peace with your inner self and you will be at peace with everybody.

Realize that you are not the master of what happens, you cannot control the future except in purely technical matters. Human relationship cannot be planned, it is too rich and varied. Just be understanding and compassionate, free of all self-seeking.

Q: Surely, I am not the master of what happens. Its slave rather

M: Be neither master, nor slave. Stand aloof.

Q: Does it imply avoidance of action?

M: You cannot avoid action. It happens, like everything else.

Q: My actions, surely, I can control.

M: Try. You will soon see that you do what you must.

Q: I can act according to my will.

M: You know your will only after you have acted.

Q: I remember my desires, the choices made, the decisions taken and act accordingly.

M: Then your memory decides, not you.

Q: Where do I come in?

M: You make it possible by giving it attention.

Q: Is there no such thing as free will? Am I not free to desire?

M: Oh no, you are compelled to desire. In Hinduism the very idea of free will is non-existent, so there is no word for it. Will is commitment, fixation, bondage.

Q: I am free to choose my limitations.

M: You must be free first. To be free in the world you must be free of the world. Otherwise your past decides for you and your future. Between what had happened and what must happen you are caught. Call it destiny or *karma,* but never — freedom. First return to your true being and then act from the heart of love.

Q: Within the manifested what is the stamp of the un-manifested?

M: There is none. The moment you begin to look for the stamp of the unmanifested, the manifested dissolves. If you try to understand the unmanifested with the mind, you at once go beyond the mind, like when you stir the fire with a wooden stick, you burn the stick. Use the mind to investigate the manifested. Be like the chick that pecks at the shell. Speculating about life outside the shell would have been of little use to it, but pecking at the shell breaks the shell from within and liberates the chick. Similarly, break the mind from within by investigation and exposure of its contradictions and absurdities.

Q: The longing to break the shell, where does it come from?

M: From the unmanifested.   ●●●

73

Death of the Mind is Birth of Wisdom

Questioner: Before one can realize one's true nature need not one be a person? Does not the ego have its value?

Maharaj: The person is of little use. It is deeply involved in its own affairs and is completely ignorant of its true being. Unless the witnessing consciousness begins to play on the person and it becomes the object of observation rather than the subject, realization is not feasible. It is the witness that makes realization desirable and attainable.

Q: There comes a point in a person's life when it becomes the witness.

M: Oh, no. The person by itself will not become the witness. It is like expecting a cold candle to start burning in the course of time. The person can stay in the darkness of ignorance forever, unless the flame of awareness touches it.

Q: Who lights the candle?

M: The Guru. His words, his presence. In India it is very often the *mantra*. Once the candle is lighted, the flame will consume the candle.

Q: Why is the *mantra* so effective?

M: Constant repetition of the *mantra* is something the person does not do for one's own sake. The beneficiary is not the person. Just like the candle which does not increase by burning.

Q: Can the person become aware of itself by itself?

M: Yes, it happens sometimes as a result of much suffering. The Guru wants to save you the endless pain. Such is his grace.

Even when there is no discoverable outer Guru, there is always the *sadguru,* the inner Guru, who directs and helps from within. The words 'outer' and 'inner' are relative to the body only; in reality all is one, the outer being merely a projection of the inner. Awareness comes as if from a higher dimension.

Q: Before the spark is lit and after, what is the difference?

M: Before the spark is lit there is no witness to perceive the difference. The person may be conscious, but is not aware of being conscious. It is completely identified with what it thinks and feels and experiences. The darkness that is in it is of its own creation. When the darkness is questioned, it dissolves. The desire to question is planted by the Guru. In other words, the difference between the person and the witness is as between not knowing and knowing oneself. The world seen in consciousness is to be of the nature of consciousness, when there is harmony *(sattva);* but when activity and passivity *(rajas* and *tamas)* appear, they obscure and distort and you see the false as real.

Q: What can the person do to prepare itself for the coming of the Guru.

M: The very desire to be ready means that the Guru had come and the flame is lighted. It may be a stray word, or a page in a book; the Guru's grace works mysteriously.

Q: Is there no such thing as self-preparation? We hear so much about *yoga sadhana?*

M: It is not the person that is doing *sadhana.* The person is in unrest and resistance to the very end. It is the witness that works on the person, on the totality of its illusions, past, present and future.

Q: How can we know that what you say is true? While it is self-contained and free from inner contradictions, how can we know that it is not a product of fertile imagination, nurtured and enriched by constant repetition?

M: The proof of the truth lies in its effect on the listener.

Q: Words can have a most powerful effect. By hearing, or repeating words, one can experience various kinds of trances. The listener's experiences may be induced and cannot be considered as a proof.

M: The effect need not necessarily be an experience. It can be a change in character, in motivation, in relationship to people and one's self. Trances and visions induced by words, or drugs, or any other sensory or mental means are temporary and inconclusive. The truth of what is said here is immovable and everlasting. And the proof of it is in the listener, in the deep and permanent changes in his entire being. It is not something he can doubt, unless he doubts his own existence, which is unthinkable. When my experience becomes your own experience also, what better proof do you want.?

Q: The experiencer is the proof of his experience.

M: Quite, but the experiencer needs no proof. 'I am, and I know I am'. You cannot ask for further proofs.

Q: Can there be true knowledge of things?

M: Relatively — yes. Absolutely — there are no things. To know that nothing *is* is true knowledge.

Q: What is the link between the relative and the absolute?

M: They are identical.

Q: From which point of view are they identical?

M: When the words are spoken, there is silence. When the relative is over, the absolute remains. The silence before the words were spoken, is it different from the silence that comes after? The silence is one and without it the words could not have been heard. It is always there — at the back of the words. Shift your attention from words to silence and you will hear it. The mind craves for experience, the memory of which it takes for knowledge. The *gnani* is beyond all experience and his memory is empty of the past. He is entirely unrelated to anything in particular. But the mind craves for formulations and definitions, always eager to squeeze reality into a verbal shape. Of everything it wants an idea, for without ideas the mind is not. Reality is essentially alone, but the mind will not leave it alone — and deals instead with the unreal. And yet it is all the mind can do — discover the unreal as unreal.

Q: And seeing the real as real?

M: There is no such state as seeing the real. Who is to see what? You can only be the real — which you are, anyhow. The problem is only mental. Abandon false ideas, that is all. There is no need of true ideas. There aren't any.

Q: Why then are we encouraged to seek the real?

M: The mind must have a purpose. To encourage it to free itself from the unreal it is promised something in return. In reality, there is no need of purpose. Being free from the false is good in itself, it wants no reward. It is just like being clean — which is its own reward.

Q: Is not self-knowledge the reward?

M: The reward of self-knowledge is freedom from the personal self. You cannot know the knower, for you are the knower. The fact of knowing proves the knower. You need no other proof. The knower of the known is not knowable. Just like the light is known in colours only, so is the knower known in knowledge.

Q: Is the knower an inference only?

M: You know your body, mind and feelings. Are you an inference only?

Q: I am an inference to others, but not to myself.

M: So am I. An inference to you, but not to myself. I know myself by being myself. As you know yourself to be a man by being one. You do not keep on reminding yourself that you are a man. It is only when your humanity is questioned that you assert it. Similarly, I know that I am all. I do not need to keep on repeating: 'I am all, I am all'. Only when you take me to be a particular, a person, I protest. As you are a man all the time, so I am what I am — all the time. Whatever you are changelessly, that you are beyond all doubt.

Q: When I ask how do you know that you are a *gnani,* you answer: 'I find no desire in me. Is this not a proof?'

M: Were I full of desires, I would have still been what I am.

Q: Myself, full of desires and you, full of desires; what difference would there be?

M: You identify yourself with your desires and become their slave. To me desires are things among other things, mere clouds in the mental sky, and I do not feel compelled to act on them.

Q: The knower and his knowledge, are they one or two?

M: They are both. The knower is the unmanifested, the known is the manifested. The known is always on the move, it changes, it has no shape of its own, no dwelling place. The knower is the immutable support of all knowledge. Each needs the other, but reality lies beyond. The *gnani* cannot be known, because there is·nobody to be known. When there is a person, you can tell something about it, but when there is no self-identification with the particular, what can be said? You may tell a *gnani* anything; his question will always be: 'about whom are you talking? There is no such person'. Just as you cannot say anything about the universe because it includes everything, so nothing can be said about a *gnani,* for he is all and yet nothing in particular. You need a hook to hang your picture on; when there is no hook, on what will the picture hang? To locate a thing you need space, to place an event you need time; but the timeless and spaceless defies all handling. It makes everything perceivable, yet itself it is beyond perception. The mind cannot know what is beyond the mind, but the mind is known by what is beyond it. The *gnani* knows neither birth nor death; existence and non-existence are the same to him.

Q: When your body dies, you remain.

M: Nothing dies. The body is just imagined. There is no such thing.

Q: Before another·century will pass, you will be dead to all around you. Your body will be covered with flowers, then burnt and the ashes scattered. That will be our experience. What will be yours?

M: Time will come to an end. This is called the Great Death *(mahamrityu),* the death of time.

Q: Does it mean that the universe and its contents will come to an end?

M: The universe is your personal experience. How can it be affected? You might have been delivering a lecture for two hours; where has it gone when it is over? It has merged into silence in which the beginning, middle and end of the lecture are all together. Time has come to a stop, it was, but is no more. The silence after a life of talking and the silence after a life of silence is the same silence. Immortality is freedom from the feeling: 'I am'. Yet it is not extinction. On the contrary, it is a state infinitely more real, aware and happy than you can possibly think of. Only self-consciousness is no more.

Q: Why does the Great Death of the mind coincide with the 'small death' of the body?

M: It does not! You may die a hundred deaths without a break in the mental turmoil. Or, you may keep your body and die only in the mind. The death of the mind is the birth of wisdom.

Q: The person goes and only the witness remains.

M: Who remains to say: 'I am the witness'. When there is no 'I am', where is the witness? In the timeless state there is no self to take refuge in.

The man who carries a parcel is anxious not to lose it — he is parcel-conscious. The man who cherishes the feeling 'I am' is self-conscious. The *gnani* holds on to nothing and cannot be said to be conscious. And yet he is not unconscious. He is the very heart of awareness. We call him *digambara* clothed in space, the Naked One, beyond all appearance. There is no name and shape under which he may be said to exist, yet he is the only one that truly *is*.

Q: I cannot grasp it.

M: Who can? The mind has its limits. It is enough to bring you to the very frontiers of knowledge and make you face the immensity of the unknown. To dive in it is up to you.

Q: What about the witness? Is it real or unreal?

M: It is both. The last remnant of illusion, the first touch of the real. To say: I am only the witness is both false and true: false because of the 'I am', true because of the witness. It is better to say: 'there is witnessing'. The moment you say: 'I am', the entire universe comes into being along with its creator.

Q: Another question: can we visualize the person and the self as two brothers small and big? The little brother is mischievous and selfish, rude and restless, while the big brother is intelligent and kind, reasonable and considerate, free from body-consciousness with its desires and fears. The big brother knows the little one, but the small one is ignorant of the big one and thinks itself to be entirely on its own. The Guru comes and tells the smaller one: 'You are not alone, you come from a very good family, your brother is a very remarkable man, wise and kind, and he loves you very much. Remember him, think of him, find him, serve him, and you will become one with him'. Now, the question is are there two in us, the personal and the individual, the false self and the true self, or is it only a simile?

M: It is both. They appear to be two, but on investigation they are found to be one. Duality lasts only as long as it is not questioned. The trinity: mind, self and spirit *(vyakti, vyakta, avyakta)*, when looked into, becomes unity. These are only modes of experiencing: of attachment, of detachment, of transcendence.

Q: Your assumption that we are in a dream state makes your position unassailable. Whatever objection we raise, you just deny its validity. One cannot discuss with you!

M: The desire to discuss is also mere desire. The desire to know, to have the power, even the desire to exist are desires only. Everybody desires to *be,* to survive, to continue, for no one is sure of himself. But everybody is immortal. You make yourself mortal by taking yourself to be the body.

Q: Since you have found your freedom, will you not give me a little of it?

M: Why little? Take the whole. Take it, it is there for the taking. But you are afraid of freedom!

Q: Swami Ramdas had to deal with a similar request. Some devotees collected round him one day and began to ask for liberation. Ramdas listened smilingly and then suddenly he became serious and said: You can have it, here and now, freedom absolute and permanent. Who wants it, come forward. Nobody moved. Thrice he repeated the offer. None accepted. Then he said: 'The offer is withdrawn'.

M: Attachment destroys courage. The giver is always ready to give. The taker is absent. Freedom means letting go. People just do not care to let go everything. They do not know that the finite is the price of the infinite, as death is the price of immortality. Spiritual maturity lies in the readiness to let go everything. The giving up is the first step. But the real giving up is in realizing that there is nothing to give up, for nothing is your own. It is like deep sleep — you do not give up your bed when you fall asleep — you just forget it.   ●●●

74

Truth is Here and Now

Questioner: My question is: What is the proof of truth? Followers of every religion, metaphysical or political, philosophical or ethical, are convinced that their's is the only truth, that all else is false and they take their own unshakable conviction for the proof of truth. 'I am convinced, so it must be true', they say. It seems to me, that no philosophy or religion, no doctrine or ideology, however complete, free from inner contradictions and emotionally appealing, can be the proof of its own truth. They are like clothes men put on, which vary with times and circumstances and follow the fashion trends.

Now, can there be a religion or philosophy which is true and which does not depend on somebody's conviction? Nor on scriptures, because they again depend on somebody's faith in them? Is there a truth which does not depend on trusting, which is not subjective?

Maharaj: What about science?

Q: Science is circular, it ends where it starts, with the senses. It deals with experience, and experience is subjective. No two persons can have the same experience, though they may express it in the same words.

M: You must look for truth beyond the mind.

Q: Sir, I have had enough of trances. Any drug can induce them cheaply and quickly. Even the classical *samadhis,* caused by breathing or mental exercises, are not much different. There are oxygen *samadhis* and carbon dioxide *samadhis* and self-induced *samadhis,* caused by·repetition of a formula or a chain of thoughts. Monotony is soporific. I cannot accept *samadhi,* however glorious, as a proof of truth.

M: *Samadhi* is beyond experience. It is a qualityless state.

Q: The absence of experience is due to inattention. It reappears with attention. Closing one's eyes does not disprove light. Attributing reality to negative states will not take us far. The very negation contains an affirmation.

M: In a way you are right. But don't you see, you are asking for the proof of truth, without explaining what is the truth you have in mind and what proof will satisfy you? You can prove anything, provided you trust your proof. But what will prove that your proof is true? I can easily drive you into an admission that you know only that you exist — that you are the only proof you can have of anything. But I do not identify mere existence with reality. Existence is momentary, always in time and space, while reality is changeless and all-pervading.

Q: Sir, I do not know what is truth and what can prove it. Do not throw me on my own resources. I have none. Here you are the truth-knower, not me.

M: You refuse testimony as the proof of truth: the experience of others is of no use to you, you reject all inference from the concurring statements of a vast number of independent witnesses; so it is for you to tell me what is the proof that will satisfy you, what is your test of a valid proof?

Q: Honestly, I do not know what makes a proof.

M: Not even your own experience?

Q: Neither my experience, nor even existence. They depend on my being conscious.

M: And your being conscious depends on what?

Q: I do not know. Formerly, I would have said: on my body; now

I can see that the body is secondary, not primary, and cannot be considered as an evidence of existence.

M: I am glad you have abandoned the I-am-the-body idea, the main source of error and suffering.

Q: I have abandoned it intellectually, but the sense of being the particular, a person, is still with me. I can say: 'I am', but what I am I cannot say. I know I exist, but I do not know what exists. Whichever way I put it, I face the unknown.

M: Your very being is the real.

Q: Surely, we are not talking of the same thing. I am not some abstract being. I am a person, limited and aware of its limitations. I am a fact, but a most unsubstantial fact I am. There is nothing I can build on my momentary existence as a person.

M: Your words are wiser than you are! As a person, your existence is momentary. But are you a person only? Are you a person at all?

Q: How am I to answer? My sense of being proves only that I am; it does not prove anything which is independent of me. I am relative, both creature and creator of the relative. The absolute proof of the absolute truth — what is it, where is it? Can the mere feeling 'I am' be the proof of reality?

M: Of course not. 'I am' and 'the world is' are related and conditional. They are due to the tendency of the mind to project names and shapes.

Q: Names and shapes and ideas and convictions, but not truth. But for you, I would have accepted the relativity of everything, including truth, and learnt to live by assumptions. But then I meet you and hear you talking of the Absolute as within my reach and also as supremely desirable. Words like peace, bliss, eternity, immortality, catch my attention, as offering freedom from pain and fear. My inborn instincts: pleasure seeking and curiosity are roused and I begin to explore the realm you have opened. All seems most attractive and naturally I ask. Is it attainable? Is it real?

M: You are like a child that says: Prove that the sugar is sweet then only I shall have it. The proof of the sweetness is in the mouth not in the sugar. To know it is sweet, you must taste it, there is no other way. Of course, you begin by asking: Is it sugar? Is it sweet? and you accept my assurance until you taste it. Then only all doubts dissolve and your knowledge becomes first hand and unshakable. I do not ask you to believe me. Just trust me enough to begin with. Every step proves or disproves itself. You seem to want the proof of truth to precede fitruth. And what will be the proof of the proof? You see, you are falling into a regress. To cut it you must put a stop to asking for proofs and accept, for a moment only, something as true. It does not really matter what it is. It may be God, or me, or your own self. In each case you accept something, or somebody, unknown as true. Now, if you act on the truth you have accepted, even for a moment, very soon you will be brought to the next step. It is like climbing a tree in the dark — you can get hold of the next branch only when you are perched on the previous one. In science it is called the experimental approach. To prove a theory you carry out an experiment according to the operational instructions, left by those who have made the experiment before you. In spiritual search the chain of experiments one has to make is called Yoga.

Q: There are so many Yogas, which to choose?

M: Of course, every *gnani* will suggest the path of his own attainment as the one he knows most intimately. But most of them are very liberal and adapt their advice to the needs of the enquirer. All the paths take you to the purification of the mind. The impure mind is opaque to truth; the pure mind is transparent. Truth can be seen through it easily and clearly.

Q: I am sorry, but I seem unable to convey my difficulty. I am asking about the proof of truth and am being given the methods of attaining it. Assuming I follow the methods and attain some most wonderful and desirable state, how do I come to know that my state is true? Every religion begins with faith and promises some ecstasy. Is the ecstasy of the real, or the product of faith? For, if it is an induced state, I shall have nothing to do with it. Take Christianity that says: Jesus is your Saviour, believe and be saved from sin. When I ask a sinning Christian how is it that he has not been saved from sin inspite of his faith in Christ, he answers: My faith is not perfect. Again we are in the vicious circle — without perfect faith — no salvation, without salvation — no perfect faith, hence no salvation. Conditions are imposed which are unfulfillable and then we are blamed for not fulfilling them.

M: You do not realize that your present waking state is one of ignorance. Your question about the proof of truth is born from ignorance of reality. You are contacting your sensory and mental states in consciousness, at the point of 'I am', while reality is not mediated, not contacted, not experienced. You are taking duality so much for granted, that you do not even notice it, while to me variety and diversity do not create separation. You imagine reality to stand apart from names and forms, while to me names and forms are the ever changing expressions of reality and not apart from it. You ask for the proof of truth while to me all existence is the proof. You separate existence from being and being from reality, while to me it is all one. However much you are convinced of the truth of your waking state, you do not claim it to be permanent and changeless, as I do when I talk of mine. Yet I see no difference between us, except that you are imagining things, while I do not.

Q: First you disqualify me from asking about truth, then you accuse me of imagination! What is imagination to you is reality to me.

M: Until you investigate. I am not accusing you of anything. I am only asking you to question wisely. Instead of searching for the proof of truth, which you do not know, go through the proofs you have of what you believe to know. You will find you know nothing for sure — you trust on hearsay. To know the truth, you must pass through your own experience.

Q: I am mortally afraid of *samadhis* and other trances, whatever their cause. A drink, a smoke, a fever, a drug, breathing, singing, shaking, dancing, whirling, praying, sex or fasting, *mantras* or some vertiginous abstraction can dislodge me from my waking state and give me some experience, extraordinary because unfamiliar. But when the cause ceases, the effect dissolves and only a memory remains, haunting but fading.

Let us give up all means and their results, for the results are bound by the means; let us put the question anew; can truth be found?

M: Where is the dwelling place of truth where you could go in search of it? And how will you know that you have found it? What touchstone do you bring with you to test it? You are back at your initial question: What is the proof of truth? There must be something wrong with the question itself, for you tend to repeat it again and again. Why do you ask what are the proofs of truth? Is it not because you do not know truth first hand and you are afraid that you may be deceived? You imagine that truth is a thing which carries the name 'truth' and that it is advantageous to have it, provided it is genuine. Hence your fear of being cheated. You are shopping for truth, but you do not trust the merchants. You are afraid of forgeries and imitations.

Q: I am not afraid of being cheated. I am afraid of cheating myself.

M: But you are cheating yourself in your ignorance of your true motives. You are asking for truth, but in fact you merely seek comfort, which you want to last for ever. Now, nothing, no state of mind, can last for ever. In time and space there is always a limit, because time and space themselves are limited. And in the timeless the words 'for ever' have no meaning. The same with the 'proof of truth'. In the realm of non-duality everything is complete, its own proof, meaning and purpose. Where all is one, no supports are needed. You imagine that permanence is the proof of truth, that what lasts longer is somehow more true. Time becomes the measure of truth. And since time is in the mind, the mind becomes the arbiter and searches within itself the proof of truth — a task altogether impossible and hopeless!

Q: Sir, were you to say: Nothing is true, all is relative, I would agree with you. But you maintain there is truth, reality, perfect knowledge, therefore I ask: What is it and how do you know? And what will make me say: Yes, Maharaj was right?

M: You are holding on to the need for a proof, a testimony, an authority. You still imagine that truth needs pointing at and telling you: 'Look, here is truth'. It is not so. Truth is not the result of an effort, the end of a road. It is here and now, in the very longing and the search for it. It is nearer than the mind and the body, nearer than the sense 'I am'. You do not see it because you look too far away from yourself, outside your innermost being. You have objectified truth and insist on your standard proofs and tests, which apply only to things and thoughts.

Q: All I can make out from what you say is that truth is beyond me and I am not qualified to talk about it.

M: You are not only qualified, but you are truth itself. Only you mistake the false for the true.

Q: You seem to say: Don't ask for proofs of truth. Concern yourself with untruth only.

M: The discovery of truth is in the discernment of the false. You can know what is not. What is — you can only be. Knowledge is relative to the known. In a way it is the counterpart of ignorance. Where ignorance is not, where is the need of knowledge? By themselves neither ignorance nor knowledge have being. They are only states of mind, which again is but an appearance of movement in consciousness which is in its essence immutable.

Q: Is truth within the realm of the mind or beyond?

M: It is neither, it is both. It cannot be put into words.

Q: This is what I hear all the time — inexpressible (anirvachaniya). It does not make me wiser.

M: It is true that it often covers sheer ignorance. The mind can operate with terms of its own making, it just cannot go beyond itself. That which is neither sensory nor mental, and yet without which neither sensory nor the mental can exist, cannot be contained in them. Do understand that the mind has its limits; to go beyond, you must consent to silence.

Q: Can we say that action is the proof of truth? It may not be verbalized, but it may be demonstrated.

M: Neither action nor inaction. It is beyond both.

Q: Can a man ever say:-'Yes, this is true'? Or is he limited to the denial of the false? In other words, is truth pure negation? Or, does a moment come when it becomes assertion?

M: Truth cannot be described, but it can be experienced.

Q: Experience is subjective, it cannot be shared. Your experiences leaves me where I am.

M: Truth can be experienced, but it is not mere experience. I know it and I can convey it, but only if you are open to it. To be open means to want nothing else.

Q: I am full of desires and fears. Does it mean that I am not eligible for truth?

M: Truth is not a reward for good behaviour, nor a prize for passing some tests. It cannot be brought about. It is the primary, the unborn, the ancient source of all that is. You are eligible because you *are*. You need not merit truth. It is your own. Just stop running away by running after. Stand still, be quiet.

Q: Sir, if you want the body to be still and the mind — quiet, tell me how it is done. In self-awareness I see the body and the mind moved by causes beyond my control. Heredity and environment dominate me absolutely. The mighty 'I am', the creator of the universe, can be wiped out by a drug temporarily, or a drop of poison — permanently.

M: Again, you take yourself to be the body.

Q: Even if I dismiss this body of bones, flesh and blood as not-me, still I remain with the subtle body made up of thoughts and feelings, memories and imaginations. If I dismiss these also as not-me, I still remain with consciousness, which also is a kind of body.

M: You are quite right, but you need not stop there. Go beyond. Neither consciousness, nor the 'I am' at the centre of it are you. Your true being is entirely unself-conscious, completely free from all self-identification with whatever it may be, gross, subtle or transcendental.

Q: I can imagine myself to be beyond. But what proof have I? To *be*, I must be somebody.

M: It is the other way round. To *be*, you must be nobody. To think yourself to be something, or somebody, is death and hell.

Q: I have read that in ancient Egypt people were admitted to some mysteries where, under the influence of drugs or incantations, they would be expelled from their bodies and could actually experience standing outside and looking at their own prostrate forms. This was intended to convince them of the reality of the after-death existence and create in them a deep concern with their ultimate destiny, so profitable to the state and temple. The self-identification with the person owning the body remained.

M: The body is made of food, as the mind is made of thoughts. See them as they are. Non-identification, when natural and spontaneous, is liberation. You need not know what you are. Enough to know what you are not. What you are you will never know, for every discovery reveals new dimensions to conquer. The unknown has no limits.

Q: Does it imply ignorance for ever?

M: It means that ignorance never was. Truth is in the discovery, not in the discovered. And to discovery there is no beginning and no end. Question the limits, go beyond, set yourself tasks apparently impossible — this is the way.   ●●●

75

In Peace and Silence you Grow

Questioner: The Indian tradition tells us that the Guru is indispensable. What is he indispensable for? A mother is indispensable for giving the child a body. But the soul she does not give. Her role is limited. How is it with the Guru? Is his role also limited, and if so, to what? Or is he indispensable generally, even absolutely?

Maharaj: The innermost light, shining peacefully and timelessly in the heart, is the real Guru. All others merely show the way.

Q: I am not concerned with the inner Guru, only with the one that shows the way. There are people who believe that without a Guru Yoga is inaccessible. They are ever in search of the right Guru, changing one for another. Of what value are such Gurus?

M: They are temporary, time-bound Gurus. You find them in every walk of life. You need them for acquiring any knowledge or skill.

Q: A mother is only for a lifetime, she begins at birth and ends at death. She is not for ever.

M:. Similarly, the time-bound Guru is not for ever. He fulfils his purpose and yields his place to the next. It is quite natural and there is no blame attached to it.

Q: For every kind of knowledge, or skill, do I need a separate Guru?

M: There can be no rule in these matters, except one 'the outer is transient, the innermost — permanent and changeless', though ever new in appearance and action.

Q: What is the relation between the inner and the outer Gurus?

M: The outer represent the inner, the inner accepts the outer — for a time.

Q: Whose is the effort?

M: The disciple's, of course. The outer Guru gives the instructions, the inner sends the strength; the alert application is the disciple's. Without will, intelligence and energy on the part of the disciple the outer Guru is helpless. The inner Guru bids his chance. Obtuseness and wrong pursuits bring about a crisis and the disciple wakes up to his own plight. Wise is he who does not wait for a shock, which can be quite rude.

Q: Is it a threat?

M: Not a threat, a warning. The inner Guru is not committed to non-violence. He can be quite violent at times, to the point of destroying the obtuse or perverted personality. Suffering and death, as life and happiness, are his tools of work. It is only in duality that non-violence becomes the unifying law.

Q: Has one to be afraid of his own self?

M: Not afraid, for the self means well. But it must be taken seriously. It calls for attention and obedience; when it is not listened to, it turns from persuasion to compulsion, for while it can wait, it shall not be denied. The difficulty lies not with the Guru, inner or outer. The Guru is always available. It is the ripe disciple that is lacking. When a person is not ready, what can be done?

Q: Ready or willing?

M: Both. It comes to the same. In India we call it *adhikari*. It means both capable and entitled.

Q: Can the outer Guru grant initiation *(diksha)*?

M: He can give all kinds of initiations, but the initiation into Reality must come from within.

Q: Who gives the ultimate initiation?

M: It is self-given.

Q: I feel we are running in circles. After all, I know one self only, the present, empirical self. The inner or higher self is but an idea conceived to explain and encourage. We talk of it as having independent existence. It hasn't.

M: The outer self and the inner both are imagined. The obsession of being an 'I' needs another obsession with a 'super-I' to get cured, as one needs another thorn to remove a thorn, or another poison to neutralize a poison. All assertion calls for a denial, but this is the first step only. The next is to go beyond both.

Q: I do understand that the outer Guru is needed to call my attention to myself and to the urgent need of doing something about myself. I also understand how helpless he is when it comes to any deep change in me. But here you bring in the *sadguru,* the inner Guru, beginningless, changeless, the root of being, the standing promise, the certain goal. Is he a concept or a reality?

M: He is the only reality. All else is shadow, cast by the body-mind *(deha-buddhi)* on the face of time. Of course, even a shadow is related to reality, but by itself it is not real.

Q: I am the only reality I know. The *sadguru* is there as long as I think of him. What do I gain by shifting reality to him?

M: Your loss is your gain. When the shadow is seen to be a shadow only, you stop following it. You turn round and discover the sun which was there all the time — behind your back!

Q: Does the inner Guru also teach?

M: He grants the conviction that you are the eternal, change-less, reality-consciousness-love, within and beyond all appearances.

Q: A conviction is not enough. There must be certainty.

M: Quite right. But in this case certainty takes the shape of courage. Fear ceases absolutely. This state of fearlessness is so unmistakably new, yet felt deeply as one's own, that it cannot be denied. It is like loving one's own child. Who can doubt it?

Q: We hear of progress in our spiritual endeavours. What kind of progress do you have in mind?

M: When you go·beyond progress, you will know what is progress.

Q: What makes us progress?

M: Silence is the main factor. In peace and silence you grow.

Q: The mind is so absolutely restless. For quieting it what is the way?

M: Trust the teacher. Take my own case. My Guru ordered me to attend to the sense 'I am' and to give attention to nothing else. I just obeyed. I did not follow any particular course of breathing, or meditation, or study of scriptures. Whatever happened, I would turn away my attention from it and remain with the sense 'I am', it may look too simple, even crude. My only reason for doing it was that my Guru told me so. Yet it worked! Obedience is a powerful solvent of all desires and fears.

Just turn away from all that occupies the mind; do whatever work you have to complete, but avoid new obligations; keep empty, keep available, resist not what comes uninvited.

In the end you reach a state of non-grasping, of joyful non-attachment, of inner ease and freedom indescribable, yet wonderfully real.

Q: When a truth-seeker earnestly practises his Yogas, does his inner Guru guide and help him or does he leave him to his own resources, just waiting for the outcome?

M: All happens by itself. Neither the seeker, nor the Guru do anything. Things happen as they happen; blame or praise are apportioned later, after the sense of doership appearing.

Q: How strange! Surely the doer comes before the deed.

M: It is the other way round; the deed is a fact, the doer a mere concept. Your very language shows that while the deed is certain, the doer is dubious; shifting responsibility is a game peculiarly human. Considering the endless list of factors required for anything to happen, one can only admit that everything is responsible for everything, however remote. Doership is a myth born from the illusion of 'me' and 'the mine'.

Q: How powerful the illusion?

M: No doubt, because based on reality.

Q: What is real in it?

M: Find out, by discerning and rejecting all that is unreal.

Q: I have not understood well the role of the inner self in spiritual endeavour. Who makes the effort? Is it the outer self, or the inner?

M: You have invented words like effort, inner, outer, self, etc. and seek to impose them on reality. Things just happen to be as they are, but we want to build them into a pattern, laid down by the structure of our language. So strong is this habit, that we tend to deny reality to what cannot be verbalized. We just refuse to see that words are mere symbols, related by convention and habit to repeated experiences.

Q: What is the value of spiritual books?

M: They help in dispelling ignorance. They are useful in the beginning, but become a hindrance in the end. One must know when to discard them.

Q: What is the link between *atma* and *sattva,* between the self and the universal harmony?

M: As between the sun and its rays. Harmony and beauty, understanding and affection are all expressions of reality. It is reality in action, the impact of the spirit on matter. *Tamas* obscures, *rajas* distorts, *sattva* harmonizes. With the maturing of the *sattva* all desires and fears come to an end. The real being is reflected in the mind undistorted. Matter is redeemed, spirit — revealed.

The two are seen as one. They were always one, but the imperfect mind saw them as two. Perfection of the mind is the human task, for matter and spirit meet in the mind.

Q: I feel like a man before a door. I know the door is open but it is guarded by the dogs of desire and fear. What am I to do?

M: Obey the teacher and brave the dogs. Behave as if they were not there. Again, obedience is the golden rule. Freedom is won by obedience. To escape from prison one must unquestioningly obey instructions sent by those who work for one's release.

Q: The words of the Guru, when merely heard, have little power. One must have faith to obey them. What creates such faith?

M: When time comes, faith comes. Everything comes in time. The Guru is always ready to share, but there are no takers.

Q: Yes, Sri Ramana Maharshi used to say: Gurus there are many, but where are the disciples?

M: Well, in the course of time everything happens. All will come through, not a single soul *(jiva)* shall be lost.

Q: I am very much afraid of taking intellectual understanding for realization. I may talk of truth without knowing it, and may know it without a single word said.

I understand these conversations are going to be published. What will be their effect on the reader?

M: In the attentive and thoughtful reader they will ripen and bring out flowers and fruits. Words based on truth, if fully tested, have their own power. ●●●

76

To Know that You do not Know, is True Knowledge

Maharaj: There is the body. Inside the body appears to be an observer and outside — a world under observation. The observer and his observation as well as the world observed appear and disappear together. Beyond it all, there is void. This void is one for all.

Questioner: What you say appears simple, but not everyone would say it. It is you, and you alone, who talks of the three and the void beyond. I see the world only, which includes all.

M: Even the 'I am'?

Q: Even the 'I am'. The 'I am' is there because the world is there.

M: And the world is there because the 'I am' is there.

Q: Yes, it goes both ways. I cannot separate the two, nor go beyond, I cannot say something *is*, unless I experience it, as I cannot say something *is not*, because I do not experience it. What is it that you experience that makes you speak with such assurance?

M: I know myself as I am — timeless, spaceless, causeless. You happen not to know, being engrossed as you are in other things.

Q: Why am I so engrossed?

M: Because you are interested.

Q: What makes me interested?

M: Fear of pain, desire for pleasure. Pleasant is the ending of pain and painful the end of pleasure. They just rotate in endless succession. Investigate the vicious circle till you find yourself beyond it.

Q: Don't I need your grace to take me beyond?

M: The grace of your Inner Reality is timelessly with you. Your very asking for grace is a sign of it. Do not worry about my grace, but do what you are told. The doing is the proof of earnestness, not the expecting of grace.

Q: What am I to be earnest about?

M: Assiduously investigate everything that crosses your field of attention. With practice the field will broaden and investigation deepen, until they become spontaneous and limitless.

Q: Are you not making realization the result of practice? Practice operates within the limitations of physical existence. How can it give birth to the unlimited?

M: Of course, there can be no causal connection between practice and wisdom. But the obstacles to wisdom are deeply affected by practice.

Q: What are the obstacles?

M: Wrong ideas and desires leading to wrong actions, causing dissipation and weakness of mind and body. The discovery and abandonment of the false remove what prevents the real entering the mind.

Q: I can distinguish two states of mind: 'I am' and 'the world is; they arise and subside together. People say: 'I am, because the world is'. You seem to say: 'The world is, because 'I am'. Which is true?

M: Neither. The two are one and the same state, in space and time. Beyond, there is the timeless.

Q: What is the connection between time and the timeless?

M: The timeless knows the time, the time does not know the timeless. All consciousness is in time and to it the timeless appears unconscious. Yet, it is what makes consciousness possible. Light shines in darkness. In light darkness is not visible. Or, you can put it the other way — in the endless ocean of light, clouds of consciousness appear — dark and limited, perceivable by contrast. These are mere attempts to express in words something very simple, yet altogether inexpressible.

Q: Words should serve as a bridge to cross over.

M: Word refers to a state of mind, not to reality. The river, the two banks, the bridge across — these are all in the mind. Words alone cannot take you beyond the mind. There must be the immense longing for truth, or absolute faith in the Guru. Believe me, there is no goal, nor a way to reach it. You are the way and the goal, there is nothing else to reach except yourself. All you need is to understand and understanding is the flowering of the mind. The tree is perennial, but the flowering and the fruit-bearing come in season. The seasons change, but not the tree. You are the tree. You have grown numberless branches and leaves in the past and you may grow them also in the future — yet you remain. Not what was, or shall be, must you know, but what *is*. Yours is the desire that creates the universe. Know the world as your own creation and be free.

Q: You say the world is the child of love. When I know the horrors the world is full of, the wars, the concentration camps, the inhuman exploitations, how can I own it as my own creation? However limited I am, I could not have created so cruel a world.

M: Find to whom this cruel world appears and you will know why it appears so cruel. Your questions are perfectly legitimate, but just cannot be answered unless you know whose is the world. To find out the meaning of a thing you must ask its maker. I am telling you: You are the maker of the world in which you live — you alone can change it, or unmake it.

Q: How can you say I have made the world? I hardly know it.

M: There is nothing in the world that you cannot know, when you know yourself. Thinking yourself to be the body you know the world as a collection of material things. When you know yourself as a centre of consciousness, the world appears as the ocean of the mind. When you know yourself as you are in reality, you know the world as yourself.

Q: It all sounds very beautiful, but does not answer my question Why is there so much suffering in the world?

M: If you stand aloof as observer only, you will not suffer. You will see the world as a show. a most entertaining show indeed.

Q: Oh, no! This *lila* theory I shall not have. The suffering is too acute and all-pervading. What a perversion to be entertained by a spectacle of suffering! What a cruel God are you offering me!

M: The cause of suffering is in the identification of the perceiver with the perceived. Out of it desire is born and with desire blind action, unmindful of results. Look round and you will see — suffering is a man-made thing.

Q: Were a man to create his own sorrow only, I would agree with you. But in his folly he makes others suffer. A dreamer has his own private nightmare and none suffers but himself. But what kind of dream is it that plays havoc in the lives of others?

M: Descriptions are many and contradictory. Reality is simple — all is one, harmony is the eternal law, none compels to suffer. It is only when you try to describe and explain, that the words fail you.

Q: I remember Gandhiji telling me once that the Self is not bound by the law of non-violence *(ahimsa)*. The Self has the freedom to impose suffering on its expressions in order to set them right.

M: On the level of duality it may be so, but in reality there is only the source, dark in itself, making everything shine. Unperceived, it causes perception. Unfelt, it causes feeling. Unthinkable, it causes thought. Non-being, it gives birth to being. It is the immovable background of motion. Once you are there you are at home everywhere.

Q: If I am that, then what causes me to be born?

M: The memory of the past unfulfilled desires traps energy, which manifests itself as a person. When its charge gets exhausted, the person dies. Unfulfilled desires are carried over into the next birth. Self-identification with the body creates ever fresh desires and there is no end to them, unless this mechanism of bondage is clearly seen. It is clarity that is liberating, for you cannot abandon desire, unless its causes and effects are clearly seen. I do not say that the same person is reborn. It dies and dies for good. But its memories remain and their desires and fears. They supply the energy for a new person. The real takes no part in it, but makes it possible by giving it the light.

Q: My difficulty is this. As I can see, every experience is its own reality. It is there — experienced. The moment I question it and ask to whom it happens, who is the observer and so on, the experience is over and all I can investigate is only the memory of it. I just cannot investigate the living moment — the *now*. My awareness is of the past, not of the present. When I am aware, I do not really live in the *now*, but only in the past. Can there really be an awareness of the present?

M: What you are describing is not awareness at all, but only thinking about the experience. True awareness *(samvid)* is a state of pure witnessing, without the least attempt to do anything about the event witnessed. Your thoughts and feelings, words and actions may also be a part of the event; you watch all unconcerned in the full light of clarity and understanding. You understand precisely what is going on, because it does not affect you. It may seem to be an attitude of cold aloofness, but it is not really so. Once you are in it, you will find that you love what you see, whatever may be its nature. This choiceless love is the touchstone of awareness. If it is not there, you are merely interested — for some personal reasons.

Q: As long as there are pain and pleasure, one is bound to be interested.

M: And as long as one is conscious, there will be pain and pleasure. You cannot fight pain and pleasure on the level of consciousness. To go beyond them you must go beyond consciousness, which is possible only when you look at consciousness as something that happens to you and not in you, as something external, alien, superimposed. Then, suddenly you are free of consciousness, really alone, with nothing to intrude. And that is your true state. Consciousness is an itching rash that makes you scratch. Of course, you cannot step out of consciousness for the very idea of stepping out is in consciousness. But if you learn to look at your consciousness as a sort of fever, personal and private, in which you are enclosed like a chick in its shell, out of this very attitude will come the crisis which will break the shell.

Q: Buddha said that life is suffering.

M: He must have meant that all consciousness is painful, which is obvious.

Q: And does death offer delivery?

M: One who believes himself as having been born is very much afraid of death. On the other hand, to him who knows himself truly, death is a happy event.

Q: The Hindu tradition says that suffering is brought by destiny and destiny is merited. Look at the immense calamities, natural or man-made, floods and earthquakes, wars and revolutions. Can we dare to think that each suffers for his own sins, of which he can have no idea? The billions who suffer, are they all criminals justly punished?

M: Must one suffer only for one's own sins? Are we really separate? In this vast ocean of life we suffer for the sins of others, and make others suffer for our sins. Of course, the law of balance rules supreme and accounts are squared in the end. But while life lasts, we affect each other deeply.

Q: Yes, as the poet says: 'No man is an island'.

M: At the back of every experience is the Self and its interest in the experience. Call it desire, call it love — words do not matter.

Q: Can I desire suffering? Can I deliberately ask for pain? Am I not like a man who made for himself a downy bed hoping for a good night of sleep and then he is visited by a nightmare and he tosses and screams in his dream? Surely, it is not the love that produces nightmares.

M: All suffering is caused by selfish isolation, by insularity and greed. When the cause of suffering is seen and removed, suffering ceases.

Q: I may remove my causes of sorrow, but others will be left to suffer.

M: To understand suffering, you must go beyond pain and pleasure. Your own desires and fears prevent you from understanding and thereby helping others. In reality there are no others, and by helping yourself you help everybody else. If you are serious about the sufferings of mankind, you must perfect the only means of help you have — yourself.

Q: You keep on saying that I am the creator, preserver and destroyer of this world, omnipresent, omniscient, omnipotent. When I ponder over what you say, I ask myself: 'How is it that there is so much evil in my world'.

M: There is no evil, there is no suffering; the joy of living is paramount. Look, how everything clings to life, how dear the existence is.

Q: On the screen of my mind images follow each other in endless succession. There is nothing permanent about me.

M: Have a better look at yourself. The screen is there — it does not change. The light shines steadily. Only the film in between keeps moving and causes pictures to appear. You may call the film — destiny (prarabdha).

Q: What creates destiny?

M: Ignorance is the cause of inevitability.

Q: Ignorance of what?

M: Ignorance of yourself primarily. Also, ignorance of the true nature of things, of their causes and effects. You look round without understanding and take appearances for reality. You believe you know the world and yourself — but it is only your ignorance that makes you say: I know. Begin with the admission that you do not know and start from there.

There is nothing that can help the world more than your putting an end to ignorance. Then, you need not do anything in particular to help the world. Your very being is a help, action or no action.

Q: How can ignorance be known? To know ignorance presupposes knowledge.

M: Quite right. The very admission: 'I am ignorant' is the dawn of knowledge. An ignorant man is ignorant of his ignorance. You can say that ignorance does not exist, for the moment it is seen it is no more. Therefore, you may call it unconsciousness or blindness. All you see around and within you is what you do not know and do not understand, without even knowing that you do not know and do not understand. To know that you do not know and do not understand is true knowledge, the knowledge of an humble heart.

Q: Yes, Christ said: Blessed are the poor in spirit. . . .

M: Put it as you like; the fact is that knowledge is of ignorance only. You know that you do not know.

Q: Will ignorance ever end?

M: What is wrong with not knowing? You need not know all. Enough to know what you need to know. The rest can look after itself, without your knowing how it does it. What is important is that your unconscious does not work against the conscious, that there is integration on all levels. To know is not so very important.

Q: What you say is correct psychologically. But when it comes to knowing others, knowing the world, my knowing that I do not know does not help much.

M: Once you are inwardly integrated, outer knowledge comes to you spontaneously. At every moment of your life you know what you need to know. In the ocean of the universal mind all knowledge is contained; it is yours on demand. Most of it you may never need to know — but it is yours all the same.

As with knowledge, so it is with power.

Whatever you feel needs be done happens unfailingly. No doubt, God attends to this business of managing the universe; but He is glad to have some help. When the helper is selfless and intelligent, all the powers of the universe are for him to command.

Q: Even the blind powers of nature?

M: There are no blind powers. Consciousness is power. Be aware of what needs be done and it will be done. Only keep alert — and quiet. Once you reach your destination and know your real nature, your existence becomes a blessing to all. You may not know, nor will the world know, yet the help radiates. There are people in the world who do more good than all the statesmen and philanthropists put together. They radiate light and peace with no intention or knowledge. When others tell them about the miracles they worked, they also are wonderstruck. Yet, taking nothing as their own, they are neither proud, nor do they crave for reputation. They are just unable to desire anything for themselves, not even the joy of helping others knowing that God is good they are at peace.   ●●●

77

'I' and 'Mine' are False Ideas

Questioner: I am very much attached to my family and possessions. How can I conquer this attachment?

Maharaj: This attachment is born along with the sense of 'me'
and 'mine'. Find the true meaning of these words and you will be
free of all bondage. You have a mind which is spread in time.
One after another all things happen to you and the memory remains. There is nothing wrong in it. The problem arises only
when the memory of past pains and pleasures — which are essential to all organic life — remains as a reflex, dominating behaviour. This reflex takes the shape of 'I' and uses the body and
the mind for its purposes, which are invariably in search for
pleasure or flight from pain. When you recognize the 'I' as it is, a
bundle of desires and fears, and the sense of 'mine', as embracing all things and people needed for the purpose of avoiding
pain and securing pleasure, you will see that the 'I' and the
'mine' are false ideas, having no foundation in reality. Created
by the mind, they rule their creator as long as it takes them to be
true; when questioned, they dissolve.

The 'I' and 'mine', having no existence in themselves, need a
support which they find in the body. The body becomes their
point of reference. When you talk of 'my' husband and 'my' children, you mean the body's husband and the body's children.
Give up the idea of being the body and face the question: Who
am I? At once a process will be set in motion which will bring
back reality, or, rather, will take the mind to reality. Only, you
must not be afraid.

Q: What am I to be afraid of?

M: For reality to be, the ideas of 'me' and 'mine' must go. They
will go if you let them. Then your normal natural state reappears,

in which you are neither the body nor the mind, neither the 'me' nor the 'mine', but in a different state of being altogether. It is pure awareness of being, without being this or that, without any self-identification with anything in particular, or in general. In that pure light of consciousness there is nothing, not even the idea of nothing. There is only light.

Q: There are people whom I love. Must I give them up?

M: You only let go your hold on them. The rest is up to them. They may lose interest in you, or may not.

Q: How could they? Are they not my own?

M: They are your body's, not your own. Or, better, there is none who is not your own.

Q: And what about my possessions?

M: When the 'mine' is no more, where are your possessions?

Q: Please tell me, must I lose all by losing the 'I'?

M: You may or you may not. It will be all the same to you. Your loss will be somebody's gain. You will not mind.

Q: If I do not mind, I shall lose all!

M: Once you have nothing you have no problems.

Q: I am left with the problem of survival.

M: It is the body's problem and it will solve it by eating, drinking and sleeping. There is enough for all, provided all share.

Q: Our society is based on grabbing, not on sharing.

M: By sharing you will change it.

Q: I do not feel like sharing. Anyhow, I am being taxed out of my possessions.

M: This is not the same as voluntary sharing. Society will not change by compulsion. It requires a change of heart. Understand that nothing is your own, that all belongs to all. Then only society will change.

Q: One man's understanding will not take the world far.

M: The world in which you live will be affected deeply. it will be a healthy and happy world, which will radiate and communicate, increase and spread. The power of a true heart is immense.

Q: Please tell us more.

M: Talking is not my hobby. Sometimes I talk, sometimes I do not. My talking, or not talking, is a part of a given situation and does not depend on me. When there is a situation in which I have to talk, I hear myself talking. In some other situation I may not hear myself talking. It is all the same to me. Whether I talk or not, the light and love of being what I am are not affected, nor are they under my control. They are, and I know they are. There is a glad awareness, but nobody who is glad. Of course, there is a sense of identity, but it is the identity of a memory track, like the identity of a sequence of pictures on the ever-present screen. Without the light and the screen there can be no picture. To know the picture as the play of light on the screen, gives freedom from the idea that the picture is real. All you have to do is to understand that you love the self and the self loves you, and that the sense 'I am' is the link between you both, a token of identity in spite of apparent diversity. Look at the 'I am' as a sign of love between the inner and the outer, the real and the appearance. Just like in a dream all is different, except the sense of 'I', which enables you to say 'I dreamt', so does the sense of 'I am' enable you to say 'I am my real Self again. I do nothing, nor is anything done to me. I am what I am and nothing can affect me. I appear to depend on everything, but in fact all depends on me.

Q: How can you say you do nothing? Are you not talking to me?

M: I do not have the feeling that I am talking. There is talking going on, that is all.

Q: I talk.

M: Do you? You hear yourself talking and you say: I talk.

Q: Everybody says: 'I work, I come, I go'.

M: I have no objection to the conventions of your language, but they distort and destroy reality. A more accurate way of saying would have been: 'There is talking, working, coming, going'. For anything to happen, the entire universe must coincide. It is wrong to believe that anything in particular can cause an event. Every cause is universal. Your very body would not exist without the entire universe contributing to its creation and survival. I am fully aware that things happen as they happen because the world is as it is. To affect the course of events I must bring a new factor into the world and such factor can only be myself, the power of love and understanding focussed in me.

When the body is born, all kinds of things happen to it and you take part in them, because you take yourself to be the body You are like the man in the cinema house, laughing and crying with the picture, though knowing fully well that he is all the time in his seat and the picture is but the play of light. It is enough to shift attention from the screen to oneself to break the spell. When the body dies, the kind of life you live now — succession of physical and mental events — comes to an end. It can end even now — without waiting for the death of the body — it is enough to shift attention to the Self and keep it there. All happens as if there is a mysterious power that creates and moves everything. Realize that you are not the mover, only the observer, and you will be at peace.

Q: Is that power separate from me?

M: Of course not. But you must begin by being the dispassionate observer. Then only will you realize your full being as the universal lover and actor. As long as you are enmeshed in the tribulations of a particular personality, you can see nothing beyond it. But ultimately you will come to see that you are neither the particular nor the universal, you are beyond both. As the tiny point of a pencil can draw innumerable pictures, so does the dimensionless point of awareness draw the contents of the vast universe. Find that point and be free.

Q: Out of what do I create this world?

M: Out of your own memories. As long as you are ignorant of yourself as the creator, your world is limited and repetitive. Once you go beyond your self-identification with your past, you are free to create a new world of harmony and beauty. Or you just remain — beyond being and non-being.

Q: What will remain with me if I let go my memories?

M: Nothing will remain.

Q: I am afraid.

M: You will be afraid until you experience freedom and its blessings. Of course, some memories are needed to identify and guide the body and such memories do remain, but there is no attachment left to the body as such; it is no longer the ground for desire or fear. All this is not very difficult to understand and practise, but you must be interested. Without interest nothing can be done.

Having seen that you are a bundle of memories held together by attachment, step out and look from the outside. You may perceive for the first time something which is not memory. You cease to be a Mr-so-and-so, busy about his own affairs. You are at last at peace. You realize that nothing was ever wrong with the world — you alone were wrong and now it is all over. Never again will you be caught in the meshes of desire born of ignorance.   •••

78
All Knowledge is Ignorance

Questioner: Are we permitted to request you to tell us the manner of your realization?

Maharaj: Somehow it was very simple and easy in my case. My Guru, before he died, told me: Believe me, you are the Supreme Reality. Don't doubt my words, don't disbelieve me. I am telling you the truth — act on it. I could not forget his words and by not forgetting — I have realized.

Q: But what were you actually doing?

M: Nothing special. I lived my life, plied my trade, looked after my family, and every free moment I would spend just remembering my Guru and his words. He died soon after and I had only the memory to fall back on. It was enough.

Q: It must have been the grace and power of your Guru.

M: His words were true and so they came true. True words always come true. My Guru did nothing; his words acted because they were true. Whatever I did, came from within, un-asked and unexpected.

Q: The Guru started a process without taking any part in it?

M: Put it as you like. Things happen as they happen — who can tell why and how? I did nothing deliberately. All came by itself — the desire to let go, to be alone, to go within.

Q: You made no efforts whatsoever?

M: None. Believe it or not, I was not even anxious to realize. He only told me that I am the Supreme and then died. I just could not disbelieve him. The rest happened by itself. I found myself changing — that is all. As a matter of fact, I was astonished. But a desire arose in me to verify his words. I was so sure that he could not possibly have told a lie, that I felt I shall either realize the full meaning of his words or die. I was feeling quite determined, but did not know what to do. I would spend hours thinking of him and his assurance, not arguing, but just remembering what he told me.

Q: What happened to you then? How did you know that you are the Supreme?

M: Nobody came to tell me. Nor was I told so inwardly. In fact, it was only in the beginning when I was making efforts, that I was passing through some strange experiences; seeing lights, hearing voices, meeting gods and goddesses and conversing with them. Once the Guru told me: 'You are the Supreme Reality', I ceased having visions and trances and became very quiet and simple. I found myself desiring and knowing less and less, until I could say in utter astonishment: 'I know nothing, I want nothing.'

Q: Were you genuinely free of desire and knowledge, or did you impersonate a *gnani* according to the image given to you by your Guru?

M: I was not given any image, nor did I have one. My Guru never told me what to expect.

Q: More things may happen to you. Are you at the end of your journey?

M: There was never any journey. I am, as I always was.

Q: What was the Supreme Reality you were supposed to reach?

M: I was undeceived, that is all. I used to create a world and populate it — now I don't do it any more.

Q: Where do you live, then?

M: In the void beyond being and non-being, beyond consciousness. This void is also fulness; do not pity me. It is like a man saying: 'I.have done my work, there is nothing left to do'.

Q: You are giving a certain date to your realization. It means something did happen to you at that date. What happened?

M: The mind ceased producing events. The ancient and ceaseless search stopped — I wanted nothing, expected nothing — accepted nothing as my own. There was no 'me' left to strive for. Even the bare 'I am' faded away. The other thing that I noticed was that I lost all my habitual certainties. Earlier I was sure of so many things, now I am sure of nothing. But I feel that I have lost nothing by not knowing, because all my knowledge was false. My not knowing was in itself knowledge of the fact that all knowledge is ignorance, that 'I do not know' is the only true statement the mind can make. Take the idea 'I was born'. You may take it to be true. It is not. You were never born, nor will you ever die. It is the idea that was born and shall die, not you. By identifying yourself with it you became mortal. Just like in a cinema all is light, so does consciousness become the vast world. Look closely, and you will see that all names and forms are but transitory waves on the ocean of consciousness, that only consciousness can be said to *be,* not its transformations.

In the immensity of consciousness a light appears, a tiny point that moves rapidly and traces shapes, thoughts and feelings, concepts and ideas, like the pen writing on paper. And the ink that leaves a trace is memory. You are that tiny point and by your movement the world is ever re-created. Stop moving, and there will be no world. Look within and you will find that the point of light is the reflection of the immensity of light in the body, as the sense 'I am'. There is only light, all else appears.

Q: Do you know that light? Have you seen it?

M: To the mind it appears as darkness. It can be known only through its reflections. All is seen in daylight — except daylight.

Q: Have I to understand that our minds are similar?

M: How can it be? You have your own private mind, woven with memories, held together by desires and fears. I have no mind of my own; what I need to know the universe brings before me, as it supplies the food I eat.

Q: Do you know all you want to know?

M: There is nothing I want to know. But what I need to know, I come to know.

Q: Does this knowledge come to you from within or from outside?

M: It does not apply. My inner is outside and my outer is inside. I may get from you the knowledge needed at the moment, but you are not apart from me.

Q: What is *turiya*, the fourth state we hear about?

M: To be the point of light tracing the world is *turiya*. To be the light itself is *turiyatita*. But of what use are names when reality is so near?

Q: Is there any progress in your condition? When you compare yourself yesterday with yourself today, do you find yourself changing, making progress? Does your vision of reality grow in width and depth?

M: Reality is immovable and yet in constant movement. It is like a mighty river — it flows and yet it is there — eternally. What ' flows is not the river with its bed and banks, but its water, so does the *sattva guna*, the universal harmony, play its games against *tamas* and *rajas*, the forces of darkness and despair. In *sattva* there is always change and progress, in *rajas* there is change and regress, while *tamas* stands for chaos. The three Gunas play eternally against each other — it is a fact and there can be no quarrel with a fact.

Q: Must I always go dull with *tamas* and desperate with *rajas*? What about *sattva*?

M: *Sattva* is the radiance of your real nature. You can always find it beyond the mind and its many worlds. But if you want a world, you must accept the three *gunas* as inseparable — matter — energy — life — one in essence, distinct in appearance. They mix and flow — in consciousness. In time and space there is eternal flow, birth and death again, advance, retreat, another advance, again retreat — apparently without a beginning and without end; reality being timeless, changeless, bodyless, mindless awareness is bliss.

Q: I understand that, according to you, everything is a state of consciousness. The world is full of things — a grain of sand is a thing, a planet is a thing. How are they related to consciousness?

M: Where consciousness does not reach, matter begins. A thing is a form of being which we have not understood. It does not change — it is always the same — it appears to be there on its own — something strange and alien. Of course it is in the *chit*, consciousness, but appears to be outside because of its apparent changelessness. The foundation of things is in memory — without memory there would be no recognition. Creation — reflection — rejection: *Brahma* — *Vishnu* — *Shiva*: this is the eternal process. All things are governed by it.

Q: Is there no escape?

M: I am doing nothing else, but showing the escape. Understand that the One includes the Three and that you are the One, and you shall be free of the world process.

Q: What happens then to my consciousness?

M: After the stage of creation, comes the stage of examination and reflection and, finally, the stage of abandonment and forgetting. The consciousness remains, but in a latent, quiet state.

Q: Does the state of identity remain?

M: The state of identity is inherent in reality and never fades. But identity is neither the transient personality *(vyakti)*, nor the karma-bound individuality *(vyakta)*. It is what remains when all self-identification is given up as false — pure consciousness, the sense of being all there is, or could be. Consciousness is pure in the beginning and pure in the end; in between it gets contaminated by imagination which is at the root of creation. At all times consciousness remains the same. To know it as it is, is realization and timeless peace.

Q: Is the sense 'I am' real or unreal?

M: Both. It is unreal when we say: 'I am this, I am that'. It is real when we mean 'I am not this, nor that'.

The knower comes and goes with the known, and is transient; but that which knows that it does not know, which is free of memory and anticipation, is timeless.

Q: Is 'I am' itself the witness, or are they separate?

M: Without one the other cannot be. Yet they are not one. It is like the flower and its colour. Without flower — no colours; without colour — the flower remains unseen. Beyond is the light which on contact with the flower creates the colour. Realize that your true nature is that of pure light only, and both the perceived and the perceiver come and go together. That which makes both possible, and yet is neither, is your real being, which means not being a 'this' or 'that', but pure awareness of being and not-being. When awareness is turned on itself, the feeling is of not knowing. When it is turned outward, the knowables come into being. To say: 'I know myself' is a contradiction in terms for what is 'known' cannot be 'myself'.

Q: If the self is for ever the unknown, what then is realized in self-realization?

M: To know that the known cannot be me nor mine, is liberation enough. Freedom from self-identification with a set of memories and habits, the state of wonder at the infinite reaches of the being, its inexhaustible creativity and total transcendence, the absolute fearlessness born from the realization of the illusoriness and transiency of every mode of consciousness — flow from a deep and inexhaustible source. To know the source as source and appearance as appearance, and oneself as the source only is self-realization.

Q: On what side is the witness? Is it real or unreal?

M: Nobody can say: 'I am the witness'. The 'I am' is always witnessed. The state of detached awareness is the witness-consciousness, the 'mirror-mind'. It rises and sets with its object and thus it is not quite the real. Whatever its object, it remains the same, hence it is also real. It partakes of both the real and the unreal and is therefore a bridge between the two.

Q: If all happens only to the 'I am', if the 'I am' is the known and the knower and the knowledge itself, what does the witness do? Of what use is it?

M: It does nothing and is of no use whatsoever.

Q: Then why do we talk of it?

M: Because it is there. The bridge serves one purpose only — to cross over. You don't build houses on a bridge. The 'I am' looks at things, the witness sees through them. It sees them as they are — unreal and transient. To say 'not me, not mine' is the task of the witness.

Q: Is it the manifested *(saguna)* by which the unmanifested *(nirguna)* is represented?

M: The unmanifested is not represented. Nothing manifested can represent the unmanifested.

Q: Then why do you talk of it?

M: Because it is my birthplace. ●●●

79

Person, Witness and the Supreme

Questioner: We have a long history of drug-taking behind us, mostly drugs of the consciousness-expanding variety. They gave us the experience of other states of consciousness, high and low, and also the conviction, that drugs are unreliable and, at best, transitory and, at worst, destructive of organism and personality. We are in search of better means for developing consciousness and transcendence. We want the fruits of our search to stay with us and enrich our lives, instead of turning to pale memories and helpless regrets. If by the spiritual we mean self-investigation and development, our purpose in coming to India is definitely spiritual. The happy hippy stage is behind us; we are serious now and on the move. We know there is reality to be found, but we do not know how to find and hold on to it. We need no convincing, only guidance. Can you help us?

Maharaj: You do not need help, only advice. What you seek is already in you. Take my own case. I did nothing for my realization. My teacher told me that the reality is within me; I looked within and found it there, exactly as my teacher told me. To see reality is as simple as to see one's face in a mirror. Only the mirror must be clear and true. A quiet mind, undistorted by desires and fears, free from ideas and opinions, clear on all the levels, is needed to reflect the reality. Be clear and quiet — alert and detached, all else will happen by itself.

Q: You had to make your mind clear and quiet before you could realize the truth. How did you do it?

M: I did nothing. It just happened. I lived my life, attending to my family's needs. Nor did my Guru do it. It just happened, as he said it will.

Q: Things do not just happen. There must be a cause for everything.

M: All that happens is the cause of all that happens. Causes are numberless; the idea of a sole cause is an illusion.

Q: You must have been doing something specific — some meditation or Yoga. How can you say that realization will happen on its own?

M: Nothing specific. I just lived my life.

Q: I am amazed!.

M: So was I. But what was there to be amazed at? My teacher's words came true. So what? He knew me better than I knew myself, that is all. Why search for causes? In the very beginning I was giving some attention and time to the sense 'I am', but only in the beginning. Soon after my Guru died, I lived on. His words proved to be true. That is all. It is all one process. You tend to separate things in time and then look for causes.

Q: What is your work now? What are you doing?

M: You imagine being and doing as identical. It is not so. The mind and the body move and change and cause other minds and bodies to move and change and that is called doing, action. I see that it is in the nature of action to create further action, like fire that continues by burning. I neither act nor cause others to act; I am timelessly aware of what is going on.

Q: In your mind, or also in other minds?

M: There is only one mind, which swarms with ideas; 'I am this, I am that, this is mine, that is mine'. I am not the mind, never was, nor shall be.

Q: How did the mind come into being?

M: The world consists of matter, energy and intelligence. They manifest themselves in many ways. Desire and imagination create the world and intelligence reconciles the two and causes a sense of harmony and peace: To me it all happens; I am aware, yet unaffected.

Q: You cannot be aware, yet unaffected. There is a contradiction in terms. Perception is change. Once you have experienced a sensation, memory will not allow you to return to the former state.

M: Yes, what is added to memory cannot be erased easily. But it can surely be done and, in fact, I am doing it all the time. Like a bird on its wings, I leave no footprints.

Q: Has the witness name and form, or is it beyond these?

M: The witness is merely a point in awareness. It has no name and form. It is like the reflection of the sun in a drop of dew. The drop of dew has name and form, but the little point of light is caused by the sun. The clearness and smoothness of the drop is a necessary condition but not sufficient by itself. Similarly clarity and silence of the mind are necessary for the reflection of reality to appear in the mind, but by themselves they are not sufficient. There must be reality beyond it. Because reality is timelessly present, the stress is on the necessary conditions.

Q: Can it happen that the mind is clear and quiet and yet no reflection appears?

M: There is destiny to consider. The unconscious is in the grip of destiny; it is destiny, in fact. One may have to wait. But however heavy may be the hand of destiny, it can be lifted by patience and self-control. Integrity and purity remove the obstacles and the vision of reality appears in the mind.

Q: How does one gain self-control? I am so weak-minded!

M: Understand first that you are not the person you believe yourself to be. What you think yourself to be is mere suggestion or imagination. You have no parents, you were not born, nor will you die. Either trust me when I tell you so, or arrive to it by study and investigation. The way of total faith is quick, the other is slow but steady. Both must be tested in action. Act on what you think is true — this is the way to truth.

Q: Are deserving the truth and destiny one and the same?

M: Yes, both are in the unconscious. Conscious merit is mere vanity. Consciousness is always of obstacles; when there are no obstacles, one goes beyond it.

Q: Will the understanding that I am not the body give me the strength of character needed for self-control?

M: When you know that you are neither body nor mind, you will not be swayed by them. You will follow truth, wherever it takes you, and do what needs be done, whatever the price to pay.

Q: Is action essential for self-realization?

M: For realization, understanding is essential. Action is only incidental. A man of steady understanding will not refrain from action. Action is the test of truth.

Q: Are tests needed?

M: If you do not test yourself all the time, you will not be able to distinguish between reality and fancy. Observation and close reasoning help to some extent, but reality is paradoxical. How do you know that you have realized unless you watch your thoughts and feelings, words and actions and wonder at the changes occurring in you without your knowing why and how? It is exactly because they are so surprising that you know that they are real. The foreseen and expected is rarely true.

Q: How does the person come into being?

M: Exactly as a shadow appears when light is intercepted by the body, so does the person arise when pure self-awareness is obstructed by the 'I am-the-body', idea. And as the shadow changes shape and position according to the lay of the land, so does the person appear to rejoice and suffer, rest and toil, find and lose according to the pattern of destiny. When the body is no more, the person disappears completely without return, only the witness remains and the Great Unknown.

The witness is that which says 'I know'. The person says 'I do'. Now, to say 'I know' is not untrue — it is merely limited. But to say 'I do' is altogether false, because there is nobody who does; all happens by itself, including the idea of being a doer.

Q: Then what is action?

M: The universe is full of action, but there is no actor. There are numberless persons small and big and very big, who, through identification, imagine themselves as acting, but it does not change the fact that the world of action *(mahadakash)* is one single whole in which all depends on, and affects all. The stars affect us deeply and we affect the stars. Step back from action to consciousness, leave action to the body and the mind; it is their domain. Remain as pure witness, till even witnessing dissolves in the Supreme.

Imagine a thick jungle full of heavy timber. A plank is shaped out of the timber and a small pencil to write on it. The witness reads the writing and knows that while the pencil and the plank are distantly related to the jungle, the writing has nothing to do with it. It is totally super-imposed and its disappearance just does not matter. The dissolution of personality is followed always by a sense of great relief, as if a heavy burden has fallen off.

Q: When you say, I am in the state beyond the witness, what is the experience that makes you say so? In what way does it differ from the stage of being a witness only?

M: It is like washing printed cloth. First the design fades, then the background and in the end the cloth is plain white. The personality gives place to the witness, then the witness goes and pure awareness remains. The cloth was white in the beginning and is white in the end; the patterns and colours just happened — for a time.

Q: Can there be awareness without an object of awareness?

M: Awareness with an object we called witnessing. When there is also self-identification with the object, caused by desire or fear, such a state is called a person. In reality there is only one state; when distorted by self-identification it is called a person, when coloured with the sense of being, it is the witness; when colourless and limitless, it is called the Supreme.

Q: I find that I am always restless, longing, hoping, seeking, finding, enjoying, abandoning, searching again. What is it that keeps me on the boil?

M: You are really in search of yourself, without knowing it. You are love-longing for the love-worthy, the perfectly lovable. Due to ignorance you are looking for it in the world of opposites and contradictions. When you find it within, your search will be over.

Q: There will be always this sorrowful world to contend with.

M: Don't anticipate. You do not know. It is true that all manifestation is in the opposites. Pleasure and pain, good and bad, high and low, progress and regress, rest and strife — they all come and go together — and as long as there is a world, its contradictions will be there. There may also be periods of perfect harmony, of bliss and beauty, but only for a time. What is perfect, returns to the source of all perfection and the opposites play on.

Q: How am I to reach perfection?

M: Keep quiet. Do your work in the world, but inwardly keep quiet. Then all will come to you. Do not rely on your work for realization. It may profit others, but not you. Your hope lies in keeping silent in your mind and quiet in your heart. Realized people are very quiet.   ●●●

80

Awareness

Questioner: Does it take time to realize the Self, or time cannot help to realize? Is self-realization a matter of time only, or does it depend on factors other than time?

Maharaj: All waiting is futile. To depend on time to solve our problems is self-delusion. The future, left to itself merely repeats the past. Change can only happen now, never in the future.

Q: What brings about a change?

M: With crystal clarity see the need of change. This is all.

Q: Does self-realization happen in matter, or beyond? Is it not an experience depending on the body and the mind for its occurrence?

M: All experience is illusory, limited and temporal. Expect nothing from experience. Realization by itself is not an experience, though it may lead to a new dimension of experiences. Yet the new experiences, however interesting, are not more real than the old. Definitely realization is not a new experience. It is the discovery of the timeless factor in every experience. It is awareness, which makes experience possible. Just like in all the colours light is the colourless factor, so in every experience awareness is present, yet it is not an experience.

Q: If awareness is not an experience, how can it be realized?

M: Awareness is ever there. It need not be realized. Open the shutter of the mind, and it will be flooded with light.

Q: What is matter?

M: What you do not understand is matter.

Q: Science understands matter.

M: Science merely pushes back the frontiers of our ignorance.

Q: And what is nature?

M: The totality of conscious experiences is nature. As a conscious self you are a part of nature. As awareness, you are beyond. Seeing nature as mere consciousness is awareness.

Q: Are there levels of awareness?

M: There are levels in consciousness, but not in awareness. It is of one block, homogeneous. Its reflection in the mind is love and understanding. There are levels of clarity in understanding and intensity in love, but not in their source. The source is simple and single, but its gifts are infinite. Only do not take the gifts for the source. Realize yourself as the source and not as the river; that is all.

Q: I am the river too.

M: Of course, you are. As an 'I am' you are the river, flowing between the banks of the body. But you are also the source and the ocean and the clouds in the sky. Wherever there is life and consciousness, you are. Smaller than the smallest, bigger than the biggest, you *are*, while all else appears.

Q: The sense of being and the sense of living — are they one and the same, or different?

M: The identity in space creates one, the continuity in time creates the other.

Q: You said once that the seer, seeing and the seen are one single thing, not three. To me the three are separate. I do not doubt your words, only I do not understand.

M: Look closely and you will see that the seer and the seen appear only when there is seeing. They are attributes of seeing. When you say 'I am seeing this'. 'I am' and 'this' come with seeing, not before. You cannot have an unseen 'this' nor an unseeing 'I am'.

Q: I can say: 'I do not see'.

M: The 'I am seeing this' has become 'I am seeing my not seeing', or 'I am seeing darkness'. The seeing remains. In the triplicity: the known, knowing and the knower, only the knowing is a fact. The 'I am' and 'this' are doubtful. Who knows? What is known? There is no certainty, except that there is knowing.

Q: Why am I sure of knowing, but not of the knower?

M: Knowing is a reflection of your true nature along with being and loving. The knower and the known are added by the mind. It is in the nature of the mind to create a subject-object duality, where there is none.

Q: What is the cause of desire and fear?

M: Obviously, the memory of past pains and pleasures. There is no great mystery about it. Conflict arises only when desire and fear refer to the same object.

Q: How to put an end to memory?

M: It is neither necessary, nor possible. Realize that all happens in consciousness and you are the root, the source, the foundation of consciousness. The world is but a succession of experiences and you are what makes them conscious, and yet remain beyond all experience. It is like the heat, the flame and the burning wood. The heat maintains the flame, the flame consumes the wood. Without heat there would be neither flame nor fuel. Similarly, without awareness there would be no consciousness, nor life, which transforms matter into a vehicle of consciousness.

Q: You maintain that without me there would be no world, and that the world and my knowledge of the world are identical. Science has come to a quite different conclusion: the world exists as something concrete and continuous, while I am a by-product of biological evolution of the nervous system, which is primarily not so much a seat of consciousness, as a mechanism of survival as individual and species. Yours is altogether a subjective view, while science tries to describe everything in objective terms. Is this contradiction inevitable?

M: The confusion is apparent and purely verbal. What is, *is*. It is neither subjective nor objective. Matter and mind are not separate, they are aspects of one energy. Look at the mind as a function of matter and you have science; look at matter as the product of the mind and you have religion.

Q: But what is true? What comes first, mind or matter?

M: Neither comes first, for neither appears alone. Matter is the shape, mind is the name. Together they make the world. Pervading and transcending is Reality, pure being — awareness — bliss, your very essence.

Q: All I know is the stream of consciousness, an endless succession of events. The river of time flows, bringing and carrying away relentlessly. Transformation of the future into past is going on all the time.

M: Are you not the victim of your language? You speak about the flow of time, as if you were stationary. But the events you have witnessed yesterday somebody else may see tomorrow. It is you who are in movement and not time. Stop moving and time will cease.

Q: What does it mean — time will cease?

M: Past and future will merge in the eternal *now*.

Q: But what does it mean in actual experience? How do you know that for you time has ceased?

M: It may mean that past and future do not matter any more. It may also mean that all that happened and will happen becomes an open book to be read at will.

Q: I can imagine a sort of cosmic memory, accessible with some training. But how can the future be known? The unexpected is inevitable.

M: What is unexpected on one level may be certain to happen, when seen from a higher level. After all, we are within the limits of the mind. In reality nothing happens, there is no past nor future; all appears and nothing is.

Q: What does it mean, nothing is? Do you turn blank, or go to sleep? Or do you dissolve the world and keep us all in abeyance, until we are brought back to life at the next flicker of your thought?

M: Oh, no, it is not that bad. The world of mind and matter, of names and shapes, continues, but it does not matter to me at all. It is like having a shadow. It is there — following me wherever I go, but not hindering me in any way. It remains a world of experiences, but not of names and forms related to me by desires and fears. The experiences are qualityless, pure experiences, if I may say so. I call them experiences for the lack of a better word. They are like the waves on the surface of the ocean, the ever-present, but not affecting its peaceful power.

Q: You mean to say an experience can be nameless, formless, undefined?

M: In the beginning all experience is such. It is only desire and fear, born of memory, that give it name and form and separate it from other experiences.

It is not a conscious experience, for it is not in opposition to other experiences, yet it is an experience all the same.

Q: If it is not conscious, why talk about it?

M: Most of your experiences are unconscious. The conscious ones are very few. You are unaware of the fact because to you only the conscious ones count. Become aware of the unconscious.

Q: Can one be aware of the unconscious? How is it done?

M: Desire and fear are the obscuring and distorting factors. When mind is free of them the unconscious becomes accessible.

Q: Does it mean that the unconscious becomes conscious?

M: It is rather the other way round. The conscious becomes one with the unconscious. The distinction ceases, whichever way you look at it.

Q: I am puzzled. How can one be aware and yet unconscious?

M: Awareness is not limited to consciousness. It is of all that is. Consciousness is of duality. There is no duality in awareness. It is one single block of pure cognition. In the same way one can talk of the pure being and pure creation — nameless, formless, silent and yet absolutely real, powerful, effective. Their being indescribable does not affect them in the least. While they are unconscious, they are essential. The conscious cannot change fundamentally, it can only modify. Any thing, to change, must pass through death, through obscuration and dissolution. Gold jewellery must be melted down before it is cast into another shape. What refuses to die cannot be reborn.

Q: Barring the death of the body, how does one die?

M: Withdrawal, aloofness, letting go is death. To live fully, death is essential; every ending makes a new beginning.

On the other hand, do understand, that only the dead can die, not the living. That which is alive in you, is immortal.

Q: From where does desire draw its energy?

M: Its name and shape it draws from memory. The energy flows from the source.

Q: Some desires are altogether wrong. How can wrong desires flow from a sublime source?

M: The source is neither right nor wrong. Nor is desire by itself right or wrong. It is nothing but striving for happiness. Having identified yourself with a speck of a body you feel lost and search desperately for the sense of fulness and completeness, you call happiness.

Q: When did I lose it? I never had it.

M: You had it before you woke up this morning. Go beyond your consciousness and you will find it.

Q: How am I to go beyond?

M: You know it already; do it.

Q: That's what you say. I know nothing about it.

M: Yet I repeat — you know it. Do it. Go beyond, back to your normal, natural, supreme state.

Q: I'm puzzled.

M: A speck in the eye makes you think you are blind. Wash it out and look.

Q: I do look! I see only darkness.

M: Remove the speck and your eyes will be flooded with light. The light is there — waiting. The eyes are there — ready. The darkness you see is but the shadow of the tiny speck. Get rid of it and come back to your natural state.   ●●●

81

Root Cause of Fear

Maharaj: Where do you come from?

Questioner: I am from the United States, but I live mostly in Europe. To India I came recently. I was in Rishikesh, in two Ashrams. I was taught meditation and breathing.

M: How long were you there?

Q: Eight days in one, six days in another. I was not happy there and I left. Then for three weeks I was with the Tibetan Lamas. But they were all wrapped up in formulas and rituals.

M: And what was the net result of it all?

Q: Definitely there was an increase of energy. But before I left for Rishikesh, I did some fasting and dieting at a Nature Cure Sanatorium at Pudukkotai in South India. It has done me enormous good.

M: Maybe the access of energy was due to better health.

Q: I cannot say. But as a result of all these attempts some fires started burning in various places in my body and I heard chants and voices where there were none.

M: And what are you after now?

Q: Well, what are we all after? Some truth, some inner certainty, some real happiness. In the various schools of self-realization there is so much talk of awareness, that one ends with the impression that awareness itself is the supreme reality. Is it so? The body is looked after by the brain, the brain is illumined by consciousness; awareness watches over consciousness; is there anything beyond awareness?

M: How do you know that you are aware?

Q: I feel that I am. I cannot express it otherwise.

M: When you follow it up carefully from brain through consciousness to awareness, you find that the sense of duality persists. When you go beyond awareness, there is a state of non-duality, in which there is no cognition, only pure being, which may be as well called non-being, if by being you mean being something in particular.

Q: What you call pure being is it universal being, being everything?

M: Everything implies a collection of particulars. In pure being the very idea of the particular is absent.

Q: Is there any relationship between pure being and particular being?

M: What relationship can there be between what *is* and what merely appears to be? Is there any relationship between the ocean and its waves? The real enables the unreal to appear and causes it to disappear. The succession of transient moments creates the illusion of time, but the timeless reality of pure being is not in movement, for all movement requires a motionless background. It is itself the background. Once you have found it in yourself, you know that you had never lost that independent being, independent of all divisions and separations. But don't look for it in consciousness, you will not find it there. Don't look for it anywhere, for nothing contains it. On the contrary, it contains everything and manifests everything. It is like the daylight that makes everything visible while itself remaining invisible.

Q: Sir, of what use to me is your telling me that reality cannot be found in consciousness? Where else am I to look for it? How do you apprehend it?

M: It is quite simple. If I ask you what is the taste of your mouth, all you can do is to say: it is neither sweet nor bitter, nor sour nor astringent; it is what remains when all these tastes are not. Similarly, when all distinctions and reactions are no more, what remains is reality, simple and solid.

Q: All that I understand is that I am in the grip of a beginningless illusion. And I do not see how it can come to an end. If it could, it would — long ago. I must have had as many opportunities in the past as I shall have in the future. What could not happen cannot happen. Or, if it did, it could not last. Our very deplorable state after all these untold millions of years carries, at best, the promise of ultimate extinction, or, which is worse, the threat of an endless and meaningless repetition.

M: What proof have you that your present state is beginningless and endless? How were you before you were born? How will you be after death? And of your present state — how much do you know? You do not know even what was your condition before you woke up this morning? You only know a little of your present state and from it you draw conclusions for all times and places. You may be just dreaming and imagining your dream to be eternal.

Q: Calling it a dream does not change the situation. I repeat my question: what hope is left which the eternity behind me could not fulfil? Why should my future be different from my past?

M: In your fevered state, you project a past and a future and take them to be real. In fact, you know only your present moment. Why not investigate what is now, instead of questioning the imaginary past and future? Your present state is neither beginningless nor endless. It is over in a flash. Watch carefully from where it comes and where it goes. You will soon discover the timeless reality behind it.

Q: Why have I not done it before?

M: Just as every wave subsides into the ocean, so does every moment return to its source. Realization consists in discovering the source and abiding there.

Q: Who discovers?

M: The mind discovers.

Q: Does it find the answers?

M: It finds that it is left without questions, that no answers are needed.

Q: Being born is a fact. Dying is another fact. How do they appear to the witness?

M: A child was born; a man has died — just events in the course of time.

Q: Is there any progress in the witness? Does awareness evolve?

M: What is seen may undergo many changes when the light of awareness is focussed on it, but it is the object that changes, not the light. Plants grow in sunlight, but the sun does not grow. By themselves both the body and the witness are motionless, but when brought together in the mind, both appear to move.

Q: Yes, I can see that what moves and changes is the 'I am' only. Is the 'I am' needed at all?

M: Who needs it? It is there — now. It had a beginning it will have an end.

Q: What remains when the 'I am' goes?

M: What does not come and go — remains. It is the ever-greedy mind that creates ideas of progress and evolution towards perfection. It disturbs and talks of order, destroys and seeks security.

Q: Is there progress in destiny, in *karma*?

M: *Karma* is only a store of unspent energies, of unfulfilled desires and fears not understood. The store is being constantly replenished by new desires and fears. It need not be so for ever. Understand the root cause of your fears — estrangement from yourself: and of desires — the longing for the self, and your *karma* will dissolve like a dream. Between earth and heaven life goes on. Nothing is affected, only bodies grow and decay.

Q: Between the person and the witness, what is the relation?

M: There can be no relation between them because they are one. Don't separate and don't look for relationship.

Q: If the seer and the seen are one, how did the separation occur?

M: Fascinated by names and forms, which are by their very nature distinct and diverse, you distinguish what is natural and separate what is one. The world is rich in diversity, but your feeling strange and frightened is due to misapprehension. It is the body that is in danger, not you.

Q: I can see that the basic biological anxiety, the flight instinct, takes many shapes and distorts my thoughts and feelings. But how did this anxiety come into being?

M: It is a mental state caused by the 'I am-the-body' idea. It can be removed by the contrary idea: 'I am-not-the-body'. Both the ideas are false, but one removes the other. Realize that no ideas are your own, they all come to you from outside. You must think it all out for yourself, become yourself the object of your meditation. The effort to understand yourself is Yoga. Be a Yogi, give your life to it, brood, wonder, search, till you come to the root of error and to the truth beyond the error.

Q: In meditation, who meditates, the person or the witness?

M: Meditation is a deliberate attempt to pierce into the higher states of consciousness and finally go beyond it. The art of meditation is the art of shifting the focus of attention to ever subtler levels, without losing one's grip on the levels left behind. In a way it is like having death under control. One begins with the lowest levels: social circumstances, customs and habits; physical surroundings, the posture and the breathing of the body; the senses, their sensations and perceptions; the mind, its thoughts and feelings; until the entire mechanism of personality is grasped and firmly held. The final stage of meditation is reached when the sense of identity goes beyond the 'I-am-so-and-so', beyond 'so-I-am', beyond 'I-am-the-witness-only', beyond 'there-is', beyond all ideas into the impersonally personal pure being. But you must be energetic when you take to meditation. It is definitely not a part-time occupation.

Limit your interests and activities to what is needed for you and your dependents' barest needs. Save all your energies and time for breaking the wall your mind had built around you. Believe me, you will not regret.

Q: How do I come to know that my experience is universal?

M: At the end of your meditation all is known directly, no proofs whatsoever are required. Just as every drop of the ocean carries the taste of the ocean, so does every moment carry the taste of eternity. Definitions and descriptions have their place as useful incentives for further search, but you must go beyond them into what is undefinable and indescribable, except in negative terms.

After all, even universality and eternity are mere concepts, the opposites of being place and time-bound. Reality is not a concept, nor the manifestation of a concept. It has nothing to do with concepts. Concern yourself with your mind, remove its distortions and impurities. Once you had the taste of your own self, you will find it everywhere and at all times. Therefore, it is so important that you should come to it. Once you know it, you will never lose it.

But you must give yourself the opportunity through intensive, even arduous meditation.

Q: What exactly do you want me to do?

M: Give your heart and mind to brooding over the 'I am', what is it, how is it, what is its source, its life, its meaning. It is very much like digging a well. You reject all that is not water, till you reach the life-giving spring.

Q: How shall I know that I am moving in the right direction?

M: By your progress in intentness, in clarity and devotion to the task.

Q: We, Europeans, find it very difficult to keep quiet. The world is too much with us.

M: Oh, no, you are dreamers too. We differ only in the contents of our dreams. You are after perfection — in the future. We are intent on finding it — in the now. The limited only is perfectible. The unlimited is already perfect. You are perfect, only you don't know it. Learn to know yourself and you will discover wonders

All you need is already within you, only you must approach your self with reverence and love. Self-condemnation and self-distrust are grievous errors. Your constant flight from pain and search for pleasure is a sign of love you bear for your self; all I plead with you is this: make love of your self perfect. Deny yourself nothing — give your self infinity and eternity and discover that you do not need them; you are beyond.   •••

82

Absolute Perfection is Here and Now

Questioner: The war is on. What is your attitude to it?

Maharaj: In some place or other, in some form or other, the war is always on. Was there a time when there was no war? Some say it is the will of God. Some say it is God's play. It is another way of saying that wars are inevitable and nobody is responsible.

Q: But what is your own attitude?

M: Why impose attitudes on me? I have no attitude to call my own.

Q: Surely somebody is responsible for this horrible and senseless carnage. Why do people kill each other so readily?

M: Search for the culprit within. The ideas of 'me' and 'mine' are at the root of all conflict. Be free of them and you will be out of conflict.

Q: What of it that I am out of conflict? It will not affect the war. If I am the cause of war, I am ready to be destroyed. Yet, it stands to reason that the disappearance of a thousand like me will not stop wars. They did not start with my birth nor will end with my death. I am not responsible. Who is?

M: Strife and struggle are a part of existence. Why don't you enquire who is responsible for existence?

Q: Why do you say that existence and conflict are inseparable? Can there be no existence without strife? I need not fight others to be myself.

M: You fight others all the time for your survival as a separate body-mind, a particular name and form. To live you must destroy. From the moment you were conceived you started a war with your environment — a merciless war of mutual extermination, until death sets you free.

Q: My question remains unanswered. You are merely describing what I know — life and its sorrows. But who is responsible, you do not say. When I press you, you throw the blame on God, or *karma,* or on my own greed and fear — which merely invites further questions. Give me the final answer.

M: The final answer is this: nothing is. All is a momentary appearance in the field of the universal consciousness; continuity as name and form is a mental formation only, easy to dispel.

Q: I am asking about the immediate, the transitory, the appearance. Here is a picture of a child killed by soldiers. It is a fact — staring at you. You cannot deny it. Now, who is responsible for the death of the child?

M: Nobody and everybody. The world is what it contains and each thing affects all others. We all kill the child and we all die with it. Every event has innumerable causes and produces numberless effects. It is useless to keep accounts, nothing is traceable.

Q: Your people speak of *karma* and retribution.

M: It is merely a gross approximation: in reality we are all creators and creatures of each other, causing and bearing each other's burden.

Q: So, the innocent suffers for the guilty?

M: In our ignorance we are innocent; in our actions we are guilty. We sin without knowing and suffer without understanding. Our only hope: to stop, to look, to understand and to get out of the traps of memory. For memory feeds imagination and im-. agination generates desire and fear.

Q: Why do I imagine at all?

M: The light of consciousness passes through the film of memory and throws pictures on your brain. Because of the deficient and disordered state of your brain, what you perceive is distorted and coloured by feelings of like and dislike. Make your thinking orderly and free from emotional overtones, and you will see people and things as they are, with clarity and charity.

The witness of birth, life and death is one and the same. It is the witness of pain and of love. For while the existence in limitation and separation is sorrowful, we love it. We love it and hate it at the same time. We fight, we kill, we destroy life and property and yet we are affectionate and self-sacrificing. We nurse the child tenderly and orphan it too. Our life is full of contradictions. Yet we cling to it. This clinging is at the root of everything. Still, it is entirely superficial. We hold on to something or somebody, with all our might and next moment we forget it; like a child that shapes its mud-pies and abandons them light-heartedly. Touch them — it will scream with anger, divert the child and he forgets them. For our life is *now*, and the love of it is *now*. We love variety, the play of pain and pleasure, we are fascinated by contrasts. For this we need the opposites and their apparent separation. We enjoy them for a time and then get tired and crave for the peace and silence of pure being. The cosmic heart beats ceaselessly. I am the witness and the heart too.

Q: I can see the picture, but who is the painter? Who is responsible for this terrible and yet adorable experience?

M: The painter is in the picture. You separate the painter from the picture and look for him. Don't separate and don't put false questions. Things are as they are and nobody in particular is responsible. The idea of personal responsibility comes from the illusion of agency. 'Somebody must have done it, somebody is responsible'. Society as it is now, with its framework of laws and customs, is based on the idea of a separate and responsible personality, but this is not the only form a society can take. There may be other forms, where the sense of separation is weak and responsibility diffused.

Q: An individual with a weak sense of personality — is he nearer self-realization?

M: Take the case of a young child. The sense of 'I-am' is not yet formed, the personality is· rudimentary. The obstacles to self-knowledge are few, but the power and the clarity of awareness, its width and depth are lacking. In the course of years awareness will grow stronger, but also the latent personality will emerge and obscure and complicate. Just as the harder the wood, the hotter the flame, so the stronger the personality, the brighter the light generated from its destruction.

Q: Have you no problems?

M: I do have problems. I told you already. To be, to exist with a name and form is painful, yet I love it.

Q: But you love everything!

M: In existence everything is contained. My very nature is to love; even the painful is lovable.

Q: It does not make it less painful. Why not remain in the unlimited?

M: It is the instinct of exploration, the love of the unknown, that brings me into existence. It is in the nature of being to see adventure in becoming, as it is in the very nature of becoming to seek peace in being. This alteration of being and becoming is inevitable; but my home is beyond.

Q: Is your home in God?

M: To love and worship a god is also ignorance. My home is beyond all notions, however sublime.

Q: But God is not a notion! It is the reality beyond existence.

M: You may use any word you like. Whatever you may think of, am beyond it.

Q: Once you know your home, why not stay in it? What takes you out of it?

M: Out of love for corporate existence one is born and once

born, one gets involved in destiny. Destiny is inseparable from becoming. The desire to be the particular makes you into a person with all its personal past and future. Look at some great man, what a wonderful man he was! And yet how troubled was his life and limited its fruits. How utterly dependent is the personality of man and how indifferent is its world. And yet we love it and protect it for its very insignificance.

Q: The war is on and there is chaos and you are being asked to take charge of a feeding centre. You are given what is needed, it is only a question of getting through the job. Will you refuse it?

M: To work, or not to work, is one and the same to me. I may take charge, or may not. There may be others, better endowed for such tasks, than I am — professional caterers for instance. But my attitude is different. I do not look at death as a calamity, as I do not rejoice at the birth of a child. The child is out for trouble while the dead is out of it. Attachment to life is attachment to sorrow. We love what gives us pain. Such is our nature.

For me the moment of death will be a moment of jubilation, not of fear. I cried when I was born and I shall die laughing.

Q: What is the change in consciousness at the moment of death?

M: What change do you expect? When the film projection ends, all remains the same as when it started. The state before you were born was also the state after death, if you remember.

Q: I remember nothing.

M: Because you never tried. It is only a question of tuning in the mind. It requires training, of course.

Q: Why don't you take part in social work?

M: But I am doing nothing else all the time! And what is the social work you want me to do? Patchwork is not for me. My stand is clear: produce to distribute, feed before you eat, give before you take, think of others, before you think of yourself. Only a selfless society based on sharing can be stable and happy. This is the only practical solution. If you do not want it — fight.

Q: It is all a matter of *gunas*. Where *tamas* and *rajas* predominate, there must be war. Where *sattva* rules, there will be peace.

M: Put it whichever way you like, it comes to the same. Society is built on motives. Put goodwill into the foundations and you will not need specialized social workers.

Q: The world is getting better.

M: The world had all the time to get better, yet it did not. What hope is there for the future? Of course, there have been and will be periods of harmony and peace, when *sattva* was in ascendence, but things get destroyed by their own perfection. A perfect society is necessarily static and, therefore, it stagnates and decays. From the summit all roads lead downwards. Societies are like people — they are born, they grow to some point of relative perfection and then decay and die.

Q: Is there not a state of absolute perfection which does not decay?

M: Whatever has a beginning must have an end. In the timeless all is perfect, here and now.

Q: But shall we reach the timeless in due course?

M: In due course we shall come back to the starting point. Time cannot take us out of time, as space cannot take us out of space. All you get by waiting is more waiting. Absolute perfection is here and now, not in some future, near or far. The secret is in action — here and now. It is your behaviour that blinds you to yourself. Disregard whatever you think yourself to be and act as if you were absolutely perfect — whatever your idea of perfection may be. All you need is courage.

Q: Where do I find such courage?

M: In yourself, of course. Look within.

Q: Your grace will help

M: My grace is telling you now: look within. All you need you have. Use it. Behave as best you know, do what you think you should. Don't be afraid of mistakes; you can always correct them, only intentions matter. The shape things take is not within your power; the motives of your actions are.

Q: How can action born from imperfection lead to perfection?

M: Action does not lead to perfection; perfection is expressed in action. As long as you judge yourself by your expressions, give them utmost attention; when you realize your own being, your behaviour will be perfect — spontaneously.

Q: If I am timelessly perfect, then why was I born at all? What is the purpose of this life?

M: It is like asking: what does it profit gold to be made into an ornament? The ornament gets the colour and the beauty of gold; gold is not enriched. Similarly, reality expressed in action makes the action meaningful and beautiful.

Q: What does the real gain through its expressions?

M: What can it gain? Nothing whatsoever. But it is in the nature of love to express itself, to affirm itself, to overcome difficulties. Once you have understood that the world is love in action, you will look at it quite differently. But first your attitude to suffering must change. Suffering is primarily a call for attention, which itself is a movement of love. More than happiness, love wants growth, the widening and deepening of consciousness and being. Whatever prevents becomes a cause of pain and love does not shirk from pain. *Sattva*, the energy that works for righteousness and orderly development, must not be thwarted. When obstructed it turns against itself and becomes destructive. Whenever love is withheld and suffering allowed to spread, war becomes inevitable. Our indifference to our neighbour's sorrow brings suffering to our door.   ●●●

83

The True Guru

Questioner: You were saying the other day that at the root of your realization was the trust in your Guru. He assured you that you were already the Absolute Reality and there was nothing more to be done. You trusted him and left it at that, without straining, without striving. Now, my question is: without trust in your Guru would you have realized? After all, what you are, You are, whether your mind trusts or not; would doubt obstruct the action of the Guru's words and make them inoperative?

Maharaj: You have said it — they would have been made inoperative — for a time.

Q: And what would happen to the energy, or power in the Guru's words?

M: It would remain latent, unmanifested. But the entire question is based on a misunderstanding. The master, the disciple, the love and trust between them, these are one fact, not so many independent facts. Each is a part of the other. Without love and trust there would have been no Guru nor disciple, and no relationship between them. It is like pressing a switch to light an electric lamp. It is because the lamp, the wiring, the switch, the transformer, the transmission lines and the power house form a single whole, that you get the light. Any one factor missing and there would be no light. You must not separate the inseparable. Words do not create facts; they either describe them or distort. The fact is always non-verbal.

Q: I still do not understand; can the Guru's word remain unfulfilled or will it invariably prove true?

M: Words of a realized man never miss their purpose. They wait for the right conditions to arise which may take some time, and this is natural, for there is a season for sowing and a season for harvesting. But the word of a Guru is a seed that cannot perish. Of course, the Guru must be a real one, who is beyond the body and the mind, beyond consciousness itself, beyond space and time, beyond duality and unity, beyond understanding and description. The good people, who have read a lot and have a lot to say, may teach you many useful things, but they are not the real Gurus whose words invariably come true. They also may tell you that you are the ultimate reality itself, but what of it?

Q: Nevertheless, if for some reason I happen to trust them and obey, shall I be the loser?

M: If you are able to trust and obey, you will soon find your real Guru, or, rather, he will find you.

Q: Does every knower of the Self become a Guru, or can one be a knower of Reality without being able to take others to it?

M: If you know what you teach, you can teach what you know. Here seership and teachership are one. But the Absolute Reality is beyond both. The self-styled Gurus talk of ripeness and effort, of merits and achievements, of destiny and grace; all these are mere mental formations, projections of an addicted mind. Instead of helping, they obstruct.

Q: How can I make out whom to follow and whom to mistrust?

M: Mistrust all, until you are convinced. The true Guru will never humiliate you, nor will he estrange you from yourself. He will constantly bring you back to the fact of your inherent perfection and encourage you to seek within. He knows you need nothing, not even him, and is never tired of reminding you. But the self-appointed Guru is more concerned with himself than with his disciples.

Q: You said that reality is beyond the knowledge and the teaching of the real. Is not the knowledge of reality the supreme itself and teaching the proof of its attainment?

M: The knowledge of the real, or the self, is a state of mind. Teaching another is a movement in duality. They concern the mind only; *sattva* is a Guna all the same.

Q: What is real then?

M: He who knows the mind as non-realized and realized, who

knows ignorance and knowledge as states of mind, he is the real. When you are given diamonds mixed with gravel, you may either miss the diamonds or find them. It is the seeing that matters. Where is the greyness of the gravel and the beauty of the diamond, without the power to see? The known is but a shape and knowledge is but a name. The knower is but a state of mind. The real is beyond.

Q: Surely, objective knowledge and ideas of things and self-knowledge are not one and the same thing. One needs a brain, the other does not.

M: For the purpose of discussion you can arrange words and give them meaning, but the fact remains that all knowledge is a form of ignorance. The most accurate map is yet only paper. All knowledge is in memory; it is only recognition, while reality is beyond the duality of the knower and the known.

Q: Then by what is reality known?

M: How misleading is your language! You assume, unconsciously, that reality also is approachable through knowledge. And then you will bring in a knower of reality beyond reality! Do understand that to *be,* reality need not be known. Ignorance and knowledge are in the mind, not in the real.

Q: If there is no such thing as the knowledge of the real, then how do I reach it?

M: You need not reach out for what is already with you. Your very reaching out makes you miss it. Give up the idea that you have not found it and just let it come into the focus of direct perception, here and now, by removing all that is of the mind.

Q: When all that can go, goes, what remains?

M: Emptiness remains, awareness remains, pure light of the conscious being remains. It is like asking what remains of a room when all the furniture is removed? A most serviceable room remains. And when even the walls are pulled down, space remains. Beyond space and time is the *here* and the *now* of reality.

Q: Does the witness remain?

M: As long as there is consciousness, its witness is also there. The two appear and disappear together.

Q: If the witness too is transient, why is he given so much importance?

M: Just to break the spell of the known, the illusion that only the perceivable is real.

Q: Perception is primary, the witness — secondary.

M: This is the heart of the matter. As long as you believe that only the outer world is real, you remain its slave. To become free, your attention must be drawn to the 'I am', the witness. Of course, the knower and the known are one not two, but to break the spell of the known the knower must be brought to the forefront. Neither is primary, both are reflections in memory of the ineffable experience, ever new and ever now, untranslatable, quicker than the mind.

Q: Sir, I am an humble seeker, wandering from Guru to Guru in search of release. My mind is sick, burning with desire, frozen with fear. My days flit by, red with pain, grey with boredom. My age is advancing, my health decaying, my future dark and frightening. At this rate I shall live in sorrow and die in despair. Is there any hope for me? Or have I come too late?

M: Nothing is wrong with you, but the ideas you have of yourself are altogether wrong. It is not you who desires, fears and suffers, it is the person built on the foundation of your body by circumstances and influences. You are not that person. This must be clearly established in your mind and never lost sight of. Normally, it needs a prolonged sadhana, years of austerities and meditation.

Q: My mind is weak and vaccilating. I have neither the strength nor the tenacity for sadhana. My case is hopeless.

M: In a way yours is a most hopeful case. There is an alternative to sadhana, which is trust. If you cannot have the conviction born from fruitful search, then take advantage of my discovery, which I am so eager to share with you. I can see with the utmost clarity that you have never been, nor are, nor will be estranged from reality, that you are the fulness of perfection here and now and that nothing can deprive you of your heritage, of what you are. You are in no way different from me, only you do not know it. You do not know what you are and therefore you imagine yourself to be what you are not. Hence desires and fear and over-whelming despair. And meaningless activity in order to escape.

Just trust me and live by trusting me. I shall not mislead you. You are the Supreme Reality beyond the world and its creator, beyond consciousness and its witness, beyond all assertions and denials. Remember it, think of it, act on it. Abandon all sense of separation, see yourself in all and act accordingly. With action bliss will come and, with bliss, conviction. After all, you doubt yourself because you are in sorrow. Happiness, natural, spontaneous and lasting cannot be imagined. Either it is there, or it is not. Once you begin to experience the peace, love and happiness which need no outer causes, all your doubts will dissolve. Just catch hold of what I told you and live by it.

Q: You are telling me to live by memory?

M: You are living by memory anyhow. I am merely asking you to replace the old memories by the memory of what I told you. As you were acting on your old memories, act on the new one. Don't be afraid. For some time there is bound to be a conflict be-tween the old and the new, but if you put yourself resolutely on the side of the new, the strife will soon come to an end and you will realize the effortless state of being oneself, of not being de-ceived by desires and fears born of illusion.

Q: Many Gurus have the habit of giving tokens of their grace — their head cloth, or their sticks, or begging bowl, or robe, thus transmitting or confirming the self-realization of their disciples. I can see no value in such practices. It is not self-realization that is transmitted, but self-importance. Of what earthly use is being told something very flattering, but not true? On one hand you are warning me against the many self-styled Gurus, on the other you want me to trust you. Why do you claim to be an exception?

M: I do not ask you to trust me. Trust my words and remember them, I want your happiness, not mine. Distrust those who put a distance between you and your true being and offer themselves as a go-between. I do nothing of the kind. I do not even make any promises. I merely say: if you trust my words and put them to test, you will for yourself discover how absolutely true they are. If you ask for a proof before you venture, I can only say:

am the proof. I did trust my teacher's words and kept them in my mind and I did find that he was right, that I was, am and shall be the Infinite Reality, embracing all; transcending all.

As you say, you have neither the time nor the energy for lengthy practices. I offer you an alternative. Accept my words on trust and live anew, or live and die in sorrow.

Q: It seems too good to be true.

M: Don't be misled by the simplicity of the advice. Very few are those who have the courage to trust the innocent and the simple. To know that you are a prisoner of your mind, that you live in an imaginary world of your own creation is the dawn of wisdom. To want nothing of it, to be ready to abandon it entirely, is earnestness. Only such earnestness, born of true despair, will make you trust me.

Q: Have I not suffered enough?

M: Suffering has made you dull, unable to see its enormity. Your first task is to see the sorrow in you and around you; your next to long intensely for liberation. The very intensity of longing will guide you; you need no other guide.

Q: Suffering has made me dull, indifferent even to itself.

M: Maybe it is not sorrow but pleasure that made you dull. Investigate.

Q: Whatever may be the cause; I am dull. I have neither the will nor the energy.

M: Oh, no. You have enough for the first step. And each step will generate enough energy for the next. Energy comes with confidence and confidence comes with experience.

Q: Is it right to change Gurus?

M: Why not change? Gurus are like milestones? It is natural to move on from one to another. Each tells you the direction and the distance, while the sadguru, the eternal Guru, is the road itself. Once you realize that the road is the goal and that you are always on the road, not to reach a goal, but to enjoy its beauty and its wisdom, life ceases to be a task and becomes natural and simple, in itself an ecstacy.

Q: So, there is no need to worship, to pray, to practis Yoga?

M: A little of daily sweeping, washing and bathing can do no harm. Self-awareness tells you at every step what needs be done. When all is done, the mind remains quiet.

Now you are in the waking state, a person with name and shape, joys and sorrows. The person was not there before you were born, nor will be there after you die. Instead of struggling with the person to make it become what it is not, why not go beyond the waking state and leave the personal life altogether? It does not mean the extinction of the person; it means only seeing it in right perspective.

Q: One more question. You said that before I was born I was one with the pure being of reality; if so, who decided that I should be born?

M: In reality you were never born and never shall die. But now you imagine that you are, or have a body and you ask what has brought about this state. Within the limits of illusion the answer is: desire born from memory attracts you to a body and makes you think as one with it. But this is true only from the relative point of view. In fact, there is no body, nor a world to contain it; there is only a mental condition, a dream-like state, easy to dispel by questioning its reality.

Q: After you die, will you come again? If I live long enough, will I meet you again.

M: To you the body is real, to me there is none. I, as you see me, exist in your imagination only. Surely, you will see me again, if and when you need me. It does not affect me, as the Sun is not affected by sunrises and sunsets. Because it is not affected, it is certain to be there when needed.

You are bent on knowledge, I am not. I do not have that sense of insecurity that makes crave to know. I am curious, like a child is curious. But there is no anxiety to make me seek refuge in knowledge. Therefore, I am not concerned whether I shall be re-born, or how long will the world last. These are questions born of fear. ●●●

84

Your Goal is Your Guru

Questioner: You were telling us that there are many self-styled Gurus, but a real Guru is very rare. There are many *gnanis* who imagine themselves realized, but all they have is book knowledge and a high opinion of themselves. Sometimes they impress, even fascinate, attract disciples and make them waste their time in useless practices. After some years, when the disciple takes stock of himself, he finds no change. When he complains to his teacher, he gets the usual rebuke that he did not try hard enough. The blame is on the lack of faith and love in the heart of the disciple, while in reality the blame is on the Guru, who had no business in accepting disciples and raising their hopes. How to protect oneself from such Gurus?

Maharaj: Why be so concerned with others? Whoever may be the Guru, if he is pure of heart and acts in good faith, he will do his disciples no harm. If there is no progress, the fault lies with the disciples, their laziness and lack of self-control. On the other hand, if the disciple is earnest and applies himself intelligently and with zest to his *sadhana*, he is bound to meet a more qualified teacher, who will take him further. Your question flows from three false assumptions: that one needs concern oneself with others; that one can evaluate another and that the progress of the disciple is the task and responsibility of his Guru. In reality, the Guru's role is only to instruct and encourage; the disciple is totally responsible for himself.

Q: We are told that total surrender to the Guru is enough, that the Guru will do the rest.

M: Of course, when there is total surrender, complete relinquishment of all concern with one's past, present and future, with one's physical and spiritual security and standing, a new

life dawns, full of love and beauty; then the Guru is not important, for the disciple has broken the shell of self-defence. Complete self-surrender by itself is liberation.

Q: When both the disciple and his teacher are inadequate,
what will happen?

M: In the long run all will be well. After all, the real Self of both is
not affected by the comedy they play for a time. They will sober
up and ripen and shift to a higher level of relationship.

Q: Or, they may separate.

M: Yes, they may separate. After all, no relationship is forever.
Duality is a temporary state.

Q: Is it by accident that I met you and by another accident shall
we separate never to meet again? Or is my meeting you a part
of some cosmic pattern, a fragment in the great drama of our
lives?

M: The real is meaningful and the meaningful relates to reality.
If our relationship is meaningful to you and me, it cannot be accidental. The future affects the present as much, as the past.

Q: How can I make out who is a real saint and who is not?

M: You cannot, unless you have a clear insight into the heart of
man. Appearances are deceptive. To see clearly, your mind
must be pure and unattached. Unless you know yourself well,
how can you know another? And when you know yourself — you
are the other.

Leave others alone for some time and examine yourself.
There are so many things you do not know about yourself —
what are you, who are you, how did you come to be born, what
are you doing now and why, where are you going, what is the
meaning and purpose of your life, your death, your future? Have
you a past, have you a future? How did you come to live in turmoil and sorrow, while your entire being strives for happiness
and peace? These are weighty matters and have to be attended
to first. You have no need, nor time for finding who is a *gnani*
and who is not?

Q: I must select my guru rightly.

M: Be the right man and the right Guru will surely find you.

Q: You are not answering my question: how to find the right Guru?

M: But I did answer your question. Do not look for a Guru, do not even think of one. Make your goal your Guru. After all, the Guru is but a means to an end, not the end itself. He is not important, it is what you expect of him that matters to you. Now, what do you expect?

Q: By his grace I shall be made happy, powerful and peaceful.

M: What ambitions! How can a person limited in time and space, a mere body-mind, a gasp of pain between birth and death, be happy? The very conditions of its arising make happiness impossible. Peace, power, happiness, these are never personal states, nobody can say 'my peace', 'my power' — because 'mine' implies exclusivity, which is fragile and insecure.

Q: I know only my conditioned existence; there is nothing else.

M: Surely, you cannot say so. In deep sleep you are not conditioned. How ready and willing you are to go to sleep, how peaceful, free and happy you are when asleep!

Q: I know nothing of it.

M: Put it negatively. When you sleep, you are not in pain, nor bound, nor restless.

Q: I see your point. While awake, I know that I am, but am not happy; in sleep I am, I am happy, but I don't know it. All I need is to know that I am free and happy.

M: Quite so. Now, go within, into a state which you may compare to a state of waking sleep, in which you are aware of yourself, but not of the world. In that state you will know, without the least trace of doubt, that at the root of your being you are free and happy. The only trouble is that you are addicted to experience and you cherish your memories. In reality it is the other way round; what is remembered is never real; the real is *now*.

Q: All this I grasp verbally, but it does not become a part of myself. It remains as a picture in my mind to be looked at. Is it not the task of the Guru to give life to the picture?

M: Again, it is the other way round. The picture is alive; dead is the mind. As the mind is made of words and images, so is every reflection in the mind. It covers up reality with verbalization and then complains. You say a Guru is needed, to do miracles with you. You are playing with words only. The Guru and the disciple are one single thing, like the candle and its flame. Unless the disciple is earnest, he cannot be called a disciple. Unless a Guru is all love and self-giving, he cannot be called a Guru. Only Reality begets reality, not the false.

Q: I can see that I am false. Who will make me true?

M: The very words you said will do it. The sentence: 'I can see that I am false' contains all you need for liberation. Ponder over it, go into it deeply, go to the root of it; it will operate. The power is in the word, not in the person.

Q: I do not grasp you fully. On one hand you say a Guru is needed; on the other — the Guru can only give advice, but the effort is mine. Please state clearly — can one realize the Self without a Guru, or is the finding of a true Guru essential?

M: More essential is the finding of a true disciple. Believe me a true disciple is very rare, for in no time he goes beyond the need for a Guru, by finding his own self. Don't waste your time on trying to make out whether the advice you get flows from knowledge only, or from valid experience? Just follow it faithfully. Life will bring you another Guru, if another one is needed. Or deprive you of all outer guidance and leave you to your own lights. It is very important to understand that it is the teaching that matters, not the person of the Guru. You get a letter that makes you laugh or cry. It is not the postman who does it. The Guru only tells you the good news about your real Self and shows you the way back to it. In a way the Guru is its messenger. There will be many messengers, but the message is one: be what you are. Or, you can put it differently: until you realize yourself, you cannot know who is your real Guru. When you realize, you find that all the Gurus you had have contributed to your awakening. Your realization is the proof that your Guru was real. Therefore, take him as he is, do what he tells you, with earnestness and zeal and trust your heart to warn you if anything goes wrong. If doubt sets in, don't fight it. Cling to what is doubtless and leave the doubtful alone.

Q: I have a Guru and I love him very much. But whether he is my true Guru I do not know.

M: Watch yourself. If you see yourself changing, growing, it means you have found the right man. He may be beautiful or ugly, pleasant or unpleasant, flattering you or scolding; nothing matters except the one crucial fact of 'inward growth. If you don't, well, he may be your friend, but not your Guru.

Q: When I meet a European with some education and talk to him about a Guru and his teachings, his reaction is: 'the man must be mad to teach such nonsense'. What am I to tell him?

M: Take him to himself. Show him, how little he knows himself, how he takes the most absurd statements about himself for holy truth. He is told that he is the body, was born, will die, has parents, duties, learns to like what others like and fear what others fear. Totally a creature of heredity and society, he lives by memory and acts by habits. Ignorant of himself and his true interests, he pursues false aims and is always frustrated. His life and death are meaningless and painful, and there seems to be no way out. Then tell him, there is a way out within his easy reach, not a conversion to another set of ideas, but a liberation from all ideas and patterns of living. Don't tell him about Gurus and disciples — this way of thinking is not for him. His is an inner path, he is moved by an inner urge and guided by an inner light. Invite him to rebel and he will respond. Do not try to impress on him that so-and-so is a realized man and can be accepted as a Guru. As long as he does not trust himself, he cannot trust another. And confidence will come with experience.

Q: How strange! I cannot imagine life without a Guru.

M: It is a matter of temperament. You too are right. For you, singing the praises of God is enough. You need not desire realization, nor take up a sadhana. God's name is all the food 'you need. Live on it.

Q: This constant repetition of a few words, is it not a kind of madness?

M: It is madness, but it is a deliberate madness. All repetiveness is tamas, but repeating the name of God is sattva-tamas due to its high purpose. Because of the presence of sattva, the tamas will wear out and will take the shape of complete dispassion, detachment, relinquishment, aloofness, immutability.

Tamas becomes the firm foundation on which an integrated life can be lived.

Q: The immutable — does it die?

M: It is the changing that dies. The immutable neither lives nor dies; it is the timeless witness of life and death. You cannot call it dead, for it is aware. Nor can you call it alive, for it does not change. It is just like your tape-recorder. It records, it reproduces — all by itself. You only listen. Similarly, I watch all that happens, including my talking to you. It is not me who talks, the words appear in my mind and then I hear them said.

Q: Is it not the case with everybody.

M: Who said no? But you insist that you think, you speak, while to me there is thinking, there is speaking.

Q: There are two cases to consider. Either I have found a Guru, or I have not. In each case what is the right thing to do?

M: You are never without a Guru, for he is timelessly present in your heart. Sometimes he externalizes himself and comes to you as an uplifting and reforming factor in your life, a mother, a wife, a teacher; or he remains as an inner urge towards righteousness and perfection. All you have to do is to obey him and do what he tells you. What he wants you to do is simple, learn self-awareness, self-control, self-surrender. It may seem arduous, but it is easy if you are earnest. And quite impossible if you are not. Earnestness is both necessary and sufficient. Everything yields to earnestness.

Q: What makes one earnest?

M: Compassion is the foundation of earnestness. Compassion for yourself and others, born of suffering, your own and of others.

Q: Must I suffer to be earnest?

M: You need not, if you are sensitive and respond to the sorrows of others, as Buddha did. But if you are callous and without pity, your own suffering will make you ask the inevitable questions.

Q: I find myself suffering, but not enough. Life is unpleasant, but bearable. My little pleasures compensate me for my small pains and on the whole I am better off than most of the people I know. I know that my condition is precarious, that a calamity can overtake me any moment. Must I wait for a crisis to put me on my way to truth?

M: The moment you have seen how fragile is your condition, you are already alert. Now, keep alert, give attention, enquire, investigate, discover your mistakes of mind and body and abandon them.

Q: Where is the energy to come from? I am like a paralyzed man in a burning house.

M: Even paralyzed people sometimes find their legs in a moment of danger! But you are not paralyzed, you merely imagine so. Make the first step and you will be on your way.

Q: I feel that my hold on the body is so strong that I just cannot give up the idea that I am the body. It will cling to me as long as the body lasts. There are people who maintain that no realization is possible while alive and I feel inclined to agree with them.

M: Before you agree or disagree, why not investigate the very idea of a body? Does the mind appear in the body or the body in the mind? Surely there must be a mind to conceive the 'I-am-the-body' idea. A body without a mind cannot be 'my body'. 'My body' is invariably absent when the mind is in abeyance. It is also absent when the mind is deeply engaged in thoughts and feelings. Once you realize that the body depends on the mind, and the mind on consciousness, and consciousness on awareness and not the other way round, your question about waiting for self-realization till you die is answered. It is not that you must be free from 'I-am-the-body' idea first, and then realize the self. It is definitely the other way round — you cling to the false, because you do not know the true. Earnestness, not perfection, is a precondition to self-realization. Virtues and powers come with realization, not before.   ●●●

85

'I am': The Foundation of all Experience

Questioner: I hear you making statements about yourself like: 'I am timeless, immutable beyond attributes', etc. How do you know these things? And what makes you say them?

Maharaj: I am only trying to describe the state before the 'I am' arose, but the state itself, being beyond the mind and its language, is indescribable.

Q: The 'I am' is the foundation of all experience. What you are trying to describe must also be an experience, limited and transitory. You speak of yourself as immutable. I hear the sound of the word, I remember its dictionary meaning, but the experience of being immutable I do not have. How can I break through the barrier and know personally, intimately, what it means to be immutable?

M: The word itself is the bridge. Remember it, think of it, explore it, go round it, look at it from all directions, dive into it with earnest perseverance: endure all delays and disappointments till suddenly the mind turns round, away from the word, towards the reality beyond the word. It is like trying to find a person knowing his name only. A day comes when your enquiries bring you to him and the name becomes reality. Words are valuable, for between the word and its meaning there is a link and if one investigates the word assiduously, one crosses beyond the concept into the experience at the root of it. As a matter of fact, such repeated attempts to go beyond the words is what is called meditation. *Sadhana* is but a persistent attempt to cross over from the verbal to the non-verbal. The task seems hopeless until suddenly all becomes clear and simple and so wonderfully easy. But, as long as you are interested in your present way of living, you will shirk from the final leap into the unknown.

Q: Why should the unknown interest me? Of what use is the unknown?

M: Of no use whatsoever. But it is worthwhile to know what keeps you within the narrow confines of the known. It is the full and correct knowledge of the known that takes you to the unknown. You cannot think of it in terms of uses and advantages; to be quiet and detached, beyond the reach of all self-concern, all selfish consideration, is an inescapable condition of liberation. You may call it death; to me it is living at its most meaningful and intense, for I am one with life in its totality and fulness — intensity, meaningfulness, harmony; what more do you want?

Q: Nothing more is needed, of course. But you are talking of the knowable.

M: Of the unknowable only silence talks. The mind can talk only of what it knows. If you diligently investigate the knowable, it dissolves and only the unknowable remains. But with the first flicker of imagination and interest the unknowable is obscured and the known comes to the fore-front. The known, the changing, is what you live with — the unchangeable is of no use to you. It is only when you are satiated with the changeable and long for the unchangeable, that you are ready for the turning round and stepping into what can be described, when seen from the level of the mind, as emptiness and darkness. For the mind craves for content and variety, while reality is, to the mind, contentless and invariable.

Q: It looks like death to me.

M: It is. It is also all-pervading, all-conquering, intense beyond words. No ordinary brain can stand it without being shattered; hence the absolute need for *sadhana*. Purity of body and clarity of mind, non-violence and selflessness in life are essential for survival as an intelligent and spiritual entity.

Q: Are there entities in Reality?

M: Identity is Reality, Reality is identity. Reality is not a shapeless mass, a wordless chaos. It is powerful, aware, blissful; compared to it your life is like a candle to the sun.

Q: By the grace of God and your teacher's you lost all desire and fear and reached the immovable state. My question is simple — how do you know that your state is immovable?

M: Only the changeable can be thought of and talked about. The unchangeable can only be realized in silence. Once realized, it will deeply affect the changeable, itself remaining unaffected.

Q: How do you know that you are the witness?

M: I do not know, I am. I am, because to *be* everything must be witnessed.

Q: Existence can be also accepted on hearsay.

M: Still, finally you come to the need of a direct witness. Witnessing, if not personal and actual, must be at least possible and feasible. Direct experience is the final proof.

Q: Experience may be faulty and misleading.

M: Quite, but not the fact of an experience. Whatever may be the experience, true or false, the fact of an experience taking place cannot be denied. It is its own proof. Watch yourself closely and you will see that whatever be the content of consciousness, the witnessing of it does not depend on the content. Awareness is itself and does not change with the event. The event may be pleasant or unpleasant, minor or important, awareness is the same. Take note of the peculiar nature of pure awareness, its natural self-identity, without the least trace of self-consciousness, and go to the root of it and you will soon realize that awareness is your true nature and nothing you may be aware of, you can call your own.

Q: Is not consciousness and its content one and the same?

M: Consciousness is like a cloud in the sky and the water drops are the content. The cloud needs the sun to become visible, and consciousness needs being focussed in awareness.

Q: Is not awareness a form of consciousness?

M: When the content is viewed without likes and dislikes, the consciousness of it is awareness. But still there is a difference between awareness as reflected in consciousness and pure awareness beyond consciousness. Reflected awareness, the sense: 'I am aware' is the witness, while pure awareness is the essence of reality. Reflection of the sun in a drop of water is a reflection of the sun, no doubt, but not the sun itself. Between awareness reflected in consciousness as the witness and pure awareness there is a gap, which the mind cannot cross.

Q: Does it not depend on the way you look at it? The mind says there is difference. The heart says there is none.

M: Of course there is no difference. The real sees the real in the unreal. It is the mind that creates the unreal and it is the mind that sees the false as false.

Q: I understood that the experience of the real follows the seeing of the false as false.

M: There is no such thing as the experience of the real. The real is beyond experience. All experience is in the mind. You know the real by being real.

Q: If the real is beyond words and mind, why do we talk so much about it?

M: For the joy of it, of course. The real is bliss supreme. Even to talk of it is happiness.

Q: I hear you talking of the unshakable and blissful. What is in your mind when you use these words?

M: There is nothing in my mind. As you hear the words, so do I hear them. The power that makes everything happen makes them also happen.

Q: But you are speaking, not me.

M: That is how it appears to you. As I see it, two body-minds exchange symbolic noises. In reality nothing happens.

Q: Listen, Sir. I am coming to you because I am in trouble. I am a poor soul lost in a world I do not understand. I am afraid of Mother Nature who wants me to grow, procreate and die. When I ask for the meaning and the purpose of all this, she does not answer. I have come to you because I was told that you are kind and wise. You talk about the changeable as false and transient and this I can understand. But when you talk of the immutable, I feel lost. 'Not this, not that, beyond knowledge, of no use' — why talk of it all? Does it exist, or is it a concept only, a verbal opposite to the changeable?

M: It is, it alone *is*. But in your present state it is of no use to you. Just like the glass of water near your bed is of no use to you, when you dream that you are dying of thirst in a desert. I am trying to wake you up, whatever your dream.

Q: Please don't tell me that I am dreaming and that I will soon wake up. I wish it were so. But I am awake and in pain. You talk of a painless state, but you add that I cannot have it in my present condition. I feel lost.

M: Don't feel lost. I only say that to find the immutable and blissful you must give up your hold on the mutable and painful. You are concerned with your own happiness and I am telling you that there is no such thing. Happiness is never your own, it is where the 'I' is not. I do not say it is beyond your reach; you have only to reach out beyond yourself, and you will find it.

Q: If I have to go beyond myself, why did I get the 'I am' idea in the first instance?

M: The mind needs a centre to draw a circle. The circle may grow bigger and with every increase there will be a change in the sense 'I am'. A man who took himself in hand, a Yogi, will draw a spiral, yet the centre will remain, however vast the spiral. A day comes when the entire enterprise is seen as false and is given up. The central point is no more and the universe becomes the centre.

Q: Yes, maybe. But what am I to do now?

M: Assiduously watch your ever-changing life, probe deeply into the motives beyond your actions and you will soon prick the bubble in which you are enclosed. A chic needs the shell to grow, but a day comes when the shell must be broken. If it is not, there will be suffering and death.

Q: Do you mean to say that if I do not take to Yoga, I am doomed to extinction?

M: There is the Guru who will come to your rescue. In the meantime be satisfied with watching the flow of your life; if your watchfulness is deep and steady, ever turned towards the source, it will gradually move upstream till suddenly it becomes the source. Put your awareness to work, not your mind. The mind is not the right instrument for this task. The timeless can be reached only by the timeless. Your body and your mind are both subject to time; only awareness is timeless, even in the now. In awareness you are facing facts and reality is fond of facts.

Q: You rely entirely on my awareness to take me over and not on the Guru and God.

M: God gives the body and the mind and the Guru shows the way to use them. But returning to the source is your own task.

Q: God has created me, he will look after me.

M: There are innumerable gods, each in his own universe. They create and re-create eternally. Are you going to wait for them to save you? What you need for your salvation is already within your reach. Use it. Investigate what you know to its very end and you will reach the unknown layers of your being. Go further and the unexpected will explode in you and shatter all.

Q: Does it mean death?

M: It means life — at last.   ●●●

86

The Unknown is the Home of the Real

Questioner: Who is the Guru and who is the supreme Guru?

Maharaj: All that happens in your consciousness is your Guru. And pure awareness beyond consciousness is the supreme Guru.

Q: My Guru is Sri Babaji. What is your opinion of him?

M: What a question to ask! The space in Bombay is asked what is its opinion of the space in Poona. The names differ, but not the space. The word 'Babaji' is merely an address. Who lives under the address? You ask questions when you are in trouble. Enquire who is giving trouble and to whom.

Q: I understand everybody is under the obligation to realize. Is it his duty, or is it his destiny?

M: Realization is of the fact that you are not a person. Therefore, it cannot be the duty of the person whose destiny is to disappear. Its destiny is the duty of him who imagines himself to be the person. Find out who he is and the imagined person will dissolve. Freedom is from something. What are you to be free from? Obviously, you must be free from the person, you take yourself to be, for it is the idea you have of yourself that keeps you in bondage.

Q: How is the person removed?

M: By determination. Understand that it must go and wish it to go — it shall go if you are earnest about it. Somebody, anybody, will tell you that you are pure consciousness, not a body-mind. Accept it as a possibility and investigate earnestly. You may discover that it is not so, that you are not a person bound in space and time. Think of the difference it would make!

Q: If I am not a person, then what am I?

M: Wet cloth looks, feels, smells differently as long as it is wet. When dry it is again the normal cloth. Water has left it and who can make out that it was wet? Your real nature is not like what you appear to be. Give up the idea of being a person, that is all. You need not become what you are anyhow. There is the identity of what you are and there is the person superimposed on it. All you know is the person, the identity — which is not a person — you do not know, for you never doubted, never asked yourself the crucial question — 'Who am I'. The identity is the witness of the person and *sadhana* consists in shifting the emphasis from the superficial and changeful person to the immutable and ever-present witness.

Q: How is it that the question 'Who am I' attracts me little? I prefer to spend my time in the sweet company of saints.

M: Abiding in your own being is also holy company. If you have no problem of suffering and release from suffering, you will not find the energy and persistence needed for self-enquiry. You cannot manufacture a crisis. It must be genuine.

Q: How does a genuine crisis happen?

M: It happens every moment, but you are not alert enough. A shadow on your neighbour's face, the immense and all-pervading sorrow of existence is a constant factor in your life, but you refuse to take notice. You suffer and see others suffer, but you don't respond.

Q: What you say is true, but what can I do about it? Such indeed is the situation. My helplessness and dullness are a part of it.

M: Good enough. Look at yourself steadily — it is enough. The door that locks you in, is also the door that lets you out. The 'I am' is the door. Stay at it until it opens. As a matter of fact, it is open, only you are not at it. You are waiting at the non-existent painted doors, which will never open.

Q: Many of us were taking drugs at some time, and to some extent. People told us to take drugs in order to break through into higher levels of consciousness. Others advised us to have abundant sex for the same purpose. What is your opinion in the matter?

M: No doubt, a drug that can affect your brain can also affect your mind, and give you all the strange experiences promised. But what are all the drugs compared to the drug that gave you this most unusual experience of being born and living in sorrow and fear, in search of happiness, which does not come, or does not last. You should enquire into the nature of this drug and find an antidote.

Birth, life, death — they are one. Find out what had caused them. Before you were born, you were already drugged. What kind of drug was it? You may cure yourself of all diseases, but if you are still under the influence of the primordial drug, of what use are the superficial cures?

Q: Is it not *karma* that causes rebirth?

M: You may change the name, but the fact remains. What is the drug which you call *karma* or destiny? It made you believe yourself to be what you are not. What is it, and can you be free of it? Before you go further you must accept, at least as a working theory, that you are not what you appear to be, that you are under the influence of a drug. Then only you will have the urge and the patience to examine the symptoms and search for their common cause. All that a Guru can tell you is: 'My dear Sir, you are quite mistaken about yourself. You are not the person you think yourself to be.' Trust nobody, not even yourself. Search, find out, remove and reject every assumption till you reach the living waters and the rock of truth. Until you are free of the drug, all your religions and sciences, prayers and Yogas are of no use to you, for based on a mistake, they strengthen it. But if you stay with the idea that you are not the body nor the mind. not even their witness, but altogether beyond, your mind will grow in clarity, your desires — in purity, your actions — in charity and that inner distillation will take you to another world, a world of truth and fearless love. Resist your old habits of feeling and thinking; keep on telling yourself: 'No, not so, it cannot be so; I am not like this, I do not need it, I do not want it', and a day will surely come when the entire structure of error and despair will collapse and the ground will be free for a new life. After all, you must remember, that all your preoccupations with yourself are only during waking hours and partly in your dreams; in sleep all is put aside and forgotten. It shows how little important is your waking life, even to yourself, that merely lying down and closing the eyes can end it. Each time you go to sleep you do so without the least certainty of waking up and yet you accept the risk.

Q: When you sleep, are you conscious or unconscious?

M: I remain conscious, but not conscious of being a particular person.

Q: Can you give us the taste of the experience of self-realization?

M: Take the whole of it! It is here for the asking. But you do not ask. Even when you ask, you do not take. Find out what prevents you from taking.

Q: I know what prevents — my ego.

M: Then get busy with your ego — leave me alone. As long as you are locked up within your mind, my state is beyond your grasp.

Q: I find I have no more questions to ask.

M: Were you really at war with your ego, you would have put many more questions. You are short of questions because you are not really interested. At present you are moved by the pleasure-pain principle which is the ego. You are going along with the ego, you are not fighting it. You are not even aware how totally you are swayed by personal, considerations. A man should be always in revolt against himself, for the ego, like a crooked mirror, narrows down and distorts. It is the worst of all the tyrants, it dominates you absolutely.

Q: When there is no 'I' who is free?

M: The world is free of a mighty nuisance. Good enough.

Q: Good for whom?

M: Good for everybody. It is like a rope stretched across the street, it snarls up the traffic. Roll up, it is there, as mere identity, useful when needed. Freedom from the ego-self is the fruit of self-enquiry.

Q: There was a time when I was most displeased with myself.

Now I have met my Guru and I am at peace, after having surrendered myself to him completely.

M: If you watch your daily life you will see that you have surrendered nothing. You have merely added the word 'surrender' to your vocabulary and made your Guru into a peg to hang your problems on. Real surrender means doing nothing, unless prompted by the Guru. You step, so to say, aside and let your Guru live your life. You merely watch and wonder how easily he solves the problems which to you seemed insoluble.

Q: As I sit here, I see the room, the people. I see you too. How does it look at your end? What do you see?

M: Nothing. I look, but I do not see in the sense of creating images clothed with judgements. I do not describe nor evaluate. I look. I see you, but neither attitude nor opinion cloud my vision. And when I turn my eyes away, my mind does not allow memory to linger; it is at once free and fresh for the next impression.

Q: As I am here, looking at you, I cannot locate the event in space and time. There is something eternal and universal about the transmission of wisdom that is taking place. Ten thousand years earlier, or later, make no difference — the event itself is timeless.

M: Man does not change much over the ages. Human problems remain the same and call for the same answers. Your being conscious of what you call transmission of wisdom shows that wisdom has not yet been transmitted. When you have it, you are no longer conscious of it. What is really your own, you are not conscious of. What you are conscious of is neither you nor yours. Yours is the power of perception, not what you perceive. It is a mistake to take the conscious to be the whole of man. Man is the unconscious, conscious and the super-conscious, but you are not the man. Yours is the cinema screen, the light as well as the seeing power, but the picture is not you.

Q: Must I search for the Guru, or shall I stay with whomever I have found?

M: The very question shows that you have not yet found one. As long as you have not realized, you will move from Guru to Guru, but when you have found yourself, the search will end. A Guru is a milestone. When you are on the move, you pass so many milestones. When you have reached your destination, it is the last alone that mattered. In reality all mattered at their own time and none matters now.

Q: You seem to give no importance to the Guru. He is merely an incident among others.

M: All incidents contribute, but none is crucial. On the road each step helps you to reach your destination, and each is as crucial as the other, for each step must be made, you cannot skip it. If you refuse to make it, you are stuck!

Q: Everybody sings the glories of the Guru, while you compare him to a milestone. Don't we need a Guru?

M: Don't we need a milestone? Yes and no. Yes, if we are uncertain, no if we know our way. Once we are certain in ourselves, the Guru is no longer needed, except in a technical sense. Your mind is an instrument, after all, and you should know how to use it. As you are taught the uses of your body, so you should know how to use your mind.

Q: What do I gain by learning to use my mind?

M: You gain freedom from desire and fear, which are entirely due to wrong uses of the mind. Mere mental knowledge is not enough. The known is accidental, the unknown is the home of the real. To live in the known is bondage, to live in the unknown is liberation.

Q: I have understood that all spiritual practice consists in the elimination of the personal self Such practice demands iron determination and relentless application. Where to find the integrity and energy for such work?

M: You find it in the company of the wise.

Q: How do I know who is wise and who is merely clever?

M: If your motives are pure, if you seek truth and nothing else, you will find the right people. Finding them is easy, what is difficult is to trust them and take full advantage of their advice and guidance.

Q: Is waking state more important for spiritual practice than sleep?

M: On the whole we attach too much importance, to the waking state. Without sleep the waking state would be impossible; without sleep one goes mad or dies; why attach so much importance to waking consciousness, which is obviously dependent on the unconscious? Not only the conscious but the unconscious as well should be taken care of in our spiritual practice.

Q: How does one attend to the unconscious?

M: Keep the 'I am' in the focus of awareness, remember that you *are*, watch yourself ceaselessly and the unconscious will flow into the conscious without any special effort on your part. Wrong desires and fears, false ideas, social inhibitions are blocking and preventing its free interplay with the conscious. Once free to mingle, the two become one and the one becomes all. The person merges into the witness, the witness into awareness, awareness into pure being, yet identity is not lost, only its limitations are lost. It is transfigured, and becomes the real Self, the *sadguru,* the eternal friend and guide. You cannot approach it in worship. No external activity can reach the inner self; worship and prayers remain on the surface only; to go deeper meditation is essential, the striving to go beyond the states of sleep, dream and waking. In the beginning the attempts are irregular, then they recur more often, become regular, then continuous and intense, until all obstacles are conquered.

Q: Obstacles to what?

M: To self-forgetting.

Q: If worship and prayers are ineffectual why do you worship daily, with songs and music, the image of your Guru!

M: Those who want it, do it. I see no purpose in interfering.

Q: But you take part in it.

M: Yes, it appears so. But why be so concerned with me? Give all your attention to the question: 'What is it that makes me conscious?', until your mind becomes the question itself and cannot think of anything else.

Q: All and sundry are urging me to meditate. I find no zest in meditation, but I am interested in many others things; some I want very much and my mind goes to them; my attempts at meditation are so half-hearted, what am I to do?

M: Ask yourself: 'to whom it all happens?' Use everything as an opportunity to go within. Light your way by burning up obstacles in the intensity of awareness. When you happen to desire or fear, it is not the desire or fear that are wrong and must go, but the person who desires and fears. There is no point in fighting desires and fears which may be perfectly natural and justified; it is the person, who is swayed by them, that is the cause of mistakes, past and future. This person should be carefully examined and its falseness seen; then its power over you will end. After all, it subsides each time you go to sleep. In deep sleep you are not a self-conscious person, yet you are alive. When you are alive and conscious, but no longer self-conscious, you are not a person any more. During the waking hours you are, as if, on the stage, playing a role, but what are you when the play is over? You are what you are; what you were before the play began you remain when it is over. Look at yourself as performing on the stage of life. The performance may be splendid or clumsy, but you are not in it, you merely watch it; with interest and sympathy, of course, but keeping in mind all the time that you are only watching while the play — life — is going on.

Q: You are always stressing the cognition aspect of reality. You hardly ever mention affection, and will — never?

M: Will, affection, bliss, striving and enjoying are so deeply tainted with the personal, that they cannot be trusted. The clarification and purification needed at the very start of the journey, only awareness can give. Love and will shall have their turn, but the ground must be prepared. The sun of awareness must rise first — all else will follow.   ●●●

87

Keep the Mind Silent and You shall Discover

Questioner: Once I had a strange experience. I was not, nor was the world, there was only light — within and without — and immense peace. This lasted for four days and then I returned to the every-day consciousness.

Now I have a feeling that all I know is merely a scaffolding, covering and hiding the building under construction. The architect, the design, the plans, the purpose — nothing I know; some activity is going on, things are happening; that is all I can say. I am that scaffolding, some thing very flimsy and short-lived; when the building is ready, the scaffolding will be dismantled and removed. The 'I am' and 'What am I' are of no importance, because once the building is ready, the 'I' will go as a matter of course, leaving no questions about itself to answer.

Maharaj: Are you not aware of all this? Is not the fact of awareness the constant factor?

Q: My sense of permanency and identity is due to memory, which is so evanescent and unreliable. How little I remember, even of the recent past! I have lived a life-time, and now what is left with me? A bundle of events, at best a short story.

M: All this takes place within your consciousness.

Q: Within and without. In daytime — within; in the night — without. Consciousness is not all. So many things happen beyond its reach. To say that what I am not conscious of does not exist, is altogether wrong.

M: What you say is logical, but actually you know only what is in your consciousness. What you claim exists outside conscious experience is inferred.

Q: It may be inferred and yet it is more real than the sensory.

M: Be careful. The moment you start talking you create a verbal universe, a universe of words, ideas, concepts and abstractions, interwoven and inter-dependent, most wonderfully generating, supporting and explaining each other and yet all without essence or substance, mere creations of the mind. Words create words, reality is silent.

Q: When you talk, I hear you. Is it not a fact?

M: That you hear is a fact. What you hear — is not. The fact can be experienced, and in that sense the sound of the word and the mental ripples it causes are experienced. There is no other reality behind it. Its meaning is purely conventional, to be remembered; a language can be easily forgotten, unless practised.

Q: If words have no reality in them why talk at all.

M: They serve their limited purpose of inter-personal communication. Words do not convey facts, they signal them. Once you are beyond the person, you need no words.

Q: What can take me beyond the person? How to go beyond consciousness?

M: Words and questions come from the mind and hold you there. To go beyond the mind, you must be silent and quiet. Peace and silence, silence and peace — this is the way beyond. Stop asking questions.

Q: Once I give up asking questions, what am I to do?

M: What can you do but wait and watch?

Q: What am I to wait for?

M: For the centre of your being to emerge into consciousness. The three states — sleeping, dreaming and waking are all in consciousness, the manifested; what you call unconsciousness will also be manifested — in time; beyond consciousness altogether lies the unmanifested. And beyond all, and pervading all, is the heart of being which beats steadily — manifested-unmanifested; manifested-unmanifested (saguna-nirguna).

Q: On the verbal level it sounds all right. I can visualize myself as the seed of being, a point in consciousness, with my sense 'I am' pulsating, appearing and disappearing alternately. But what am I to do to realize it as a fact, to go beyond into the changeless, wordless Reality?

M: You can do nothing. What time has brought about, time will take away.

Q: Why then all these exhortations to practise Yoga and seek reality? They make me feel empowered and responsible, while in fact it is time that does all.

M: This is the end of Yoga — to realize independence. All that happens, happens in and to the mind, not to the source of the 'I am'. Once you realize that all happens by itself, (call it destiny, or the will of God or mere accident), you remain as witness only, understanding and enjoying, but not perturbed.

Q: If I cease trusting words altogether, what will be my condition?

M: There is a season for trusting and for distrusting. Let the seasons do their work, why worry?

Q: Somehow I feel responsible for what happens around me.

M: You are responsible only for what you can change. All you can change is only your attitude. There lies your responsibility.

Q: You are advising me to remain indifferent to the sorrows of others!

M: It is not that you are not indifferent. All the sufferings of mankind do not prevent you from enjoying your next meal. The witness is not indifferent. He is the fulness of understanding and compassion. Only as the witness you can help another.

Q: All my life I was fed on words. The number of words I have heard and read goes into billions. Did it benefit me? Not at all!

M: The mind shapes the language and the language shapes the mind. Both are tools, use them but don't misuse them. Words can bring you only upto their own limit; to go beyond, you must abandon them. Remain as the silent witness only.

Q: How can I? The world disturbs me greatly.

M: It is because you think yourself big enough to be affected by the world. It is not so. You are so small that nothing can pin you down. It is your mind that gets caught, not you. Know yourself as you *are* — a mere point in consciousness, dimensionless and timeless. You are like the point of the pencil — by mere contact with you the mind draws its picture of the world. You are single and simple — the picture is complex and extensive. Don't be misled by the picture — remain aware of the tiny point — which is everywhere in the picture.

What is, can cease to be; what is not, can come to be; but what neither is nor is not, but on which being and non-being depend, is unassailable; know yourself to be the cause of desire and fear, itself free from both.

Q: How am I the cause of fear?

M: All depends on you. It is by your consent that the world exists. Withdraw your belief in its reality and it will dissolve like a dream. Time can bring down mountains; much more you, who are the timeless source of time. For, without memory and expectation there can be no time.

Q: Is the 'I am' the Ultimate?

M: Before you can say: 'I am', you must be there to say it. Being need not be self-conscious. You need not know to be, but you must *be* to know.

Q: Sir, I am getting drowned in a sea of words! I can see that all depends on how the words are put together, but there must be somebody to put them together — meaningfully. By drawing words at random the Ramayana, Mahabharata and Bhagavata could never be produced. The theory of accidental emergence is not tenable. The origin of the meaningful must be beyond it. What is that power that creates order out of chaos? Living is more than being, and consciousness is more than living. Who is the conscious living being?

M: Your question contains its answer: a conscious living being is a conscious living being. The words are most appropriate, but you do not grasp their full import. Go deep into the meaning of the words: being, living, conscious, and you will stop running in circles, asking questions, but missing answers. Do understand that you cannot ask a valid question about yourself, because you do not know whom you are asking about. In the question 'Who am I?' the 'I' is not known and the question can be worded as: "I do not know what I mean by 'I'" What you are, you must find out. I can only tell you what you are not. You are not of the world, you are not even in the world. The world is not, you alone are. You create the world in your imagination like a dream. As you cannot separate the dream from yourself, so you cannot have an outer world independent of yourself. You are independent, not the world. Don't be afraid of a world you yourself have created. Cease from looking for happiness and reality in a dream and you will wake up. You need not know all the 'why' and 'how', there is no end to questions. Abandon all desires, keep your mind silent and you shall discover.   ●●●

88
Knowledge by the Mind, not True Knowledge

Questioner: Do you experience the three states of waking, dreaming and sleeping just as we do, or otherwise?

Maharaj: All the three states are sleep to me. My waking state is beyond them. As I look at you, you all seem asleep, dreaming up words of your own. I am aware, for I imagine nothing. It is not *samadhi*, which is but a kind of sleep. It is just a state unaffected by the mind, free from the past and future. In your case it is distorted by desire and fear, by memories and hopes; in mine it is as it is — normal. To be a person is to be asleep.

Q: Between the body and pure awareness stands the 'inner organ', *antahkarana*, the 'subtle body', the 'mental body', whatever the name. Just as a whirling mirror converts sunlight into a manifold pattern of streaks and colours, so does the subtle body convert the simple light of the shining Self into a diversified world. Thus have I understood your teaching. What I cannot grasp is how did this subtle body arise in the first instance?

M: It is created with the emergence of the 'I am' idea. The two are one.

Q: How did the 'I am' appear?

M: In your world everything must have a beginning and an end. If it does not, you call it eternal. In my view there is no such thing as beginning or end — these are all related to time. Timeless being is entirely in the *now*.

Q: The *antahkarana,* or the 'subtle body', is it real or unreal?

M: It is momentary. Real when present, unreal when over.

Q: What kind of reality? Is it momentary?

M: Call it empirical, or actual, or factual. It is the reality of immediate experience, here and now, which cannot be denied. You can question the description and the meaning, but not the event itself. Being and not-being alternate and their reality is momentary. The Immutable Reality lies beyond space and time. Realize the momentariness of being and not-being and be free from both.

Q: Things may be transient, yet they are very much with us, in endless repetition.

M: Desires are strong. It is desire that causes repetition. There is no recurrence where desire is not.

Q: What about fear?

M: Desire is of the past, fear is of the future. The memory of past suffering and the fear of its recurrence make one anxious about the future.

Q: There is also the fear of the unknown.

M: Who has not suffered is not afraid.

Q: We are condemned to fear?

M: Until we can look at fear and accept it as the shadow of personal existence, as persons we are bound to be afraid. Abandon all personal equations and you shall be free from fear. It is not difficult. Desirelessness comes on its own when desire is recognized as false. You need not struggle with desire. Ultimately, it is an urge to happiness, which is natural as long as there is sorrow. Only see that there is no happiness in what you desire.

Q: We settle for pleasure.

M: Each pleasure is wrapped in pain. You soon discover that you cannot have one without the other.

Q: There is the experiencer and there is his experience. What created the link between the two?

M: Nothing created it. It is. The two are one.

Q: I feel there is a catch somewhere, but I do not know where.

M: The catch is in your mind, which insists on seeing duality where there is none.

Q: As I listen to you, my mind is all in the now and I am astonished to find myself without questions.

M: You can know reality only when you are astonished.

Q: I can make out that the cause of anxiety and fear is memory. What are the means for putting an end to memory?

M: Don't talk of means, there are no means. What you see as false, dissolves. It is the very nature of illusion to dissolve on investigation. Investigate — that is all. You cannot destroy the false, for you are creating it all the time. Withdraw from it, ignore it, go beyond, and it will cease to be.

Q: Christ also speaks of ignoring evil and being child-like.

M: Reality is common to all. Only the false is personal.

Q: As I watch the *sadhakas* and enquire into the theories by which they live, I find they have merely replaced material cravings by 'spiritual' ambitions. From what you tell us it looks as if the words: 'spiritual' and 'ambition' are incompatible. If 'spirituality' implies freedom from ambition, what will urge the seeker on? The Yogas speak of the desire for liberation as essential. Is it not the highest form of ambition?

M: Ambition is personal, liberation is from the personal. In liberation both the subject and the object of ambition are no longer. Earnestness is not a yearning for the fruits of one's endeavours. It is an expression of an inner shift of interest away from the false, the unessential, the personal.

Q: You told us the other day that we cannot even dream of perfection before realization, for the Self is the source of all perfections and not the mind. If it is not excellence in virtue that is essential for liberation, then what is?

M: Liberation is not the result of some means skilfully applied, nor of circumstances. It is beyond the causal process. Nothing can compel it, nothing can prevent it.

Q: Then why are we not free here and now?

M: But we are free 'here and now'. It is only the mind that imagines bondage.

Q: What will put an end to imagination?

M: Why should you want to put an end to it? Once you know your mind and its miraculous powers, and remove what poisoned it — the idea of a separate and isolated person — you just leave it alone to do its work among things for which it is well suited. To keep the mind in its own place and on its own work is the liberation of the mind.

Q: What is the work of the mind?

M: The mind is the wife of the heart and the world their home — to be kept bright and happy.

Q: I have not yet understood why, if nothing stands in the way of liberation, it does not happen here and now.

M: Nothing stands in the way of your liberation and it can happen here and now, but for your being more interested in other things. And you cannot fight with your interests. You must go with them, see through them and watch them reveal themselves as mere errors of judgement and appreciation.

Q: Will it not help me if I go and stay with some great and holy man?

M: Great and holy people are always within your reach, but you do not recognize them. How will you know who is great and holy? By hearsay? Can you trust others in these matters, or even yourself? To convince you beyond the shadow of doubt you need more than a commendation, more even than a momentary rapture. You may come across a great and holy man or woman and not even know for a long time your good fortune. The infant son of a great man for many years will not know the greatness of his father. You must mature to recognize greatness and purify your heart for holiness. Or you will spend your time and money in vain and also miss what life offers you. There are good people among your friends — you can learn much from them. Running after saints is merely another game to play. Remember yourself instead and watch your daily life relentlessly. Be earnest, and you shall not fail to break the bonds of inattention and imagination.

Q: Do you want me to struggle all alone?

M: You are never alone. There are powers and presences who serve you all the time most faithfully. You may or may not perceive them, nevertheless they are real and active. When you realize that all is in your mind and that you are beyond the mind, that you are truly alone; then all is you.

Q: What is omniscience? Is God omniscient? Are you omniscient? We hear the expression — universal witness. What does it mean? Does self-realization imply omniscience? Or is it a matter of specialized training?

M: To lose entirely all interest in knowledge results in omniscience. It is but the gift of knowing what needs be known, at the right moment, for error-free action. After all, knowledge is needed for action and if you act rightly, spontaneously, without bringing in the conscious, so much the better.

Q: Can one know the mind of another person?

M: Know your own mind first. It contains the entire universe and with place to spare!

Q: Your working theory seems to be that the waking state is not basically different from dream and the dreamless sleep. The three states are essentially a case of mistaken self-identification with the body. Maybe it is true, but, I feel, it is not the whole truth.

M: Do not try to know the truth, for knowledge by the mind is not true knowledge. But you can know what is not true — which is enough to liberate you from the false. The idea that you know what is true is dangerous, for it keeps you imprisoned in the mind. It is when you do not know, that you are free to investigate. And there can be no salvation, without investigation, because non-investigation is the main cause of bondage.

Q: You say that the illusion of the world begins with the sense 'I am', but when I ask about the origin of the sense 'I am', you answer that it has no origin, for on investigation it dissolves. What is solid enough to build the world on cannot be mere illusion. The 'I am' is the only changeless factor I am conscious of; how can it be false?

M: It is not the 'I am' that is false, but what you take yourself to be. I can see, beyond the least shadow of doubt, that you are not what you believe yourself to be. Logic or no logic, you cannot deny the obvious. You are nothing that you are conscious of. Apply yourself diligently to pulling apart the structure you have built in your mind. What the mind has done the mind must undo.

Q: You cannot deny the present moment, mind or no mind. What is now, is. You may question the appearance, but not the fact. What is at the root of the fact?

M: The 'I am' is at the root of all appearance and the permanent link in the succession of events that we call life; but I am beyond the 'I am'.

Q: I have found that the realized people usually describe their state in terms borrowed from their religion. You happen to be a Hindu, so you talk of *Brahma, Vishnu* and *Shiva* and use Hindu approaches and imagery. Kindly tell us, what is the experience behind your words? What reality do they refer to?

M: It is my way of talking, a language I was taught to use.

Q: But what is behind the language?

M: How can I put it into words, except in negating them? Therefore, I use words like timeless, spaceless, causeless. These too are words, but as they are empty of meaning, they suit my purpose.

Q: If they are meaningless, why use them?

M: Because you want words where no words apply.

Q: I can see your point. Again, you have robbed me of my question!   ●●●

89

Progress in Spiritual Life

Questioner: We are two girls from England, visiting India. We know little about Yoga and we are here because we were told that spiritual teachers play an important role in Indian life.

Maharaj: You are welcome. There is nothing new you will find here. The work we are doing is timeless. It was the same ten thousand years ago and will be the same ten thousand years hence. Centuries roll on, but the human problem does not change — the problem of suffering and the ending of suffering.

Q: The other day seven young foreigners have turned up asking for a place to sleep for a few nights. They came to see their Guru who was lecturing in Bombay. I met him — a very pleasant looking young man is he — apparently very matter-of-fact and efficient, but with an atmosphere of peace and silence about him. His teaching is traditional with stress on *karma Yoga,* selfless work, service of the Guru etc. Like the Gita, he says that selfless work will result in salvation. He is full of ambitious plans: training workers who will start spiritual centres in many countries. It seems he gives them not only the authority, but also the power to do the work in his name.

M: Yes, there is such a thing as transmission of power.

Q: When I was with them I had a strange feeling of becoming invisible. The devotees, in their surrender to their Guru surrendered me also! Whatever I did for them was their Guru's doing and I was not considered, except as a mere instrument. I was merely a tap to turn left or right. There was no personal relationship whatsoever. They tried a little to convert me to their faith; as soon as they felt resistance, they just dropped me from the field of their attention. Even between themselves they did not appear very much related; it is their common interest in their Guru that kept them together. I found it rather cold, almost inhuman. To consider oneself an instrument in God's hands is one thing; to be denied all attention and consideration because 'all is God' may lead to indifference verging on cruelty. After all, all wars are made 'in the name of God'. The entire history of mankind is a succession of 'holy wars'. One is never so impersonal as in war!

M: To insist, to resist, are contained in the will to *be*. Remove the will to *be* and what remains? Existence and non-existence relate to something in space and time; here and now, there and then, which again are in the mind. The mind plays a guessing game; it is ever uncertain; anxiety-ridden and restless. You resent being treated as mere instrument of some god, or Guru, and insist on being treated as a person, because you are not sure of your own existence and do not want to give up the comfort and assurance of a personality. You may not be what you believe yourself to be, but it gives you continuity, your future flows into the present and becomes the past without jolts. To be denied personal existence is frightening, but you must face it and find your identity with the totality of life. Then the problem of who is used by whom is no more.

Q: All the attention I got was an attempt to convert me to their faith. When I resisted, they lost all interest in me.

M: One does not become a disciple by conversion, or by accident. There is usually an ancient link, maintained through many lives and flowering as love and trust, without which there is no discipleship.

Q: What made you decide to become a teacher?

M: I was made into one by being called so. Who am I to teach and whom? What I am, you are, and what you are — I am. The 'I am' is common to us all; beyond the 'I am' there is the immensity of light and love. We do not see it because we look elsewhere; I can only point out at the sky; seeing of the star is your own work. Some take more time before they see the star, some take less; it depends on the clarity of their vision and their earnestness in search. These two must be their own — I can only encourage.

Q: What am I expected to do when I become a disciple?

M: Each teacher has his own method, usually patterned on his

Guru's teachings and on the way he himself has realized, and his own terminology as well. Within that framework adjustments to the personality of the disciple are made. The disciple is given full freedom of thought and enquiry and encouraged to question to his heart's content. He must be absolutely certain of the standing and the competence of his Guru, otherwise his faith will not be absolute nor his action complete. It is the absolute in you that takes you to the absolute beyond you — absolute truth, love, selflessness are the decisive factors in self-realization. With earnestness these can be reached.

Q: I understand one must give up one's family and possessions to become a disciple.

M: It varies with the Guru. Some expect their mature disciples to become ascetics and recluses; some encourage family life and duties. Most of them consider a model family life more difficult than renunciation, suitable for a personality more mature and better balanced. At the early stages the discipline of monastic life may be advisable. Therefore, in the Hindu culture students up to the age of 25 are expected to live like monks — in poverty, chastity and obedience — to give them a chance to build a character able to meet the hardships and temptations of married life.

Q: Who are the people in this room? Are they your disciples?

M: Ask them. It is not on the verbal level that one becomes a disciple, but in the silent depths of one's being. You do not become a disciple by choice; it is more a matter of destiny than self-will. It does not matter much who is the teacher — they all wish you well. It is the disciple that matters — his honesty and earnestness. The right disciple will always find the right teacher.

Q: I can see the beauty and feel the blessedness of a life devoted to search for truth under a competent and loving teacher. Unfortunately, we have to return to England.

M: Distance does not matter. If your desires are strong and true, they will mould your life for their fulfilment. Sow your seed and leave it to the seasons.

Q: What are the signs of progress in spiritual life?

M: Freedom from all anxiety; a sense of ease and joy; deep

peace within and abundant energy without.

Q: How did you get it?

M: I found it all in the holy presence of my Guru — I did nothing on my own. He told me to be quiet — and I did it — as much.as I could.

Q: Is your presence as powerful as his?

M: How am I to know? For me — his is the only presence. If you are with me, you are with him.

Q: Each Guru will refer me to his own Guru. Where is the starting point?

M: There is a power in the universe working for enlightenment — and liberation. We call it *Sadashiva,* who is ever present in the hearts of men. It is the unifying factor. Unity — liberates. Freedom — unites. Ultimately nothing is mine or yours — everything is ours. Just be one with yourself and you will be one with all, at home in the entire universe.

Q: You mean to say that all these glories will come with the mere dwelling on the feeling 'I am'?

M: It is the simple that is certain, not the complicated. Somehow, people do not trust the simple, the easy, the always available. Why not give an honest trial to what I say? It may look very small and insignificant, but it is like a seed that grows into a mighty tree. Give yourself a chance!

Q: I see so many people sitting here — quietly. What for have they come?

M: To meet themselves. At home the world is too much with them. Here nothing disturbs them; they have a chance to take leave of their daily worries and contact the essential in themselves.

Q: What is the course of training in self-awareness?

M: There is no need of training. Awareness is always with you. The same attention that you give to the outer, you turn to the inner. No new, or special kind of awareness is needed.

Q: Do you help people personally?

M: People do come to discuss their problems. Apparently they derive some help, or they would not come.

Q: Are the talks with people always in public, or will you talk to them privately also?

M: It is according to their wish. Personally, I make no distinction between public and private.

Q: Are you always available, or have you other work to do?

M: I am always available, but the hours in the morning and late afternoon are the most convenient.

Q: I understand that no work ranks higher than the work of a spiritual teacher.

M: The motive matters supremely.   ●●●

90
Surrender to Your Own Self

Questioner: I was born in the United States, and the last four-teen months I have spent in Sri Ramanashram; now I am on my way back to the States where my mother is expecting me.

Maharaj: What are your plans?

Q: I may qualify as a nurse, or just marry and nave babies.

M: What makes you want to marry?

Q: Providing a spiritual home is the highest form of social ser-vice I can think of. But, of course, life may shape otherwise. I am ready for whatever comes.

M: These fourteen months at Sri Ramanashram, what did they give you? In what way are you different from what you were when you arrived there?

Q: I am no longer afraid. I have found some peace.

M: What kind of peace is it? The peace of having what you want, or not wanting what you do not have?

Q: A little of both, I believe. It was not easy at all. While the Ashram is a very peaceful place, inwardly I was in agonies.

M: When you realize that the distinction between inner and outer is in the mind only, you are no longer afraid.

Q: Such realization comes and goes with me. I have not yet reached the immutability of absolute completeness.

M: Well, as long as you believe so, you must go on with your *sadhana*, to disperse the false idea of not being complete. *Sadhana* removes the super-impositions. When you realize yourself as less than a point in space and time, something too small to be cut and too short-lived to be killed, then, and then only, all fear goes. When you are smaller than the point of the needle, then the needle cannot pierce you — you pierce the needle!

Q: Yes, that is how I feel sometimes — indomitable. I am more than fearless — I am fearlessness itself.

M: What made you go to the Ashram?

Q: I had an unhappy love affair and suffered hell. Neither drink nor drugs could help me. I was groping and came across some books on Yoga. From book to book, from clue to clue — I came to Ramanashram.

M: Were the same tragedy happen to you again, would you suffer as much, considering your present state of mind?

Q: Oh no, I would not let myself suffer again. I would kill myself.

M: So you are not afraid to die!

Q: I am afraid of dying, not of death itself. I imagine the dying process to be painful and ugly.

M: How do you know? It need not be so. It may be beautiful and peaceful. Once you know that death happens to the body and not to you, you just watch your body falling off like a discarded garment.

Q: I am fully aware that my fear of death is due to apprehension and not knowledge.

M: Human beings die every second, the fear and the agony of dying hangs over the world like a cloud. No wonder you too are afraid. But once you know that the body alone dies and not the continuity of memory and the sense of 'I am' reflected in it, you are afraid no longer.

Q: Well, let us die and see.

M: Give attention and you will find that birth and death are one, that life pulsates between being and not being, and that each needs the other for completeness. You are born to die and you die to be reborn.

Q: Does not detachment stop the process?

M: With detachment the fear goes, but not the fact.

Q: Shall I be compelled to be reborn? How dreadful!

M: There is no compulsion. You get what you want. You make your own plans and you carry them out.

Q: Do we condemn ourselves to suffer?

M: We grow through investigation, and to investigate we need experience. We tend to repeat what we have not understood. If we are sensitive and intelligent, we need not suffer. Pain is a call for attention and the penalty of carelessness. Intelligent and compassionate action is the only remedy.

Q: It is because I have grown in intelligence that I would not tolerate my suffering again. What is wrong with suicide?

M: Nothing wrong, if it solves the problem. What, if it does not? Suffering caused by extraneous factors — some painful and incurable disease, or unbearable calamity — may provide some justification, but where wisdom and compassion are lacking, suicide can not help. A foolish death means foolishness reborn. Besides there is the question of *karma* to consider. Endurance is usually the wisest course.

Q: Must one endure suffering, however acute and hopeless?

M: Endurance is one thing and helpless agony is another. Endurance is meaningful and fruitful, while agony is useless.

Q: Why worry about *karma*? It takes care of itself, anyhow.

M: Most of our *karma* is collective. We suffer for the sins of others, as others suffer for ours. Humanity is one. Ignorance of this fact does not change it. We could have been much happier people ourselves, but for our indifference to the sufferings of others.

Q: I find I have grown much more responsive.

M: Good. When you say it, what do you have in mind? Yourself, as a responsive person within a female body?

Q: There is a body and there is compassion and there is memory and a number of things and attitudes; collectively they may be called a person.

M: Including the 'I am' idea?

Q: The 'I am' is like a basket that holds the many things that make a person.

M: Or, rather, it is the willow of which the basket is woven. When you think of yourself as a woman, do you mean that you are a woman, or that your body is described as female?

Q: It depends on my mood. Sometimes I feel myself to be a mere centre of awareness.

M: Or, an ocean of awareness. But are there moments when you are neither man nor woman, not the accidental, occasioned by circumstances and conditions?

Q: Yes, there are, but I feel shy to talk about it.

M: A hint is all that one can expect. You need not say more.

Q: Am I allowed to smoke in your presence? I know that it is not the custom to smoke before a sage and more so for a woman.

M: By all means, smoke, nobody will mind. We understand.

Q: I feel the need of cooling down.

M: It is very often so with Americans and Europeans. After a stretch of *sadhana* they become charged with energy and frantically seek an outlet. They organize communities, become teachers of Yoga, marry, write books — anything except keeping quiet and turning their energies within, to find the source of the inexhaustible power and learn the art of keeping it under control.

Q: I admit that now I want to go back and live a very active life because I feel full of energy.

M: You can do what you like, as long as you do not take your-self to be the body and the mind. It is not so much a question of actual giving up the body and all that goes with it, as a clear un-derstanding that you are not the body, a sense of aloofness, of emotional non-involvement.

Q: I know what you mean. Some four years ago I passed through a period of rejection of the physical; I would not buy myself clothes, would eat the simplest of foods, sleep on bare planks. It is the acceptance of the privations that matters, not the actual discomfort. Now I have realized that welcoming life as it comes and loving all it offers, is the best of it. I shall accept with a glad heart whatever comes and make the best of it. If I can do nothing more than give life and true culture to a few chil-dren — good enough; though my heart goes out to every child, I cannot reach all.

M: You are married and a mother only when you are man-woman conscious. When you do not take yourself to be the body, then the family life of the body, however intense and in-teresting, is seen only as a play on the screen of the mind, with the light of awareness as the only reality.

Q: Why do you insist on awareness as the only real? Is not the object of awareness as real, while it lasts?

M: But it does not last! Momentary reality is secondary; it de-pends on the timeless.

Q: Do you mean continuous, or permanent?

M: There can be no continuity in existence. Continuity implies identity in past, present and future. No such identity is possible, for the very means of identification fluctuate and change. Con-tinuity, permanency, these are illusions created by memory, mere mental projections of a pattern where no pattern can be; abandon all ideas of temporary or permanent, body or mind, man or woman; what remains? What is the state of your mind when all separation is given up? I am not talking of giving up dis-tinctions, for without them there is no manifestation.

Q: When I do not separate, I am happily at peace. But some-how I lose my bearings again and again and begin to seek hap-piness in outer things. Why is my inner peace not steady, I can-not understand.

M: Peace, after all, is also a condition of the mind.

Q: Beyond the mind is silence. There is nothing to be said about it.

M: Yes, all talk about silence is mere noise.

Q: Why do we seek worldly happiness, even after having tasted one's own natural spontaneous happiness?

M: When the mind is engaged in serving the body, happiness is lost. To regain it, it seeks pleasure. The urge to be happy is right, but the means of securing it are misleading, unreliable and destructive of true happiness.

Q: Is pleasure always wrong?

M: The right state and use of the body and the mind are intensely pleasant. It is the search for pleasure that is wrong. Do not try to make yourself happy, rather question your very search for happiness. It is because you are not happy that you want to be happy. Find out why you are unhappy. Because you are not happy you seek happiness in pleasure; pleasure brings in pain and therefore you call it worldly; you then long for some other pleasure, without pain, which you call divine. In reality, pleasure is but a respite from pain. Happiness is both worldly and unworldly, within and beyond all that happens. Make no distinction, don't separate the inseparable and do not alienate yourself from life.

Q: How well I understand you now! Before my stay at Ramanashram I was tyrannized by conscience, always sitting in judgement over myself. Now I am completely relaxed, fully accepting myself as I am. When I return to the States, I shall take life as it comes, as Bhagavan's grace, and enjoy the bitter along with the sweet. This is one of the things I have learnt in the Ashram — to trust Bhagavan. I was not like this before. I could not trust.

M: Trusting Bhagavan is trusting yourself. Be aware that whatever happens, happens to you, by you, through you, that you are the creator, enjoyer and destroyer of all you perceive and you will not be afraid. Unafraid, you will not be unhappy, nor will you seek happiness.

In the mirror of your mind all kinds of pictures appear and disappear. Knowing that they are entirely your own creations, watch them silently come and go, be alert, but not perturbed. This attitude of silent observation is the very foundation of Yoga. You see the picture, but you are not the picture.

Q: I find that the thought of death frightens me because I do not want to be reborn. I know that none compels, yet the pressure of unsatisfied desires is overwhelming and I may not be able to resist.

M: The question of resistance does not arise. What is born and reborn is not you. Let it happen, watch it happen.

Q: Why then be at.all concerned?

M: But you are concerned! And you will be concerned as long as the picture clashes with your own sense of truth, love and beauty. The desire for harmony and peace is ineradicable. But once it is fulfilled, the concern ceases and physical life becomes effortless and below the level of attention. Then, even in the body you are not born. To be embodied or bodyless is same to you. You reach a point when nothing can happen to you. Without body, you cannot be killed; without possessions you cannot be robbed; without mind, you cannot be deceived. There is no point where a desire or fear can hook on. As long as no change can happen to you, what else matters?

Q: Somehow I do not like the idea of dying.

M: It is because you are so young. The more you know yourself the less you are afraid. Of course, the agony of dying is never pleasant to look at, but the dying man is rarely conscious.

Q: Does he return to consciousness?

M: It is very much like sleep. For a time the person is out of focus and then it returns.

Q: The same person?

M: The person, being a creature of circumstances, necessarily changes along with them, like the flame that changes with the fuel. Only the process goes on and on, creating time and space.

Q: Well, God will look after me. I can leave everything to Him.

M: Even faith in God is only a stage on the way. Ultimately you abandon all, for you come to something so simple that there are no words to express it.

Q: I am just beginning. At the start I had no faith, no trust; I was afraid to let things happen. The world seemed to be a very dangerous and inimical place. Now, at least I can talk of trusting the Guru or God. Let me grow. Don't drive me on. Let me proceed at my own pace.

M: By all means proceed. But you don't. You are still stuck in the ideas of man and woman, old and young, life and death. Go on, go beyond. A thing recognized is a thing transcended.

Q: Sir, wherever I go people take it to be their duty to find faults with me and goad me on. I am fed up with this spiritual fortune making. What is wrong with my present that it should be sacrificed to a future, however glorious? You say reality is in the now. I love my now. I want it. I do not want to be eternally anxious about my stature and its future. I do not want to chase the more and the better. Let me love what I have.

M: You are quite right; do it. Only be honest — just love what you love — don't strive and strain.

Q: This is what I call surrender to the Guru.

M: Why exteriorize? Surrender to your own self, of which everything is an expression.   ●●●

91

Pleasure and Happiness

Questioner: A friend of mine, a young man of about twenty-five, was told that he is suffering from an incurable heart disease. He wrote to me that instead of slow death he preferred suicide. I replied that a disease incurable by Western medicine may be cured in some other way. There are yogic powers that can bring almost instantaneous changes in the human body. Effects of repeated fasting also verge on the miraculous. I wrote to him not to be in a hurry to die; rather to give a trial to other approaches.

There is a Yogi living not far from Bombay who possesses some miraculous powers. He has specialized in the control of the vital forces governing the body. I met some of his disciples and sent through them to the Yogi my friend's letter and photo. Let us see what happens.

Maharaj: Yes, miracles often take place. But there must be the will to live. Without it the miracle will not happen.

Q: Can such a desire be instilled?

M: Superficial desire, yes. But it will wear out. Fundamentally, nobody can compel another to live. Besides, there were cultures in which suicide had its acknowledged and respected place.

Q: Is it not obligatory to live out one's natural span of life?

M: Natural — spontaneously — easy — yes. But disease and suffering are not natural. There is noble virtue in unshakable endurance of whatever comes, but there is also dignity in the refusal of meaningless torture and humiliation.

Q: I was given a book written by a *siddha*. He describes in it many of his strange, even amazing experiences. According to him the way of a true *sadhaka* ends with his meeting his Guru and surrendering to him body, mind and heart. Henceforth the Guru takes over and becomes resposible for even the least event in the disciple's life, until the two become one. One may call it realization through identification. The disciple is taken over by a power he cannot control, nor resist, and feels as helpless as a leaf in the storm. The only thing that keeps him safe from madness and death is his faith in the love and power of his Guru.

M: Every teacher teaches according to his own experience. Experience is shaped by belief and belief is shaped by experience. Even the Guru is shaped by the disciple to his own image. It is the disciple that makes the Guru great. Once the Guru is seen to be the agent of a liberating power, which works both from within and without, whole-hearted surrender becomes natural and easy. Just as a man gripped by pain puts himself completely in the hands of a surgeon, so does the disciple entrust himself without reservation to his Guru. It is quite natural to seek help when its need is felt acutely. But, however powerful the Guru may be, he should not impose his will on the disciple. On the other hand, a disciple that distrusts and hesitates is bound to remain unfulfilled for no fault of his Guru.

Q: What happens then?

M: Life teaches, where all else fails. But the lessons of life take a long time to come. Much delay and trouble is saved by trusting and obeying. But such trust comes only when indifference and restlessness give place to clarity and peace. A man who keeps himself in low esteem, will not be able to trust himself, nor anybody else. Therefore, in the beginning the teacher tries his best to reassure the disciple as to his high origin, noble nature and glorious destiny. He relates to him the experiences of some saints as well as his own, instilling confidence in himself and in his infinite possibilities. When self-confidence and trust in the teacher come together, rapid and far-going changes in the disciple's character and life can take place.

Q: I may not want to change. My life is good enough as it is.

M: You say so because you have not seen how painful is the life you live. You are like a child sleeping with a lollypop in its mouth. You may feel happy for a moment by being totally self-centered, but it is enough to have a good look at human faces to perceive the universality of suffering. Even your own happiness is so vulnerable and short-lived, at the mercy of a bank-crash, or a stomach ulcer. It is just a moment of respite, a mere gap between two sorrows. Real happiness is not vulnerable, because it does not depend on circumstances.

Q: Are you talking from your own experience? Are you too unhappy?

M: I have no personal problems. But the world is full of living beings whose lives are squeezed between fear and craving. They are like the cattle driven to the slaughter house, jumping and frisking, carefree and happy, yet dead and skinned within an hour.

You say you are happy. Are you really happy, or are you merely trying to convince yourself. Look at yourself fearlessly and you will at once realize that your happiness depends on conditions and circumstances, hence it is momentary, not real. Real happiness flows from within.

Q: Of what use is your happiness to me? It does not make me happy.

M: You can have the whole of it and more for the mere asking But you do not ask; you don't seem to want.

Q: Why do you say so? I do want to be happy.

M: You are quite satisfied with pleasures. There is no place for happiness. Empty your cup and clean it. It cannot be filled otherwise. Others can give you pleasure, but never happiness.

Q: A chain of pleasurable events is good enough.

M: Soon it ends in pain, if not in disaster. What is Yoga after all, but seeking lasting happiness within?

Q: You can speak only for the East. In the West the conditions are different and what you say does not apply.

M: There is no East or West in sorrow and fear. The problem is universal — suffering and the ending of suffering. The cause of suffering is dependence and independence is the remedy. Yoga is the science and the art of self-liberation through self-understanding.

Q: I do not think I am fit for Yoga.

M: What else are you fit for? All your going and coming, seeking pleasure, loving and hating — all this shows that you struggle against limitations, self-imposed or accepted. In your ignorance you make mistakes and cause pain to yourself and others, but the urge is there and shall not be denied. The same urge that seeks birth, happiness and death shall seek understanding and liberation. It is like a spark of fire in a cargo of cotton. You may not know about it, but sooner or later the ship will burst in flames. Liberation is a natural process and in the long run, inevitable. But it is within your power to bring it into the now.

Q: Then why are so few liberated people in the world?

M: In a forest only some of the trees are in full bloom at a given moment, yet every one will have its turn.

Sooner or later your physical and mental resources will come to an end. What will you do then? Despair? All right, despair. You will get tired of despairing and begin to question. At that moment you will be fit for conscious Yoga.

Q: I find all this seeking and brooding most unnatural.

M: Yours is the naturalness of a born cripple. You may be unaware but it does not make you normal. What it means to be natural or normal you do not know, nor do you know that you do not know.

At present you are drifting and therefore in danger, for to a drifter any moment anything may happen. It would be better to wake up and see your situation. That you *are* — you know. What you are — you don't know. Find out what you are.

Q: Why is there so much suffering in the world?

M: Selfishness is the cause of suffering. There is no other cause.

Q: I understood that suffering is inherent in limitation.

M: Differences and distinctions are not the causes of sorrow. Unity in diversity is natural and good. It is only with separateness and self-seeking that real suffering appears in the world ●●●

92

Go Beyond the I-am-the-body Idea

Questioner: We are like animals, running about in vain pursuits and there seems to be no end to it. Is there a way out?

Maharaj: Many ways will be offered to you which will but take you round and bring you back to your starting point. First realize that your problem exists in your waking state only, that however painful it is, you are able to forget it altogether when you go to sleep. When you are awake you are conscious; when you are asleep, you are only alive. Consciousness and life — both you may call God; but you are beyond both, beyond God, beyond being and not-being. What prevents you from knowing yourself as all and beyond all, is the mind based on memory. It has power over you as long as you trust it; don't struggle with it; just disregard it. Deprived of attention, it will slow down and reveal the mechanism of its working. Once you know its nature and purpose, you will not allow it to create imaginary problems.

Q: Surely, not all problems are imaginary. There are real problems.

M: What problems can there be which the mind did not create? Life and death do not create problems; pains and pleasures come and go, experienced and forgotten. It is memory and anticipation that create problems of attainment or avoidance, coloured by like and dislike. Truth and love are man's real nature and mind and heart are the means of its expression.

Q: How to bring the mind under control? And the heart, which does not know what it wants?

M: They cannot work in darkness. They need the light of pure awareness to function rightly. All effort at control will merely subject them to the dictates of memory. Memory is a good servant, but a bad master. It effectively prevents discovery. There is no place for effort in reality. It is selfishness, due to a self-identification with the body, that is the main problem and the cause of all other problems. And selfishness cannot be removed by effort, only by clear insight into its causes and effects. Effort is a sign of conflict between incompatible desires. They should be seen as they are — then only they dissolve.

Q: And what remains?

M: That which cannot change, remains. The great peace, the deep silence, the hidden beauty of reality remain. While it can not be conveyed through words, it is waiting for you to experience for yourself.

Q: Must not one be fit and eligible for realization? Our nature is animal to the core. Unless it is conquered, how can we hope for reality to dawn?

M: Leave the animal alone. Let it be. Just remember what you are. Use every incident of the day to remind you that without you as the witness there would be neither animal nor God. Understand that you are both, the essence and the substance of all there is, and remain firm in your understanding.

Q: Is understanding enough? Don't I need more tangible proofs?

M: It is your understanding that will decide about the validity of proofs. But what more tangible proof do you need than your own existence? Wherever you go you find yourself. However far you reach out in time, you are there.

Q: Obviously, I am not all-pervading and eternal. I am only here and now.

M: Good enough. The 'here' is everywhere and the now — always. Go beyond 'I-am-the-body' idea and you will find that space and time are in you and not you in space and time. Once you have understood this, the main obstacle to realization is removed.

Q: What is the realization which is beyond understanding?

M: Imagine a dense forest full of tigers and you in a strong steel cage. Knowing that you are well protected by the cage, you watch the tigers fearlessly. Next you find the tigers in the cage and yourself roaming about in the jungle. Last — the cage disappears and you ride the tigers!

Q: I attended one of the group meditation sessions, held recently in Bombay, and witnessed the frenzy and self-abandon of the participants. Why do people go for such things?

M: These are all inventions of a restless mind pampering to people in search of sensations. Some of them help the unconscious to disgorge suppressed memories and longings and to that extent they provide relief. But ultimately they leave the practitioner where he was — or worse.

Q: I have read recently a book by a Yogi on his experiences in meditation. It is full of visions and sounds, colours and melodies; quite a display and a most gorgeous entertainment! In the end they all faded out and only the feeling of utter fearlessness remained. No wonder — a man who passed through all these experiences unscathed need not be afraid of anything! Yet I was wondering of what use is such book to me?

M: Of no use, probably, since it does not attract you. Others may be impressed. People differ. But all are faced with the fact of their own existence. 'I am' is the ultimate fact; 'Who am I?' is the ultimate question to which everybody must find an answer.

Q: The same answer?

M: The same in essence, varied in expression.

Each seeker accepts, or invents, a method which suits him, applies it to himself with some earnestness and effort, obtains results according to his temperament and expectations, casts them into the mould of words, builds them into a system, establishes a tradition and begins to admit others into his 'school of Yoga'. It is all built on memory and imagination. No such school is valueless, nor indispensable; in each one can progress up to the point, when all desire for progress must be abandoned to make further progress possible. Then all schools are given up, all effort ceases; in solitude and darkness the last step is made which ends ignorance and fear forever.

The true teacher, however, will not imprison his disciple in a prescribed set of ideas, feelings and actions; on the contrary, he will show him patiently the need to be free from all ideas and set patterns of behaviour, to be vigilant and earnest and go with life wherever it takes him, not to enjoy or suffer, but to understand and learn.

Under the right teacher the disciple learns to learn, not to remember and obey. *Satsang*, the company of the noble, does not mould, it liberates. Beware of all that makes you dependent. Most of the so-called 'surrenders to the Guru' end in disappointment, if not in tragedy. Fortunately, an earnest seeker will disentangle himself in time, the wiser for the experience.

Q: Surely, self-surrender has its value.

M: Self-surrender is the surrender of all self-concern. It cannot be done, it happens when you realize your true nature. Verbal self-surrender, even when accompanied by feeling, is of little value and breaks down under stress. At the best it shows an apsiration, not an actual fact.

Q: In the Rigveda there is the mention of the *adhi yoga*, the Primordial Yoga, consisting of the marriage of *pragna* with *Prana*, which, as I understand, means the bringing together of wisdom and life. Would you say it means also the union of *Dharma* and *Karma*, righteousness and action?

M: Yes, provided by righteousness you mean harmony with one's true nature and by action — only unselfish and desireless action.

In *adhi yoga* life itself is the Guru and the mind — the disciple. The mind attends to life, it does not dictate. Life flows naturally and effortlessly and the mind removes the obstacles to its even flow.

Q: Is not life by its very nature repetitive? Will not following life lead to stagnation?

M: By itself life is immensely creative. A seed, in course of time, becomes a forest. The mind is like a forester — protecting and regulating the immense vital urge of existence.

Q: Seen as the service of life by the mind, the *adhi yoga* is a perfect democracy: Everyone is engaged in living a life to his best capacity and knowledge, everyone is a disciple of the same Guru.

M: You may say so. It may be so — potentially. But unless life is loved and trusted, followed with eagerness and zest, it would be fanciful to talk of Yoga, which is a movement in consciousness, awareness in action.

Q: Once I watched a mountain-stream flowing between the boulders. At each boulder the commotion was different, according to the shape and size of the boulder. Is not every person a mere commotion over a body, while life is one and eternal?

M: The commotion and the water are not separate. It is the disturbance that makes you aware of water. Consciousness is always of movement, of change. There can be no such thing as changeless consciousness. Changelessness wipes out consciousness immediately. A man deprived of outer or inner sensations blanks out, or goes beyond consciousness and unconsciousness into the birthless and deathless state. Only when spirit and matter come together consciousness is born.

Q: Are they one or two?

M: It depends on the words you use: they are one, or two, or three. On investigation three become two and two become one. Take the simile of face — mirror — image. Any two of them presuppose the third which unites the two. In *sadhana* you see the three as two, until you realize the two as one.

A long as you are engrossed in the world, you are unable to know yourself: to know yourself, turn away your attention from the world and turn it within.

Q: I cannot destroy the world.

M: There is no need. Just understand that what you see is not what is. Appearances will dissolve on investigation and the underlying reality will come to the surface. You need not burn the house to get out of it. You just walk out. It is only when you cannot come and go freely that the house becomes a jail. I move in and out of consciousness easily and naturally and therefore to me the world is a home, not a prison.

Q: But ultimately is there a world, or is there none?

M: What you see is nothing but your self. Call it what you like, it does not change the fact. Through the film of destiny your own light depicts pictures on the screen. You are the viewer, the

light, the picture and the screen. Even the film of destiny
(prarabdha) is self-selected and self-imposed. The spirit is a
sport and enjoys to overcome obstacles. The harder the task
the deeper and wider his self-realization.   •••

93

Man is not the Doer

Questioner: From the beginning of my life I am pursued by a
sense of incompleteness. From school to college, to work, to
marriage, to affluence, I imagined that the next thing will surely
give me peace, but there was no peace. This sense of unfulfil-
ment keeps on growing as years pass by.

Maharaj: As long as there is the body and the sense of identity
with the body, frustration is inevitable. Only when you know
yourself as entirely alien to and different from the body, will you
find respite from the mixture of fear and craving inseparable
from 'I-am-the-body' idea. Merely assuaging fears and satisfy-
ing desires will not remove this sense of emptiness you are trying to escape from; only self-knowledge can help you. By self-
knowledge I mean full knowledge of what you are not. Such
knowledge is attainable and final; but to the discovery of what
you *are* there can be no end. The more you discover, the more
there remains to discover.

Q: For this we must have different parents and schools, live in a
different society.

M: You cannot change your circumstances, but your attitudes you can change. You need not be attached to the non-essentials. Only the necessary is good. There is peace only in the essential.

Q: It is truth I seek, not peace.

M: You cannot see the true unless you are at peace. A quiet mind is essential for right perception, which again is required for self-realization.

Q: I have so much to do. I just cannot afford to keep my mind quiet.

M: It is because of your illusion that you are the doer. In reality things are done to you, not by you.

Q: If I just let things happen, how can I be sure that they will happen my way? Surely I must bend them to my desire.

M: Your desire just happens to you along with its fulfilment, or non-fulfilment. You can change neither. You may believe that you exert yourself, strive and struggle. Again, it all merely happens, including the fruits of the work. Nothing is by you and for you. All is in the picture exposed on the cinema screen, nothing in the light, including what you take yourself to be, the person. You are the light only.

Q: If I am light only, how did I come to forget it?

M: You have not forgotten. It is in the picture on the screen that you forget and then remember. You never cease to be a man because you dream to be a tiger. Similarly you are pure light appearing as a picture on the screen and also becoming one with it.

Q: Since all happens, why should I worry?

M: Exactly. Freedom is freedom from worry. Having realized that you cannot influence the results, pay no attention to your desires and fears. Let them come and go. Don't give them the nourishment of interest and attention.

Q: If I turn my attention from what happens, what am I to live by?

M: Again it is like asking: 'What shall I do, if I stop dreaming?' Stop and see. You need not be anxious: 'What next?' There is always the next. Life does not begin nor end: immovable — it

moves, momentary — it lasts. Light can not be exhausted even
if innumerable pictures are projected by it. So does life fill every
shape to the brim and return to its source, when the shape
breaks down.

Q: If life is so wonderful, how could ignorance happen?

M: You want to treat the disease without having seen the patient! Before you ask about ignorance, why don't you enquire
first, who is the ignorant? When you say you are ignorant, you do
not know that you have imposed the concept of ignorance over
the actual state of your thoughts and feelings. Examine them as
they occur, give them your full attention and you will find that
there is nothing like ignorance, only inattention. Give attention to
what worries you, that is all. After all, worry is mental pain and
pain is invariably a call for attention. The moment you give attention, the call for it ceases and the question of ignorance dissolves. Instead of waiting for an answer to your question, find out
who is asking the question and what makes him ask it. You will
soon find that it is the mind, goaded by fear of pain, that asks
the question. And in fear there is memory and anticipation, past
and future. Attention brings you back to the present, the now,
and the presence in the now is a state ever at hand, but rarely
noticed.

Q: You are reducing sadhana to simple attention. How is it that
other teachers teach complete, difficult and time-consuming
courses?

M: The Gurus usually teach the sadhanas by which they themselves have reached their goal, whatever their goal may be.
This is but natural, for their own sadhana they know intimately. I
was taught to give attention to my sense of 'I am' and I found it
supremely effective. Therefore, I can speak of it with full confidence. But often people come with their bodies, brain and
minds so mishandled, perverted and weak, that the state of
formless attention is beyond them. In such cases, some simpler
token of earnestness is appropriate. The repetition of a mantra,
or gazing at a picture will prepare their body and mind for a
deeper and more direct search. After all, it is earnestness that is
indispensable, the crucial factor. Sadhana is only a vessel and it
must be filled to the brim with earnestness, which is but love in

action. For nothing can be done without love.

Q: We love only ourselves.

M: Were it so, it would be splendid! Love your self wisely and you will reach the summit of perfection. Everybody loves his body, but few love their real being.

Q: Does my real being need my love?

M: Your real being is love itself and your many loves are its reflections according to the situation at the moment.

Q: We are selfish, we know only self-love.

M: Good enough for a start. By all means wish yourself well. Think over, feel out deeply what is really good for you and strive for it earnestly. Very soon you will find that the real is your only good.

Q: Yet I do not understand why the various Gurus insist on prescribing complicated and difficult sadhanas. Don't they know better?

M: It is not what you do, but what you stop doing that matters. The people who begin their sadhana are so feverish and restless, that they have to be very busy to keep themselves on the track. An absorbing routine is good for them. After some time they quieten down and turn away from effort. In peace and silence the skin of the 'I' dissolves and the inner and the outer become one. The real sadhana is effortless.

Q: I have sometimes the feeling that space itself is my body.

M: When you are bound by the illusion: 'I am this body', you are merely a point in space and a moment in time. When the self-identification with the body is no more, all space and time are in your mind, which is a mere ripple in consciousness, which is awareness reflected in nature. Awareness and matter are the active and the passive aspects of pure being, which is in both and beyond both. Space and time are the body and the mind of the universal existence. My feeling is that all that happens in space and time happens to me, that every experience is my experience every form is my form. What I take myself to be, becomes my body and all that happens to that body becomes my mind. But at the root of the universe there is pure awareness, beyond space and time, here and now. Know it to be your real being and act accordingly.

Q: What difference will it make in action what I take myself to *be*. Actions just happen according to circumstances.

M: Circumstances and conditions rule the ignorant. The knower of reality is not compelled. The only law he obeys is that of love.   ●●●

94

You are Beyond Space and Time

Questioner: You keep on saying that I was never born and will never die. If so, how is it that I see the world as one which has been born and will surely die?

Maharaj: You believe so because you have never questioned your belief that you are the body which, obviously, is born and dies. While alive, it attracts attention and fascinates so completely that rarely does one perceive one's real nature. It is like seeing the surface of the ocean and completely forgetting the immensity beneath. The world is but the surface of the mind and the mind is infinite. What we call thoughts are just ripples in the mind. When the mind is quiet it reflects reality. When it is motionless through and through, it dissolves and only reality remains. This reality is so concrete, so actual, so much more tangible than mind and matter, that compared to it even diamond is soft like butter. This overwhelming actuality makes the world dream-like, misty, irrelevant.

Q: This world, with so much suffering in it, how can you see it as irrelevant. What callousness!

M: It is you who is callous, not me. If your world is so full of suffering, do something about it; don't add to it through greed or indolence. I am not bound by your dreamlike world. In my world the seeds of suffering, desire and fear are not sown and suffering does not grow. My world is free from opposites, of mutually destructive discrepancies; harmony pervades; its peace is rocklike; this peace and silence are my body.

Q: What you say reminds me of the *dharmakaya* of the Buddha.

M: May be. We need not run off with terminology. Just see the person you imagine yourself to be as a part of the world you perceive within your mind and look at the mind from the outside, for you are not the mind. After all, your only problem is the eager self-identification with whatever you perceive. Give up this habit, remember that you are not what you perceive, use your power of alert aloofness. See yourself in all that lives and your behaviour will express your vision. Once you realize that there is nothing in this world, which you can call your own, you look at it from the outside as you look at a play on the stage, or a picture on the screen, admiring and enjoying, but really unmoved. As long as you imagine yourself to be something tangible and solid, a thing among things, actually existing in time and space, shortlived and vulnerable, naturally you will be anxious to survive and increase. But when you know yourself as beyond space and time — in contact with them only at the point of here and now, otherwise all-pervading and all-containing, unapproachable, unassailable, invulnerable — you will be afraid no longer. Know yourself as you are — against fear there is no other remedy.

You have to learn to think and feel on these lines, or you will remain indefinitely on the personal level of desire and fear, gaining and losing, growing and decaying. A personal problem cannot be solved on its own level. The very desire to live is the messenger of death, as the longing to be happy is the outline of sorrow. The world is an ocean of pain and fear, of anxiety and despair. Pleasures are like the fishes, few and swift, rarely come, quickly gone. A man of low intelligence believes, against all evidence, that he is an exception and that the world owes him happiness. But the world cannot give what it does not have; unreal to the core, it is of no use for real happiness. It cannot be otherwise. We seek the real because we are unhappy with the unreal. Happiness is our real nature and we shall never rest until we find it. But rarely we know where to seek it. Once you have understood that the world is but a mistaken view of reality, and is not what it appears to be, you are free of its obsessions. Only what is compatible with your real being can make you happy and the world, as you perceive it, is its outright denial.

Keep very quiet and watch what comes to the surface of the mind. Reject the known, welcome the so far unknown and reject it in its turn. Thus you come to a state in which there is no knowledge, only being, in which being itself is knowledge. To know by being is direct knowledge. It is based on the identity of the seer and the seen. Indirect knowledge is based on sensation and memory, on proximity of the perceiver and his percept, confined with the contrast between the two. The same with happiness. Usually you have to be sad to know gladness and glad to know sadness. True happiness is uncaused and this cannot disappear for lack of stimulation. It is not the opposite of sorrow, it includes all sorrow and suffering.

Q: How can one remain happy among so much suffering?

M: One cannot help it — the inner happiness is overwhelmingly real. Like the sun in the sky, its expressions may be clouded, but it is never absent.

Q: When we are in trouble, we are bound to be unhappy.

M: Fear is the only trouble. Know yourself as independent and you will be free from fear and its shadows.

Q: What is the difference between happiness and pleasure?

M: Pleasure depends on things, happiness does not.

Q: If happiness is independent, why are we not always happy?

M: As long as we believe that we need things to make us happy, we shall also believe that in their absence we must be miserable. Mind always shapes itself according to its beliefs. Hence the importance of convincing oneself that one need not be prodded into happiness; that, on the contrary, pleasure is a

distraction and a nuisance, for it merely increases the false conviction that one needs to have and do things to be happy when
in reality it is just the opposite.

But why talk of happiness at all? You do not think of happiness except when you are unhappy. A man who says: 'Now I am
happy', is between two sorrows — past and future. This happiness is mere excitement caused by relief from pain. Real happiness is utterly unselfconscious. It is best expressed negatively
as: 'there is nothing wrong with me. I have nothing to worry
about'. After all, the ultimate purpose of all *sadhana* is to reach a
point, when this conviction, instead of being only verbal, is
based on the actual and ever-present experience.

Q: Which experience?

M: The experience of being empty, uncluttered by memories
and expectations; it is like the happiness of open spaces, of
being young, of having all the time and energy for doing things,
for discovery, for adventure.

Q: What remains to discover?

M: The universe without and the immensity within as they are in
reality, in the great mind and heart of God. The meaning and
purpose of existence, the secret of suffering, life's redemption
from ignorance.

Q: If being happy is the same as being free from fear and
worry, cannot it be said that absence of trouble is the cause of
happiness?

M: A state of absence, of non-existence cannot be a cause; the
pre-existence of a cause is implied in the notion. Your natural
state, in which nothing exists, cannot be a cause of becoming;
the causes are hidden in the great and mysterious power of
memory. But your true home is in nothingness, in emptiness of
all content.

Q: Emptiness and nothingness — how dreadful!

M: You face it most cheerfully, when you go to sleep! Find out
for yourself the state of wakeful sleep and you will find it quite in
harmony with your real nature. Words can only give you the idea
and the idea is not the experience. All I can say is that true happiness has no cause and what has no cause is immovable.

Which does not mean it is perceivable, as pleasure. What is perceivable is pain and pleasure; the state of freedom from sorrow can be described only negatively. To know it directly you must go beyond the mind addicted to causality and the tyranny of time.

Q: If happiness is not conscious and consciousness — not happy, what is the link between the two?

M: Consciousness being a product of conditions and circumstances, depends on them and changes along with them. What is independent, uncreated, timeless and changeless, and yet ever new and fresh, is beyond the mind. When the mind thinks of it, the mind dissolves and only happiness remains.

Q: When all goes, nothingness remains.

M: How can there be nothing without something? Nothing is only an idea, it depends on the memory of something. Pure being is quite independent of existence, which is definable and describable.

Q: Please tell us: beyond the mind does consciousness continue, or does it end with the mind?

M: Consciousness comes and goes, awareness shines immutably.

Q: Who is aware in awareness?

M: When there is a person, there is also consciousness. 'I am', mind, consciousness denote the same state. If you say 'I am aware', it only means: 'I am conscious of thinking about being aware'. There is no 'I am' in awareness.

Q: What about witnessing?

M: Witnessing is of the mind. The witness goes with the witnessed. In the state of non-duality all separation ceases.

Q: What about you? Do you continue in awareness?

M: The person, the 'I am this body, this mind, this chain of memories, this bundle of desires and fears' disappears, but something you may call identity, remains. It enables me to become a person when required. Love creates its own necessities, even of becoming a person.

Q: It is said that Reality manifests itself as existence — consciousness — bliss. Are they absolute or relative?

M: They are relative to each other and depend on each other. Reality is independent of its expressions.

Q: What is the relation between reality and its expressions?

M: No relation. In reality all is real and identical. As we put it, *saguna* and *nirguna* are one in *Parabrahman*. There is only the Supreme. In movement, it is *saguna*. Motionless, it is *nirguna*. But it is only the mind that moves or does not move. The real is beyond, you are beyond. Once you have understood that nothing perceivable, or conceivable can be yourself, you are free of your imaginations. To see everything as imagination, born of desire, is necessary for self-realization. We miss the real by lack of attention and create the unreal by excess of imagination.

You have to give your heart and mind to these things and brood over them repeatedly. It is like cooking food. You must keep it on the fire for some time before it is ready.

Q: Am I not under the sway of destiny, of my *karma*? What can I do against it? What I am and what I do is pre-determined. Even my so-called free choice is predetermined; only I am not aware of it and imagine myself to be free.

M: Again, it all depends how you look at it. Ignorance is like a fever — it makes you see things which are not there. *Karma* is the divinely prescribed treatment. Welcome it and follow the instructions faithfully and you will get well. A patient will leave the hospital after he recovers. To insist on immediate freedom of choice and action will merely postpone recovery. Accept your destiny and fulfil it — this is the shortest way to freedom from destiny, though not from love and its compulsions. To act from desire and fear is bondage, to act from love is freedom. ●●●

95

Accept Life as it Comes

Questioner: I was here last year. Now I am again before you. What makes me come I really do not know, but somehow I cannot forget you.

Maharaj: Some forget, some do not, according to their destinies, which you may call chance, if you prefer.

Q: Between chance and destiny there is a basic difference.

M: Only in your mind. In fact, you do not know what causes what? Destiny is only a blanket word to cover up your ignorance. Chance is another word.

Q: Without knowledge of causes and their results can there be freedom?

M: Causes and results are infinite in number and variety. Everything affects everything. In this universe, when one thing changes, everything changes. Hence the great power of man in changing the world by changing himself.

Q: According to your own words, you have, by the grace of your Guru, changed radically some forty years ago. Yet the world remains as it had been before.

M: My world has changed completely. Yours remains the same, for you have not changed.

Q: How is it that your change has not affected me?

M: Because there was no communion between us. Do not consider yourself as separate from me and we shall at once share in the common state.

Q: I have some property in the United States which I intend to sell and buy some land in the Himalayas. I shall build a house, lay out a garden, get two-three cows and live quietly. People tell me that property and quiet are not compatible, that I shall at once get into trouble with officials, neighbours and thieves. Is it inevitable?

M: The least you can expect is an endless succession of visitors who will make your abode into a free and open guesthouse. Better accept your life as it shapes, go home and look after your wife with love and care. Nobody else needs you. Your dreams of glory will land you in more trouble.

Q: It is not glory that I seek. I seek Reality.

M: For this you need a well-ordered and quiet life, peace of mind and immense earnestness. At every moment whatever comes to you unasked, comes from God and will surely help you, if you make the fullest use of it. It is only what you strive for, out of your own imagination and desire, that gives you trouble.

Q: Is destiny the same as grace?

M: Absolutely. Accept life as it comes and you will find it a blessing.

Q: I can accept my own life. How can I accept the sort of life others are compelled to live?

M: You are accepting it anyhow. The sorrows of others do not interfere with your pleasures. If you were really compassionate, you would have abandoned long ago all self-concern and entered the state from which alone you can really help.

Q: If I have a big house and enough land, I may create an Ashram, with individual rooms; common meditation hall, canteen, library, office etc.

M: Ashrams are not made, they happen. You cannot start nor prevent them, as you cannot start or stop a river. Too many factors are involved in the creation of a successful Ashram and your inner maturity is only one of them. Of course, if you are ignorant of your real being, whatever you do must turn to ashes. You cannot imitate a Guru and get away with it. All hypocrisy will end in disaster.

Q: What is the harm in behaving like a saint even before being one?

M: Rehearsing saintliness is a *sadhana*. It is perfectly allright provided no merit is claimed.

Q: How can I know whether I am able to start an Ashram unless I try?

M: As long as you take yourself to be a person, a body and a mind, separate from the stream of life, having a will of its own, pursuing its own aims, you are living merely on the surface and whatever you do will be short-lived and of little value, mere straw to feed the flames of vanity. You must put in true worth before you can expect something real. What is your worth?

Q: By what measure shall I measure it?

M: Look at the content of your mind. You are what you think about. Are you not most of the time busy with your own little person and its daily needs?

The value of regular meditation is that it takes you away from the humdrum of daily routine and reminds you that you are not what you believe yourself to be. But even remembering is not enough — action must follow conviction. Don't be like the rich man who has made a detailed will, but refuses to die.

Q: Is not gradualness the law of life?

M: Oh, no. The preparation alone is gradual, the change itself is sudden and complete. Gradual change does not take you to a new level of conscious being. You need courage to let go.

Q: I admit it is courage that I lack.

M: It is because you are not fully convinced. Complete conviction generates both desire and courage. And meditation is the art of achieving faith through understanding. In meditation you consider the teaching received, in all its aspects and repeatedly, until out of clarity confidence is born and, with confidence, action. Conviction and action are inseparable. If action does not follow conviction, examine your convictions, don't accuse yourself of lack of courage. Self-depreciation will take you nowhere. Without clarity and emotional assent of what use is will?

Q: What do you mean by emotional assent? Am I not to act against my desires?

M: You will not act against your desires. Clarity is not enough. Energy comes from love — you must love to act — whatever the shape and object of your love. Without clarity and charity courage is destructive. People at war are often wonderfully courageous, but what of it?

Q: I see quite clearly that all I want is a house in a garden where I shall live in peace. Why should I not act on my desire?

M: By all means, act. But do not forget the inevitable, unexpected. Without rain your garden will not flourish. You need courage for adventure.

Q: I need time to collect my courage, don't hustle me. Let me ripen for action.

M: The entire approach is wrong. Action delayed is action abandoned. There may be other chances for other actions, but the present moment is lost — irretrievably lost. All preparation is for the future — you cannot prepare for the present.

Q: What is wrong with preparing for the future?

M: Acting in the now is not much helped by your preparations. Clarity is now, action is now. Thinking of being ready impedes action. And action is the touchstone of reality.

Q: Even when we act without conviction?

M: You cannot live without action, and behind each action there is some fear or desire. Ultimately, all you do is based on your conviction that the world is real and independent of yourself. Were you convinced of the contrary, your behaviour would have been quite different.

Q: There is nothing wrong with my convictions; my actions are shaped by circumstances.

M: In other words, you are convinced of the reality of your circumstances, of the world in which you live. Trace the world to its source and you will find that before the world was, you were and when the world is no longer, you remain. Find your timeless being and your action will bear it testimony. Did you find it?

Q: No, I did not.

M: Then what else have you to do? Surely, this is the most urgent task. You cannot see yourself as independent of everything unless you drop everything and remain unsupported and undefined. Once you know yourself, it is immaterial what you do, but to realize your independence, you must test it by letting go all you were dependent on. The realized man lives on the level of the absolutes; his wisdom, love and courage are complete, there is nothing relative about him. Therefore he must prove himself by tests more stringent, undergo trials more demanding. The tester, the tested and the set up for testing are all within; it is an inner drama to which none can be a party.

Q: Crucifixion, death and resurrection — we are on familiar grounds! I have read, heard and talked about it endlessly, but to do it I find myself incapable.

M: Keep quiet, undisturbed, and the wisdom and the power will come on their own. You need not hanker. Wait in silence of the heart and mind. It is very easy to be quiet, but willingness is rare. You people want to become supermen overnight. Stay without ambition, without the least desire, exposed, vulnerable, unprotected, uncertain and alone, completely open to and welcoming life as it happens, without the selfish conviction that all must yield you pleasure or profit, material or so-called spiritual.

Q: I respond to what you say, but I just do not see how it is done.

M: If you know how to do it, you will not do it. Abandon every attempt, just *be;* don't strive, don't struggle, let go every support, hold on to the blind sense of being, brushing off all else. This is enough.

Q: How is this brushing done? The more I brush off, the more it comes to the surface.

M: Refuse attention, let things come and go. Desires and thoughts are also things. Disregard them. Since immemorial time the dust of events was covering the clear mirror of your mind, so that only memories you could see. Brush off the dust before it has time to settle; this will lay bare the old layers until the true nature of your mind is discovered. It is all very simple and comparatively easy; be earnest and patient, that is all. Dispassion, detachment, freedom from desire and fear, from all self-concern, mere awareness — free from memory and expectation — this is the state of mind to which discovery can happen. After all, liberation is but the freedom to discover.   •••

96

Abandon Memories and Expectations

Questioner: I am an American by birth and for the last one year I was staying in an Ashram in Madhya Pradesh, studying Yoga in its many aspects. We had a teacher, whose Guru, a disciple of the great Sivananda Saraswati, stays in Monghyr. I stayed at Ramanashram also. While in Bombay I went through an intensive course of Burmese meditation managed by one Goenka. Yet I have not found peace. There is an improvement in self-control and day-to-day discipline, but that is all. I cannot say exactly what caused what. I visited many holy places. How each acted on me, I cannot say.

Maharaj: Good results will come, sooner or later. At Sri Ramanashram did you get some instructions?

Q: Yes, some English people were teaching me and also an Indian follower of *gnana yoga,* residing there permanently, was giving me lessons.

M: What are your plans?

Q: I have to return to the States because of visa difficulties. I intend to complete my B.Sc., study Nature Cure and make it my profession.

M: A good profession, no doubt.

Q: Is there any danger in pursuing the path of Yoga at all cost?

M: Is a match-stick dangerous when the house is on fire? The search for reality is the most dangerous of all undertakings for it will destroy the world in which you live. But if your motive is love of truth and life, you need not be afraid.

Q: I am afraid of my own mind. It is so unsteady!

M: In the mirror of your mind images appear and disappear. The mirror remains. Learn to distinguish the immovable in the movable, the unchanging in the changing, till you realize that all differences are in appearance only and oneness is a fact. This basic identity — you may call God, or *Brahman,* or the matrix *(Prakriti),* the words matters little — is only the realization that all is one. Once you can say with confidence born from direct experience: 'I am the world, the world is myself', you are free from desire and fear on one hand and become totally responsible for the world on the other. The senseless sorrow of mankind becomes your sole concern.

Q: So even a *gnani* has his problems!

M: Yes, but they are no longer of his own creation. His suffering is not poisoned by a sense of guilt. There is nothing wrong with suffering for the sins of others. Your Christianity is based on this.

Q: Is not all suffering self-created?

M: Yes, as long as there is a separate self to create it. In the end you know that there is no sin, no guilt, no retribution, only life in its endless transformations. With the dissolution of the personal 'I' personal suffering disappears. What remains is the great sadness of compassion, the horror of the unnecessary pain.

Q: Is there anything unnecessary in the scheme of things?

M: Nothing is necessary, nothing is inevitable. Habit and passion blind and mislead. Compassionate awareness heals and redeems. There is nothing we can do, we can only let things happen according to their nature.

Q: Do you advocate complete passivity?

M: Clarity and charity is action. Love is not lazy and clarity directs. You need not worry about action, look after your mind and heart. Stupidity and selfishness are the only evil.

Q: What is better — repetition of God's name, or meditation?

M: Repetition will stabilize your breath. With deep and quiet breathing vitality will improve, which will influence the brain and help the mind to grow pure and stable and fit for meditation. Without vitality little can be done, hence the importance of its protection and increase. Posture and breathing are a part of

Yoga, for the body must be healthy and well under control, but too much concentration on the body defeats its own purpose, for it is the mind that is primary in the beginning. When the mind has been put to rest and disturbs no longer the inner space (chidakash), the body acquires a new meaning and its transformation becomes both necessary and possible.

Q: I have been wandering all over India, meeting many Gurus and learning in driblets several Yogas. Is it all right to have a taste of everything?

M: No, this is but an introduction. You will meet a man who will help you find your own way.

Q: I feel that the Guru of my own choice can not be my real Guru. To be real he must come unexpected and be irresistible.

M: Not to anticipate is best. The way you respond is decisive.

Q: Am I the master of my responses?

M: Discrimination and dispassion practised now will yield their fruits at the proper time. If the roots are healthy and well-watered, the fruits are sure to be sweet. Be pure, be alert, keep ready.

Q: Are austerities and penances of any use?

M: To meet all the vicissitudes of life is penance enough! You need not invent trouble. To meet cheerfully whatever life brings is all the austerity you need.

Q: What about sacrifice?

M: Share willingly and gladly all you have with whoever needs — don't invent self-inflicted cruelties.

Q: What is self-surrender?

M: Accept what comes.

Q: I feel I am too weak to stand on my own legs. I need the holy company of a Guru and of good people. Equanimity is beyond me. To accept what comes as it comes, frightens me. I think of my returning to the States with horror.

M: Go back and make the best use of your opportunities. Get your B.Sc. degree first. You can always return to India for your Nature Cure studies.

Q: I am quite aware of the opportunities in the States. It is the loneliness that frightens me.

M: You have always the company of your own self — you need not feel alone. Estranged from it even in India you will feel lonely. All happiness comes from pleasing the self. Please it, after return to the States, do nothing that may be unworthy of the glorious reality within your heart and you shall be happy and remain happy. But you must seek the self and, having found it, stay with it.

Q: Will compete solitude be of any benefit?

M: It depends on your temperament. You may work with others and for others, alert and friendly, and grow more fully than in solitude, which may make you dull or leave you at the mercy of your mind's endless chatter. Do not imagine that you can change through effort. Violence, even turned against yourself, as in austerities and penance, will remain fruitless.

Q: Is there no way of making out who is realized and who is not?

M: Your only proof is in yourself. If you find that you turn to gold, it will be a sign that you have touched the philosopher's stone. Stay with the person and watch what happens to you. Don't ask others. Their man may not be your Guru. A Guru may be universal in his essence, but not in his expressions. He may appear to be angry or greedy or over-anxious about his Ashram or his family, and you may be misled by appearances, while others are not.

Q: Have I not the right to expect all-round perfection, both inner and outer?

M: Inner — yes. But outer perfection depends on circumstances, on the state of the body, personal and social, and other innumerable factors.

Q: I was told to find a *gnani* so that I may learn from him the art of achieving *gnana* and now I am told that the entire approach is false, that I cannot make out a *gnani*, nor can *gnana* be conquered by appropriate means. It is all so confusing!

M: It is all due to your complete misunderstanding of reality. Your mind is steeped in the habits of evaluation and acquisition and will not admit that the incomparable and unobtainable are waiting timelessly within your own heart for recognition. All you have to do is to abandon all memories and expectations. Just keep yourself ready in utter nakedness and nothingness.

Q: Who is to do the abandoning?

M: God will do it. Just see the need of being abandoned. Don't resist, don't hold on to the person you take yourself to be. Because you imagine yourself to be a person you take the *gnani* to be a person too, only somewhat different, better informed and more powerful. You may say that he is eternally conscious and happy, but it is far from expressing the whole truth. Don't trust definitions and descriptions — they are grossly misleading.

Q: Unless I am told what to do and how to do it, I feel lost.

M: By all means do feel lost! As long as you feel competent and confident, reality is beyond your reach. Unless you accept inner adventure as a way of life, discovery will not come to you.

Q: Discovery of what?

M: Of the centre of your being, which is free of all directions, all means and ends.

Q: Be all, know all, have all?

M: Be nothing, know nothing, have nothing. This is the only life worth living, the only happiness worth having.

Q: I may admit that the goal is beyond my comprehension. Let me know the way at least.

M: You must find your own way. Unless you find it yourself it will not be your own way and will take you nowhere. Earnestly live your truth as you have found it — act on the little you have understood. It is earnestness that will take you through, not cleverness — your own or another's.

Q: I am afraid of mistakes. So many things I tried — nothing came out of them.

M: You gave too little of yourself, you were merely curious, not earnest.

Q: I don't know any better.

M: At least that much you know. Knowing them to be superficial, give no value to your experiences, forget them as soon as they are over. Live a clean, selfless life, that is all.

Q: Is morality so important? '

M: Don't cheat, don't hurt — is it not important? Above all you need inner peace — which demands harmony between the inner and the outer. Do what you believe in and believe in what you do. All else is waste of energy and time.   •••

97
Mind and the World are not Separate

Questioner: I see here pictures of several saints and I am told that they are your spiritual ancestors. Who are they and how did it all begin?

Maharaj: We are called collectively the 'Nine Masters'. The legend says that our first teacher was Rishi Dattatreya, the great incarnation of the Trinity of Brahma, Vishnu and Shiva. Even the 'Nine Masters' (Navnath) are mythological.

Q: What is the peculiarity of their teaching?

M: Its simplicity, both in theory and practice.

Q: How does one become a Navnath? By initiation or by succession?

M: Neither. The Nine Masters' tradition, Navnath Parampara, is like a river — it flows into the ocean of reality and whoever enters it is carried along.

Q: Does it imply acceptance by a living master belonging to the same tradition?

M: Those who practise the *sadhana* of focussing their minds on 'I am' may feel related to others who have followed the same *sadhana* and succeeded. They may decide to verbalize their sense of kinship by calling themselves Navnaths. It gives them the pleasure of belonging to an established tradition.

Q: Do they in any way benefit by joining?

M: The circle of *satsang*, the 'company of saints', expands in numbers as time passes.

Q: Do they get hold thereby of a source of power and grace from which they would have been barred otherwise?

M: Power and grace are for all and for the asking. Giving oneself a particular name does not help. Call yourself by any name — as long as you are intensely mindful of yourself, the accumulated obstacles to self-knowledge are bound to be swept away.

Q: If I like your teaching and accept your guidance, can I call myself a Navnath?

M: Please your word-addicted mind! The name will not change you. At best it may remind you to behave. There is a succession of Gurus and their disciples, who in turn train more disciples and thus the line is maintained. But the continuity of tradition is informal and voluntary. It is like a family name, but here the family is spiritual.

Q: Do you have to realize to join the Sampradaya?

M: The Navnath Sampradaya is only a tradition, a way of teaching and practice. It does not denote a level of consciousness. If you accept a Navnath Sampradaya teacher as your Guru, you join his Sampradaya. Usually you receive a token of his grace — a look, a touch, or a word, sometimes a vivid dream or a strong remembrance. Sometimes the only sign of grace is a significant and rapid change in character and behaviour.

Q: I know you now for some years and I meet you regularly. The thought of you is never far from my mind. Does it make me belong to your Sampradaya?

M: Your belonging is a matter of your own feeling and conviction. After all, it is all verbal and formal. In reality there is neither Guru nor disciple, neither theory nor practice, neither ignorance nor realization. It all depends on what you take yourself to be. Know yourself correctly. There is no substitute to self-knowledge.

Q: What proof will I have that I know myself correctly?

M: You need no proofs. The experience is unique and unmistakable. It will dawn on you suddenly, when the obstacles are removed to some extent. It is like a frayed rope snapping. Yours is to work at the strands. The break is bound to happen. It can be delayed, but not prevented.

Q: I am confused by your denial of causality. Does it mean that none is responsible for the world as it is?

M: The idea of responsibility is in your mind. You think there must be something or somebody solely responsible for all that happens. There is a contradiction between a multiple universe and a single cause. Either one or the other must be false. Or both. As I see it, it is all day-dreaming. There is no reality in ideas. The fact is that without you, neither the universe nor its cause could have come into being.

Q: I cannot make out whether I am the creature or the creator of the universe.

M: 'I am' is an ever-present fact, while 'I am created' is an idea. Neither God nor the universe have come to tell you that they have created you. The mind obsessed by the idea of causality invents creation and then wonders 'who is the creator?' The mind itself is the creator. Even this is not quite true, for the created and its creator are one. The mind and the world are not separate. Do understand that what you think to be the world is your own mind.

Q: Is there a world beyond, or outside the mind??

M: All space and time are in the mind. Where will you locate a superamental world? There are many levels of the mind and each projects its own version, yet all are in the mind and created by the mind.

Q: What is your attitude to sin? How do you look at a sinner, somebody who breaks the law, inner or outer? Do you want him

to change or you just pity him? Or, are you indifferent to him because of his sins?

M: I know no sin, nor sinner. Your distinction and valuation do not bind me. Everybody behaves according to his nature. It cannot be helped, nor need it be regretted.

Q: Others suffer

M: Life lives on life. In nature the process is compulsory, in society it should be voluntary. There can be no life without sacrifice. A sinner refuses to sacrifice and invites death. This is as it is, and gives no cause for condemnation or pity.

Q: Surely you feel at least compassion when you see a man steeped in sin.

M: Yes, I feel I am that man and his sins are my sins.

Q: Right, and what next?

M: By my becoming one with him he becomes one with me. It is not a conscious process, it happens entirely by itself. None of us can help it. What needs changing shall change anyhow; enough to know oneself as one is, here and now. Intense and methodical investigation into one's mind is Yoga.

Q: What about the chains of destiny forged by sin?

M: When ignorance, the mother of sin, dissolves, destiny, the compulsion to sin again, ceases.

Q: There are retributions to make.

M: With ignorance coming to an end all comes to an end. Things are then seen as they are and they are good.

Q: If a sinner, a breaker of the law, comes before you and asks for your grace, what will be your response?

M: He will get what he asks for.

Q: In spite of being a very bad man?

M: I know no bad people, I only know myself. I see no saints nor sinners, only living beings. I do not hand out grace. There is nothing I can give, or deny, which you do not have already in equal measure. Just be aware of your riches and make full use of them. As long as you imagine that you need my grace, you will be at my door begging for it.

My begging for grace from you would make as little sense! We are not separate, the real is common.

Q: A mother comes to you with a tale of woe. Her only son has taken to drugs and sex and is going from bad to worse. She is asking for your grace. What shall be your response?

M: Probably I shall hear myself telling her that all will be well.

Q: That's all?

M: That's all. What more do you expect?

Q: But will the son of the woman change?

M: He may or he may not.

Q: The people who collect round you, and who know you for many years, maintain that when you say 'it will be all right' it invariably happens as you say.

M: You may as well say that it is the mother's heart that saved the child. For everything there are innumerable causes.

Q: I am told that the man who wants nothing for himself is all-powerful. The entire universe is at his disposal.

M: If you believe so, act on it. Abandon every personal desire and use the power thus saved for changing the world!

Q: All the Buddhas and Rishis have not succeeded in changing the world.

M: The world does not yield to changing. By its very nature it is painful and transient. See it as it is and divest yourself of all desire and fear. When the world does not hold and bind you, it becomes an abode of joy and beauty. You can be happy in the world only when you are free of it.

Q: What is right and what is wrong?

M: Generally, what causes suffering is wrong and what removes it, is right. The body and the mind are limited and therefore vulnerable; they need protection which gives rise to fear. As long as you identify yourself with them you are bound to suffer; realize your independence and remain happy. I tell you, this is the secret of happiness. To believe that you depend on things and people for happiness is due to ignorance of your true nature; to know that you need nothing to be happy, except self-knowledge, is wisdom.

Q: What comes first, being or desire?

M: With being arising in consciousness, the ideas of what you are arise in your mind as well as what you should be. This brings forth desire and action and the process of becoming begins. Becoming has, apparently, no beginning and no end, for it re-starts every moment. With the cessation of imagination and de-sire, becoming ceases and the being this or that merges into pure being, which is not describable, only experienceable.

The world appears to you so overwhelmingly real, because you think of it all the time; cease thinking of it and it will dissolve into thin mist. You need not forget; when desire and fear end, bondage also ends. It is the emotional involvement, the pattern of likes and dislikes which we call character and temperament, that create the bondage.

Q: Without desire and fear what motive is there for action?

M: None, unless you consider love of life, of righteousness, of beauty, motive enough.

Do not be afraid of freedom from desire and fear. It enables you to live a life so different from all you know, so much more in-tense and interesting, that, truly, by losing all you gain all.

Q: Since you count your spiritual ancestry from Rishi Datta-treya, are we right in believing that you and all your predeces-sors are reincarnations of the Rishi?

M: You may believe in whatever you like and if you act on your belief, you will get the fruits of it; but to me it has no importance. I am what I am and this is enough for me. I have no desire to iden-tify myself with anybody, however illustrious. Nor do I feel the need to take myths for reality. I am only interested in ignorance and the freedom from ignorance. The proper role of a Guru is to dispel ignorance in the hearts and minds of his disciples. Once the disciple has understood, the confirming action is up to him. Nobody can act for another. And if he does not act rightly, it only means that he has not understood and that the Guru's work is not over.

Q: There must be some hopeless cases too?

M: None is hopeless. Obstacles can be overcome. What life cannot mend, death will end, but the Guru cannot fail.

Q: What gives you the assurance?

M: The Guru and man's inner reality are really one and work together towards the same goal — the redemption and salvation
of the mind. They cannot fail. Out of the very boulders that obstruct them they build their bridges. Consciousness is not the
whole of being — there are other levels on which man is much
more co-operative. The Guru is at home on all levels and his
energy and patience are inexhaustible.

Q: You keep on telling me that I am dreaming and that it is high
time I should wake up. How does it happen that the Maharaj,
who has come to me in my dreams, has not succeeded in waking me up? He keeps on urging and reminding, but the dream
continues.

M: It is because you have not really understood that you are
dreaming. This is the essence of bondage — the mixing of the
real with unreal. In your present state only the sense 'I am' refers
to reality; the 'what' and the 'how I am' are illusions imposed by
destiny, or accident.

Q: When did the dream begin?

M: It appears to be beginningless, but in fact it is only now.
From moment to moment you are renewing it. Once you have
seen that you are dreaming, you shall wake up. But you do no
see, because you want the dream to continue. A day will come
when you will long for the ending of the dream, with all your
heart and mind, and be willing to pay any price; the price will be
dispassion and detachment, the loss of interest in the dream itself.

Q: How helpless I am. As long as the dream of existence lasts, I
want it to continue. As long as I want it to continue, it will last.

M: Wanting it to continue is not inevitable. See clearly your
condition, your very clarity will release you.

Q: As long as I am with you, all you say seems pretty obvious;
but as soon as I am away from you I run about restless and anxious.

M: You need not keep away from me, in your mind at least. But
your mind is after the world's welfare!

Q: The world is full of troubles, no wonder my mind too is full of them.

M: Was there ever a world without troubles? Your being as a person depends on violence to others. Your very body is a battlefield, full of the dead and dying. Existence implies violence.

Q: As a body — yes. As a human being — definitely no. For humanity non-violence is the law of life and violence of death.

M: There is little of non-violence in nature.

Q: God and nature are not human and need not be humane. I am concerned with man alone. To be human I must be compassionate absolutely.

M: Do you realize that as long as you have a self to defend, you must be violent?

Q: I do. To be truly human I must be self-less. As long as I am selfish, I am sub-human, a humanoid only.

M: So, we are all sub-human and only a few are human. Few or many, it is again 'clarity and charity' that make us human. The sub-human — the 'humanoids' — are dominated by *tamas* and *rajas* and the humans by *sattva*. Clarity and charity is *sattva* as it affects mind and action. But the real is beyond *sattva*. Since I have known you, you seem to be always after helping the world. How much did you help?

Q: Not a bit. Neither the world has changed, nor have I. But the world suffers and I suffer along with it. To struggle against suffering is a natural reaction. And what is civilization and culture, philosophy and religion, but a revolt against suffering. Evil and the ending of evil — is it not your own main preoccupation? You may call it ignorance — it comes to the same.

M: Well, words do not matter, nor does it matter in what shape you are just now. Names and shapes change incessantly. Know yourself to be the changeless witness of the changeful mind. That is enough.   ●●●

98

Freedom from Self-identification

Maharaj: Can you sit on the floor? Do you need a pillow? Have you any questions to ask? Not that you need to ask, you can as well be quiet. To be, just *be,* is important. You need not ask anything, nor do anything. Such apparently lazy way of spending time is highly regarded in India. It means that for the time being you are free from the obsession with 'what next'. When you are not in a hurry and the mind is free from anxieties, it becomes quiet and in the silence something may be heard which is ordinarily too fine and subtle for perception. The mind must be open and quiet to see. What we are trying to do here is to bring our minds into the right state for understanding what is real.

Questioner: How do we learn to cut out worries?

M: You need not worry about your worries. Just *be.* Do not try to be quiet; do not make 'being quiet' into a task to be performed. Don't be restless about 'being quiet', miserable about 'being happy'. Just be aware that you are and remain aware — don't say: 'yes, I am; what next?' There is no 'next' in 'I am'. It is a timeless state.

Q: If it is a timeless state, it will assert itself anyhow.

M: You are what you are, timelessly, but of what use is it to you unless you know it and act on it? Your begging bowl may be of pure gold, but as long as you do not know it, you are a pauper. You must know your inner worth and trust it and express it in the daily sacrifice of desire and fear.

Q: If I know myself, shall I not desire and fear?

M: For some time the mental habits may linger in spite of the new vision, the habit of longing for the known past and fearing the unknown future. When you know these are of the mind only, you can go beyond them. As long as you have all sorts of ideas about yourself, you know yourself through the mist of these ideas; to know yourself as you are, give up all ideas. You cannot imagine the taste of pure water, you can only discover it by abandoning all flavourings.

As long as you are interested in your present way of living, you will not abandon it. Discovery cannot come as long as you cling to the familiar. It is only when you realize fully the immense sorrow of your life and revolt against it, that a way out can be found.

Q: I can now see that the secret of India's eternal life lies in these dimensions of existence, of which India was always the custodian.

M: It is an open secret and there were always people willing and ready to share it. Teachers — there are many, fearless disciples — very few.

Q: I am quite willing to learn.

M: Learning words is not enough. You may know the theory, but without the actual experience of yourself as the impersonal and unqualified centre of being, love and bliss, mere verbal knowledge is sterile.

Q: Then, what am I to do?

M: Try to be, only to be. The all-important word is 'try'. Allot enough time daily for sitting quietly and trying, just trying, to go beyond the personality, with its addictions and obsessions. Don't ask how, it cannot be explained. You just keep on trying until you succeed. If you persevere, there can be no failure. What matters supremely is sincerity, earnestness; you must really have had surfeit of being the person you are, now see the urgent need of being free of this unnecessary self-identification with a bundle of memories and habits. This steady resistance against the unnecessary is the secret of success.

After all, you are what you are every moment of your life, but you are never conscious of it, except, maybe, at the point of awakening from sleep. All you need is to be aware of being, not as a verbal statement, but as an ever-present fact. The awareness that you *are* will open your eyes to what you are. It is all very simple. First of all, establish a constant contact with your self, be with yourself all the time. Into self-awareness all blessings flow. Begin as a centre of observation, deliberate cognizance, and grow into a centre of love in action. 'I am' is a tiny seed which will grow into a mighty tree — quite naturally, without a trace of effort.

Q: I see so much evil in myself. Must I not change it?

M: Evil is the shadow of inattention. In the light of self-awareness it will wither and fall off.

All dependence on another is futile, for what others can give others will take away. Only what is your own at the start will remain your own in the end. Accept no guidance but from within, and even then sift out all memories for they will mislead you. Even if you are quite ignorant of the ways and the means, keep quiet and look within; guidance is sure to come. You are never left without knowing what your next step should be. The trouble is that you may shirk it. The Guru is there for giving you courage because of his experience and success. But only what you discover through your own awareness, your own effort, will be of permanent use to you.

Remember, nothing you perceive is your own. Nothing of value can come to you from outside; it is only your own feeling and understanding that are relevant and revealing. Words, heard or read, will only create images in your mind, but you are not a mental image. You are the power of perception and action behind and beyond the image.

Q: You seem to advise me to be self-centered to the point of egoism. Must I not yield even to my interest in other people?

M: Your interest in others is egoistic, self-concerned, self-oriented. You are not interested in others as persons, but only as far as they enrich, or ennoble your own image of yourself. And the ultimate in selfishness is to care only for the protection, preservation and multiplication of one's own body. By body I mean all that is related to your name and shape — your family, tribe, country, race, etc. To be attached to one's name and shape is selfishness. A man who knows that he is neither body nor mind cannot be selfish, for he has nothing to be selfish for.

Or, you may say, he is equally 'selfish' on behalf of everybody he meets; everybody's welfare is his own. The feeling 'I am the world, the world is myself' becomes quite natural; once it is established, there is just no way of being selfish. To be selfish means to covet, acquire, accumulate on behalf of the part against the whole.

Q: One may be rich with many possessions, by inheritance, or marriage, or just good luck.

M: If you do not hold on to, it will be taken away from you.

Q: In your present state can you love another person as a person?

M: I am the other person, the other person is myself; in name and shape we are different, but there is no separation. At the root of our being we are one.

Q: Is it not so whenever there is love between people?

M: It is, but they are not conscious of it. They feel the attraction, but do not know the reason.

Q: Why is love selective?

M: Love is not selective, desire is selective. In love there are no strangers. When the centre of selfishness is no longer, all desires for pleasure and fear of pain cease; one is no longer interested in being happy; beyond happiness there is pure intensity, inexhaustible energy, the ecstasy of giving from a perennial source.

Q: Mustn't I begin by solving for myself the problem of right and wrong?

M: What is pleasant people take it to be good and what is painful they take it to be bad.

Q: Yes, that is how it is with us, ordinary people. But how is it with you, at the level of oneness? For you what is good and what is bad?

M: What increases suffering is bad and what removes it is good.

Q: So you deny goodness to suffering itself. There are religions in which suffering is considered good and noble.

M: *Karma*, or destiny, is an expression of a beneficial law: the universal trend towards balance, harmony and unity. At every moment, whatever happens now, is for the best. It may appear painful and ugly, a suffering bitter and meaningless, yet considering the past and the future it is for the best, as the only way out of a disastrous situation.

Q: Does one suffer only for one's own sins?

M: One suffers along with what one thinks oneself to be. If you feel one with humanity, you suffer with humanity.

Q: And since you claim to be one with the universe, there is no limit in time or space to your suffering!

M: To be is to suffer. The narrower the circle of my self-identification, the more acute the suffering caused by desire and fear.

Q: Christianity accepts suffering as purifying and ennobling, while Hinduism looks at it with distaste.

M: Christianity is one way of putting words together and Hinduism is another. The real is, behind and beyond words, incommunicable, directly experienced, explosive in its effect on the mind. It is easily had when nothing else is wanted. The unreal is created by imagination and perpetuated by desire.

Q: Can there be no suffering that is necessary and good?

M: Accidental or incidental pain is inevitable and transitory; deliberate pain, inflicted with even the best of intentions, is meaningless and cruel.

Q: You would not punish crime?

M: Punishment is but legalized crime. In a society built on prevention, rather than retaliation, there would be very little crime. The few exceptions will be treated medically, as of unsound mind and body.

Q: You seem to have little use for religion.

M: What is religion? A cloud in the sky. I live in the sky, not in the clouds, which are so many words held together. Remove the verbiage and what remains? Truth remains. My home is in the unchangeable, which appears to be a state of constant reconciliation and integration of opposites. People come here to learn about the actual existence of such a state, the obstacles to its emergence, and, once perceived, the art of stabilising it in consciousness, so that there is no clash between understanding and living. The state itself is beyond the mind and need not be learnt. The mind can only focus the obstacles; seeing an obstacle as an obstacle is effective, because it is the mind acting on the mind. Begin from the beginning: give attention to the fact that you *are*. At no time can you say 'I was not' all you can say: 'I do not remember'. You know how unreliable is memory. Accept that, engrossed in petty personal affairs you have forgotten what you are; try to bring back the lost memory through the elimination of the known. You cannot be told what will happen, nor is it desirable; anticipation will create illusions. In the inner search the unexpected is inevitable; the discovery is invariably beyond all imagination. Just as an unborn child cannot know life after birth, for it has nothing in its mind with which to form a valid picture, so is the mind unable to think of the real in terms of the unreal, except by negation: 'Not this, not that'. The acceptance of the unreal as real is the obstacle; to see the false as false and abandon the false brings reality into being. The states of utter clarity, immense love, utter fearlessness; these are mere words at the present, outlines without colour, hints at what can be. You are like a blind man expecting to see as a result of an operation — provided you do not shirk the operation! The state I am in words do not matter at all. Nor is there any addiction to words. Only facts matter.

Q: There can be no religion without words.

M: Recorded religions are mere heaps of verbiage. Religions show their true face in action, in silent action. To know what man believes, watch how he acts. For most of the people service of their bodies and their minds is their religion. They may have religious ideas, but they do not act on them. They play with them, they are often very fond of them, but they will not act on them.

Q: Words are needed for communication.

M: For exchange of information — yes. But real communication between people is not verbal. For establishing and maintaining relationship affectionate awareness expressed in direct action is required. Not what you say, but what you do is that matters. Words are made by the mind and are meaningful only on the level of the mind. The word 'bread': neither can you eat nor live by it; it merely conveys an idea. It acquires meaning only with the actual eating. In the same sense am I telling you that the Normal State is not verbal. I may say it is wise love expressed in action, but these words convey little, unless you experience them in their fulness and beauty.

Words have their limited usefulness, but we put no limits to them and bring ourselves to the brink of disaster. Our noble ideas are finely balanced by ignoble actions. We talk of God, Truth and Love, but instead of direct experience we have definitions. Instead of enlarging and deepening action we chisel our definitions. And we imagine that we know what we can define!

Q: How can one convey experience except through words?

M: Experience cannot be conveyed through words. It comes with action. A man who is intense in his experience will radiate confidence and courage. Others too will act and gain experience born out of action. Verbal teaching has its use, it prepares the mind for voiding itself of its accumulations.

A level of mental maturity is reached when nothing external is of any value and the heart is ready to relinquish all. Then the real has a chance and it grasps it. Delays, if any, are caused by the mind being unwilling to see or to discard.

Q: Are we so totally alone?

M: Oh, no, we are not. Those who have, can give. And such givers are many. The world itself is a supreme gift, maintained by loving sacrifice. But the right receivers, wise and humble, are so few. 'Ask and you shall be given' is the eternal law.

So many words you have learnt, so many you have spoken. You know everything, but you do not know yourself. For the self is not known through words — only direct insight will reveal it. Look within, search within.

Q: It is very difficult to abandon words. Our mental life is one continuous stream of words.

M: It is not a matter of easy, or difficult. You have no alternative. Either you try or you don't. It is up to you.

Q: I have tried many times and failed.

M: Try again. If you keep on trying, something may happen. But if you don't, you are stuck. You may know all the right words, quote the scriptures, be brilliant in your discussions and yet remain a bag of bones. Or you may be inconspicuous and humble, an insignificant person altogether, yet glowing with loving kindness and deep wisdom.   •••

99
The Perceived can not be the Perceiver

Questioner: I have been moving from place to place investigating the various Yogas available for practice and I could not decide which will suit me best. I should be thankful for some competent advice. At present, as a result of all this searching, I am just tired of the idea of finding truth. It seems to me, both unnecessary and troublesome. Life is enjoyable as it is and I see no purpose in improving on it.

Maharaj: You are welcome to stay in your contentment, but can you? Youth, vigour, money — all will pass away sooner than you expect. Sorrow, shunned so far, will pursue you. If you want to be beyond suffering, you must meet it half way and embrace it. Relinquish your habits and addictions, live a simple and sober life, don't hurt a living being; this is the foundation of Yoga. To find reality you must be real in the smallest daily action; there can be no deceit in the search for truth. You say you find your life enjoyable. Maybe it is — at present. But who enjoys it?

Q: I confess I do not know the enjoyer, nor the enjoyed. I only know the enjoyment.

M: Quite right. But enjoyment is a state of mind — it comes and goes. Its very impermanence makes it perceivable. You cannot be conscious of what does not change. All consciousness is consciousness of change. But the very perception of change — does it not necessitate a changeless background?

Q: Not at all. The memory of the last state — compared to the actuality of the present state gives the experience of change.

M: Between the remembered and the actual there is a basic difference which can be observed from moment to moment. At no point of time is the actual the remembered. Between the two there is a difference in kind, not merely in intensity. The actual is unmistakably so. By no effort of will or imagination can you interchange the two. Now, what is it that gives this unique quality to the actual?

Q: The actual is real, while there is a good deal of uncertainty about the remembered.

M: Quite so, but why? A moment back the remembered was actual, in a moment the actual will be the remembered. What makes the actual unique? Obviously, it is your sense of being present. In memory and anticipation there is a clear feeling that it is a mental state under observation, while in the actual the feeling is primarily of being present and aware.

Q: Yes, I can see. It is awareness that makes the difference between the actual and the remembered. One thinks of the past or the future, but one is present in the *now*.

M: Wherever you go, the sense of here and now you carry with you all the time. It means that you are independent of space and time, that space and time are in you, not you in them. It is your self-identification with the body, which, of course, is limited in space and time, that gives you the feeling of finiteness. In reality you are infinite and eternal.

Q: This infinite and eternal self of mine, how am I to know it?

M: The self you want to know, is it some second self? Are you made of several selves? Surely, there is only one self and you are that self. The self you are is the only self there is. Remove and abandon your wrong ideas about yourself and there it is, in all its glory. It is only your mind that prevents self-knowledge.

Q: How am I to be rid of the mind? And is life without mind at all possible on the human level?

M: There is no such thing as mind. There are ideas and some of them are wrong. Abandon the wrong ideas, for they are false and obstruct your vision of yourself.

Q: Which ideas are wrong and which are true?

M: Assertions are usually wrong and denials — right.

Q: One cannot live by denying everything!

M: Only by denying can one live. Assertion is bondage. To question and deny is necessary. It is the essence of revolt and without revolt there can be no freedom.

There is no second, or higher self to search for. You are the highest self, only give up the false ideas you have about your self. Both faith and reason tell you that you are neither the body, nor its desires and fears, nor are you the mind with its fanciful ideas, nor the role society compels you to play, the person you are supposed to be. Give up the false and the true will come into its own.

You say you want to know your self. You *are* your self — you cannot be anything but what you are. Is knowing separate from being? Whatever you can know with your mind is of the mind, not you; about yourself you can only say: 'I am, I am aware, I like it'.

Q: I find being alive a painful state.

M: You cannot be alive for you are life itself. It is the person you imagine yourself to be that suffers, not you. Dissolve it in awareness. It is merely a bundle of memories and habits. From the awareness of the unreal to the awareness of your real nature there is a chasm which you will easily cross, once you have mastered the art of pure awareness.

Q: All I know is that I do not know myself.

M: How do you know that you do not know your self? Your direct insight tells you that yourself you know first, for nothing exists to you without your being there to experience its existence. You imagine you do not know your self, because you cannot describe your self. You can always say: 'I know that I am' and you will refuse as untrue the statement: 'I am not'. But whatever can be described cannot be your self, and what you are cannot be described. You can only know your self by being yourself without any attempt at self-definition and self-description. Once you have understood that you are nothing perceivable or conceivable, that whatever appears in the field of consciousness cannot be your self, you will apply yourself to the eradication of all self-identification, as the only way that can take you to a deeper realization of your self. You literally progress by rejection — a veritable rocket. To know that you are neither in the body nor in the mind, though aware of both, is already self-knowledge.

Q: If I am neither the body nor mind, how am I aware of them? How can I perceive something quite foreign to myself?

M: 'Nothing is me,' is the first step. 'Everything is me' is the next. Both hang on the idea: 'there is a world'. When this too is given up, you remain what you are — the non-dual Self. You are *it* here and now, but your vision is obstructed by your false ideas about your self.

Q: Well, I admit that I am, I was, I shall be; at least from birth to death. I have no doubts of my being, here and now. But I find that it is not enough. My life lacks joy, born of harmony between the inner and the outer If I alone am and the world is merely a projection, then why is there disharmony?

M: You create disharmony and then complain! When you desire and fear, and identify yourself with your feelings, you create sorrow and bondage. When you create, with love and wisdom, and remain unattached to your creations, the result is harmony and peace. But whatever be the condition of your mind, in what way does it reflect on you? It is only your self-identification with your mind that makes you happy or unhappy. Rebel against your slavery to your mind, see your bonds as self-created and break the chains of attachment and revulsion. Keep in mind your goal of freedom, until it dawns on you that you are already free, that freedom is not something in the distant future to be earned with painful efforts, but perennially one's own, to be used! Liberation is not an acquisition but a matter of courage, the courage to believe that you are free already and to act on it.

Q: If I do as I like, I shall have to suffer.

M: Nevertheless, you are free. The consequences of your action will depend on the society in which you live and its conventions.

Q: I may act recklessly.

M: Along with courage will emerge wisdom and compassion and skill in action. You will know what to do and whatever you do will be good for all.

Q: I find that the various aspects of myself are at war between themselves and there is no peace in me. Where are freedom and courage, wisdom and compassion? My actions merely increase the chasm in which I exist.

M: It is all so, because you take yourself to be somebody, or something. Stop, look, investigate, ask the right questions, come to the right conclusions and have the courage to act on them and see what happens. The first steps may bring the roof down on your head, but soon the commotion will clear and there will be peace and joy. You know so many things about yourself, but the knower you do not know. Find out who you are, the knower of the known. Look within diligently, remember to remember that the perceived cannot be the perceiver Whatever you see, hear or think of, remember — you are not what happens, you are he to whom it happens. Delve deeply into the sense 'I am' and you will surely discover that the perceiving centre is universal, as universal as the light that illumines the world. All that happens in the universe happens to you, the silent witness. On the other hand, whatever is done, is done by you, the universal and inexhaustible energy.

Q: It is, no doubt, very gratifying to hear that one is the silent witness as well as the universal energy. But how is one to cross over from a verbal statement to direct knowledge? Hearing is not knowing.

M: Before you can know anything directly, nonverbally, you must know the knower. So far, you took the mind for the knower, but it is just not so. The mind clogs you up with images and ideas, which leave scars in memory. You take remembering to be knowledge. True knowledge is ever fresh, new, unexpected.

It wells up from within. When you know what you are, you also are what you know. Between knowing and being there is no gap.

Q: I can only investigate the mind with the mind.

M: By all means use your mind to know your mind. It is perfectly legitimate and also the best preparation for going beyond the mind. Being, knowing and enjoying is your own. First realize your own being. This is easy because the sense 'I am' is always with you. Then meet yourself as the knower, apart from the known. Once you know yourself as pure being, the ecstacy of freedom is your own.

Q: Which Yoga is this?

M: Why worry? What makes you come here is your being displeased with your life as you know it, the life of your body and mind. You may try to improve them, through controlling and bending them to an ideal, or you may cut the knot of self-identification altogether and look at your body and mind as something that happens without committing you in any way.

Q: Shall I call the way of control and discipline *raja yoga* and the way of detachment — *gnana yoga*? And the worship of an ideal — *bhakti yoga*?

M: If it pleases you. Words indicate, but do not explain. What I teach is the ancient and simple way of liberation through understanding. Understand your own mind and its hold on you will snap. The mind misunderstands, misunderstanding is its very nature. Right understanding is the only remedy, whatever name you give it. It is the earliest and also the latest, for it deals with the mind as it is.

Nothing you do will change you, for you need no change. You may change your mind or your body, but it is always something external to you that has changed, not yourself. Why bother at all to change? Realize once for all that neither your body nor your mind, nor even your consciousness is yourself and stand alone in your true nature beyond consciousness and unconsciousness. No effort can take you there, only the clarity of understanding. Trace your misunderstandings and abandon them, that is all. There is nothing to seek and find, for there is nothing lost. Relax and watch the 'I am'. Reality is just behind it. Keep quiet, keep silent; it will emerge, or, rather, it will take you in.

Q: Must I not get rid of my body and mind first?

M: You cannot, for the very idea binds you to them. Just understand and disregard.

Q: I am unable to disregard, for I am not integrated.

M: Imagine you are completely integrated, your thought and action fully co-ordinated. How will it help you? It will not free you from mistaking yourself to be the body or the mind. See them correctly as 'not you', that is all.

Q: You want me to remember to forget!

M: Yes, it looks so. Yet, it is not hopeless. You can do it. Just set about it in earnest. Your blind groping is full of promise. Your very searching is the finding. You cannot fail.

Q: Because we are disintegrated, we suffer.

M: We shall suffer as long as our thoughts and actions are prompted by desires and fears. See their futility and the danger and chaos they create will subside. Don't try to reform yourself, just see the futility of all change. The changeful keeps on changing while the changeless is waiting. Do not expect the changeful, to take you to the changeless — it can never happen. Only when the very idea of changing is seen as false and abandoned, the changeless can come into its own.

Q: Everywhere I go, I am told that I must change profoundly before I can see the real. This process of deliberate, self-imposed change is called Yoga.

M: All change affects the mind only. To be what you are, you must go beyond the mind, into your own being. It is immaterial what is the mind that you leave behind, provided you leave it behind for good. This again is not possible without self-realization.

Q: What comes first — the abandoning of the mind or self-realization?

M: Self-realization definitely comes first. The mind cannot go beyond itself by itself. It must explode.

Q: No exploration before explosion?

M: The explosive power comes from the real. But you are well advised to have your mind ready for it. Fear can always delay it, until another opportunity arises.

Q: I thought there is always a chance.

M: In theory — yes. In practice a situation must arise, when all the factors necessary for self-realization are present. This need not discourage you. Your dwelling on the fact of 'I am' will soon create another chance. For, attitude attracts opportunity. All you know is second-hand. Only 'I am' is first-hand and needs no proofs. Stay with it.   •••

100

Understanding leads to Freedom

Questioner: In many countries of the world investigating officers follow certain practices aimed at extracting confessions from their victim and also changing his personality, if needed. By a judicious choice of physical and moral deprivations and by persuasions the old personality is broken down and a new personality established in its place. The man under investigation hears so many times repeated that he is an enemy of the State and a traitor to his country, that a day comes when something breaks down in him and he begins to feel with full conviction that he is a traitor, a rebel, altogether despicable and deserving the direst punishment. This process is known as brain-washing.

It struck me that the religious and Yogic practices are very

similar to 'brain-washing'. The same physical and mental depri-
vation, solitary confinement, a powerful sense of sin, despair
and a desire to escape through expiation and conversion,
adoption of a new image of oneself and impersonating that
image. The same repetition of set formulas: 'God is good; the
Guru (party) knows; faith will save me.' In the so-called Yogic or
religious practices the same mechanism operates. The mind is
made to concentrate on some particular idea to the exclusion of
all other ideas and concentration is powerfully reinforced by
rigid discipline and painful austerities. A high price in life and
happiness is paid and what one gets in return appears therefore, to be of great importance. This pre-arranged conversion,
obvious or hidden, religious or political, ethical or social, may
look genuine and lasting, yet there is a feeling of artificiality
about it.

Maharaj: You are quite right. By undergoing so many hardships
the mind gets dislocated and immobilized. Its condition becomes precarious; whatever it undertakes, ends in a deeper
bondage.

Q: Then why are *sadhanas* prescribed?

M: Unless you make tremendous efforts, you will not be convinced that effort will take you nowhere. The self is so self-
confident, that unless it is totally discouraged, it will not give up.
Mere verbal conviction is not enough. Hard facts alone can
show the absolute nothingness of the self-image.

Q: The brain-washer drives me mad, and the Guru drives me
sane. The driving is similar. Yet the motive and the purpose are
totally different. The similarities are, perhaps merely verbal.

M: Inviting, or compelling to suffer contains in it violence and
the fruit of violence cannot be sweet.

There are certain life situations, inevitably painful, and you
have to take them in your stride. There are also certain situations
which you have created, either deliberately or by neglect. And
from these you have to learn a lesson so that they are not repeated again.

Q: It seems that we must suffer, so that we learn to overcome
pain.

M: Pain has to be endured. There is no such thing as overcoming the pain and no training is needed. Training for the future, developing attitudes is a sign of fear.

Q: Once I know how to face pain, I am free of it, not afraid of it, and therefore happy. This is what happens to a prisoner. He accepts his punishment as just and proper and is at peace with the prison authorities and the State. All religions do nothing else but preach acceptance and surrender. We are being encouraged to plead guilty, to feel responsible for all the evils in the world and point at ourselves as their only cause. My problem is: I cannot see much difference between brain-washing and *sadhana*, except that in the case of *sadhana* one is not physically constrained. The element of compulsive suggestion is present in both.

M: As you have said, the similarities are superficial. You need not harp on them.

Q: Sir, the similarities are not superficial. Man is a complex being and can be at the same time the accuser and the accused, the judge, the warden and the executioner. There is not much that is voluntary in a 'voluntary' *sadhana*. One is moved by forces beyond one's ken and control. I can change my mental metabolism as little as the physical, except by painful and protracted efforts — which is Yoga. All I am asking is: does Maharaj agree with me that Yoga implies violence?

M: I agree that Yoga, as presented by you, means violence and I never advocate any form of violence. My path is totally non-violent. I mean exactly what I say: non-violent. Find out for yourself what it is. I merely say: it is non-violent.

Q: I am not misusing words. When a Guru asks me to meditate sixteen hours a day for the rest of my life, I cannot do it without extreme violence to myself. Is such a Guru right or wrong?

M: None compels you to meditate sixteen hours a day, unless you feel like doing so. It is only a way of telling you: 'remain with yourself, don't get lost among others'. The teacher will wait, but the mind is impatient.

It is not the teacher, it is the mind that is violent and also afraid of its own violence. What is of the mind is relative, it is a mistake to make it into an absolute.

Q: If I remain passive, nothing will change. If I am active, I must be violent. What is it I can do which is neither sterile nor violent?

M: Of course, there is a way which is neither violent nor sterile and yet supremely effective. Just look at yourself as you are, see yourself as you are, accept yourself as you are and go ever deeper into what you are. Violence and non-violence describe your attitude to others; the self in relation to itself is neither violent nor non-violent, it is either aware or unaware of itself. If it knows itself, all it does will be right; if it does not, all it does will be wrong.

Q: What do you mean by saying: I know myself as I am?

M: Before the mind — I am. 'I am' is not a thought in the mind; the mind happens to me, I do not happen to the mind. And since time and space are in the mind, I am beyond time and space, eternal and omnipresent.

Q: Are you serious? Do you really mean that you exist everywhere and at all times?

M: Yes, I do. To me it is as obvious, as the freedom of movement is to you. Imagine a tree asking a monkey: 'Do you seriously mean that you can move from place to place?' And the monkey saying: 'Yes, I do.'

Q: Are you also free from causality? Can you produce miracles?

M: The world itself is a miracle. I am beyond miracles — I am absolutely normal. With me everything happens as it must. I do not interfere with creation. Of what use are small miracles to me when the greatest of miracles is happening all the time? Whatever you see it is always your own being that you see. Go ever deeper into yourself, seek within, there is neither violence nor non-violence in self-discovery. The destruction of the false is not violence.

Q: When I practise self-enquiry, or go within with the idea that it will profit me in some way or other, I am still escaping from what I am.

M: Quite right. True enquiry is always into something, not out of something. When I enquire how to get, or avoid something, I am not really enquiring. To know anything I must accept it — totally.

Q: Yes, to know God I must accept God — how frightening!

M: Before you can accept God, you must accept yourself, which is even more frightening. The first steps in self-acceptance are not at all pleasant, for what one sees is not a happy sight. One needs all the courage to go further. What helps is silence. Look at yourself in total silence, do not describe yourself. Look at the being you believe you are and remember — you are not what you see. 'This I am not — what am I?' is the movement of self-enquiry. There are no other means to liberation, all means delay. Resolutely reject what you are not, till the real Self emerges in its glorious nothingness, its 'not-a-thing-ness.'

Q: The world is passing through rapid and critical changes. We can see them with great clarity in the United States, though they happen in other countries. There is an increase in crime on one hand and more genuine holiness on the other. Communities are being formed and some of them are on a very high level of integrity and austerity. It looks as if evil is destroying itself by its own successes, like a fire which consumes its fuel, while the good, like life, perpetuates itself.

M: As long as you divide events into good and evil, you may be right. In fact, good becomes evil and evil becomes good by their own fulfilment.

Q: What about love?

M: When it turns to lust, it becomes destructive.

Q: What is lust?

M: Remembering — imagining — anticipating. It is sensory and verbal. A form of addiction.

Q: Is *brahmacharya,* continence, imperative in Yoga?

M: A life of constraint and suppression is not Yoga. Mind must be free of desires and relaxed. It comes with understanding, not with determination, which is but another form of memory. An understanding mind is free of desires and fears.

Q: How can I make myself understand?

M: By meditating which means giving attention. Become fully aware of your problem, look at it from all sides, watch how it affects your life. Then leave it alone. You can't do more than that.

Q: Will it set me free?

M: You are free from what you have understood. The outer expressions of freedom may take time to appear, but they are already there. Do not expect perfection. There is no perfection in manifestation. Details must clash. No problem is solved completely, but you can withdraw from it to a level on which it does not operate.   ●●●

101

Gnani does not Grasp, nor Hold

Questioner: How does the *gnani* proceed when he needs something to be done? Does he make plans, decide about details and execute them?

Maharaj: *Gnani* understands a situation fully and knows at once what needs be done. That is all. The rest happens by itself, and to a large extent unconsciously. The *gnani's* identity with all that is, is so complete, that as he responds to the universe, so does the universe respond to him. He is supremely confident that once a situation has been cognized, events will move in adequate response. The ordinary man is personally concerned, he counts his risks and chances, while the *gnani* remains aloof, sure that all will happen as it must; and it does not matter much what happens, for ultimately the return to balance and harmony is inevitable. The heart of things is at peace.

Q: I have understood that personality is an illusion, and alert detachment, without loss of identity, is our point of contact with the reality. Will you, please, tell me — at this moment are you a person or a self-aware identity?

M: I am both. But the real self cannot be described except in terms supplied by the person, in terms of what I am not. All you can tell about the person is not the self, and you can tell nothing about the self, which would not refer to the person, as it is, as it could be, as it should be. All attributes are personal. The real is beyond all attributes.

Q: Are you sometimes the self and sometimes the person?

M: How can I be? The person is what I appear to be to other persons. To myself I am the infinite expanse of consciousness in which innumerable persons emerge and disappear in endless succession.

Q: How is it that the person, which to you is quite illusory, appears real to us?

M: You, the self, being the root of all being, consciousness and joy, impart your reality to whatever you perceive. This imparting of reality takes place invariably in the now, at no other time, because past and future are only in the mind. 'Being' applies to the now only.

Q: Is not eternity endless too?

M: Time is endless, though limited, eternity is in the split moment of the *now*. We miss it because the mind is ever shuttling between the past and the future. It will not stop to focus the *now*. It can be done with comparative ease, if interest is aroused.

Q: What arouses interest?

M: Earnestness, the sign of maturity.

Q: And how does maturity come about?

M: By keeping your mind clear and clean, by living your life in full awareness of every moment as it happens, by examining and dissolving one's desires and fears as soon as they arise.

Q: Is such concentration at all possible?

M: Try. One step at a time is easy. Energy flows from earnestness.

Q: I find I am not earnest enough.

M: Self-betrayal is a grievous matter. It rots the mind like cancer. The remedy lies in clarity and integrity of thinking. Try to understand that you live in a world of illusions, examine them and uncover their roots. The very attempt to do so will make you earnest, for there is bliss in right endeavour.

Q: Where will it lead me?

M: Where can it lead you if not to its own perfection? Once you are well-established in the *now*, you have nowhere else to go What you are timelessly, you express eternally.

Q: Are you one or many?

M: I am one, but appear as many.

Q: Why does one appear at all?

M: It is good to be, and to be conscious.

Q: Life is sad.

M: Ignorance causes sorrow. Happiness follows understand-ing.

Q: Why should ignorance be painful?

M: It is at the root of all desire and fear, which are painful states and the source of endless errors.

Q: I have seen people supposed to have realized, laughing and crying. Does it not show that they are not free of desire and fear?

M: They may laugh and cry according to circumstances, but inwardly they are cool and clear, watching detachedly their own spontaneous reactions. Appearances are misleading and more so in the case of a *gnani*.

Q: I do not understand you.

M: The mind cannot understand, for the mind is trained for grasping and holding while the *gnani* is not grasping and not holding.

Q: What am I holding on to, which you do not?

M: You are a creature of memories; at least you imagine your-self to be so. I am entirely unimagined. I am what I am, not iden-tifiable with any physical or mental state.

Q: An accident would destroy your equanimity.

M: The strange fact is that it does not. To my own surprise, I remain as I am — pure awareness, alert to all that happens.

Q: Even at the moment of death?

M: What is it to me that the body dies?

Q: Don't you need it to contact the world?

M: I do not need the world. Nor am I in one. The world you think of is in your own mind. I can see it through your eyes and mind, but I am fully aware that it is a projection of memories; it is touched by the real only at the point of awareness, which can be only now.

Q: The only difference between us seems to be that while I keep on saying that I do not know my real self, you maintain that you know it well; is there any other difference between us?

M: There is no difference between us; nor can I say that I know myself, I know that I am not describable nor definable. There is a vastness beyond the farthest reaches of the mind. That vastness is my home; that vastness is myself. And that vastness is also love.

Q: You see love everywhere, while I see hatred and suffering. The history of humanity is the history of murder, individual and collective. No other living being so delights in killing.

M: If you go into the motives, you will find love, love of oneself and of one's own. People fight for what they imagine they love.

Q: Surely their love must be real enough when they are ready to die for it.

M: Love is boundless. What is limited to a few cannot be called love.

Q: Do you know such unlimited love?

M: Yes, I do.

Q: How does it feel?

M: All is loved and lovable. Nothing is excluded.

Q: Not even the ugly and the criminal?

M: All is within my consciousness; all is my own. It is madness to split oneself through likes and dislikes. I am beyond both. I am not alienated.

Q: To be free from like and dislike is a state of indifference.

M: It may look and feel so in the beginning. Persevere in such indifference and it will blossom into an all-pervading and all-embracing love.

Q: One has such moments when the mind becomes a flower and a flame, but they do not last and the life reverts to its daily greyness.

M: Discontinuity is the law, when you deal with the concrete. The continuous cannot be experienced, for it has no borders. Consciousness implies alterations, change following change, when one thing or state comes to an end and another begins; that which has no borderline cannot be experienced in the common meaning of the word. One can only *be* it, without knowing, but one can know what it is not. It is definitely not the entire content of consciousness which is always on the move.

Q: If the immovable cannot be known, what is the meaning and purpose of its realization?

M: To realize the immovable means to become immovable. And the purpose is the good of all that lives.

Q: Life is movement. Immobility is death. Of what use is death to life?

M: I am talking of immovability, not of immobility. You become immovable in righteousness. You become a power which gets all things right. It may or may not imply intense outward activity, but the mind remains deep and quiet.

Q: As I watch my mind I find it changing all the time, mood succeeding mood in infinite variety, while you seem to be perpetually in the same mood of cheerful benevolence.

M: Moods are in the mind and do not matter. Go within, go beyond. Cease being fascinated by the content of your consciousness. When you reach the deep layers of your true being, you will find that the mind's surface-play affects you very little.

Q: There will be play all the same?

M: A quiet mind is not a dead mind.

Q: Consciousness is always in movement — it is an observable fact. Immovable consciousness is a contradiction. When you talk of a quiet mind, what is it? Is not mind the same as consciousness?

M: We must remember that words are used in many ways, according to the context. The fact is that there is little difference between the conscious and the unconscious — they are essentially the same. The waking state differs from deep sleep in the presence of the witness. A ray of awareness illumines a part of our mind and that part becomes our dream or waking consciousness, while awareness appears as the witness. The witness usually knows only consciousness. *Sadhana* consists in the witness turning back first on his conscious, then upon himself in his own awareness. Self-awareness is Yoga.

Q: If awareness is all-pervading, then a blind man, once realized, can see?

M: You are mixing sensation with awareness. The *gnani* knows himself as he is. He is also aware of his body being crippled and his mind being deprived of a range of sensory perceptions. But he is not affected by the availability of eyesight, nor by its absence.

Q: My question is more specific; when a blind man becomes a *gnani* will his eyesight be restored to him or not?

M: Unless his eyes and brain undergo a renovation, how can he see?

Q: But will they undergo a renovation?

M: They may or may not. It all depends on destiny and grace. But a *gnani* commands a mode of spontaneous, non-sensory perception, which makes him know things directly, without the intermediary of the senses. He is beyond the perceptual and the conceptual, beyond the categories of time and space, name and shape. He is neither the perceived nor the perceiver, but the simple and the universal factor that makes perceiving possible. Reality is within consciousness, but it is not consciousness nor any of its contents.

Q: What is false, the world, or my knowledge of it?

M: Is there a world outside your knowledge? Can you go beyond what you know? You may postulate a world beyond the mind, but it will remain a concept, unproved and unprovable. Your experience is your proof, and it is valid for you only. Who else can have your experience, when the other person is only as real as he appears in your experience?

Q: Am I so hopelessly lonely?

M: You are, as a person. In your real being you are the whole.

Q: Are you a part of the world which I have in consciousness, or are you independent?

M: What you see is yours and what I see is mine. The two have little in common.

Q: There must be some common factor which unites us.

M: To find the common factor you must abandon all distinctions. Only the universal is in common.

Q: What strikes me as exceedingly strange is that while you say that I am merely a product of my memories and woefully limited, I create a vast and rich world in which everything is contained, including you and your teaching. How this vastness is created and contained in my smallness is what I find hard to understand. May be you are giving me the whole truth, but I am grasping only a small part of it.

M: Yet, it is a fact — the small projects the whole, but it cannot contain the whole. However great and complete is your world, it is self-contradictory and transitory and altogether illusory.

Q: It may be illusory yet it is marvellous. When I look and listen, touch, smell and taste, think and feel, remember and imagine, I cannot but be astonished at my miraculous creativity. I look through a microscope or telescope and see wonders, I follow the track of an atom and hear the whisper of the stars. If I am the sole creator of all this, then I am God indeed! But if I am God, why do I appear so small and helpless to myself?

M: You are God, but you do not know it.

Q: If I am God, then the world I create must be true.

M: It is true in essence, but not in appearance. Be free of desires and fears and at once your vision will clear and you shall see all things as they are. Or, you may say that the *satoguna* creates the world, the *tamoguna* obscures it and the *rajoguna* distorts.

Q: This does not tell me much, because if I ask what are the *gunas*, the answer will be: what creates — what obscures — what distorts. The fact remains — something unbelievable happened to me, and I do not understand what has happened, how and why.

M: Well, wonder is the dawn of wisdom. To be steadily and consistently wondering is *sadhana*.

Q: I am in a world which I do not understand and therefore, I am afraid of it. This is everybody's experience.

M: You have separated yourself from the world, therefore it pains and frightens you. Discover your mistake and be free of fear.

Q: You are asking me to give up the world, while I want to be happy in the world.

M: If you ask for the impossible, who can help you? The limited is bound to be painful and pleasant in turns. If you seek real happiness, unassailable and unchangeable, you must leave the world with its pains and pleasures behind you.

Q: How is it done?

M: Mere physical renunciation is only a token of earnestness, but earnestness alone does not liberate. There must be understanding which comes with alert perceptivity, eager enquiry and deep investigation. You must work relentlessly for your salvation from sin and sorrow.

Q: What is sin?

M: All that binds you.   ●●●

Nisarga Yoga

In the humble abode of Sri Nisargadatta Maharaj, but for the electric lights and the noises of the street traffic, one would not know in which period of human history one dwells. There is an atmosphere of timelessness about his tiny room; the subjects discussed are timeless — valid for all times; the way they are expounded and examined is also timeless; the centuries, millennia and *yugas* fall off and one deals with matters immensely ancient and eternally new.

The discussions held and teachings given would have been the same ten thousand years ago and will be the same ten thousand years hence. There will always be conscious beings wondering about the fact of their being conscious and enquiring into its cause and aim. Whence am I? Who am I? Whither am I? Such questions have no beginning and no end. And it is crucial to know the answers, for without a full understanding of oneself, both in time and in timelessness, life is but a dream, imposed on us by powers we do not know, for purposes we cannot grasp.

Maharaj is not a learned man. There is no erudition behind his homely Marathi; authorities he does not quote, scriptures are rarely mentioned; the astonishingly rich spiritual heritage of India is implicit in him rather than explicit. No rich Ashram was ever built round him and most of his followers are humble working people cherishing the opportunity of spending an hour with him from time to time.

Simplicity and humility are the keynotes of his life and teachings; physically and inwardly he never takes the higher seat; the essence of being on which he talks, he sees in others as clearly as he sees it in himself. He admits that while he is aware of it, others are not yet, but this difference is temporary and of little importance, except to the mind and its ever-changing content.

When asked about his Yoga, he says he has none to offer, no system to propound, no theology, cosmogony, psychology or philosophy. He knows the real nature — his own and his listeners'

— and he points it out. The listener cannot see it because he cannot see the obvious, simply and directly. All he knows, he knows with his mind, stimulated by the senses. That the mind is a sense in itself, he does not even suspect.

The *Nisarga Yoga, the 'natural' Yoga of Maharaj, is disconcertingly simple — the mind, which is all-becoming, must recognize and penetrate its own being, not as being this or that, here or there, then or now, but just timeless being.

This timeless being is the source of both life and consciousness. In terms of time, space and causation it is all-powerful, being the causeless cause; all-pervading, eternal, in the sense of being beginningless, endless and ever-present. Uncaused, it is free; all-pervading, it knows; undivided, it is happy. It lives, it loves, and it has endless fun, shaping and re-shaping the universe. Every man has it, every man *is* it, but not all know themselves as they are, and therefore identify themselves with the name and shape of their bodies and the contents of their consciosness.

To rectify this misunderstanding of one's reality, the only way is to take full cognizance of the ways of one's mind and to turn it into an instrument of self-discovery. The mind was originally a tool in the struggle for biological survival. It had to learn the laws and ways of Nature in order to conquer it. That it did, and is doing, for mind and Nature working hand-in-hand can raise life to a higher level. But, in the process the mind acquired the art of symbolic thinking and communication, the art and skill of language. Words became important. Ideas and abstractions acquired an appearance of reality, the conceptual replaced the real, with the result that man now lives in a verbal world, crowded with words and dominated by words.

Obviously, for dealing with things and people words are exceedingly useful. But they make us live in a world totally symbolic and, therefore, unreal. To break out from this prison of the verbal mind into reality, one must be able to shift one's focus from the word to what it refers to, the thing itself.

The most commonly used word and most pregnant with feelings, and ideas is the word 'I'. Mind tends to include in it anything and everything, the body as well as the Absolute. In practice it stands as a pointer to an experience which is direct, immediate and immensely significant. To *be*, and to know that one *is*, is most important. And to be of interest, a thing must be related to one's conscious existence, which is the focal point of every

* *nisarga* natural state, innate disposition.

desire and fear. For, the ultimate aim of every desire is to enhance and intensify this sense of existence, while all fear is, in its essence, the fear of self-extinction.

To delve into the sense of 'I' — so real and vital — in order to reach its source is the core of the *Nisarga Yoga*. Not being continuous, the sense of 'I' must have a source from which it flows and to which it returns. This timeless source of conscious being is what Maharaj calls the self-nature, self-being, *swarupa*.

As to methods of realizing one's supreme identity with the self-being, Maharaj is peculiarly non-committal. He says that each has his own way to reality, and that there can be no general rule. But, for all the gateway to reality, by whatever road one arrives to it, is the sense of 'I am'. It is through grasping the full import of the 'I am', and going beyond it to its source, that one can realize the supreme state, which is also the primordial and the ultimate. The difference between the beginning and the end lies only in the mind. When the mind is dark or turbulent, the source is not perceived. When it is clear and luminous, it becomes a faithful reflection of the source. The source is always the same — beyond darkness and light, beyond life and death, beyond the conscious and the unconscious.

This dwelling on the sense 'I am' is the simple, easy and natural Yoga, the *Nisarga Yoga*. There is no secrecy in it and no dependence; no preparation is required and no initiation. Whoever is puzzled by his very existence as a conscious being and earnestly wants to find his own source, can grasp the ever-present sense of 'I am' and dwell on it assiduously and patiently, till the clouds obscuring the mind dissolve and the heart of being is seen in all its glory.

The *Nisarga Yoga*, when persevered in and brought to its fruition, results in one becoming conscious and active in what one always was unconsciously and passively. There is no difference in kind — only in manner — the difference between a lump of gold and a glorious ornament shaped out of it. Life goes on, but it is spontaneous and free, meaningful and happy.

Maharaj most lucidly describes this natural, spontaneous state, but as the man born blind cannot visualize light and colours, so is the unenlightened mind unable to give meaning to such descriptions. Expressions like dispassionate happiness, affectionate detachment, timelessness and causelessness of things and being—they all sound strange and cause no response. Intuitively we feel they have deep meaning, and they even create in us a strange longing for the ineffable, a forerunner of things to come, but that is all. As Maharaj puts it: words are pointers, they show the direction but they will not come along with us. Truth is the fruit of earnest action, words merely point the way.

Maurice Frydman

Navanath Sampradaya

Hinduism comprises numerous sects, creeds and cults and the origin of most of them is lost in the antiquity. The Nath Sampradaya, later known as the [1]Navnath Sampradaya, is one of them. Some scholars are of the view that this sect originated with the teachings of the mythical Rishi Dattatreya, who is believed to be a combined incarnation of the holy trinity of Brahma, Vishnu and Shiva. The unique spiritual attainments of this legendary figure are mentioned in the Bhagavata Purana, the Mahabharata and also in some later Upanishads. Others hold that it is an offshoot of the Hatha Yoga.

Whatever be its origin, the teachings of the Nath Sampradaya have, over the centuries, become labyrinthine in complexity and have assumed different forms in different parts of India. Some Gurus of the Sampradaya lay stress on *bhakti*, devotion; others on *jnana*, knowledge; still others on *yoga*, the union with the ultimate. In the fourteenth century we find Svatmarama Svami, the great Hathayogin, bemoaning 'the darkness arising out of multiplicity of opinions' to dispel which he lit the lamp of his famous work Hathayogapradipika.

According to some learned commentators, the Nath Gurus propound that the entire creation is born out of *nada* (sound), the divine principle, and *bindu* (light), the physical principle and the Supreme Reality from which these two principles emanate is Shiva. Liberation according to them is merging of the soul into Shiva through the process of [2]*laya*, dissolution of the human ego, the sense of I-ness.

In the day-today instructions to their devotees, however, the Nath Gurus seldom refer to the metaphysics discovered by the scholars in their teachings. In fact their approach is totally non-metaphysical, simple and direct. While the chanting of sacred hyms and devotional songs as well as the worship of the idols is a traditional feature of the sect, its teaching emphasizes that the Supreme Reality can be realized only within the heart.

[1] The Navnath Sampradaya, or the tradition of Nine Masters (*nava*, nine, *natha*, master, *sampradaya*, tradition).

[2] *laya*, dissolution

The Nath Sampradaya came to be known as Navnath Sampradaya when, sometime in the remote past, the followers of the sect chose nine of their early Gurus as examplars of their creed. But there is no unanimity regarding the names of these nine Masters. The most widely accepted list however is as follows:
1. Matsyendranath, 2. Gorakhnath, 3. Jalandharnath, 4. Kantinath, 5. Gahininath, 6. Bhartrinath, 7. Revananath, 8. Charpatnath and 9. Naganath.

Of these nine Masters, Gahininath and Revananath had large followings in the Southern part of India, including Maharashtra, the state to which Sri Nisargadatta Maharaj belongs. Revananath is said to have founded a sub-sect of his own and chose Kadasiddha as his chief disciple and successor. The latter initiated Lingajangam Maharaj and Bhausahib Maharaj and entrusted to their care his Ashram and the propagation of his teaching. Bhausahib Maharaj later established what came to be known as Inchegeri Sampradaya, a new movement within the traditional fold. Among his disciples were Amburao Maharaj, Girimalleshwar Maharaj, Siddharameshwar Maharaj and the noted philosopher Dr. R.D. Ranade. Sri Nisargadatta Maharaj is the direct disciple and successor of Siddharameshwar Maharaj.

It may be mentioned here that, though officially the current Guru of the Inchegeri branch of the Navnath Sampradaya, Sri Nisargadatta does not seem to attach much importance to sects, cults and creeds, including his own. In answer to a questioner who wished to join the Navnath Sampradaya he said:-

The Navnath Sampradaya is only a tradition, a way of teaching and practice. It does not denote a level of consciousness. If you accept a Navnath Sampradaya teacher as your Guru, you join his Sampradaya . . . . . . Your belonging is a matter of your own feeling and conviction. After all it is all verbal and formal. In reality there is neither Guru nor disciple, neither theory nor practice, neither ignorance nor realization. It all depends upon what you take yourself to be. Know yourself correctly. There is no substitute for self-knowledge.

The teaching of Nath Sampradaya offers the seeker the royal road to liberation, a road in which all the four by-lanes of *bhakti, jnana, karma* and *dhyana* seem to unite. Adinath Bhairava, said to be a manifestation of Lord Shiva, in his hagiography, entitled Nathlingamrita, claims that the path shown by the Nath sect is the best of all and it leads direct to liberation.

o o o

Glossary

Adhar

Support.

Adhi-Yoga

The Supreme Yoga *(adhi,* above, supreme + *yoga).*

Ahimsa

Harmlessness, abstaining from hurting others in thought, word or deed, (negative participle *a,* un + *himsa,* killing, hurting).

Akash

The void, ether as an element of space, sky, (*a,* to + *kasha,* appearance).

Ananda

Bliss, happiness, (*a,* to + *nand,* to rejoice).

Anirvachaniya

Indescribable, (negative part. *a,* un + *vachaniya,* from *vach,* word, expression).

Antahkarana

The psyche, mind, (*antar,* internal + *karana,* sense organ). Mind in a collective sense, including intelligence *(buddhi),* ego *(ahamkara)* and mind *(manas).*

Anubhava

Direct perception, experience, cognition, (*anu,* after + *bhav,* to happen). The experience that is attained at the end of an action, perception, feeling or thought is *anubhava.* In all experiences there is no experiencer other than 'I'. Thus all *anubhava* leads to the I-principle — 'I am'.

Atma, Atman

The Supreme Self, the individual soul, (*atm,* belonging to oneself). *Atman* is beyond all the three *gunas* of *Prakriti.* It is not the *atman* that acts but only *Prakriti.*

Atma-Bhakti

Worship of the Supreme, (*atman* + *bhakti,* from *bhaj,* to worship, adore).

Atma-Prakash

The light of the Self.

Atmaram

Rejoicing the Self, (*atma,* the self + *ram, raman,* to enjoy).

Avatara
Incarnation, (*ava*, off, down, *avataran*, descent).

Avyakta
The unmanifested, (neg. part. *a*, un + *vyakta*, manifest). Opposite —
'vyakta'.

Bhajan
Devotional practice, prayer (*bhaj*, to adore).

Bhakti
Devotion, adoration, (*bhaj*, to adore). Hence 'Bhakta', a devotee.

Bhoga, Bhogi
Experience of worldly joys and sorrows, (*bhuj*, to enjoy, to endure).
'Bhogi', one involved in worldly joys and sorrows. 'Bhoga Marga', the
path of worldly pursuits — joys and sorrows.

Brahma
One of the gods of the Hindu trinity: *Brahma*, the creator; *Vishnu*, the preserver and *Shiva* the destroyer. (*brh*, to increase. Brahma creates, increases).

Brahmacharya
Continence, religious studentship with celebacy. *Brahmacharya* in its
wider sense stands not only for abstinence from sexual indulgence, but
freedom from craving for all sensual enjoyments.

Brahman
The Absolute, the Ultimate Reality, whose characteristics are — absolute
existence *(sat)*, absolute consciousness *(chit)* and absolute bliss
(ananda). According to Sankaracharya *Brahman*, the Absolute, has five
different phases: *Hiranyagarbha*, the Cosmic Self, *Ishvara*, the personal
god in the form of an *Avatar*, *Jiva*, the individual soul, *Prakriti*, the
perishable Nature and *Shakti*, the creative power.

Brahmasmi
I am the Supreme, (*Brahman*, the Supreme + *asmi*, I am, *as*, to be) 'I am'
(asmi) represents the pure awareness of self-existence and is therefore
the expression of pure consciousness or the *Purusha*. When this pure
consciousness gets involved in matter the pure 'I am' changes into 'I am
that', 'I am so-and so'.

Buddhi
Intelligence, reflection of the real in the mind, (*bodhati*, to discern, to
know). Buddhi is that faculty which enables the mind to perceive objects
in the phenomenal world. As long as *buddhi* is functioning through the
medium of the mind it is not possible to know pure consciousness. (*budh*,
to wake up, observe).

Chetana
Consciousness, inner awakening (*chit*, to perceive).

Chidakash
Brahman in its aspect of limitless knowledge, the expanse of awareness,

(*chit*, to perceive + *akash*, expanse, sky). Variously used for consciousness, individual as well as universal.

Chidananda

Consciousness-Bliss, the joy of spirit, (*chit*, to perceive + *ananda*, joy).

Chidaram

Joy of consciousness, (*chit*, to perceive + *ram*, to enjoy).

Chit

Universal Consciousness, (*chit*, to perceive).

Chitta

Individual consciousness, (*chit*, to perceive). *Chitta* is of the nature of consciousness, which is immaterial but is affected by matter. It may be described as a product of both, consciousness and matter, or *Purusha* and *Prakriti*. *Chitta* comprises all the levels of mind, the lowest of which is *manas*.

Deha

Physical body.

Deha-Buddhi

The intellect that makes one identify the Self with the physical body.

Digambara

Naked, one clothed in the directions of the sky, (*dish, dik*, quarter or direction of the sky + *ambar* clothes).

Gnana

Knowledge, specially the higher knowledge derived from meditation. Mostly spelt as 'jnana' (*jna*, to know), *Gnani (Jnani)*, the knower. *Gnana* is the realization of the unity of all things in *Brahman*.

Gunas

Attributes, qualities. In Samkhya philosophy the three attributes of the Cosmic Substance *(Prakriti)* are: Illuminating *(sattva)*, activating *(rajas)* and restraining *(tamas)*.

Guru

Spiritual teacher, preceptor.

Jagrat-Sushupti

Awakened-sleep, (*jagri*, to be awake, watchful, attentive + *sushupti*, sleep).

Jiva, Jivatman

The individual soul, (*jiv*, to live). According to Vedanta *jiva* comes into being as a result of the false identification of the *atman* with body, senses and mind. *Atman* + doership is *jiva*.

Kalpana

Imagination, fancy.

Karma

Action, specially responsible action, good or evil, (*karma*, to do, perform); *karma* is of three kinds: *sanchita* (accumulated from previous births), *prarabdha* (portion of the past karma to be worked out in the present life) and *agami* (the current karma the result of which will fructify in future).

Karana

Cause, the primary cause invariably antecedant to a result, the unmanifested potential cause that in due course, takes shape as the visible effect, the material cause of the universe. *Karana* is cosmic energy in potential form.

Lila

Play, sport, the cosmos looked upon as the divine play. *Lila* does not represent the Absolute truth of the *Brahman*. It is only the partial truth, which is not different from untruth. For example, ice may be described by some as water and as vapour by others. Both statements are only partially true.

Mahadakash

The great expanse of existence, the universe of matter and energy, (*mahat*, great + *akash*, sky).

Maha-Karta

The great doer, (*maha*, great + *karta*, doer, *kar*, to do). Mind is the great doer, for it is ever busy, ever engaged in something or the other.

Maha-Mantra

The great incantation. (see Mantra).

Maha-Maya

The Great Illusion, Unreality, (*maha*, great + *maya*, illusion). *Maya* is the illusive power that veils the Reality. The nature of *Maya* is to delude. *Maya* is the totality of all mental projections.

Maha-Mrityu

The final dissolution, the great death of all creation.

Maha-Sattva

The Supreme Harmony, (*maha*, great + *sattva*, being, harmonious existence).

Maha-Tattva

The Great Reality, Supreme Consciousness, (*maha*, great + *tattva*, reality, true essence).

Maha-Vakya

The sublime pronouncement, (*vach*, word, sound, expression, *vakya*, speech, sentence, what is spoken, *Maha-vakya* — *maha*, great, sublime + *vakya*, sentence, pronouncement). Four Upanishadic declarations, expressing the highest Vedantic truths, are known as *Mahavakyas*. They are: *Prajnanam Brahman* (consciousness is Brahman), *Aham Brahmasmi* (I Am Brahman), *Tat Tvam asi* (That Thou Art) and *Ayam Atma Brahma* (the Self is Brahman).

Mana, Manas

The mind, understanding. (*man*, to think). *Manas* is the thinking faculty, the faculty of discrimination. In Nyaya philosophy *manas* is regarded as a substance distinct from *Atman*, soul.

Manana

Meditation, reflection, (*man*, to think).

Mantra

Incantation, hymn, an instrument of thought, ideal sounds visualized as letters and vocalized as syllables (*man*, to think + agential suffix *tra*). *Mantra* is a group of words whose constant repetition produces specific results.

Marga

Path.

Moksha

Emancipation, liberation from worldly existence, (*muc*, to loosen, to free). 'Mukta', a liberated person.

Moksha-Sankalpa

Determination to be free from the false, (*moksha*, emancipation + *sankalpa*, determination).

Mumukshattva

Right desire, which consists of earnetsness to know the Ultimate Principle and thereby to attain liberation. In Vedanta one of the four qualifications of the seeker of the Truth, viz. right discrimination *(viveka)*, right dispassion *(vairagya)*, right conduct *(sat-sampat)* and right desire *(mumukshatva)*. *Mumukshattva* is intense longing for liberation.

Neti-Neti

Not this; not this, the analytic process of progressively negating all names and forms. *(nama-rupa)* of which the world is made, in order to arrive at the eternal, Ultimate Truth.

Nirguna

The Unconditioned, without attributes, (*nir*, without + *guna*, attribute).

Nirvana

Final dissolution, extinction of the flame of life (*nis*, out + *vana*, blown — root *va*, to blow). Hence emancipation from matter and re-union with the Supreme Spirit *(Brahman)*. 'Nirvani', the seeker of Nirvana.

Nirvikalpa

Free of ideation, without modifications of the mind, (*nir*, without + *vikalpa*, doubts, ideation, fancy).

Nisarga

Natural, innate, inborn.

Nivritti

Liberation from worldly existence, renunciation, (*nir*, without + *vritti*, from *vart*, to turn, revolve, the mode of life).

Parabrahman

The Supreme Reality, (*para*, beyond + *Brahman*, Ultimate Reality).

Paramakash

The great expanse, the timeless and spaceless Reality (*param*, highest, most distant, greatest + *akash*, the void). Hence the Absolute Being.

Paramartha

The sublime truth (*para*, beyond + *artha*, purpose, true knowledge).

Pragna

Un-selfconscious knowledge, cognitive consciousness, pure awareness. Also written as 'prajna' (*prajin*, wise, *pra*, high + *jna*, to know). Prajna stands for higher consciousness.

Prakriti

The Cosmic Substance. the original uncaused cause of phenomenal existence, which is formless, limitless, immobile, eternal and all-pervasive, (*pra*, before, first + *kar*, to make). It is also called 'Avyakta'.

Pralaya

Complete dissolution, when the cosmos merges into the Unmanifested Absolute of the Supreme Reality, (*pra*, before + *laya*, extinction).

Prana

The breath of life, vital principle, (*pra*, before + *ana*, breath).

Prarabdha

Destiny, what is begun as an undertaking, (*pra, prak*, before + *abdham, addhi*, reservoir). Hence the store of *sanchita karma* (*karma* of past lives) that has become the destiny in the present life.

Pravritti

Continued activity, predeliction towards worldly life, (*pra*, before + *vritti*, mode of life).

Premakash

Brahman in its aspect of limitless love, (*prem*, love + *akash*, expanse, sky). It is another name for *Chidakash*, but it lays stress on the love aspect and not on the knowledge aspect. Love is the expression of the Self through the heart. *Premakash* is the heart + I am — I am the heart.

Puja

Worship, adoration (*pu, puyati, puta* to purify).

Purna

Full, complete, absolute, infinite — used for *Brahman*.

Purusha

The Cosmic Spirit, the eternal and efficient cause of the universe that gives appearance of consciousness to all manifestations of matter (*prakriti*). The bondage of *Purusha* in matter is due to 'I' - consciousness born of *Chitta-vrittis*, which give rise to innumerable desires.

Rajas

Motivity, activity, energy, (*ra(n)j*, to be coloured, affected, moved). One of the three constituents of the Cosmic Substance (*sattva, rajas* and *tamas*) without which the other two could not be manifest. In Yoga-egoism.

Sad-Chit

The transcendental condition of the universal potentiality, (*sat*, being + *chit*, consciousness).

Sadanubhava

Experience of the Everlasting Reality, (*sada*, always + *anubhava*, experience.

Sadashiva

The perpetual beatitude, ever prosperous, (*sada*, always + *shiva*, gracious. auspicious).

Saccitananda

The Ultimate Principle with the three attributes in absolute perfection (*sat*, being + *chit*, consciousness + *ananda*, bliss).

Sadguru

The true spiritual teacher (*sat*, true, transcendental being + *guru*, teacher).

Sadhana

The practice which produces success 'Siddhi', (*sadh*, to go straight to the goal, to be successful).

Sadhu

An ascetic, (*sadh*, to go straight to the goal).

Saguna

Manifested condition with the three 'gunas' — *sattva*, *rajas* and *tamas*. The Supreme Absolute conceived of as possessing qualities like love, mercy etc., as distinguished from the Undifferentiated Absolute of the Advaita Vedanta.

Samadhi

Superconscious state, profound meditation, trance, rapturous absorption, (*sam*, together + *a*, to + *dhi*, placing, putting together). A practice of Yoga in which the seeker *(sadhaka)* becomes one with the object of his meditation *(sadhya)*, thus attaining unqualified bliss. *Samadhi* is of five types: *savikalpa*, visualizing a sense object (usually an ideal or a god) in the dualistic sphere; *nirvikalpa*, beyond all doubts, names and forms; *nissankalpa*, all desires cease coming up in the form of 'sankalpa', *nirvrittik*, even involuntary mentations *(vrittis)* cease; *nirvasana*, even the instinctive upsurge of 'vasanas' is stilled.

Samskara

Mental impression, memory (*sans*, together + *kara*, action; to put together). Also called *vasana*, residual impression.

Samvid

True awareness.

Sat

The transcendental aspect of the Ultimate Principle in active condition. (participle of root *as*, to be). Opposite — 'asat'.

Sat-Sang

Association with the true and the wise people, (*sat,* true, wise + *sang,* association).

Sattva

Being, existence, true essence, (*sat,* being + abstract formative *tva*). In Yoga the quality of purity or goodness. 'Sattvic', pure, true.

Sattvanubhava

Experience *(anubhava)* of the true harmony of the universe (*sattva,* being).

Satyam-Shivam-Sundaram

The true, the good, the beautiful — *satyam* (abstract from *sat,* true), *shivam* (*shiva,* auspicious, propitious), *sundaram* (*sundar,* beautiful).

Satyakama

He who longs for the Sublime Truth, (*satya,* truth, Brahman + *kama, kamana,* desire).

Shiva

One of the gods of the Hindu trinity — *Brahma,* the creator; *Vishnu,* the preserver and *Shiva,* the destroyer. Shiva actually means auspicious, propitious. Destruction of the cosmos by the god Shiva is a propitious act, for destruction precedes creation. *Shiva* is absolute love of the 'I-principle' in a man. As a destroyer He brings about the total annihilation of the human ego.

Shravana

Hearing of the scriptures, the act of hearing.

Siddha

The realized person, one who has attained perfection, (*sadh,* to go straight to the goal, to be successful).

Smarana

Remembrance, mental recitation.

Soham

I am He (*so,* he + *aham,* I am).

Sutratma

The connecting link between all beings, (*sutra,* thread, string + *atma,* soul). The string-like supporter of the manifested worlds, hence the Pure Consciousness which is the substratum of all beings. Maharaj uses the word for the accumulated *karma* from life to life.

Swarga

The celestial regions.

Swarupa

One's own form, nature, character, (*sva,* one's own + *rupa,* subtle element of form).

Tamas

Darkness, inertia, passivity. One of the three constituents *(gunas)* of the Cosmic Substance, viz., *sattva, rajas* and *tamas.*

Tat-Sat

That is the truth (*tat*, that + *sat*, truth, Being, Reality). The sacred text is 'Om Tat Sat' in which *Brahman* is identified by each of the three words.

Tattva

The true essence, Reality, (*tad*, *tat*, that + *tva*, abstract suffix, i.e. 'that-ness').

Turiya

The superconscious state of *samadhi*, (*turiya*, fourth) the fourth state of soul in which it becomes one with Brahman, the highest awareness.

Turiyatita

Beyond the highest awareness (*turiya* + *atita*, gone beyond).

Tyaga

Renunciation. Tyaga is the renunciation of the fruits of all works, i.e. the *tyagi* should perform *karma* with detachment and with no desire for results.

Uparati

Rest, repose, tolerance and renunciation of all sectarian observances, (*upa*, towards, under, down + *rati*, rest, repose, from root *ram*, to make content). In Vedanta one of the six acquirements (*sat-sampat*): viz. *sama*, tranquillity; *dama*, self-restraint: *uprati*, tolerance; *titiksha*, endurance; *sraddha*, faith and *samadhana*, equipoise.

Vairagya

Absence of worldly desires, (*vi*, apart without + *raga*, desire). Indifference to the unreal and transitory. Hence complete absence of any attraction towards objects which give pleasure.

Vishnu

One of the gods of the Hindu trinity — *Brahma*, *Vishnu* and *Shiva*.

Viveka

Discrimination, right discrimination between the true and the false, the real and the unreal, (*vi*, away, without + *veka* from root *vic*, to sift, sever, separate). *Viveka* is an expression of the spiritual consciousness hidden behind the mind. *Viveka* leads to *vairagya*.

Vyakta

Manifest matter, the evolved Nature, (*vi*, apart, away, without + *akta*, passive participle of *anj*, to anoint). Hence evolved, annointed product. Opposite — 'Avyakta'.

Vyakti

Person, the outer self.

Vyaktitva

Personality, limited self-indentification with the body.

Yoga

One of the six systems of the Hindu philosophy (from *yuj*, to yoke or join). Yoga teaches the means by which the individual spirit (*jivatma*) can be

joined or united with the Universal Spirit (Paramatma). The Yoga system
is believed to have been founded by Patanjali.

Yoga-Bhrashta

One who has fallen from the high state of Yoga.

Yoga-Kshetra

The field for Yoga, the physical body in a philosophical sense (*kshetra*,
field).

Yoga-Sadhana

Spiritual practices of Yoga.

Yogi

One who practises Yoga.

Other talks of Sri Nisargadatta Maharaj.

Self Knowledge and Self Realization.
The Ultimate Medicine as Prescribed by Sri Nisargadatta Maharaj.
The Nectar of Immortality.

Of Related Interest

By Ramesh S. Balsekar

Ramesh Balsekar, in his well-received scholarly writings, reaches beyond the communication of past knowledge to a creative exploration of the teachings of Nisargadatta Maharaj. In his contemplations upon the sentience of the human spirit, Balsekar has used Maharaj's wisdom as the touchstone for his own ventures into the realm of conscious and unconscious

CONSCIOUSNESS SPEAKS. Recommended both for the newcomer to Advaita (non-duality) and the more knowledgeable student of the subject. 392 pages. Paperback.

EXPERIENCING THE TEACHING. In this book many facets of Advaita are examined and illuminated through a series of 24 dialogues. 142 pages. Paperback.

THE FINAL TRUTH; A GUIDE TO ULTIMATE UNDERSTANDING. Comprehensive and powerful look at Advaita from the arising of I AM to the final dissolution into identification as Pure Consciousness. 240 pages. Paperback.

FROM CONSCIOUSNESS TO CONSCIOUSNESS. This wonderful book explores the heart of the guru/disciple relationship. 80 pages. Paperback.

A DUET OF ONE: THE ASHTAVAKRA GITA DIALOGUE. Here the most beautiful of the Advaitic texts, *The Ashtavakra Gita* is used as a vehicle for an illuminating look at the nature of duality and dualism. 224 pages. Paperback.

Available from

THE ACORN PRESS, P. O. Box 3279, Durham, NC 27715-3279. Phone: (919) 471-3842. FAX (919) 477-2622.